J.C. Ryle
Best Sermons Ever!

Duties of Parents, Thoughts for Young Men, Victory, and More!

By *J.C. Ryle*

BISHOP OF LIVERPOOL

*From the 1887 Edition of "The Upper Room",
with two bonus sermons that have resonated through the ages.*

The book's body text is in the public domain. Please copy, replicate,
and distribute freely to further walking in Christ.

~ ※ ~

TABLE OF CONTENTS

THE UPPER ROOM 3
Preface 3
CHAPTER I 3
Acts 1:13 "They Went Up Into An Upper Room." 3
CHAPTER II 9
Colossians 4:14 "Luke, The Beloved Physician." 9
CHAPTER III 14
Eccles. 12:12 Simplicity In Preaching. 14
CHAPTER IV 23
1 Cor. 15:3-4 Foundation Truths. 23
CHAPTER V 31
Jer. 6:16 The Good Way. 31
CHAPTER VI 40
Acts 17:26 "One Blood." 40
CHAPTER VII 48
John 7:37-38 "Let Any Man Come." 48
CHAPTER VIII 61
1 John 5:4-5 Victory. 61
CHAPTER IX 70
Acts 17:16-17 Athens. 70
CHAPTER X 80
Acts 26:24-29 Portraits. 80
CHAPTER XI 87
John 6:68 "To Whom?" 87
CHAPTER XII 94
Heb. 4:14 Our Profession. 94
CHAPTER XIII 106
Matt. 8:11 Many. 106
CHAPTER XIV 116
2 Sam. 23:4-5 Without Clouds. 116
CHAPTER XV 122
Canticles 4:12 The Lord's Garden. 122
CHAPTER XVI 129
Prov. 22:6 The Duties Of Parents. 129
CHAPTER XVII 146
Phil. 1:1 The Rights And Duties Of Lay Churchmen. 146
CHAPTER XVIII 160
John 3:3; 2 Cor. 5:17 Questions About Regeneration. 160
CHAPTER XIX 167
Tit. 2:6 Thoughts For Young Men. 167
CHAPTER XX 195
Questions About The Lord's Supper. 195
CHAPTER XXI 210
1 Thess. 2:1-2 "For Kings." 210
Bonus Sermon: A Call to Prayer 215
Bonus Sermon: On Christmas 231

THE UPPER ROOM

Being a Few Truths for the Times

Preface

The volume now in the reader's hands requires little introductory explanation. It contains a very miscellaneous selection of papers which I have sent forth from time to time, in one shape or another, during a forty-five years' ministry. Some of these papers are not known beyond a small circle of kind friends. Not a few of them are the substance of pulpit addresses delivered on important public occasions, and composed with more than ordinary pains. All of them, I venture humbly to think, will be found to contain some useful truths for the times, and words in season.

I have reached an age when I cannot reasonably expect to write much more. There are many thoughts in this volume which I do not wish to leave behind me in the precarious form of separate single sermons, addresses, lectures, and tracts. I have therefore resolved to gather them together in the volume I now send forth, which I heartily pray God to bless, and to make it a permanent blessing to many souls.

Palace, Liverpool, December 1, 1887
—J. C.

CHAPTER I[1]

Acts 1:13
"They Went Up Into An Upper Room."

WE are told in these simple words what the Apostles did immediately after the Ascension of our Lord Jesus Christ into heaven. Fresh from the wonderful and touching sight of their beloved Master being taken away from them,—with the message brought by angels, bidding them expect His Second Advent, still ringing in their ears,—they returned from Mount Olivet to Jerusalem, and went at once "into an upper room." Simple as the words are, they are full of suggestive thoughts, and deserve the close attention of all into whose hands this volume may fall.

Let us fix our eyes for a few minutes on the first place of meeting of Christians for worship of which we have any record. Let us examine the first congregation which assembled after the great Head of the Church had left the world, and left His people to themselves. Let us see who these first worshippers were, and how they behaved, and what they did. I venture to think that a little quiet contemplation of the subject may do us good.

This "upper room," we should remember, was the forerunner of every church and cathedral which has been reared in Christendom within the last eighteen centuries. St. Paul's, and York, and Lincoln, and all the stately ministers of our own land; St. Sophia at Constantinople, St. Isaac at St. Petersburg, St. Stephen's at Vienna, Notre Dame at Paris, St. Peter's at Rome, all are descendants from this "upper room." Not one can trace its

---

[1] The substance of this paper was originally delivered as a sermon at the consecration of St. Agnes' Church, Liverpool.

pedigree beyond that little chamber. Here it was that professing Christians, when left alone by their Master, first began to pray together, to worship, and to exhort one another. This room was the cradle of the infant Church of Christ, and the beginning of all our services. From this room the waters of the everlasting gospel first began to flow, which have now spread so widely throughout the world, however adulterated and corrupted they may have been in some ages and in some parts of the earth. I invite my readers, then, to come with me and examine this upper room as it appeared on Ascension day.

I. There are certain points arising naturally out of the text before us which appear to demand special notice. Let us see what they are.

Concerning the shape and size and form of this room, we know nothing at all. It was probably like many other "upper rooms" in Jerusalem. But whether it was lofty, or low, or square, or round; whether it stood east and west, or north and south; whether it was ornamented or decorated or perfectly plain, we have not the slightest information, and the matter signifies very little. But it is a striking and noteworthy fact that in the original Greek it is called the upper room, and not an upper room, as our Authorized Version calls it. I venture to think that there is much in this. I believe there is the highest probability that this was the very room in which our Lord first appointed the Sacrament of the Lord's Supper, and in which the Apostles first heard those well-known words, "Take, eat; this is My body,"—"Drink ye all of this, for this is My blood,"—those famous words which have been the cause of so much unhappy controversy with some, but the source of such mighty comfort to others.—I believe it was the same room in which the disciples were "in the habit of abiding" during the fifty days between the Resurrection and Pentecost. Here, again, the original Greek helps us to a conclusion, if literally translated. I believe it is the same room in which the disciples were assembled with "the doors shut for fear of the Jews," when the Lord Jesus suddenly appeared in the midst of them after His resurrection, and said, "Peace be unto you: as My Father sent Me, so send I you;" and "breathed on them, saying, Receive ye the Holy Ghost" (John 20:21-22).—I believe it is the same room in which, a week afterwards, He appeared again, and rebuked the scepticism[2] of doubting Thomas, saying, "Be not faithless, but believing."—I believe it is the same room in which our Lord appeared, and did eat before His disciples, and said, "Handle Me, and see: a spirit hath not flesh and bones, as ye see Me have" (Luke 24:39). On all these points I freely grant that I have nothing but conjectures to put before my readers. But they are conjectures which appear to me to be founded on the highest possible probability, and as such I think they demand our reverent consideration. But we may now turn boldly from conjectures, and look at things which are most plainly and unmistakably revealed.

(1) Let us then, first and foremost, look at the worshippers who were gathered together in this first place of Christian worship.

Peter was there, that warm-hearted, impulsive, but unstable Apostle, who, forty days before, denied his Master three times, and then repented with bitter tears, and who had been graciously raised by our Lord, and commanded to "feed His sheep" (John 21:16-17).

James was there, who had been the favoured companion of Peter and John on three important occasions, and who was the first of the Apostles to seal his faith with his blood, and drink of the cup which his Master drank (Matt. 20:23).

John was there, the other son of Zebedee, the beloved Apostle, whose head lay on our Lord's breast at the Last Supper,—John, the first on the lake of Galilee, when our Lord

---

[2]An effort to keep the original spelling has been made throughout.

appeared to the disciples as they were fishing, who cried out with instinctive love, "It is the Lord,"—John, who at one time wished to call down fire from heaven on a village of the Samaritans, but lived to write three Epistles brimming over with love (John 21:7; Luke 9:54).

Andrew was there, the first of all the Apostles whose name we know, who followed Jesus after hearing the words, "Behold the Lamb of God," and then brought his brother Peter to Jesus, saying, "We have found the Messias" (John 1:40-41).

Philip of Bethsaida was there, the first Apostle to whom Jesus said, "Follow Me,"—the Apostle who told Nathanael to "come and see" the promised Messiah (John 1:43).

Thomas was there, who was once so desponding and weak in faith, but afterwards cried out with such grand Athanasian confidence, "My Lord and my God" (John 20:28).

Bartholomew was there, who, by general consent, is the same as that very Nathanael who at first said, "Can any good thing come out of Nazareth?" Yet this is he whom our Lord pronounced to be "an Israelite without guile," and who said, "Thou art the Son of God, Thou art the King of Israel" (John 1:46-49).

Matthew the publican was there, who forsook his worldly calling at the bidding of our Lord, and sought lasting treasure in heaven, and who was afterwards privileged to hold the pen which wrote the first Gospel (Matt. 9:9).

James the son of Alphaeus was there, who had the honour of being the presiding Apostle at the first Council held in Jerusalem, and of whom St. Paul tells the Galatians that, together with Peter and John, James was a "pillar of the Church" (Gal. 2:9).

Simon Zelotes was there, of whom we know little certain except that he was also "called the Canaanite," and may possibly have lived at Cana of Galilee, and seen the first miracle our Lord worked. His name Zelotes seems to indicate that he was once a member of the famous Zealot party, a fierce advocate of Jewish home-rule, and an enemy of Roman supremacy. He was now zealous only for the kingdom of Christ.

Judas was there, the brother of James, called also Lebbaeus or Thaddaeus, the writer of the last Epistle in the New Testament, and the Apostle who asked the remarkable question," How is it that Thou wilt manifest Thyself unto us and not unto the world?" (John 14:22). In short, the whole company of the eleven faithful Apostles was assembled in that "upper room." On this occasion there were no absentees; and doubting Thomas was among the rest.

But there were others present beside the Apostles. The "women" were there of whom some had long followed our Lord and ministered to His necessities, and been last at the Cross, and first at the tomb. I have little doubt that Mary Magdalene and Salome, and Susanna, and Joanna the wife of Chuza, Herod's steward, formed part of the company (Luke 8:2-3). And Mary the mother of Jesus was there, whom our Lord had committed to the special care of John; and where he was, she was sure to be. Truly the prophecy of old Simeon had been fulfilled in her case. "The sword" of deep and keen sorrow had pierced "through her soul" (Luke 2:35). For she was only flesh and blood, like any other woman. This is the last occasion on which her name appears in the pages of Holy Scripture. From henceforth she sinks out of sight, and all stories about her after-life are mere baseless traditions.

And, finally, our Lord's "brethren" were there. They were his cousins in all probability, or the sons of Joseph by a former marriage. Never let it be forgotten that at one time they did not believe on Jesus (John 7:5); but now their unbelief was gone, and they were true disciples, while Judas Iscariot had fallen away. The mention of them teaches the grand lesson that men may begin ill, and end well, and that many who now seem faithless may one day believe. So true it is that the last are sometimes first, and the first last.

Such was the congregation which assembled in the "upper room" after the Ascension. Never, I suppose, has there been such a pure and spotless gathering of Christians from that day down to this. Never has there been, and probably never will be, such a near approach to the "one Holy Catholic Church," the "mystical body of the Son of God, which is the blessed company of all faithful people." Never has there been together so much wheat without tares, and such a singular proportion of grace, and penitence, and faith, and hope, and holiness, and love in one room together. Well would it be for the visible Church of Christ if all her assemblies were as free from unsound members, spots, and blemishes as the congregation which met together in the "upper room."

(2) We should notice, secondly, the unity which characterized this first meeting in the "upper room." We are told expressly, "that they were all there with one accord," that is, of one mind. There were no divisions among them. They believed the same thing. They loved the same Person, and at present there was no disagreement among them. There was nothing of High, or Low, or Broad in that "upper room." Heresies, and strifes, and controversies were as yet unknown. Neither about baptism, or the Lord's Supper, or vestments, or incense, was there any contention or agitation. Happy would it have been for Christendom if this blessed state of things had continued! At the end of eighteen centuries we all know, by bitter experience, that the divisions of Christians are the weakness of the Church, and the favourite argument of the world, the infidel, and the devil against revealed religion. Well may we pray, when we see this blessed picture of the upper room, that God would heal the many ecclesiastical diseases of the nineteenth century, and make Churchmen especially become more of one mind.

(3) We should notice, thirdly, the devotional habits of this first congregation in the "upper room." We are told expressly that they "were continuing in prayer and supplication." Here, again, we should mark the original Greek. The expression denotes that prayer was a continued and habitual practice at this crisis. What things these holy worshippers prayed for we are not told. Like our Lord's discourse with the two Apostles journeying to Emmaus, one would like to know what their prayers were (Luke 24:27). We need not doubt that there was much prayer for grace to be faithful and not fall away, refer wisdom to do the thing that was right in the new and difficult position which they had to take up,—for courage, for patience, for unwearied zeal, for abiding recollection of our Lord's example, our Lord's teaching, and our Lord's promises. But in perfect wisdom the Holy Ghost has thought fit to keep back these things from us, and we must not doubt that this is right. One thing, at any rate, is quite certain. We are taught clearly that nothing is such a primary duty of a Christian assembly as united prayer and supplication. Let us never forget the first charge which the meat Apostle of the Gentiles gave to Timothy when he wrote to him about his duties as a minister of the Church, "I exhort, therefore, first of all, that supplications, prayers, intercessions, and giving of thanks be made for all men; for kings and all that are in authority, that we may live a quiet and peaceable life" (1 Tim. 2:1, etc.). I dare to believe that the names of Annas, Caiaphas, and Pontius Pilate were not forgotten in the supplications and intercessions of the "upper room."

(4) We should notice, lastly, the address given in this upper room by the Apostle Peter, on one of the ten days which elapsed between the Ascension and the day of Pentecost. It is an interesting fact that this is the first address which is recorded to have been given to

any assembly of Christians after the Lord left the world. It is no less interesting that the first speaker was the Apostle Peter,—the very Apostle who, after denying his Master, had been mercifully raised again, and commended to prove his love by feeding His sheep,— the very Apostle who had received a charge before his fall, "When thou art converted, strengthen thy brethren" (Luke 22:32). There was a peculiar fitness in Peter being the first to stand up and address the little company of "one hundred and twenty names."

(a) Mark how he begins his address with a reverent reference to Holy Scripture. He puts down his foot firmly on the supremacy of God's written Word as the Church's rule of faith. He says, "This scripture had to have been fulfilled." He says, "It is written in the book of Psalms," and takes a quotation for his text. Well and wisely does the late Dean Alford remark in his Homilies on the Acts: "The first act of the Church by her first superintendent minister was an appeal to the text of Scripture. Let that never be forgotten. Would that every appeal by every one of her ministers since had been an appeal equally direct and equally justified!"

(b) Mark, next, how Peter humbly acknowledges the liability of the highest and most privileged ministers of the Church to fall. He says of Judas Iscariot, "He was numbered with us, and had obtained part of this ministry," and then mentions his miserable end. "He fell by transgression," and then "went to his own place." Let that also never be forgotten. He lays down the grand principle, which should always be remembered in the Church, that no infallibility belongs to the ministerial office. A chosen Apostle of Christ fell sadly, and so also may any successor of the Apostles. Bishops, priests, and deacons may err, and have erred greatly, like Hophni, and Phinehas, and Annas, and Caiaphas, who were in direct succession to Aaron. We are never to suppose that ordained and consecrated men can make no mistakes. We are never to follow them blindly, or to believe as a matter of course that all they say is truth. The Bible is the only infallible guide.

(c) Mark, next, how he calls upon the Church to fill up the place which Judas had left vacant, and to choose one who might be numbered with the eleven Apostles. He speaks with unfaltering confidence, like one convinced that a work was beginning which the world and the devil could never stop, and that workmen must be appointed to carry it on in regular order. He speaks with a clear foresight of the battles the Church would have to fight, but with an evident conviction that they would not be fought in vain, and that the final issue was sure. He seems to say, "Stand firm, though a standard-bearer has fallen away. Fill up the gap. Close up your ranks."

(d) Mark, lastly, how he winds up his address with a plain declaration of what a minister and successor of the Apostles ought to be. He was to be "a witness of Christ's resurrection." He was to be a witness to the fact that the foundation of the Gospel is not a vague idea of God's mercy, but an actual living Person, a Person who lived for us, died for us, and above all, rose again. Let that also never be forgotten. I affirm, without hesitation, that in these latter days we do not make enough of the resurrection of Christ. We certainly do not make as much of it as the Apostles did, judging from the Acts and the Epistles. When Paul went to Athens, we are told that "he preached Jesus and the resurrection" (Acts 27:18). When he went to Corinth, one of the first truths he proclaimed was, that "Christ rose again according to the Scriptures" (1 Cor. 15:4). When the same Paul was brought before Festus and Agrippa, Festus said that the complaint against him was about "one Jesus who was dead, whom Paul affirmed to be alive" (Acts 25:19).

Let no one misunderstand my meaning. I do not say that we dwell too much on the sacrifice and the blood of Christ, but I do contend that we dwell too little on His resurrection. Yet our Lord Himself told the Jews more than once that the resurrection would prove Him to be the Messiah. St. Paul told the Romans, in the beginning of his Epistle, that Jesus was "declared to be the Son of God with power by the resurrection from the dead" (Rom. 1:4). The resurrection completed the work of redemption, which our Lord came into the world to effect. It is written, that "He was delivered for our offences, and raised again for our justification," and the Corinthians are expressly told, "If Christ be not raised, your faith is vain; ye are yet in your sins" (Rom. 4:25; 1 Cor. 15:17). In short, Christ's resurrection is one of the grandest evidences of the truth of Christianity, a foundation proof that the salvation of sinners by the vicarious atonement is a finished work, and a miracle which the cleverest infidels have never been able to explain away. Until it is explained away, we need not be troubled by carping remarks about Balaam's ass speaking, and Jonah in the whale's belly. Well indeed would it have been for the Church if all her ministers had always been such as Peter recommended to be appointed, faithful "witnesses" to a personal Christ, His death, and His resurrection.

So much for the upper room at Jerusalem, its congregation, their unity, their prayers, and the first address delivered within its walls. So much for the first prayer meeting, the first sermon, and the first corporate action of the professing Church of which we have any record. We need not doubt for a moment that the well-known promise of our Lord Jesus Christ was fulfilled in that room, "Wheresoever two or three are gathered together in My name, there am I in the midst of them" (Matt. 18:20). The little company of worshippers did not see Him; but He was there.

II. Let me now try to draw some practical lessons for ourselves from the whole subject.

(1) In the first place, let us learn to be more thankful for the liberty of the days in which our lot is cast, and the wise toleration of the Government under which we live in this country. By the mercy of God, "we enjoy great quietness." We have no need to meet in "upper rooms" with "doors closed for fear of the Jews," and with a constant feeling that there is but a step between us and a violent death. Men may build places of worship now, if they please, as costly and magnificent as the temple of Jerusalem itself, and no one jealously prohibits or interferes with them. We need not fear Roman Emperors, nor mediaeval autocrats, nor Spanish Inquisitions. The land is before us, and men may build and worship as they please. I would to God that all wealthy laymen in this country would remember from whom riches come, and to whom they are indebted for their freedom and prosperity. I would to God that many more would honour Him with their substance, and come forward more frequently, saying, "Let me build a Church for the service of God."

(2) In the next place, let us learn the source of trite power in the Church. This little upper room was the starting-point of a movement which shook the Roman Empire, emptied the heathen temples, stopped gladiatorial combats, raised women to their true position, checked infanticide, created a new standard of morality, confounded the old Greek and Roman philosophers, and turned the world upside down. And what was the secret of this power? The unity, the soundness in the faith, the holiness, and the prayers and intercessions of the first professing Christians. Where these things are wanting, the grandest architecture and the most ornate ceremonial will do nothing to mend the world. It is the presence of Christ and the Holy Ghost which alone gives power.

(3) In the last place, let us pray for the Church of England, that she may continue faithful to the old truths which have done so much good for 300 years, truths which are embalmed in our Articles, Prayer Book, and Creeds. It is cheap and easy work to sneer at

dogma, to scoff at inspiration and the atonement, to make merry at the controversies of Christians, and to tell us that no one really believes all the Bible, or all the facts enumerated in the Belief. It is easy, I repeat, to do this. Even children can cast mud, and throw stones, and make a noise. But sneers, and mud, and noise are not arguments. I challenge those who sneer at dogma to show us a more excellent way, to show us anything that does more good in the world than the old, old story of Christ dying for our sins, and rising again for our justification.

The man of science may say, "Come with me, and look through my microscope or telescope, and I will show you things which Moses, David, and St. Paul never dreamed of. Do you expect me to believe what was written by ignorant fellows like them?" But can this man of science show us anything through his microscope or telescope which will minister to a mind diseased, bind up the wounds of a broken heart, satisfy the wants of an aching conscience, supply comfort to the mourner over a lost husband, wife, or child? No, indeed! He can do nothing of the kind! Men and women are fearfully and wonderfully made. We are not made up merely of brains, and head, and intellect, and reason. We are frail, dying creatures, who have got hearts, and feelings, and consciences; and we live in a world of sorrow, and disappointment, and sickness, and death. And what can help us in a world like this? Certainly not science alone. Nothing can help us but the doctrine of that volume which some people call an old worn-out Jewish book, the Bible. None can help us but He who was laid in the manger of Bethlehem and died on the cross to pay our debt to God, and is now at God's right hand. None but He who said, "Come unto Me, all ye that labour, and I will give you rest" (Matt. 11:28). None but He who has thrown light on the grave, and the world beyond it, and has brought life and immortality to light through the gospel and made a deeper mark on the world than all the men of science who have ever lived, from the times of Pythagoras, Aristotle, and Archimedes, down to Darwin and Huxley in the present day. Yes! I say again, let us pray that our Church may ever be faithful to her first principles, and never lend an ear to those plausible, eloquent apostles of free thought, who would fain persuade her to throw overboard her Creeds and Articles as useless lumber. Fine words and rhetorical fireworks will never satisfy humanity, check moral evil, or feed souls. Men would do well to read that striking paper which Miss Frances Power Cobbe wrote in the Contemporary Review for December 1884, and see what a ghastly world our world would be if it was a world without a faith or a creed. The age needs nothing new. It only needs the bold and steady proclamation of the old truths which were held in the "upper room" at Jerusalem.

CHAPTER II[3]

Colossians 4:14
"Luke, The Beloved Physician."

THERE are two things in the title of this paper which I shall take for granted, and not dwell on them. One is, that Luke here mentioned is the same Luke who wrote the third Gospel and the Acts of the Apostles, and was the friend and companion of St. Paul. The other is, that Luke really was a physician of the body. On both these points the consent of

---

[3] The substance of this paper was originally delivered as a sermon in Liverpool Cathedral at the opening of the Annual Conference of the British Medical Association in Liverpool, on July 31st, 1883.

learned men, who have a right to command our attention, is almost universal. I shall rigidly confine myself to two remarks which appear to grow out of the subject. For it is a significant fact, I think, that the great Apostle of the Gentiles, who was ever ministering to men's souls, makes honourable mention of one who ministered to men's bodies.

I. I remark then, for one thing, that one great feature of the Christian religion is the dignity and importance which it attaches to the human body.

Many readers of this paper need hardly be reminded that some of the schools of heathen philosophers regarded the body with contempt, as a hindrance and not a help, a clog and a drag and not an aid, to the soul. Even those nations which paid most attention to the burial of the body when dead, like the Egyptians, Greeks, and Romans, knew nothing of a future existence of the body after death, even at the most distant period. The heroes described by Homer and Viral, in the Elysian Fields, the supposed place of happiness after death, were only ghosts and airy figures, with nothing material about them. When St. Paul, on Mars Hill, spoke of the "resurrection of the dead," we are told that "some mocked" (Acts 17:32). Even Pliny, one of the most intelligent Latin writers, in his Natural History, says there were two things which were beyond the power of God,—one was to give immortality to mortals, and the other was to give bodily life again to the dead. (See Pearson on The Creed, vol. ii., p. 306, Oxford edition.)

Let us turn now to the Christian religion, and mark what a contrast it presents. Whether we look at its leading facts, or doctrines, or practical instructions for the present, or hopes for the future, the human body is continually brought to the front, and its importance magnified.

(a) Look, to begin with, at the great mysterious truth which lies at the foundation of our holy faith, the incarnation of Christ. When the Eternal Son of God came down into this sin-burdened world, to bring redemption, and change the whole condition of our fallen race, how did He come? Not as a mighty angel or a glorious spirit, as we might have expected. Nothing of the kind! He took on Him a bodily nature, just like our own, sin only excepted. He was born of a woman as an infant, and had a body that grew and increased in stature as our bodies do,—a body that could hunger and thirst, and be weary and need sleep, and feel pain, and groan in agony and suffering, like the body of any one who reads this paper. In that body He condescended to tabernacle for thirty-three years, its members daily fulfilling the Law of God perfectly, so that in His "flesh" Satan could find nothing failing or defective (John 14:30).

(b) Look, in the next place, at the great cardinal doctrine of Christ's atonement. That wondrous distinctive verity of our faith, that solution of the problem, "how can sinful man have peace with God?"—is indissolubly bound up with Christ's body. It was the death of that body on the cross which provided for fallen man a way of reconciliation with God. It was the precious lifeblood, which flowed from our Lord's crucified body on Calvary, which purchased for us redemption from the curse of a broken law. In short, it is the blood of Christ's body to which true Christians owe all their comfort while they live, and their hope when they die.

(c) Look, next, at the crowning facts of Christ's resurrection and ascension into heaven. When our Lord came forth from the grave where Joseph and Nicodemus had laid Him, on the third day, He did not come forth as a spirit. To use the words of our Fourth Article, He "took again His body, with flesh, bones, and all things appertaining to the perfection of man's nature." In that body He was seen and touched by His disciples. In that body He spoke, and ate, and drank like ourselves. And, finally, in that body He ascended into heaven, and there sits till He returns to judge all men at the last day. We have a priest and advocate with the Father who has a body.

(d) Look, next, at the practical precepts and exhortations which the Apostles are continually pressing on us in the New Testament. Mark how frequently they speak of the body and its members as "instruments of righteousness," as a part of the Christian's nature requiring his constant care, and as a means of exhibiting his sanctification and holiness. "Your body is the temple of the Holy Ghost."—"Glorify God in body and spirit, which are His."—"I pray God your whole spirit, and soul, and body, may be preserved blameless."—"Present your bodies a living sacrifice."—Let "Christ be magnified in my body."—Let the "life of Jesus be manifest in our mortal flesh."—We shall "receive the things done in the body."—Where, indeed, and how, could the graces of temperance, soberness, chastity, and self-denial be shown forth except in and through the body? (Rom. 6:13; 1 Cor. 6:19-20; 1 Thess. 5:23; Rom. 12:1; Phil. 1:20; 2 Cor. 4:11; 2 Cor. 5:10).

(e) Look, finally, at that grand distinctive hope which sustains the Christian amidst the deaths, and funerals, and pains, and partings, and sufferings of this world. That hope is the resurrection of the flesh after death. Our bodies shall live again. The grave cannot hold them. We part from those who fall asleep in Jesus in the blessed confidence that we shall meet and see them again, better, stronger, more beautiful than they ever were upon earth. For ever let us thank God that the glorious gospel which we profess to believe makes provision for our bodies as well as our souls.

But, after all, the importance which Christianity attaches to the body is not one whir greater than that which is continually attached to it by the children of this world. It is easy to sneer at the simple facts and doctrines of Christianity, and to talk great swelling words about" mind," and "thought," and "intellect," and "reason." But there is no getting over the broad fact that it is the body and not the mind, and the wants of the body, by which the world is governed.

Statesmen and politicians know this full well, and often to their cost. Their tenure of office depends in great measure on the contentment of the people. And who does not know that nothing creates popular discontent so much as high prices of corn, and general dearness of food for the body?

Merchants and ship-owners, of all men in the world, ought to know the importance of the body. Corn, and meat, and sugar, and tea, to feed the body,—cotton and wool to clothe the body,—what are these but the very articles which create the main portion of the commerce, and carrying trade, and business of a nation?

It would be waste of time to multiply arguments on this subject. In the face of such facts as these, it is the highest wisdom, both in the Church and the State, never to forget the importance of the body. To promote cleanliness, and temperance, and social purity,—to aim at the highest standard of sanitary arrangements, and to encourage every movement which can increase the health and longevity of a people,—to provide as far as possible good air, good water, good dwellings, and cheap food for every man, woman, and child in the land,—these are objects which deserve the best attention both of the Christian and the man of the world.

There is a mine of deep truth in the saying, "Sanitas sanitatum: omnia sanitas."[4] Whatever students and bookworms and philosophers may please to say, there is an indissoluble connection between the bodies and minds and souls of mankind. You cannot

---

[4]Sanity of sanity, all is sanity. First used in Benjamin Disraeli's speech of April 3, 1872.

separate them. Not one of the three can be safely neglected. The Church, which only cares for saving souls, and the State, which only cares for educating minds, are both making a vast mistake. Happy is that country where body, soul, and mind are all cared for, and a continual effort made to provide for the health of all three.

II. The other remark which I wish to make is this: Observe the honour which our Lord Jesus Christ has put on the medical profession.

It is a noteworthy fact, to begin with, that one of the four men whom our Lord chose to write the Gospels was a "physician." Not only does ecclesiastical history, with almost entire harmony, tell us this, but there is strong internal evidence in St. Luke's writings to confirm it. An ingenious writer has lately published a book which proves that many Greek phrases and expressions used in the third Gospel and the Acts are thoroughly medical, and such as a physician of that age would use in describing the symptoms of disease, or of returning health. In short, there is little room for doubt that out of the twenty-seven books which make up the little volume of the New Testament, two of the longest come from the pen of a medical man.

But, after all, there is another fact of even deeper significance which demands attention. I refer to the very large number of the cases of sickness and disease which our Lord Jesus Christ was pleased to heal during the period of His earthly ministry. No doubt, if He had thought fit, He could have shown His Divine power, and proved His Divine mission, by miracles like the plagues of Egypt, by calling fire from heaven like Elijah, by causing the earth to open and swallow up His enemies, as Dathan and Abiram were swallowed up in the wilderness. But He did not do so. The great majority of His wondrous works were works of mercy wrought on the suffering bodies of men and women. To cure the leprous, the dropsical, the palsied, the fevered, the lame, the blind, was the continual labour of love of Him who was "God manifest in the flesh." To use the deep and mysterious words quoted from Isaiah by St. Matthew, "Himself took our infirmities, and bare our sicknesses" (Matt. 8:17).

Now why was this? Why did our Lord adopt this line of action, and habitually condescend to devote time and attention to the humbling and often loathsome ills to which flesh is heir? Partly, I believe, to remind us that He came to remedy the fall of man; and that of all the consequences of the fall, none cause so much trouble, and affect all ranks and classes of society so thoroughly, as sickness. But partly also, I believe, to teach Christians in every age, that to minister to the sick is eminently a work of mercy according to Christ's mind. He that endeavours to check disease, to alleviate suffering, to lessen pain, to help the self-curative powers of nature, and to lengthen life, may surely take comfort in the thought, that, however much he may fail, he is at any rate walking in the footsteps of Jesus of Nazareth. Next to the office of him who ministers to men's souls, there is none really more useful and honourable than that of him who ministers to the soul's frail tabernacle—the body.

He that thinks of these things will not wonder that the rise and progress of Christianity in every age has done much for the office of the physician. That nothing was known of medicine or surgery before the Christian era, it would be unfair to say. The names of Podalirius and Machaon in Homer, the better-known, less mythical name of Hippocrates (no mean observer of symptoms), are familiar to students. But it is a certain fact that the sick were never so systematically cared for, and the medical profession so honourably esteemed, as they have been since the Church of Christ leavened the world. The builders of the Parthenon and Colosseum built no infirmaries. You will find no ruins of hospitals at Athens or Rome. The infidel, the sceptic, and the agnostic may sneer at Bible religion if they please, but they cannot get over the fact that medical and surgical knowledge have always advanced side by side with the gospel of Christ. Clever and ingenious as the heathen inhabitants of India, China, and Japan are at this day, it is notorious that their acquaintance with anatomy and materia medica, and their treatment of bodily diseases, are beneath contempt.

Few of us, perhaps, realize what an immense debt we owe in Christian England to the medical profession. How much the comfort of our lives depends on it, and how vastly different is the condition of those whose lot is cast in a heathen country, or an "uncivilized back settlement of a colony! He that has a good servant in his house, and a good doctor within reach, ought to be a thankful man.

Fewer still, I believe, realize what enormous strides medicine and surgery have made in the last two centuries, and are continually making in the present. Of course death still reigns, and will reign until Christ returns in glory. Kings and their subjects, rich and poor, all alike die, and will die until death is swallowed up in victory. And no marvel! The human body is a frail and delicate machine. "Strange that a harp of a thousand strings should keep in tune so long." But that the duration of life in this age is greatly increased by the advance of medical science, and that many diseases are preventable, manageable, or curable, which were once always thought fatal, are facts entirely beyond dispute. Let any one read Baxter's semi-medical sermon in the Morning Exercises, and observe his receipts for hypochondria and dyspepsia, and then say whether he ought not to be thankful that he lives in the nineteenth century. The mere fact that our ancestors knew nothing of quinine, chloroform, vaccination, the carbolic spray, the stethoscope, the laryngoscope, the ophthalmoscope, or the right treatment of the lunatic, the idiot, the deaf and dumb, and the blind, is a fact that speaks volumes to any intelligent mind.

None, perhaps, have such constant opportunities of seeing the value of a medical man's services as Christian ministers. We meet them in sick-rooms, and by the side of death-beds, and we know the self-denying labour which their profession entails, and the ungrudging and often unpaid attention which the sick almost invariably receive at their hands.

There ought always to be the utmost harmony and friendly feeling between the two professions. The sick-room is the common ground on which they meet. On that ground they can greatly help one another. I think the minister of religion can help the medical man by teaching his patients the paramount importance of obedience to orders, of submission to advice, of attention to rules about diet and sanitary matters, and by encouraging patience and quietness of spirit. I am sure the doctor can help the minister by gently and wisely reminding those whose cases are past recovery, that it is their duty to accept the inevitable, that this life is not all, that they have souls as well as bodies, and that it is wise to look calmly at their latter end, and a world to come, and to prepare to meet God.

There is much in common in the two professions, the one in caring for men's bodies, and the other in caring for men's souls. We ministers cannot command success. Too often we visit in vain, exhort in vain, advise in vain, preach in vain. We find that spiritual life and death are in higher hands than ours. The doctor finds that under the most skillful treatment people will die, and we find that under the most faithful teaching many continue unmoved in conscience, and dead in sins. Like the doctor, we often feel our ignorance, cannot diagnose or discern symptoms, and feel doubtful what to say. Both ministers and medical men have great need to be clothed with humility. But I trust, to use the words which were placed on the tomb of Sir Henry Lawrence, we both "try to do our duty," and persevere. Duties are ours, but events are God's.

That there never may be wanting in Great Britain a continual supply of able, right-minded, faithful medical men, and that we who minister to the soul, and those who minister to the body, may always work harmoniously together, and help one another, is my earnest prayer.

CHAPTER III[5]

Eccles. 12:12
Simplicity In Preaching.

KING SOLOMON says, in the book of Ecclesiastes, "Of making many books there is no end" (Eccles. 12:12). There are few subjects about which that saying is more true than that of preaching. The volumes which have been written in order to show ministers how to preach are enough to make a small library. In sending forth one more little treatise, I only propose to touch one branch of the subject. I do not pretend to consider what should be the substance and matter of a sermon. I purposely leave alone such points as "gravity, unction, liveliness, warmth," and the like, or the comparative merits of written or extempore sermons. I wish to confine myself to one point, which receives far less attention than it deserves. That point is simplicity in language and style.

I ought to be able to tell my readers something about "simplicity," if experience will give any help. I began preaching forty-five years ago, when I first took orders in a poor rural parish, and a great portion of my ministerial life has been spent in preaching to labourers and farmers. I know the enormous difficulty of preaching to such hearers, of making them understand one's meaning, and securing their attention. So far as concerns language and composition, I deliberately say that I would rather preach before the University at Oxford or Cambridge, or the Temple, or Lincoln's Inn, or the Houses of Parliament, than I would address an agricultural congregation on a fine hot afternoon in the month of August. I have heard of a labourer who enjoyed Sunday more than any other day in the week, "Because," he said, "I sit comfortably in church, put up my legs, have nothing to think about, and just go to sleep." Some of my younger friends in the ministry may some day be called to preach to such congregations as I have had, and I shall be glad if they can profit by my experience.

Before entering on the subject, I wish to clear the way by making four prefatory remarks.

(a) For one thing, I ask all my readers to remember that to attain simplicity in preaching is of the utmost importance to every minister who wishes to be useful to souls. Unless you are simple in your sermons you will never be understood, and unless you are understood you cannot do good to those who hear you. It was a true saying of Quintilian, "If you do not wish to be understood, you deserve to be neglected." Of course the first object of a minister should be to preach the truth, the whole truth, and nothing but "the

---

[5]The substance of this paper was originally addressed, as a lecture, to a clerical audience, at St. Paul's Cathedral, on behalf of the Homiletical Society. For a certain roughness and abruptness of style I must apologize. But my readers must kindly remember that the lecture was spoken and not written, and is prepared for the press from the notes of a shorthand writer.

truth as it is in Jesus." But the next thing he ought to aim at is, that his sermon may be understood; and it will not be understood by most of his hearers if it is not simple.

(b) The next thing I will say, by way of prefatory remark, is, that to attain simplicity in preaching is by no means an easy matter. No greater mistake can be made than to suppose this. "To make hard things seem hard," to use the substance of a saying of Archbishop Usher's, "is within the reach of all, but to make hard things seem easy and intelligible is a height attained by very few speakers." One of the wisest and best of the Puritans said two hundred years ago, "that the greater part of preachers shoot over the heads of the people." This is true also in 1837! I fear a vast proportion of what we preach is not understood by our hearers any more than if it were Greek. When people hear a simple sermon, or read a simple tract, they are apt to say, "How true! how plain! how easy to understand!" and to suppose that any one can write in that style. Allow me to tell my readers that it is an extremely difficult thing to write simple, clear, perspicuous, and forcible English. Look at the sermons of Charles Bradley, of Clapham. A sermon of his reads most beautifully. It is so simple and natural, that any one feels at once that the meaning is as clear as the sun at noonday. Every word is the right word, and every word is in its right place. Yet the labour those sermons cost Mr. Bradley was very great indeed. Those who have read Goldsmith's Vicar of Wakefield attentively, can hardly fail to have noticed the exquisite naturalness, ease, and simplicity of its language. And yet it is known that the pains and trouble and time bestowed upon that work were immense. Let the Vicar of Wakefield be compared with Johnson's Rasselas, which was written off in a few days, it is said, under higher pressure, and the difference is at once apparent. In fact, to use very long words, to seem very learned, to make people go away after a sermon saying, "How fine! how clever! how grand!" all this is very easy work. But to write what will strike and stick, to speak or to write that which at once pleases and is understood, and becomes assimilated with a heater's mind and a thing never forgotten—that, we may depend upon it, is a very difficult thing and a very rare attainment.

(c) Let me observe, in the next place, that when I talk of simplicity in preaching, I would not have my readers suppose I mean childish preaching. If we suppose the poor like that sort of sermon, we are greatly mistaken. If our hearers once imagine we consider them a parcel of ignorant folks for whom any kind of "infant's food" is good enough, our chance of doing good is lost altogether. People do not like even the appearance of condescending preaching. They feel we are not treating them as equals, but inferiors. Human nature always dislikes that. They will at once put up their backs, stop their ears, and take offence, and then we might as well preach to the winds.

(d) Finally, let me observe, that it is not coarse or vulgar preaching that is needed. It is quite possible to be simple, and yet to speak like a gentleman, and with the demeanour of a courteous and refined person. It is an utter mistake to imagine that uneducated and illiterate men and women prefer to be spoken to in an illiterate way, and by an uneducated person. To suppose that a lay-evangelist or Scripture-reader, who knows nothing of Latin or Greek, and is only familiar with his Bible, is more acceptable than an Oxford first-class man, or a Cambridge wrangler (if that first-class man knows how to preach), is a complete error. People only tolerate vulgarity and coarseness, as a rule, when they can get nothing else.

Having made these prefatory remarks in order to clear the way, I will now proceed to give my readers five brief hints as to what seems to me the best method of attaining simplicity in preaching.

I. My first hint is this: If you want to attain simplicity in preaching, take care that you have a clear view of the subject upon which you are going to preach. I ask your special attention to this. Of all the five hints I am about to give, this is the most important. Mind, then, when your text is chosen, that you understand it and see right through it; that you know precisely what you want to prove, what you want to teach, what you want to establish, and what you want people's minds to carry away. If you yourself begin in a fog, you may depend upon it you will leave your people in darkness. Cicero, one of the greatest ancient orators, said long ago, "No one can possibly speak clearly and eloquently about a subject which he does not understand,"—and I am satisfied that he spoke the truth. Archbishop Whately was a very shrewd observer of human nature, and he said rightly of a vast number of preachers, that "they aimed at nothing, and they hit nothing. Like men landing on an unknown island, and setting out on a journey of exploration, they set out in ignorance, and travelled on in ignorance all the day long."

I ask all young ministers especially, to remember this first hint. I repeat most emphatically, "Take care you thoroughly understand your subject. Never choose a text of which you do not quite know what it means." Beware of taking obscure passages such as those which are to be found in unfulfilled and emblematic prophecies. If a man will continually preach to an ordinary congregation about the seals and vials and trumpets in Revelation, or about Ezekiel's temple, or about predestination, free will, and the eternal purposes of God, it will not be at all surprising to any reasonable mind if he fails to attain simplicity. I do not mean that these subjects ought not to be handled occasionally, at fit times, and before a suitable audience. All I say is, that they are very deep subjects, about which wise Christians often disagree, and it is almost impossible to make them very simple. We ought to see our subjects plainly, if we wish to make them simple, and there are hundreds of plain subjects to be found in God's Word.

Beware, for the same reason, of taking up what I call fanciful subjects and accommodated texts, and then dragging out of them meanings which the Holy Ghost never intended to put into them. There is no subject needful for the soul's health which is not to be found plainly taught and set forth in Scripture. This being the case, I think a preacher should never take a text and extract from it, as a dentist would a tooth from the jaw, something which, however true in itself, is not the plain literal meaning of the inspired words. The sermon may seem very glittering and ingenious, and his people may go away saying, "What a clever parson we have got!" But if, on examination, they can neither find the sermon in the text, nor the text in the sermon, their minds are perplexed, and they begin to think the Bible is a deep book which cannot be understood. If you want to attain simplicity, beware of accommodated texts.

When I speak of accommodated texts, let me explain what I mean. I remember hearing of a minister in a northern town, who was famous for preaching in this style. Once he gave out for his text, "He that is so impoverished that he hath no oblation, chooseth unto him a tree that will not rot" (Isa. 40:20). "Here," said he, "is man by nature impoverished and undone. He has nothing to offer, in order to make satisfaction for his soul. And what ought he to do? He ought to choose a tree which cannot rot, even the cross of our Lord Jesus Christ."—On another occasion, being anxious to preach on the doctrine of indwelling sin, he chose his text out of the history of Joseph and his brethren, and gave out the words, "The old man of whom ye spake, is he yet alive?" (Gen. 43:27). Out of this question he ingeniously twisted a discourse about the infection of nature remaining in the believer,—a grand truth, no doubt, but certainly not the truth of the passage. Such instances will, I trust, be a warning to all my younger brethren. If you want to preach about the indwelling corruption of human nature, or about Christ crucified, you need not seek for such far-fetched texts as those I have named. If you want to be simple, mind you choose plain simple texts.

Furthermore, if you wish to see through your subjects thoroughly, and so to attain the foundation of simplicity, do not be ashamed of dividing your sermons and stating your divisions. I need hardly say this is a very vexed question. There is a morbid dread of "firstly, secondly, and thirdly" in many quarters. The stream of fashion runs strongly against divisions, and I must frankly confess that a lively undivided sermon is much better than one divided in a dull, stupid, illogical way. Let every man be fully persuaded in his own mind. He that can preach sermons which strike and stick without divisions, by all means let him hold on his way and persevere. But let him not despise his neighbour who divides. All I say is, if we would be simple, there must be order in a sermon as there is in an army. What wise general would mix up artillery, infantry, and cavalry in one confused mass in the day of battle? What giver of a banquet or dinner would dream of putting on the table the whole of the viands at once, the soup, the fish, the entrees, the joints, the salads, the game, the sweets, the dessert, in one huge dish? Such a host would hardly be thought to serve his dinner well. Just so I say it is with sermons. By all means let there be order—order, whether you bring out your "firstly, secondly, or thirdly," or not—order, whether your divisions are concealed or expressed—order so carefully arranged that your points and ideas shall follow one another in beautiful regularity, like regiments marching past before the Queen on a review day in Windsor Park.

For my own part, I honestly confess that I do not think I have preached two sermons in my life without divisions. I find it of the utmost importance to make people understand, remember, and carry away what I say, and I am certain that divisions help me to do so. They are, in fact, like hooks and pegs and shelves in the mind. If you study the sermons of men who have been and are successful preachers, you will always find order, and often divisions, in their sermons. I am not a bit ashamed to say that I often read the sermons of Mr. Spurgeon. I like to gather hints about preaching from all quarters. David did not ask about the sword of Goliath, Who made it? who polished it? what blacksmith forged it? He said, "There is nothing like it;" for he had once used it to cut off its owner's head. Mr. Spurgeon can preach most ably, and he proves it by keeping his enormous congregation together. We ought always to examine and analyze sermons which draw people together. Now when you read Mr. Spurgeon's sermons, note how clearly and perspicuously he divides a sermon, and fills each division with beautiful and simple ideas. How easily you grasp his meaning! How thoroughly he brings before you certain great truths, that hang to you like hooks of steel, and which, once planted in your memory, you never forget!

My first point, then, if you would be simple in your preaching, is, that you must thoroughly understand your subject, and if you want to know whether you understand it, try to divide and arrange it. I can only say for myself; that I have done this ever since I have been a minister. For forty-five years I have kept blank manuscript books in which I put down texts and heads of sermons for use when required. Whenever I get hold of a text, and see my way through it, I put it down and make a note of it. If I do not see my way through a text, I cannot preach on it, because I know I cannot be simple; and if I cannot be simple, I know I had better not preach at all.

II. The second hint I would give is this: Try to use in all your sermons, as far as you can, simple words. In saying this, however, I must explain myself. When I talk of simple words, I do not mean words of only one syllable, or words which are purely Saxon. I cannot in this matter agree with Archbishop Whately. I think he goes too far in his recommendation of Saxon, though there is much truth in what he says about it. I rather prefer the saying of that wise old heathen Cicero, when he said, that orators should try to use words which are "in daily common use" amongst the people. Whether the words are Saxon or not, or of two or three syllables, it does not matter so long as they are words commonly used and understood by the people. Only, whatever you do, beware of what the poor shrewdly call "dictionary" words, that is, of words which are abstract, or scientific, or pedantic, or complicated, or indefinite, or very long. They may seem very fine, and sound very grand, but they are rarely of any use. The most powerful and forcible words, as a rule, are very short.

Let me say one word more to confirm what I have stated about that common fallacy of the desirableness of always using Saxon English. I would remind you that a vast number of words of other than Saxon origin are used by writers of notorious simplicity. Take, for instance, the famous work of John Bunyan, and look at the very title of it, The Pilgrim's Progress. Neither of the leading words in that title is Saxon. Would he have improved matters if he had called it "The Wayfarer's Walk"? In saying this I admit freely that words of French and Latin origin are generally inferior to Saxon; and, as a rule, I should say, use strong pure Saxon words if you can. All I mean to say is, that you must not think it a matter of course that words cannot be good and simple if they are not of Saxon origin. In any case, beware of long words.

Dr. Gee, in his excellent book, Our Sermons (Longman), very ably points out the uselessness of using long words and expressions not in common use. For example, he says, "Talk of happiness rather than of felicity, talk of almighty rather than omnipotent, lessen rather than diminish, forbidden rather than proscribed, hateful rather than noxious, seeming rather than apparent, afterwards rather than subsequently, call out and draw forth instead of evoke and educe." We all need to be pulled up sharply on these points. It is very well to use fine words at Oxford and Cambridge, before classical hearers, and in preaching before educated audiences. But depend upon it, when you preach to ordinary congregations, the sooner you throw overboard this sort of English, and use plain common words, the better. One thing, at all events, is quite certain, without simple words you will never attain simplicity in preaching.

III. The third hint I would offer, if you wish to attain simplicity in preaching, is this: Take care to aim at a simple style of composition. I will try to illustrate what I mean. If you take up the sermons preached by that great and wonderful man Dr. Chalmers, you can hardly fail to see what an enormous number of lines you meet with without coming to a full stop. This I cannot but regard as a great mistake. It may suit Scotland, but it will never do for England. If you would attain a simple style of composition, beware of writing many lines without coming to a pause, and so allowing the minds of your hearers to take breath. Beware of colons and semicolons. Stick to commas and full stops, and take care to write as if you were asthmatical or short of breath. Never write or speak very long sentences or long paragraphs. Use stops frequently, and start again; and the oftener you do this, the more likely you are to attain a simple style of composition. Enormous sentences full of colons, semicolons, and parentheses, with paragraphs of two or three pages' length, are utterly fatal to simplicity. We should bear in mind that preachers have to do with hearers and not readers, and that what will "read" well will not always "speak" well. A reader of English can always help himself by looking back a few lines and refreshing his mind. A hearer of English hears once for all, and if he loses the thread of your sermon in a long involved sentence, he very likely never finds it again.

Again, simplicity in your style of composition depends very much upon the proper use of proverbs and epigrammatic sentences. This is of vast importance. Here, I think, is the value of much that you find in Matthew Henry's commentary, and Bishop Hall's Contemplations. There are some good sayings of this sort in a book not known so well as it should be, called Papers on Preaching by a Wykehamist. Take a few examples of what I mean: "What we weave in time we wear in eternity." "Hell is paved with good intentions." "Sin forsaken is one of the best evidences of sin forgiven." "It matters little how we die, but it matters much how we live." "Meddle with no man's person, but spare no man's sin." "The street is soon clean when every one sweeps before his own door." "Lying rides on debt's back: it is hard for an empty bag to stand upright." "He that begins with prayer will end with praise" "All is not gold that glitters." "In religion, as in business, there are no gains without pains." "In the Bible there are shallows where a lamb can wade, and depths where an elephant must swim." "One thief on the cross was saved, that none should despair, and only one, that none should presume."

Proverbial, epigrammatic, and antithetical sayings of this kind give wonderful perspicuousness and force to a sermon. Labour to store your minds with them. Use them judiciously, and especially at the end of paragraphs, and you will find them an immense help to the attainment of a simple style of composition. But of long, involved, complicated sentences always beware.

IV. The fourth hint I will give is this: If you wish to preach simply, use a direct style. What do I mean by this? I mean the practice and custom of saying "I" and "you." When a man takes up this style of preaching, he is often told that he is conceited and egotistical. The result is that many preachers are never direct, and always think it very humble and modest and becoming to say "we." But I remember good Bishop Villiers saying that "we" was a word kings and corporations should use, and they alone, but that parish clergymen should always talk of "I" and "you." I endorse that saying with all my heart. I declare I never can understand what the famous pulpit "we" means. Does the preacher who all through his sermon keeps saying "we" mean himself and the bishop? or himself and the Church? or himself and the congregation? or himself and the Early Fathers? or himself and the Reformers? or himself and all the wise men in the world? or, after all, does he only mean myself, plain "John Smith" or "Thomas Jones"? If he only means himself, what earthly reason can he give for using the plural number, and not saying simply and plainly "I"? When he visits his parishioners, or sits by a sick-bed, or catechises his school, or orders bread at the baker's, or meat at the butcher's, he does not say "we," but "I." Why, then, I should like to know, can he not say "I" in the pulpit? What right has he, as a modest man, to speak for any one but himself? Why not stand up on Sunday and say, "Reading in the Word of God, I have found a text containing such things as these, and I come to set them before you"?

Many people, I am sure, do not understand what the preacher's "we" means. The expression leaves them in a kind of fog. If you say, "I, your rector; I, your vicar; I, the curate of the parish," come here to talk of something that concerns your soul, something you should believe, something you should do—you are at any rate understood. But if you begin to talk in the vague plural number of what "we" ought to do, many of your hearers do not know what you are driving at, and whether you are speaking to yourself or them. I charge and entreat my younger brethren in the ministry not to forget this point. Do try to be as direct as possible. Never mind what people say of you. In this particular do not imitate Chalmers, or Melville, or certain other living pulpit celebrities. Never say "we" when you mean "I." The more you get into the habit of talking plainly to the people, in the first person singular, as old Bishop Latimer did, the simpler will your sermon be, and the more easily understood. The glory of Whitefield's sermons is their directness. But unhappily they were so badly reported, that we cannot now appreciate them.

V. The fifth and last hint I wish to give you is this: If you would attain simplicity in preaching, you must use plenty of anecdotes and illustrations. You must regard illustrations as windows through which light is let in upon your subject. Upon this point a great deal might be said, but the limits of a small treatise oblige me to touch it very briefly. I need hardly remind you of the example of Him who "spake as never man spake," our Lord and Saviour Jesus Christ. Study the four Gospels attentively, and mark what a wealth of illustration His sermons generally contain. How often you find figure upon figure, parable upon parable, in His discourses! There was nothing under His eyes apparently from which He did not draw lessons. The birds of the air, and the fish in the sea, the sheep, the goats, the cornfield, the vineyard, the ploughman, the sower, the reaper, the fisherman, the shepherd, the vinedresser, the woman kneading meal, the flowers, the grass, the bank, the wedding feast, the sepulchre, all were made vehicles for conveying thoughts to the minds of hearers. What are such parables as the prodigal son, the good Samaritan, the ten virgins, the king who made a marriage for his son, the rich man and Lazarus, the labourers of the vineyard, and others,—what are all these but stirring stories that our Lord tells in order to convey some great truth to the souls of His hearers? Try to walk in His footsteps and follow His example.

If you pause in your sermon, and say, "Now I will tell you a story," I engage that all who are not too fast asleep will prick up their ears and listen. People like similes, illustrations, and well-told stories, and will listen to them when they will attend to nothing else. And from what countless sources we can get illustrations! Take all the book of nature around us. Look at the sky above and the world beneath. Look at history. Look at all the branches of science, at geology, at botany, at chemistry, at astronomy. What is there in heaven above or earth below from which you may not bring illustrations to throw light on the message of the gospel? Read Bishop Latimer's sermons, the most popular, perhaps, that were ever preached. Read the works of Brooks, and Watson, and Swinnock, the Puritans. How full they are of illustrations, figures, metaphors, and stories! Look at Mr. Moody's sermons. What is one secret of his popularity? He fills his sermons with pleasing stories. He is the best speaker, says an Arabian proverb, who can turn the ear into an eye.

For my part, I not only try to tell stories, but in country parishes I have sometimes put before people familiar illustrations which they can see. For instance—Do I want to show them that there must have been a first great cause or Being who made this world? I have sometimes taken out my watch, and have said, "Look at this watch. How well it is made! Do any of you suppose for a moment that all the screws, all the wheels, all the pins of that watch came together by accident? Would not any one say there must have been a watchmaker? And if so, it follows most surely that there must have been a Maker of the world, whose handiwork we see graven on the face of every one of those glorious planets going their yearly rounds and keeping time to a single second. Look at the world in which you live, and the wonderful things which it contains. Will you tell me that there is no God, and that creation is the result of chance?" Or sometimes I have taken out a bunch of keys and shaken them. The whole congregation, when they hear the keys, look up. Then I say,

"Would there be need of any keys if all men were perfect and honest? What does this bunch of keys show? Why, they show that the heart of man is deceitful above all things, and desperately wicked." Illustration, I confidently assert, is one of the best receipts for making a sermon simple, clear, perspicuous, and easily understood. Lay yourselves out for it. Pick up illustrations wherever you can. Keep your eyes open, and use them well. Happy is that preacher who has an eye for similitudes, and a memory stored with well-chosen stories and illustrations. If he is a real man of God, and knows how to deliver a sermon, he will never preach to bare walls and empty benches.

But I must add a word of caution. There is a way of telling stories. If a man cannot tell stories naturally, he had better not tell them at all. Illustration, again, after all I have said in its favour, may be carried too far. I remember a notable instance of this in the case of the great Welsh preacher, Christmas Evans. There is in print a sermon of his about the wonderful miracle that took place in Gadara, when devils took possession of the swine, and the whole herd ran down violently into the sea. He paints it so minutely that it really becomes ludicrous by reason of the words put in the mouth of the swineherds who told their master of the loss he had sustained. "Oh! sir," says one, "the pigs have all gone!" "But," says the master, "where have they gone?" "They have run down into the sea." "But who drove them down?" "Oh! sir, that wonderful man." "Well, what sort of a man was he? What did he do?" "Why, sir, he came and talked such strange things, and the whole herd ran suddenly down the steep place into the sea." "What, the old black boar and all?" "Yes, sir, the old black boar has gone too; for as we looked round, we just saw the end of his tail going over the cliff." Now that is going to an extreme. So, again, Dr. Guthrie's admirable sermons are occasionally so overlade with illustrations as to remind one of cake made almost entirely of plums and containing hardly any flour. Put plenty of colour and picture into your sermon by all means. Draw sweetness and light from all sources and from all creatures, from the heavens and the earth, from history, from science. But after all there is a limit. You must be careful how you use colour, lest you do as much harm as good. Do not put on colour by spoonfuls, but with a brush. This caution remembered, you will find colour an immense aid in the attainment of simplicity and perspicuousness in preaching.

And now bear in mind that my five points are these: First: If you want to attain simplicity in preaching, you must have a clear knowledge of what you are going to preach.

Secondly: If you would attain simplicity in preaching, you must use simple words.

Thirdly: If you would attain simplicity in preaching, you must seek to acquire a simple style of composition, with short sentences and as few colons and semicolons as possible.

Fourthly: If you would attain simplicity in preaching, aim at directness.

Lastly: If you would attain simplicity in preaching, make abundant use of illustration and anecdote.

Let me add to all this one plain word of application. You will never attain simplicity in preaching without plenty of trouble. Pains and trouble, I say emphatically, pains and trouble. When Turner, the great painter, was asked by some one how it was he mixed his colours so well, and what it was that made them so different from those of other artists: "Mix them? mix them? mix them? Why, with brains, sir." I am persuaded that, in preaching, little can be done except by trouble and by pains.

I have heard that a young and careless clergyman once said to Richard Cecil, "I think I want more faith." "No," said the wise old man; "you want more works. You want more pains. You must not think that God will do work for you, though He is ready to do it by you." I entreat my younger brethren to remember this. I beg them to make time for their composition of sermons, to take trouble and to exercise their brains by reading. Only mind that you read what is useful.

I would not have you spend your time in reading the Fathers in order to help your preaching. They are very useful in their way, but there are many things more useful in modern writers, if you choose them discreetly.

Read good models, and become familiar with good specimens of simplicity in preaching. As your best model, take the English Bible. If you speak the language in which that is written, you will speak well. Read John Bunyan's immortal work, the Pilgrim's Progress. Read it again and again, if you wish to attain simplicity in preaching. Do not be above reading the Puritans. Some of them no doubt are heavy. Goodwin and Owen are very heavy, though excellent artillery in position. Read such books as Baxter, and Watson, and Traill, and Flavel, and Charnock, and Hall, and Henry. They are, to my mind, models of the best simple English spoken in old times. Remember, however, that language alters with years. They spoke English, and so do we, but their style was different from ours. Read beside them the best models of modern English that you can get at. I believe the best English writer for the last hundred years was William Cobbett, the political Radical. I think he wrote the finest simple Saxon-English the world has ever seen. In the present day I do not know a greater master of tersely spoken Saxon-English than John Bright. Among old political orators, the speeches of Lord Chatham and Patrick Henry, the American, are models of good English. Last, but not least, never forget that, next to the Bible, there is nothing in the English language which, for combined simplicity, perspicuousness, eloquence, and power, can be compared with some of the great speeches in Shakespeare. Models of this sort must really be studied, and studied "with brains," too, if you wish to attain a good style of composition in preaching. On the other hand, do not be above talking to the poor, and visiting your people from house to house. Sit down with your people by the fireside, and exchange thoughts with them on all subjects. Find out how they think and how they express themselves, if you want them to understand your sermons. By so doing you will insensibly learn much. You will be continually picking up modes of thought, and get notions as to what you should say in your pulpit.

A humble country clergyman was once asked "whether he studied the fathers." The worthy man replied, that he had little opportunity of studying the fathers, as they were generally out in the fields when he called. But he studied the mothers more, because he often found them at home, and he could talk to them.

Wittingly or unwittingly, the good man hit a nail right on the head. We must talk to our people when we are out of church, if we would understand how to preach to them in the church.

(a) I will only say, in conclusion, that whatever we preach, or whatever pulpit we occupy, whether we preach simply or not, whether we preach written or extempore, we ought to aim not merely at letting off fireworks, but at preaching that which will do lasting good to souls. Let us beware of fireworks in our preaching. "Beautiful" sermons, "brilliant" sermons, "clever" sermons, "popular" sermons, are often sermons which have no effect on the congregation, and do not draw men to Jesus Christ. Let us aim so to preach, that what we say may really come home to men's minds and consciences and hearts, and make them think and consider.

(b) All the simplicity in the world can do no good, unless you preach the simple gospel of Jesus Christ so fully and clearly that everybody can understand it. If Christ crucified has not His rightful place in your sermons, and sin is not exposed as it should be, and your people are not plainly told what they ought to believe, and be, and do, YOUR PREACHING IS OF NO USE.

(c) All the simplicity in the world, again, is useless without a good lively delivery. If you bury your head in your bosom, and mumble over your manuscript in a dull, monotonous, droning way, like a bee in a bottle, so that people cannot understand what you are speaking about, your preaching will be in vain. Depend upon it, delivery is not sufficiently attended to in our Church. In this, as in everything else connected with the science of preaching, I consider the Church of England is sadly deficient. I know that I began preaching alone in the New Forest, and nobody ever told me what was right or wrong in the pulpit. The result was that the first year of my preaching was a series of experiments. We get no help in these matters at Oxford and Cambridge. The utter want of any proper training for the pulpit is one great blot and defect in the system of the Church of England.

(d) Above all, let us never forget that all the simplicity in the world is useless without prayer for the outpouring of the Holy Spirit, and the grant of God's blessing, and a life corresponding in some measure to what we preach. Be it ours to have an earnest desire for the souls of men, while we seek for simplicity in preaching the gospel of Jesus Christ, and let us never forget to accompany our sermons by holy living and fervent prayer.

CHAPTER IV[6]

1 Cor. 15:3-4
Foundation Truths.

"I delivered unto you first of all that which I also received, how that Christ died for our sins according to the Scriptures; And that He was buried, and that He rose again the third day according to the Scriptures." —1 Cor. 15:3-4

THE text which heads this paper is taken from a passage of Scripture with which most Englishmen are only too well acquainted. It is the chapter from which the lesson has been selected, which forms part of the matchless Burial Service of the Church of England. Of all the occasional services of the Prayer Book, none, in my humble judgment, is more beautiful than this. The good old "Book of Common Prayer," we all know, has no form or comeliness in the eyes of some. We have seen the burial laws of this realm altered, and other "uses" sanctioned, and introduced into our churchyards at funerals. But of one tiling I am very certain. We shall never see the bodies of professing Christians committed to the ground with a wiser and better service than that of the Anglican Liturgy.

The starting-point of the whole argument of this chapter will be found in the two verses which form the text. The Apostle opens by reminding the Corinthians that" among the first things "which he delivered to them, when he commenced his teaching, were two great facts about Christ: one was His death, the other was His resurrection. The passage seems to me to open up two subjects of deep interest, and to them I invite the attention of all into whose hands this paper may fall.

---

[6]The substance of these pages was originally delivered as a sermon before the University of Oxford, in my turn as Select Preacher at St. Mary's in the year 1830.

I. For one thing, let us mark well the primary truths which St. Paul delivered to the Corinthians.

II. For another thing, let us try to grasp the reasons why St. Paul assigns to these truths such a singularly prominent position.

I. What, then, were the things which the Apostle preached "first of all," that is, among the first things, at Corinth?

Before I answer that question, I ask my readers to pause awhile and realize the whole position which St. Paul occupied when he left Athens and entered Corinth.

Here is a solitary Jew visiting a great heathen city for the first time, to preach an entirely new religion, to begin an aggressive Evangelistic mission. He is a member of a despised people, sneered at alike by Greeks and Romans, isolated and cut off from other nations, in their own little corner of the earth, by their peculiar laws and habits, and unknown to Gentiles either for literature, arms, arts, or science. The "bodily presence" of this bold Jew is "weak," and his "speech," compared to that of Greek rhetoricians, "contemptible" (2 Cor. 10:10). He stands almost alone in a city, famous all over the world, even in the estimate of the heathen, for luxury, immorality, and idolatry. Such was the place, and such was the man! A more remarkable position it is hard to conceive.

And what did this solitary Jew tell the Corinthians?

What did he say about the great Head and Founder of the new faith which he wanted them to receive in place of their ancient religion? Did he begin by cautiously telling them how Christ lived, and taught, and worked miracles, and spake "as no man ever spake"? Did he tell them that He had been rich as Solomon, victorious as Joshua, or learned as Moses? Nothing of the kind! The very first fact he proclaimed about Christ was that He died, and died the most ignominious death—the death of a malefactor, the death of the cross.

And why did St. Paul lay so much stress upon Christ's death rather than His life? Because, he tells the Corinthians, "He died for our sins." A deep and wonderful truth that, a truth which lay at the very foundation of the whole religion which the Apostle came to preach! For that death of Christ was not the involuntary death of a martyr, or a mere example of self-sacrifice. It was the voluntary death of a Divine Substitute for the guilty children of Adam, by which He made atonement for "the sin of the world." It was a death of such mighty influence on the position of sinful man before God, that it provided complete redemption from the consequences of the fall. In a word, St. Paul told the Corinthians that when Christ died, He died as the Representative of guilty man, to make expiation for us by the sacrifice of Himself, and to endure the penalty which we deserved. "He bore our sins in His own body on the tree." "He suffered for sins, the just for the unjust, that He might bring us to God." "He was made sin for us who knew no sin, that we might be made the righteousness of God in Him" (1 Pet. 2:24, 3:18; 2 Cor. 5:21). A great and stupendous mystery, no doubt! But it was a mystery to which every sacrifice from the time of Abel had been continually pointing for 4000 years. Christ died "according to the Scriptures."

The other great fact about Christ which St. Paul placed in the front part of his teaching was His resurrection from the dead. He boldly told the Corinthians that the same Jesus who died, and was buried, came forth alive from the grave on the third day after His death, and was seen, touched, handled, and talked to, in the body, by many competent witnesses. By this amazing miracle He proved, as He had frequently said He would, that He was the promised and long-expected Saviour foretold in prophecy, that the satisfaction for sin He had made by His death was accepted by God the Father, that the work of our redemption was completed, and that death, as well as sin, was a conquered enemy. In short, the Apostle taught that the greatest of miracles had been wrought, and that with such a Founder of the new faith which he came to proclaim, first dying for our sins, and then rising again for our justification, nothing was impossible, and nothing wanting for the salvation of man's soul.

Such were the two great truths to which St. Paul assigned the first place, when he began his campaign as a Christian teacher at Corinth,—Christ's vicarious death for our sins,—Christ's rising again from the grave. Nothing seems to have preceded them: nothing to have been placed on a level with them. No doubt it was a sore trial of faith and courage to a learned and highly-educated man like St. Paul to take up such a line. Flesh and blood might well shrink from it. He says himself, "I was with you in weakness and fear, and in much trembling" (1 Cor. 2:2-3). But by the grace of God he did not flinch. He says, "I determined not to know anything among you, save Jesus Christ and Him crucified."

Nor did the case of Corinth stand alone. Wherever the great Apostle of the Gentiles went, he preached the same doctrine, and put it in the forefront of his preaching. He addressed very different hearers, and people of very different minds. But he always used the same spiritual medicine, whether at Jerusalem, or Antioch in Pisidia, or Iconium, or Lystra, or Philippi, or Thessalonica, or Berea, or Athens, or Ephesus, or Rome. That medicine was the story of the cross and the resurrection. They crop up in all his sermons and Epistles. You never go far without coming across them. Even Festus, the Roman governor, when he tells Agrippa of Paul's case, describes it as hinging on "One Jesus, which was dead, whom Paul affirmed to be alive" (Acts 25:19).

(a) Now let us learn for one thing what were the leading principles of that religion, which eighteen centuries ago came forth from Palestine, and turned the world upside down. The veriest infidel cannot deny the effect that it produced on mankind. The world before and the world after the introduction of Christianity were as different worlds as light and darkness, night and day. It was Christianity that starved idolatry, and emptied the heathen temples,—that stopped gladiatorial combats, elevated the position of women, raised the whole tone of morality, and improved the condition of children and the poor. These are facts which we may safely challenge all the enemies of revealed religion to gainsay. They are facts which form one of the gravest difficulties of infidelity. And what did it all? Not, as some dare to say, the mere publication of a higher code of duty, a sort of improved Platonic philosophy, without root or motive. No! it was the simple story of the cross of Calvary, and the empty sepulchre in the garden, the marvellous death of One "numbered with transgressors," and the astounding miracle of His resurrection (Isa. 53:12). It was by telling how the Son of God died for our sins, and rose again for our justification, that Apostles and apostolic men changed the face of the world, gathered mighty churches, and turned countless sinners into saints.

(b) Let us learn, for another thing, what the foundation of our own personal religion must be, if we really want inward, spiritual comfort. That the early Christians possessed such comfort is as plain as the sun at noonday. We read repeatedly in the New Testament of their joy, and peace, and hope, and patience, and cheerfulness, and contentment. We read in ecclesiastical history of their courage and firmness under the fiercest persecution, of their uncomplaining endurance of sufferings, and their triumphant deaths. And what was the mainspring of their peculiar characters,—characters which excited the admiration even of their bitterest enemies, and puzzled philosophers like Pliny? There can only be one reply. These men had a firm grasp of the two great facts which St. Paul proclaimed "first" and foremost to the Corinthians, the death and resurrection of their great Head, Jesus Christ the Lord. Let us never be ashamed of walking in their steps. It is cheap and easy work to sneer at "dogmatic theology" and old-fashioned creeds and modes of faith, as if they were effete and worn-out things, unfit for this enlightened nineteenth century. But after all, what are the fruits of modern philosophy, and the teaching of cold abstractions, compared to the fruits of the despised dogmas of distinctive Christianity? If you want to see peace in life, and hope in death, and consolation felt in sorrow, you will never find such things except among those who rest on the two great facts of our text, and can say, "I live by faith in the Son of God," who died for my sins, and was raised again for my justification (Gal. 2:20).

II. Let me turn now to another view of the subject before us. We have seen what the truths were which St. Paul proclaimed "first of all" to the Corinthians, and what were the effects which they produced. Let us now try to grasp and examine the reasons why he was led to assign them such a prominent position.

The inquiry is a very interesting one. I cannot hold, with some, that St. Paul adopted this course only because he was commissioned and commanded to do so. I think the reasons lie far deeper than this. Those reasons are to be sought in the necessities and condition of fallen human nature. I believe that man's wants could never have been met and satisfied by any other message than that which St. Paul brought to Corinth; and if he had not brought it, he would have come thither in vain.

For there are three things about man in every part of the world which force themselves on our notice, whenever we sit down to examine his nature, position, and constitution. He is a creature with a sense of sin and accountableness at the bottom of his heart—a creature continually liable to sorrow and trouble from his cradle to his grave, and a creature who has before him the certainty of death, and a future state at last. These are three great facts which stare us in the face everywhere, in Europe, Asia, Africa, and America. Travel all over the world, and they meet you, both among the most highly educated Christians and the most untutored savages. Go about our own country, and study the family life of the most learned philosophers and the most ignorant peasants. Everywhere, and in every rank and class, you will have to make the same report. Everywhere you will find these three things, sorrow, death, and the sense of sin. And the position I boldly take up is this, that nothing can be imagined or conceived more admirably suited to meet the wants of human nature than the very doctrine which St. Paul began with at Corinth—the doctrine of Christ dying for our sins and rising again for us from the grave.

It fits the needs of man, just as the right key fits the lock.

Let me glance for a few minutes at the three things which I have just named, and try to show the strong light which they throw on St. Paul's choice of subjects when he began his ministry at Corinth.

(a) Consider first and foremost, the, inward sense of sin and imperfection which exists in every member of the human family, more or less. I grant freely that it differs widely in different persons. In thousands of people it seems completely gone, effaced, and dead. Early want of education, customary sin, constant neglect of all religion, habitual indulgence in fleshly lusts,—all these things have a wonderful power to blind the eye and sear the conscience. But where will you ever find a man, except among high-caste Brahmins, or half-crazy Christian fanatics, who will boldly tell you that he is perfect and faultless, and who will not confess, if you drive him into a corner, that he is not exactly what he ought to be, and that he knows better than he does? Oh, no! The vast majority of mankind have a conscience of sin, which every now and then makes them miserable. The self-imposed austerities of Hindoos, the trembling of rulers like Herod and Felix, are proofs of what I mean. Wherever there is a child of Adam, there is a creature that has in his heart of hearts a consciousness of guilt, defectiveness, and need.

And when this sense of sin is really awakened, and stirs within us, what can cure it? That is the grand question. Some talk vaguely of God's "mercy" and "goodness," though utterly unable to explain their meaning, and to show what title man has to them. Others flatter themselves that their own repentance, and tears, and prayers, and active and diligent use of the ceremonials of religion, will bring them peace. But what child of Adam ever found relief in this way? What more certain than the recorded experience of thousands, that medicines like these never healed inward misgivings and mental fears? Nothing has ever been found to do good to a sin-stricken soul but the sight of a Divine Mediator between God and man, a real living Person of almighty power and almighty mercy, bearing our sins, suffering in our stead, and taking on Himself the whole burden of our redemption. So long as man only looks within, and thinks to efface the sense of sin by vain attempts to scour and purify his own character, so long he only feels more wretched every day. Once let him look without for peace, to "the Man Christ Jesus" dying for his sins, and rest his soul on Him, and he will find, as millions have found in the last eighteen centuries, that he has got the very thing that a wounded conscience needs. In short, a believing view of Christ dying for our sins is God's appointed remedy for man's spiritual need. It is the Divine specific for that deadly plague which infects the whole family of Adam, and once seen and felt makes men and women miserable. If Paul had not proclaimed this grand specific at Corinth, he would have shown great ignorance of human nature, and been a physician of no value. And if we ministers do not proclaim it, it is because our eyes are dim, and there is little light in us.

(b) Let us consider, in the next place, the universal liability of man to sorrow. The testimony of Scripture, "that man is born to trouble," is continually echoed by thousands who know nothing of the Scriptures, but simply speak the language of their own experience. The world, nearly all men agree, is full of trouble. It is a true saying, that we come into life crying, and pass through it complaining, and leave it disappointed. Of all God's creatures, none is so vulnerable as man. Body, and mind, and affections, and family, and property, are all liable in their turn to become sources and avenues of sorrow. And from this no rank or class possesses any immunity. There are sorrows for the rich as well as the poor, for the learned as well as the unlearned, for the young as well as the old, for the castle as well as the cottage; and neither wealth, nor science, nor high position can prevent their forcing their way into our homes, and breaking in upon us sometimes like an armed man. These are ancient things, I know; the poets and philosophers of old Greece and Rome knew them as well as we do. But it is well to be put in remembrance.

For what shall best help man to meet and bear sorrow? That is the question. If our condition is such, since the Fall, that we cannot escape sorrow, what is the surest receipt for making it tolerable? The cold lessons of Stoicism have no power in them. Resignation and submission to the will of God are excellent things to talk about in fine weather. But when the storm strikes us, and hearts ache, and tears flow, and gaps are made in our family circle, and friends fail us, and money makes itself wings, and sickness lays us low, we want something more than abstract principles and general lessons. We want a living, personal Friend, a Friend to whom we can turn with firm confidence that he can help and feel.

Now it is just here, I maintain, that St. Paul's doctrine of a risen Christ comes in with a marvellous power, and exactly meets our necessities. We have One sitting at the right hand of God, as our sympathizing Friend, who has all power to help us, and can be touched with the feeling of our infirmities, even Jesus the Son of God. He knows the heart of a man and all his condition, for He Himself was born of a woman, and took part of flesh and blood. He knows what sorrow is, for He Himself in the days of His flesh wept, and groaned, and grieved. He has proved His love towards us by "bearing our manners" for thirty-three years in this world, by a thousand acts of kindness, and ten thousand words of consolation, and by finally dying for us on the cross. And He took care before He left the world to say such golden sayings as these, "Let not your heart be troubled: ye believe in God, believe also in Me." "I will not leave you comfortless, I will come to you." "Ask, and ye shall receive, that your joy may be full" (John 14:1, 18, 16:24). I can imagine no truth more suited to man's wants than this. Rules, and principles, and prescriptions, and instructions in times of sorrow are all very well in their way; but what the human heart craves is a personal friend to go to, to talk to, to lean back upon, and commune with. The risen Christ, living and interceding for us at God's right hand, is precisely the Person that we need. If St. Paul had not proclaimed Him to the Corinthians, he would have left one of man's greatest wants unsatisfied. No religion will ever satisfy man which does not meet the legitimate wants of his nature. Teachers who give no place to a living risen Christ in their system, must never be surprised if their weary hearers seek rest at the feet of human priests in the Romish Confessional.

(c) Let us consider, lastly, the certainty of death and its consequences, which every child of Adam must make up his mind to face one day.

To say that death is a serious thing, is to utter a very bald and commonplace truism. Yet it is a strange fact that the familiarity of 6000 years does not abate one jot of its seriousness. The end of each individual is still a very momentous circumstance in his history, and most men honestly confess it. To leave the world and shut our eyes on all among whom we have played our part,—to surrender our bodies, whether we like it or not, to the humiliation of disease, decay, and the grave to be obliged to drop all our schemes and plans and intentions all this is serious enough. But when to this you add the overwhelming thought that there is something beyond the grave, an undiscovered and unknown world, and an account of some sort to be rendered of our life on earth, the death of any man or woman becomes a tremendously serious event. Well may our great poet Shakespeare speak of "the dread of something after death." It is a dread which many feel far more than they would like to confess. Few are ever satisfied with Mohamedan fatalism. Not one in a thousand will ever be found to believe the doctrine of annihilation.

Now at no point do the uninspired religions of the ancients, or the systems of modern philosophy, break down so completely as in the article of death. To dwell for ever in Elysian fields, amidst shadowy, immaterial ghosts, was a consummation little valued even by Homeric heroes. The vague, rootless theory of some undefined state of rest after death, where, somehow and in some way, the souls of the good and the just, separate from their bodies, are to spend an objectless, endless existence is a miserable comforter. Homer, and Plato, and Bolingbroke, and Voltaire, and Paine are all alike cheerless and silent when they look down into an open grave.

But just at the point where all man-made systems are weakest, and fail to satisfy the wants of human nature, there the gospel which St. Paul proclaimed at Corinth is strongest. For it shows us an Almighty Saviour who not only died for our sins, and went down to the grave, but also rose again from the grave with His body, and proved that He had gained a victory over death. "Now is Christ risen from the dead, and become the first-fruits of them that slept."—"He has abolished death, and brought life and immortality to light."—"Through death He has destroyed death, and delivered them that through fear of death were all their lifetime subject to bondage" (1 Cor. 15:20; 2 Tim. 1:10; Heb. 2:15).

And thanks be to God, this blessed victory over death and the grave has not been won by Christ for Himself alone. For eighteen centuries He has enabled thousands of Christian men and women, believing and trusting themselves to Him, to face the king of terrors without fear, and to go down the valley of the shadow of death in the sure and certain hope that they will yet come forth victorious, and in the flesh see God. Read the story of the deaths of the early Christians under heathen persecutions. Mark the dying experience of those who suffered at Oxford and Smithfield, under Queen Mary, for Protestantism. Find, if you can, in the whole range of biography any death-beds of non-Christians which will bear comparison with the death-beds of Christians in the matter of peace, and hope, and strong consolation. You may search for ever and not find them. You will find yourself shut up to the conclusion that the old Scriptural truth of Christ dying and rising again is exactly the truth that fits human nature, and must have come down from God. This, and this only, will enable natural man to meet the last enemy without fear, and to say, "O death, where is thy sting? O grave, where is thy victory?" (1 Cor. 15:55).

What shall we say to these things? I know well that the human heart and its necessities are a deep and intricate subject. But, after studying men's hearts attentively for many years, I have come to one decided conviction. That conviction is, that the true reason why St. Paul preached first and foremost what he preached at Corinth, is to be found in his right knowledge of the nature, moral condition, and position of man. He was taught of God the Holy Ghost that it was the only medicine that was suited to the disease. What human nature requires is a religion for dying sinners, a mighty remedial system and a personal Redeemer; and the work of Christ is marvellously fitted to meet its requirements. We are sick of a deadly sickness, and our first want is a living physician.

It would have been worse than useless if St. Paul had begun his work at Corinth by telling men to be virtuous and moral, while he kept back Christ. It is just as useless now. It even does positive harm. To awaken human nature, and then not show it God's spiritual prescription, may lead to most mischievous consequences. I know no case so pitiable as that of the man who sees clearly sin, sorrow, and death on one side, and does not see clearly Christ dying for sins, and rising again for sinners, on the other. Such a man is just the person to sink into flat despair, or to take refuge in the delusive theology of the Church of Rome. No doubt we may sleep the sleep of unconversion for many years, and feel nothing of spiritual doubts and fears. But once let a man's conscience become uneasy, and crave peace, and I know no medicine which can cure him, and keep him from soul-ruining error, except the "first things" which St. Paul delivered at Corinth,—I mean the two doctrines of Christ's atoning death and resurrection.

And now let me wind up this paper with some words of advice to all who read it. It is advice which the times appear to me to demand. Who can tell but to some one it may be a word in season?

(a) Let me, then, advise you most strongly not to be ashamed of holding decided views about the first things, the foundation truths of religion. Your lot is cast in a day of free thought, free handling, and free inquiry. There is a widespread dislike to doctrinal decision and what is called dogmatism, and none perhaps are so exposed to its influence as the yoking. The natural generosity, unsuspiciousness, and love of fair play, of a young man's heart, make him shrink from taking up very positive theological views, and holding opinions which may even seem to be narrow, party-spirited, or illiberal. The temptation of the present day is to be content with a vague earnestness, to abstain from all sharply cut and distinct views, to be an honorary member of all schools of thought, and to maintain that no man can be unsound in the faith if he exhibits zeal and works hard.

(b) But, after all, your religion must have roots, if it is to live and bear fruit in this cold world. "Earnestness," and "zeal," and "work" are brave words; but, like cut flowers stuck in a garden, they have no power of continuance, if they have no hidden roots below. Admitting to the full that there are secondary things in religion, about which those who are young may fairly suspend their judgment and wait for light, I charge you to remember that there are first things about which you must be decided and make up your minds. You must, I say, if you want peace within, and desire to be useful. And among these first things stand forth like mountains in a plain, the two great truths which are laid down in the text which heads this paper, Christ's death for our sins, and Christ's miraculous resurrection. Grasp tightly these two great truths. Plant your feet firmly on them. Feed your own soul on them. Live on them. Die on them. Never let them go. Strive to be able to say, "I know whom I believe,"—not what, but whom. I live by faith in One who died for me, and rose again. Be decided about this at any cost, and in due time all other truths shall be added to you.

(c) Some, it may be, into whose hands this paper may have fallen are going forth from the quiet haven of a happy home into the battle and conflict of busy life. But wherever your lot may be cast, whether in town or in country, whether among rich or poor, I hope you will try to do good. And remember one chief problem you will have to be continually solving is how to help souls who are labouring under the burden of sin, crushed down with sorrow, or oppressed with the fear of death. And when that time comes, remember the word that I speak to you this day.—The only way to do good is to walk in St. Paul's steps, and to tell men first, foremost, continually, repeatedly, publicly, and from house to house, that Jesus Christ died for their sins, rose again for their justification, lives at the right hand of God to receive, to pardon, and to preserve, and will soon come again to give them a glorious resurrection. These are the truths which the Holy Ghost has always blessed, is blessing, and will bless until the Lord comes. These were St. Paul's "first things." Resolve and determine that by God's grace they shall be yours in this generation. I knew a man of God who made a great mark in his day, who said to me, thirty-five years ago, that Jeremiah was pre-eminently a book for the latter days of England. To that opinion I entirely subscribe. Holding that opinion, I ask my readers to hear a few words about the text which I have chosen. I commend it to you as a text for the times.

CHAPTER V[7]

Jer. 6:16
The Good Way.

"Thus saith the Lord, Stand ye in the ways, and see, and ask for the old paths, where is the good way, and walk therein, and ye shall find rest for your souls." —Jer. 6:16

THE book of the prophet Jeremiah receives from most Christians far less attention than it deserves. It is a noteworthy fact that hardly any portion of Holy Scripture is the subject of so few exhaustive commentaries and expositions.

I fail to see the reason of this comparative neglect. The book was written, under God's inspiration, by a Jewish priest, at a peculiar crisis, in the last days of the kingdom of Judah. Jeremiah was God's messenger to a wicked king,—a worldly aristocracy,—a corrupt people, in a rotten Church, and a dead formal priesthood. He warned his countrymen faithfully, but, like Cassandra of old, he was not believed. He lived to see the complete ruin of Church and State, the city burnt, the temple of Solomon destroyed, and the people carried into captivity. And, finally, it is a Christian tradition, that, after being dragged into Egypt by the Jewish refugees, who fled there, he died the death of a martyr.

I repeat that the writings of such a prophet as this deserve more attention than they have hitherto received.

I. First of all, you have in this text excellent general advice. Jeremiah says to you, "Stand, and see, and ask." I take these words to be a call to thought and consideration. They are as though the prophet said, "Stop and think. Stand still, pause, and reflect. Look within, behind, and before. Do nothing rashly. What are you doing? Where are you going? What will be the end and consequence of your present line of action? Stop and think."

Now to set men thinking is one great object which every teacher of religion should always keep before him. Serious thought, in short, is one of the first steps toward heaven. "I thought on my ways," says the Psalmist, "and turned my feet unto Thy testimonies" (Ps. 119:59). The prodigal son in the parable "came to himself" before he came to his father. He began to consider quietly the folly and uselessness of his conduct, and then, and not till then, he returned home, saying, "Father, I have sinned" (Luke 15:18). Want of thought is, in truth, the simple cause why many make shipwreck for ever. There are but few, I suspect, who deliberately and calmly choose evil, refuse good, turn their back on God, and resolve to serve sin as sin. The most part are what they are because they began their present course without thought. They would not take the trouble to look forward and consider the consequence of their conduct. By thoughtless actions they created habits which have become second nature to them. They have got into a groove now, and nothing but a special miracle of grace will stop them. That is a solemn charge which Isaiah brings against Israel: "My people doth not consider" (Isa. 1:3). "I never gave it a thought," is the sad excuse which I have heard many a man or woman in the lower classes make for sin. The words of Hosea are strictly true of thousands: "They consider not in their hearts" (Hos. 7:2).

There are none, we must all be aware, who bring themselves into so much trouble by want of thinking as the young. From natural high spirits and ignorance of the world, they

---

[7]The substance of this paper was originally preached in a sermon in the Chapel Royal, Whitehall, in the year 1883.

are always tempted to look only at the present and forget the future. Too often they marry in haste and repent at leisure, and lay up misery for life by wedding an uncongenial partner. Too often they choose in haste a wrong profession or business, and find, after two or three years, that they have made an irretrievable mistake, and, if I may borrow a railway phrase, have got on the wrong line of rails. Esau thought only of present gratification, and sold his birthright for a mess of pottage. Dinah had to go "to see the daughters of the land," thinking no harm, and ends by losing her own character, and bringing trouble on her father's house (Gen. 34:1-31). Lot thought only of the present advantage of settling in the well-watered valley around Sodom, and forgot the consequence of being mingled with a people who were "sinners before God exceedingly" (Gen. 13:13). All these found to their cost the folly of not considering, looking forward, and thinking. They sowed to the flesh, and they reaped a harvest of sorrow and disappointment, because they did not "stand and see."

These, no doubt, are ancient things. Every middle-aged person can shake his head over the foolishness of young people, and tell us mournfully that you "cannot put old heads on young shoulders." But the young are not the only persons who need the exhortation of the text in this day. It is pre-eminently advice for the times. Hurry is the characteristic of the age in which we live. Railways, and electric telegraphs, and general competition, appear to oblige modem Englishmen to live in a constant breathless whirl. On every side you see the many "driving furiously," like Jehu, after business or politics. They seem unable to find time for calm, quiet, serious reflection about their souls and a world to come. They have no abstract objection to the doctrines of Christianity, or to the use of means of grace, the Bible, or private prayer. But, alas, they cannot make leisure for them! They live in a perpetual hurry, and in a hurry they too often die. If ever there was an age in England when Jeremiah's advice was needed, it is now. If the prophet could rise from the dead, I believe he would cry aloud to the men of the nineteenth century, "Stop, and think,—look forward,—stand, and see."

Let me, as Christ's minister, impress on all into whose hands these pages may fall, the absolute necessity of resisting the current of the age,—the absolute necessity of making time for your souls. The restless, high-pressure hurry in which men live endangers the very foundations of personal religion. Daily private prayer and daily Bible-reading are too often jostled into a corner, and hastily slurred over. Body and mind are wearied out, when Sunday arrives, by the intense struggle of week-day life. Church services are listlessly attended, and sometimes neglected altogether. The temptation to idle away God's day, or to spend it in visiting or dining out, becomes almost irresistible. Little by little the soul gets into a languid and relaxed condition, and the fine edge of conscience becomes blunt and dull. And why? Simply because in the incessant hurry of business and politics men never find time to think. They are not wilfully and of purpose irreligious; but they give themselves no leisure to stand still and take stock of the state of their souls. Even at the end of last century William Wilberforce made this sorrowful remark about Mr. Pitt, "He was so absorbed in politics, that he had never given himself time for reflection on religion" (Life of Wilberforce, p. 41. Edition, 1872).

I ask every reader of this paper to consider his ways. Beware of the infection of the times. Remember the old Spanish proverb, "Hurry comes from the devil." Resolve by the grace of God, if you love life, that you will have regular seasons for examining yourself, and looking over the accounts of your soul. "Stand, and see" where you are going, and how matters stand between you and God. Beware of perpetual hurried prayers, hurried

Bible-reading, hurried church-going, hurried communions. Commune at least once a week with thine own heart, and be still. Cotton, and coal, and iron, and corn, and ships, and stocks, and land, and gold, and Liberalism, and Conservatism, are not the only things for which we were sent into the world. Death, and judgment, and eternity are not fancies, but stern realities. Make time to think about them. Stand still, and look them in the face. You will be obliged one day to make time to die, whether you are prepared or not. The last enemy, when he knocks at your door, will brook no delay, and will not wait for a "convenient season." He must be admitted, and you will have to go. Happy is he who, when the roar of business and politics is dying away on his ear, and the unseen world is looming large, can say, "I know whom I have believed: I have often stood and communed with Him by faith; and now I go to see as I have been seen."

II. From the general advice which Jeremiah gives in our text, I shall now pass on to the particular direction which the Lord commands him to address to the men of his generation. If they were really willing to listen to his counsel to "stand, and see," and consider their ways, then he bids them "ask for the old paths."

Now what did Jeremiah mean when he spoke of the "old paths"? I find no difficulty in answering that question. I feel no doubt that the phrase meant the old paths of faith in which the fathers of Israel had walked for 1300 years,—the paths of Abraham, Isaac, and Jacob,—the paths of Moses, and Joshua, and Samuel,—the paths of David, and Solomon, and Hezekiah, and Jehoshaphat,—the paths in which the rule of life was the Decalogue, and the rule of worship was that elaborate, typical, sacrificial system of which the essence was faith in the coming Redeemer. That this was the standard around which the men of Jeremiah's day were summoned to rally I shall never hesitate to maintain. Fallen and low as the spiritual condition of Israel often was, between the first of the Judges and the last of the Kings, I fail to see any proof that the Ten Commandments and the law of sacrifice were ever dethroned and repealed. On the contrary, I believe they were honoured and revered by every Jew who was "an Israelite indeed." In the darkest days of the Kings, I believe there were always a few who mourned secretly over the corrupt state of the nation, and, like Simeon and Anna, kept the faith and longed for better times. In a general return to the "old paths," and nothing short of the "old paths," Jeremiah declared, was the only prospect of hope for the future of his countrymen.

But is the principle laid down by Jeremiah a principle which applied to his times alone? Nothing of the kind! I am firmly persuaded that one chief medicine for the spiritual diseases of the nineteenth century is a bold and unhesitating inquiry for "old paths," old doctrines, and the faith of the days that are past. Error, no doubt, is often very ancient, yet truth is always old. Men's hearts are just what they were 6000 years ago, and need the same remedy. God in that long period has used several dispensations, and each succeeding age has enjoyed more light. But the foundation truths have always been the same, and the way by which sinners have reached heaven has always been one and the same. I say boldly that the age wants nothing new. What it wants is plain, distinct, unflinching teaching about "the old paths." Give me no modern road of man's invention. Show me where patriarchs, and prophets, and Apostles, and Fathers, and Reformers set down their feet, obtained a good report, and made a mark on the world. "The old path is the good way."

We want throughout Christendom a return to the old paths of the early Christians. The first followers of the Apostles, no doubt, were, like their teachers, "unlearned and ignorant men." They had no printed books. They had short creeds, and very simple forms of worship. I doubt much if they could have stood an examination in the Thirty-nine Articles, or the Creed of Athanasius, or even in the Church Catechism. But what they knew they knew thoroughly, believed intensely, and propagated unhesitatingly, with a burning enthusiasm. They grasped with both hands, and not with finger and thumb, the Personality, the Deity, the offices, the mediation, the atoning work, the free and full grace of our Lord Jesus Christ, and the inseparable necessity of repentance, faith, and a Christlike life of holiness, self-denial, and charity. On these truths they lived, and for them they were ready to die. Armed with these truths, without gold to bribe or the sword to compel assent, they turned the world upside down, confounded the Greek and Roman philosophers, and altered in two or three centuries the whole face of Society. Can we mend these "old paths"? Can we improve them after eighteen centuries? Does human nature require any different medicine? I believe the bones of the oldest human skeleton that ever was unearthed are just like the bones of men in these days, and I believe the moral nature and hearts of men, after the lapse of ages, are just the same. We had better ask for the "old paths."

We want throughout the Church of England a return to the old paths of our Protestant Reformers. I grant they were rough workmen, and made some mistakes. They worked under immense difficulties, and deserve tender judgment and fair consideration. But they revived out of the dust grand foundation truths which had been long buried and forgotten. They brought into just prominence such cardinal verities as the sufficiency and supremacy of Scripture, the right and duty of private judgment, and free justification by faith without the deeds of the law, and without any ordained man or any ceremony interposing between the soul and the Saviour. By embalming those truths in our Articles and Liturgy, by incessantly pressing them on the attention of our forefathers, they changed the whole character of this nation, and raised a standard of true doctrine and practice, which, after three centuries, is a power in the land, and has an insensible influence on English character to this very day. Can we mend these "old paths"? Shall we improve them either by going back behind the Reformation and increasing the ceremonials of religion on the one hand, or by adopting lower views of inspiration and the atonement on the other? I doubt it entirely. I believe the men of 300 years ago understood the real wants of human nature better than many do in 1882.

Of course I am well aware that the "old paths" for which I have been pleading are not popular in some quarters at this day. In fact, the views I have just propounded are in direct antagonism to much of the so-caned wisdom of these times. "Effete systems," "old-world creeds," "fossil theology," "exploded theories," "worn-out doctrines," "old-fashioned divinity," and the like phrases,—who does not know the heavy fire of such language which is continually poured on the "old paths" of faith in some organs of public opinion, and from some pulpits and platforms? Novelty is the idol of the day. Free handling, enlightened views, rational interpretation, science (so called) before the Bible, these are the guiding principles of many in this age. Tell them that any religious idea is old, and they seem to think it is probably false! Tell them that it is new, and it is probably true!

But I have yet to learn that all new views of religion are necessarily better than the old. It is not so in the work of men's hands. I doubt if this nineteenth century can produce an architect who could design better buildings than the Parthenon or Coliseum, or a mason who could rear fabrics which will last so long. It certainly is not so in the work of men's minds. Thucydides is not superseded by Macaulay, nor Homer by Milton. Why, then, are we to suppose that old theology is necessarily inferior to new?

For, after all, when modern scoffers at "old paths" and worn-out creeds have said their say, there remain some stern facts which can never be explained away, and some questions which can only receive one answer. I ask boldly, What extensive good has ever been done in the world, except by the theology of the "old paths"? and I confidently challenge a reply, because I know that none can be given. I affirm, unhesitatingly, that there never has been any spread of the gospel, any conversion of nations or countries, any successful evangelistic work, excepting by the old-fashioned distinct doctrines of the early Christians and the Reformers. I invite any opponent of dogmatic theology to name a single instance of a country, or town, or people, which has ever been Christianized by merely telling men that "Christ was a great moral Teacher,—that they must love one another, that they must be true, and just, and unselfish, and generous, and brotherly, and high-souled," and the like. No! no! no! Not one single victory can such teaching show us: not one trophy can such teaching exhibit. It has wrought no deliverance on the earth. The victories of Christianity, wherever they have been won, have been won by distinct doctrinal theology; by telling men of Christ's vicarious death and sacrifice; by showing them Christ's substitution on the cross, and His precious blood; by teaching them justification by faith, and bidding them believe on a crucified Saviour; by preaching ruin by sin, redemption by Christ, regeneration by the Spirit; by lifting up the brazen serpent; by telling men to look and live,—to believe, repent, and be converted. These are the "old paths." This, this is the only teaching which for eighteen centuries God has honoured with success, and is honouring at the present day both at home and abroad: Let the teachers of a broad and undogmatic theology,—or the preachers of the gospel of earnestness, and sincerity, and cold morality, or the advocates of a ceremonial, sensuous, histrionic, Sacramentarian Christianity,—let them, I say, show us at this day any English village, or parish, or city, or district, which has been evangelized, without the distinct doctrinal teaching of the "old paths." They cannot do it, and they never will. There is no getting over facts. The good that is done in the earth may be comparatively small. Evil may abound, and ignorant impatience may murmur and cry out that Christianity has failed. But, we may depend on it, if we want to do good and shake the world, we must fight with the old apostolic weapons, and stick to the "old paths."

Does any reader doubt the truth of what I am saying, and think I am going too far? I ask him to listen for a moment to the two following arguments, and overthrow them if he can.

For one thing, I bid him turn to the lives of all the most eminent saints who have adorned the Church of Christ since its great Head left the world, and summon them as witnesses. I will not weary my readers with long lists of names, for happily they are legion. Let us examine the holiest Fathers, and Schoolmen, and Reformers, and Puritans, and Anglicans, and Dissenters, and Churchmen of every school, and Christians generally of every name, and nation, and people, and tongue. Let us search their diaries, analyze their biographies, and study their letters. Let us just see what manner of men they have been in every age, who, by the consent of all their contemporaries, have been really holy, and saintly, and good. Where will you find one of them who did not cling to the "old paths" of simple faith in the atonement and sacrificial work of Christ? who did not hold certain great distinct doctrinal views, and live in the belief of them? I am satisfied you will not find one! In their clearness of perception and degree of spiritual light, in the proportion they have assigned to particular articles of faith, they may have differed widely. In their mode of expressing their theological opinions they may not have agreed. But they have always had one common stamp and mark. They have not been content with vague ideas of "earnestness, and goodness, and sincerity, and charity." They have had certain systematic, sharply-cut, and positive views of truth. They have known whom they believed, and what they believed, and why they believed. And so it always will be. You will never have Christian fruits without Christian roots, whatever novel-writers may say; you will never have eminent holiness without the "old paths" of dogmatic theology.

For another thing, I bid him turn to the death-beds of all who die with solid comfort and good hope, and appeal to them. There are few of us who are not called on occasionally, as we travel through life, to see people passing through the valley of the shadow of death, and drawing near to their latter end, and to those "things unseen which are eternal." We all of us know what a vast difference there is in the manner in which such people leave the world, and the amount of comfort and hope which they seem to feel. Can any of us say that he ever saw a person die in peace who did not know distinctly what he was resting on for acceptance with God, and could only say, in reply to inquiries, that he was "earnest and sincere"? I can only give my own experience: I never saw one. Oh, no! The story of Christ's moral teaching, and self-sacrifice, and example, and the need of being earnest, and sincere, and like Him, will never smooth down a dying pillow. Christ the Teacher, Christ the great Pattern, Christ the Prophet, will not suffice. We want something more than this! We want the old, old story of Christ dying for our sins, and rising again for our justification. We want Christ the Mediator, Christ the Substitute, Christ the Intercessor, Christ the Redeemer, in order to meet with confidence the King of Terrors, and to say, "Oh death, where is thy sting? Oh grave, where is thy victory?" Not a few, I believe, who have gloried all their lives in rejecting dogmatic religion, have discovered at last that their "broad theology" is a miserable comforter, and the gospel of mere "earnestness" is no good news at all Not a few, I firmly believe, could be named, who at the eleventh hour have cast aside their favourite, new-fashioned views, have fled for refuge to the "old paths" and the precious blood, and left the world with no other hope than the old-fashioned Evangelical doctrine of faith in a crucified Jesus. Nothing in their life's religion has given them such peace as the simple truth grasped at the eleventh hour,—

> *"Just as I am: without one plea,*
> *But that Thy blood was shed for me,*
> *And that Thou bidst me come to Thee—*
> *O Lamb of God, I come."*

Surely, when this is the case, we have no need to be ashamed of the "old paths," and of walking therein.

I ask every reader of this paper to respect the logic of facts. Give the direction of Jeremiah the attention it deserves. If you once begin to think seriously about your soul, never be ashamed of asking for "the old paths," and walking in them. Yes! do not merely look at them and talk of them, but actually walk in them. Let no scorn of the world, let no ridicule of smart writers, let no sneer of liberal critics, shake your confidence in those paths. Only try them, and you will find they are the good way, "a way of pleasantness and peace."

III. From Jeremiah's general advice and special directions let me now turn to the precious promise with which our text concludes. "Walk in the old paths," saith the Lord, "and ye shall find rest to your souls."

I cannot doubt that our Lord Jesus Christ had these words of the prophet in His mind, when He proclaimed that glorious invitation which is so wisely quoted in our Communion Service: "Come unto Me, all ye that labour and are heavy-laden, and I will give you rest" (Matt. 11:28). One thing, at any rate, is quite certain. Whether under the Old Testament or the New, nothing could be held out to man more suitable to his spiritual wants than "rest." Walk in the "old paths," is the promise, and you shall have "rest."

Let it never, never be forgotten that rest of conscience is the secret want of a vast portion of mankind. Sin and the sense of guilt are the root of all the heart-weariness in the world. Men are not at ease, because they are not at peace with God. Men often feel their sinfulness, though they know not what the feeling really means. They only know there is something wrong within, but they do not understand the cause. "Who will show us any good?" is the universal cry. But there is universal ignorance of the disease from which the cry springs. The "labouring and heavy-laden" are everywhere: they are a multitude that man can scarcely number; they are to be found in every climate, and in every country under the sun.

To what class do the labouring and heavy-laden belong? They belong to every class: there is no exception. They are to be found among masters as well as among servants, among rich as well as among poor, among kings as well as among subjects,—among learned as well as among ignorant people. In every class you will find trouble, care, sorrow, anxiety, murmuring, discontent, and unrest. What does it mean? What does it all come to? Men are "labouring and heavy-laden," and want rest.

Now, rest for the labouring and heavy-laden is one of the chief promises which the Word of God offers to man, both in the Old Testament and the New. "Come to me," says the world, "and I will give you riches and pleasure." "Come with me," says the devil, "and I will give you greatness, power, and wisdom." "Come unto Me," says the Lord Jesus Christ, "and I will give you rest." "Walk in the old paths," says the prophet Jeremiah, "and you shall find rest for your souls."

But what is the nature of that rest which the Lord Jesus promises to give? It is no mere repose of body.

A man may have that, and yet be miserable. You may place him in a palace, and surround him with every possible comfort; you may give him money in abundance, and everything that money can buy; you may free him from all care about tomorrow's bodily wants, and take away the need of labouring for a single hour: all this you may do to a man, and yet not give him true rest. Thousands know this only too well by bitter experience. Their hearts are starving in the midst of worldly plenty; their inward man is sick and weary, while their outward man is clothed in purple and fine linen, and fares sumptuously every day! Yes: a man may have houses, and lands, and money, and horses, and carriages, and soft beds, and good fare, and attentive servants, and yet not have true "rest."

The rest that Christ gives in the "old paths" is an inward thing. It is rest of heart, rest of conscience, rest of mind, rest of affection, rest of will. It is rest from a comfortable sense of sins being all forgiven, and guilt all put away. It is rest from a solid hope of good things to come, laid up beyond the reach of disease, and death, and the grave. It is rest from the well-grounded feeling, that the great business of life is settled, its great end provided for, that in time all is well done, and in eternity heaven will be our home.

Rest such as this the Lord Jesus gives to those who come to Him in the "old paths," by showing them His own finished work on the cross, by clothing them in His own perfect righteousness, and washing them in His own precious blood. When a man begins to see that the Son of God actually died for his sins, his soul begins to taste something of inward quiet and peace.

Rest such as this the Lord Jesus gives to those who come to Him in the "old paths," by revealing Himself as their ever-living High Priest in heaven, and God reconciled to them through Him. When a man beans to see that the Son of God actually lives at the right hand of the Father to intercede for him, he will begin to feel something of inward quiet and peace.

Rest such as this the Lord Jesus gives to those who come to Him in the "old paths," by implanting His Spirit in their hearts, witnessing with their spirits that they are God's children, and that old things are passed away, and all things are become new. When a man begins to feel an inward drawing towards God as a Father, and a sense of being an adopted and forgiven child, his soul begins to feel something of quiet and peace.

Rest such as this the Lord Jesus gives to those who come to Him in the "old paths," by dwelling in their hearts as King, by putting all things within in order, and giving to each faculty its place and work. When a man begins to find order in his heart in place of rebellion and confusion, his soul begins to understand something of quiet and peace. There is no true inward happiness until the true King is on the throne.

Rest such as this is the privilege of all believers in Christ. Some know more of it, and some less; some feel it only at distant intervals, and some feel it almost always. Few enjoy the sense of it without many a battle with unbelief, and many a conflict with fear: but all who truly come to Christ know something of this rest. Ask them, with all their complaints and doubts, whether they would give up Christ and go back to the world. You will get only one answer. Weak as their sense of rest may be, they have got hold of something which does them good, and that something they cannot let go.

Rest such as this is within reach of all who are willing to seek it and receive it. The poor man is not so poor but he may have it; the ignorant man is not so ignorant but he may know it; the sick man is not so weak and helpless but he may get hold of it. Faith, simple faith, is the one thing needful in order to possess Christ's rest. Faith in Christ is the grand secret of happiness. Neither poverty, nor ignorance, nor tribulation, nor distress can prevent men and women feeling rest of soul, if they will only come to Christ and believe.

Rest such as this is the possession which makes men independent. Banks may break, and money make itself wings and flee away. War, pestilence, and famine may break in on a land, and the foundations of the earth be out of course. Health and vigour may depart, and the body be crushed down by loathsome disease. Death may cut down wife, and children, and friends, until he who once enjoyed them stands entirely alone. But the man who has come to Christ by faith will still possess some thing which can never be taken from him. Like Paul and Silas, he will sing in prison; like Job, bereaved of children and property, he will bless the name of the Lord. He is the truly independent man who possesses that which nothing can take away.

Rest such as this is the possession which makes men truly rich. It lasts; it wears; it endures; it lightens the solitary home; it smoothes down the dying pillow; it goes with men when they are placed in their coffins; it abides with them when they are laid in their graves. When friends can no longer help us, and money is no longer of use,—when doctors can no longer relieve our pain, and nurses can no longer minister to our wants, when sense begins to fail, and eye and ear can no longer do their duty, then, even then, the "rest" which Christ gives in the "old paths" will be shed abroad in the heart of the believer.

The words "rich" and "poor" will change their meaning entirely one day. He is the only rich man who has come to Christ by faith, and from Christ has received rest.

This is the rest which Jeremiah was commissioned to proclaim. This is the rest which Christ offers to give to all who are labouring and heavy-laden; this is the rest for which He invites them to come to Him; this is the rest which I want all who read this paper to enjoy, and to which I bring an invitation this day. May God grant that the invitation may not be brought in vain!

(a) And now, before we part, let me ask if there is any reader who is inwardly desiring rest of soul, and yet knows not where to turn for it? Remember this day, that there is only one place where rest can be found. Governments cannot give it; education will not impart it; worldly amusements cannot supply it; money will not purchase it. It can only be found in the hand of Jesus Christ; and to His hand you must turn if you would find peace within.

There is no royal road to rest of soul. Let that never be forgotten. There is only one way to the Father,—Jesus Christ; one door into heaven,—Jesus Christ; and one path to heart-peace and rest,—Jesus Christ. By that way all labouring and heavy-laden ones must go, whatever be their rank or condition. Kings in their palaces, and paupers in the workhouse, are all on a level in this matter. All alike must walk in the "old paths," and come to Christ, if they feel soul-weary and athirst. All must drink of the same fountain, if they would have their thirst relieved.

You may not believe what I am now saying. Time will show who is right and who is wrong. Go on, if you will, imagining that true happiness is to be found in the good things of this world. Seek it, if you will, in revelling and banqueting, in dancing and merry-making, in races and theatres, in field sports and cams. Seek it, if you will, in reading and scientific pursuits, in music and painting, in politics and business. Seek it in a round of religious formalities,—in a perfunctory obedience to the requirements of a ceremonial Christianity. Seek it; but you will never overtake it, unless you change your plan. Real heart-rest is never to be found except in the "old paths," in heart-union with Jesus Christ.

The Princess Elizabeth, daughter of Charles I., lies buried in Newport Church, in the Isle of Wight. A marble monument, erected by our gracious Queen Victoria, records in a touching way the manner of her death. She languished in Carisbrook Castle during the unhappy Commonwealth wars, a prisoner, alone, and separate from all the companions of her youth, until death set her free. She was found dead one day with her head leaning on her Bible, and the Bible open at the words, "Come unto Me, all ye that labour and are heavy-laden, and I will give you rest." The monument in Newport Church records this fact. It consists of a female figure reclining her head on a marble book, with the text already quoted engraven on the book. Think what a sermon in stone that monument preaches! Think what a standing memorial it affords of the utter inability of rank and high birth to confer certain happiness! Think what a testimony it bears to the lesson before you this day,—the mighty lesson that there is no true "rest" for any one excepting in Christ! Happy will it be for your soul if that lesson is never forgotten!

(b) But who is there among the readers of this paper that has walked in the "old paths," and found the rest which Christ gives? Who is there that has tasted true peace by coming to Him, and casting his soul on Him? Let me entreat you never to leave the "old paths," and never to be tempted to think there is a better way. Stand fast in the liberty wherewith Christ has made you free. Turn not aside to right or left. Go on to the end of your days as you have begun, looking to Jesus and living on Him. Go on drawing daily full supplies of rest, peace, mercy, and grace from the great fountain of rest and peace. Remember, that if you live to the age of Methuselah, you will never be anything but a poor empty sinner, owing all you have and hope for to Christ alone.

Never be ashamed of living the life of faith in Christ. The "old paths" will bear thinking of to all eternity. The way of the world is a way which will not bear calm reflection now, and of which the end is shame and remorse. Men may ridicule and mock you, and even silence you in argument; but they can never take from you the feelings which faith in Christ gives. They can never prevent you feeling, "I was weary till I found Christ, but now I have rest of conscience. I was blind, but now I see. I was dead, but I am alive again. I was lost, but I am found."

Last, but not least, look forward with confidence to a better rest in a world to come. Yet a little time, and He that shall come will come, and will not tarry. He will gather together all who have believed in Him, and take His people to a home where the wicked shall cease from troubling, and the weary shall be at perfect rest. He shall give them a glorious body, in which they shall serve Him without distraction, and praise Him without weariness. He shall wipe away tears from all faces, and make all things new (Isa. 25:8).

There is a good time coming for all who have come to Christ in the "old paths," and committed their souls into His keeping. They will remember all the way by which they have been led, and see the wisdom of every step in the way. They will wonder that they ever doubted the kindness and love of their Shepherd. Above all, they will wonder that they could live so long without Him, and that when they heard of Him they could hesitate about coming to Him.

There is a pass in Scotland called Glencroe, which supplies a beautiful illustration of what heaven will be to the man who comes to Christ. The road through Gleneroe carries the traveller up a long and steep ascent, with many a little winding and many a little turn in its course. But when the top of the pass is reached, a stone is seen by the wayside, with these simple words engraven on it, "Rest, and be thankful." Those words describe the feelings with which every one who comes to Christ will at length enter heaven. The summit of the narrow way will be won: we shall cease from our weary journeying, and sit down in the kingdom of God. We shall look back over all the way of life with thankfulness, and see the perfect wisdom of every little winding and turn in the steep ascent by which we were led. We shall forget the toils of the upward journey in the glorious rest. Here in this world our sense of rest in Christ at best is feeble and partial; but "when that which is perfect is come, that which is in part shall be done away." Thanks be unto God, a day is coming when the end of the "old path" will be reached, and believers shall rest perfectly, and be thankful!

CHAPTER VI[8]

Acts 17:26
"One Blood."

THIS is a very short and simple text, and even a child knows the meaning of its words. But simple as it is, it supplies food for much thought, and it forms part of a speech delivered by a great man on a great occasion.

---

[8] The substance of this paper was preached as a sermon at the Chapel Royal, St. James's, London, on

The speaker is the Apostle of the Gentiles, St. Paul. The hearers are the cultivated men of Athens, and specially the Epicurean and Stoic philosophers. The place is Mars' Hill at Athens, in full view of religious buildings and statues, of which even the shattered remains are a marvel of art at this day. Never perhaps were such a place, such a man, and such an audience brought together! It was a strange scene. And how did St. Paul use the occasion? What did this Jewish stranger, this member of a despised nation, coming from an obscure corner of Asia, this little man whose "bodily presence was weak," and very unlike the ideal figure in one of Raphael's cartoons, what does he say to these intellectual Greeks?

He tells them boldly the unity of the true God. There is only one God, the maker of heaven and earth, and not many deities, as his hearers seem to think, a God who needed no temples made with hands, and was not to be represented by images made of wood or metal or stone.

Standing in front of the stately Parthenon and the splendid statue of Minerva, he sets before his refined hearers the ignorance with which they worshipped, the folly of idolatry, the coming judgment of all mankind, the certainty of a resurrection, and the absolute need of repentance. And not least, he tells the proud men of Athens that they must not flatter themselves that they were superior beings, as they vainly supposed, made of finer clay, and needing less than other races of men. No! he declares that "God has made of one blood all nations." There is no difference. The nature, the needs, the obligation to God of all human beings on the globe are one and the same.

I shall stick to that expression "one blood," and confine myself entirely to it. I see in it three great points,—

I. A point of fact;

II. A point of doctrine;

III. A point of duty.

Let me try to unfold them.

I. In the first place comes the point of fact. We are all made "of one blood." Then the Bible account of the origin of man is true. The Book of Genesis is right. The whole family of mankind, with all its thousand millions, has descended from one pair—from Adam and Eve.

This is a humbling fact, no doubt; but it is true. Kings and their subjects, rich and poor, learned and unlearned, prince and pauper, the educated Englishman and the untutored negro, the fashionable lady at the West End of London and the North American squaw,— all, all might trace their pedigree, if they could trace it through sixty centuries, to one man and one woman. No doubt in the vast period of six thousand years immense varieties of races have gradually been developed. Hot climates and cold climates have affected the colour and physical peculiarities of nations. Civilization and culture have produced their effect on the habits, demeanour, and mental attainments of the inhabitants of different parts of the globe. Some of Adam's children in the lapse of time have been greatly degraded, and some have been raised and improved. But the great fact remains the same. The story written by Moses is true. All the dwellers in Europe, Asia, Africa, and America originally sprang from Adam and Eve. We were all "made of one blood."

Now why do I dwell on all this? I do it because I wish to impress on the minds of my readers the plenary inspiration and divine authority of the Book of Genesis. I want you to hold fast the old teaching about the origin of man, and to refuse steadily to let it go.

March 2, 1884.

I need hardly remind you that you live in a day of abounding scepticism and unbelief. Clever writers and lecturers are continually pouring contempt on the Old Testament Scriptures, and especially on the Book of Genesis. The contents of that venerable document, we are frequently told, are not to be read as real historical facts, but as fictions and fables. We are not to suppose that Adam and Eve were the only man and woman originally created, and that all mankind sprang from one pair. We are rather to believe that different races of human beings have been called into existence in different parts of the globe, at different times, without any relationship to one another. In short, we are coolly informed that the narratives in the first half of Genesis are only pleasing Oriental romances, and are not realities at all! Now, when you hear such talk as this, I charge you not to be moved or shaken for a moment. Stand fast in the old paths of the faith, and especially about the origin of man. There is abundant evidence that Moses is right, and those who impugn his veracity and credibility are wrong. We are all descended from one fallen father. We are "all of one blood."

It would be easy to show, if the limits of this paper permitted, that the oldest traditions of nations all over the globe confirm the account given by Moses in the most striking manner. Geikie, in his Hours with the Bible, has briefly shown that the story of the first pair, the serpent, the fall, the flood, and the ark are found cropping up in one form or another in almost every part of the habitable world. But the strongest proof of our common origin is to be found in the painful uniformity of man's moral nature, whatever be the colour of his skin. Go where you will on the globe, and observe what men and women are everywhere. Go to the heart of Africa or China, or to the remotest island of the Pacific Ocean, and mark the result of your investigations. I boldly assert that everywhere, and in every climate, you will find the moral nature of the human race exactly the same. Everywhere you will find men and women are naturally wicked, corrupt, selfish, proud, lazy, deceitful, godless,—servants of lusts and passions. And I contend that nothing can reasonably account for this but the first three chapters of Genesis. We are what we are morally, because we have sprung from one parent, and partake of his nature. We are all descendants of one fallen Adam, and in Adam we all died. Moses is right. We are all of "one blood."

After all, if doubt remains in any man's mind, and he cannot quite believe the narratives of Genesis, I ask him to remember what a deadly blow his unbelief strikes at the authority of the New Testament. It is easy work to point out difficulties in the first book of the Bible; but it is not easy to explain away the repeated endorsement which Genesis receives from Christ and the Apostles. There is no getting over the broad fact that creation, the serpent, the fall, Cain and Abel, Enoch, Noah, the flood, the ark, Abraham, Lot, Sodom and Gomorrah, Isaac, Jacob, Esau, are all mentioned in the New Testament as historical things or historical persons. What shall we say to this fact? Were Christ and the Apostles deceived and ignorant? The idea is absurd. Did they dishonestly accommodate themselves to the popular views of their hearers, in order to procure favour with them, knowing all the time that the things and persons they spoke of were fictitious, and not historical at all? The very idea is wicked and profane. We are shut up to one conclusion, and I see no alternative. If you give up the Old Testament, you must give up the New also. There is no standing-ground between disbelief of the supernatural narratives of Genesis and disbelief of the gospel. If you cannot believe Moses, you ought not to trust Christ and the Apostles, who certainly did believe him. Are you really wiser than the Lord Jesus Christ or St. Paul? Do you know better than they? Cast such notions behind your back. Stand firm on the old foundation, and be not carried away by modern theories. And as a great cornerstone, place beneath your feet the fact of our text, the common origin of all mankind. "We are all made of one blood."

II. From the point of fact in our text I now pass on to the point of doctrine. Are we all of "one blood"? Then we all need one and the same remedy for the great family disease of our souls. The disease I speak of is sin. We inherit it from our parents, and it is a part of our nature. We are born with it, whether gentle or simple, learned or unlearned, rich or poor, as children of fallen Adam, with his blood in our veins. It is a disease which grows with our growth and strengthens with our strength, and unless cured before we die, will be the death of our souls.

Now, what is the only remedy for this terrible spiritual disease? What will cleanse us from the guilt of sin? What will bring health and peace to our poor dead hearts, and enable us to walk with God while we live, and dwell with God when we die? To these questions I give a short but unhesitating reply. For the one universal soul-disease of all Adam's children there is only one remedy. That remedy is "the precious blood of Christ." To the blood of Adam we owe the beginning of our deadly spiritual ailment. To the blood of Christ alone must we all look for a cure.

When I speak of the "blood of Christ," my readers must distinctly understand that I do not mean the literal material blood which flowed from His hands and feet and side as He hung on the cross. That blood, I doubt not, stained the fingers of the soldiers who nailed our Lord to the tree; but there is not the slightest proof that it did any good to their souls. If that blood were really in the Communion cup at the Lord's Supper, as some profanely tell us, and we touched it with our lips, such mere corporeal touch would avail us nothing. Oh no! When I speak of the "blood" of Christ as the cure for the deadly ailment which we all inherit from the blood of Adam, I mean the life-blood which Christ shed, and the redemption which Christ obtained for sinners when He died for them on Calvary,—the salvation which He procured for us by His vicarious sacrifice,—the deliverance from the guilt and power and consequences of sin, which He purchased when He suffered as our Substitute. This and this only is what I mean when I speak of "Christ's blood" as the one medicine needed by all Adam's children. The thing that we all need to save us from eternal death is not merely Christ's incarnation and life, but Christ's death. The atoning "blood" which Christ shed when He died, is the grand secret of salvation. It is the blood of the second Adam suffering in our stead, which alone can give life or health and peace to all who have the first Adam's blood in their veins.

I can find no words to express my deep sense of the importance of maintaining in our Church the true doctrine of the blood of Christ. One plague of our age is the widespread dislike to what men are pleased to call dogmatic theology. In the place of it, the idol of the day is a kind of jelly-fish Christianity,—a Christianity without bone, or muscle, or sinew, without any distinct teaching about the atonement or the work of the Spirit, or justification, or the way of peace with God,—a vague, foggy, misty Christianity, of which the only watchwords seem to be, "You must be earnest, and real, and true, and brave, and zealous, and liberal, and kind. You must condemn no man's doctrinal views. You must consider everybody is right, and nobody is wrong." And this Creedless kind of religion, we are actually told, is to give us peace of conscience! And not to be satisfied with it in a sorrowful, dying world, is a proof that you are very narrow-minded! Satisfied, indeed! Such a religion might possibly do for unfallen angels. But to tell sinful, dying men and women, with the blood of our father Adam in their veins, to be satisfied with it, is an insult to common sense, and a mockery of our distress. We need something far better than this. We need the blood of Christ.

What saith the Scripture about "that blood"? Let me try to put my readers in remembrance. Do we want to be clean and guiltless now in the sight of God? It is written that "the blood of Jesus Christ cleanseth from all sin;"—that "it justifies;" that "it makes us nigh to God;" that "through it there is redemption, even the forgiveness of sin;" that it "purges the conscience;" that "it makes peace between God and man;"—that it gives "boldness to enter into the holiest." Yes! it is expressly written of the saints in glory, that "they had washed their robes, and made them white in the blood of the Lamb," and that they had "overcome their souls' enemies by the blood of the Lamb" (1 John 1:7; Col. 1:20; Heb. 10:19; Eph. 1:7; Heb. 9:14; Eph. 2:13; Rom. 5:9; Rev. 7:14). Why, in the name of common sense, if the Bible is our guide to heaven, why are we to refuse the teaching of the Bible about Christ's blood, and turn to other remedies for the great common soul-disease of mankind? If, besides this, the sacrifices of the Old Testament did not point to the sacrifice of Christ's death on the cross, they were useless, unmeaning forms, and the outer courts of tabernacle and temple were little better than shambles. But if, as I firmly believe, they were meant to lead the minds of Jews to the better sacrifice of the true Lamb of God, they afford unanswerable confirmation of the position which I maintain this day. That position is, that the one "blood of Christ" is the spiritual medicine for all who have the "one blood of Adam" in their veins.

Does any reader of this paper want to do good in the world? I hope that many do. He is a poor style of Christian who does not wish to leave the world better, when he leaves it, than it was when he entered it. Take the advice I give you this day. Beware of being content with half-measures and inadequate remedies for the great spiritual disease of mankind. You will only labour in vain if you do not show men the blood of the Lamb. Like the fabled Sisyphus, however much you strive, you will find the stone ever rolling back upon you. Education, teetotalism, cleaner dwellings, popular concerts, blue ribbon leagues, white cross armies, penny readings, museums, all are very well in their way; but they only touch the surface of man's disease: they do not go to the root. They cast out the devil for a little season; but they do not fill his place, and prevent him coming back again. Nothing will do that but the story of the cross applied to the conscience by the Holy Ghost, and received and accepted by faith. Yes! it is the blood of Christ, not His example only, or His beautiful moral teaching, but His vicarious sacrifice that meets the wants of the soul. No wonder that St. Peter calls it "precious." Precious it has been found by the heathen abroad, and by the peer and the peasant at home. Precious it was found on a death-bed by the mighty theologian Bengel, by the unwearied labourer John Wesley, by the late Archbishop Longley, and Bishop Hamilton in our own days. May it ever be precious in our eyes! If we want to do good, we must make much of the blood of Christ. There is only one fountain that can cleanse any one's sin. That fountain is the blood of the Lamb.

III. The third and last point which arises out of our text is a point of duty. Are we all of "one blood"? Then we ought to live as if we were. We ought to behave as members of one great family. We ought to "love as brethren." We ought to put away from us anger, wrath, malice, quarrelling, as specially hateful in the sight of God. We ought to cultivate kindness and charity towards all men. The dark-skinned African negro, the dirtiest dweller in some vile slum of London, has a claim upon our attention. He is a relative and a brother, whether we like to believe it or not. Like ourselves, he is a descendant of Adam and Eve, and inherits a fallen nature and a never-dying soul.

Now what are we Christians doing to prove that we believe and realize all this? What are we doing for our brethren? I trust we do not forget that it was wicked Cain who asked that awful question, "Am I my brother's keeper?" (Gen. 4:9).

What are we doing for the heathen abroad? That is a grave question, and one which I have no room to consider fully. I only remark that we do far less than we ought to do. The nation whose proud boast it is that her flag is to be seen in every port on the globe, gives less to the cause of foreign missions than the cost of a single first-class ironclad man-of-war.

But what are we doing for the masses at home? That is a far graver question, and one which imperiously demands a reply. The heathen are out of sight and out of mind. The English masses are hard by our own doors, and their condition is a problem which politicians and philanthropists are anxiously trying to solve, and which cannot be evaded. What are we doing to lessen the growing sense of inequality between rich and poor, and to fill up the yawning gulf of discontent? Socialism, and communism, and confiscation of property are looming large in the distance, and occupying much attention in the press. Atheism and secularism are spreading fast in some quarters, and specially in overgrown and neglected parishes, Now what is the path of duty?

I answer without hesitation, that we want a larger growth of brotherly love in the land. We want men and women to grasp the great principle, that we are all of "one blood," and to lay themselves out to do good. We want the rich to care more for the poor, and the employer for the employed, and wealthy congregations for the working-class congregations in the great cities, and the West End of London to care more for the East and the South. And, let us remember, it is not merely temporal relief that is wanted. The Roman emperors tried to keep the proletarians and the lower classes quiet by the games of the circus and largesses of corn. And some ignorant modern Britons seem to think that money, cheap food, good dwellings, and recreation are healing medicines for the evils of our day in the lowest stratum of society. It is a complete mistake. What the masses want is more sympathy, more kindness, more brotherly love, more treatment as if they were really of "one blood" with ourselves. Give them that., and you will fill up half the gulf of discontent.

It is a common saying in this day, that the working classes have no religion, that they are alienated from the Church of England, that they cannot be brought to church, and that it is hopeless and useless to try to do them good. I believe nothing of the kind. I believe the working classes are not one jot more opposed to religion than the "upper ten thousand," and that they are just as open to good influences, and even more likely to be saved if they are approached in the right way. But what they do like is to be treated as "one blood," and what is wanted is a great increase of sympathy and personal friendly dealing with them.

I confess that I have immense faith in the power of sympathy and kindness. I believe the late Judge Talfourd hit the right nail on the head when he said, in almost his last charge to a Grand Jury at Stafford Assizes, "Gentlemen, the great want of the age is more sympathy between classes." I entirely agree with him; I think an increase of sympathy and fellow-feeling between high and low, rich and poor, employer and employed, parson and people, is one healing medicine which the age demands. Sympathy, exhibited in its perfection, was one secondary cause of the acceptance which Christ's gospel met with on its first appearance in the heathen world. Well says Lord Macaulay, "It was before Deity taking a human form, walking among men, partaking of their infirmities, leaning on their bosoms, weeping over their graves, slumbering in the manger, bleeding on the cross, that the prejudices of the synagogue, and the doubts of the academy, and the fasces of the lictor, and the swords of thirty legions, were humbled in the dust." And sympathy, I firmly believe, can do as much in the nineteenth century as it did in the first. If anything will melt down the cold isolation of classes in these latter days, and make our social body consist of solid cubes compacted together, instead of spheres only touching each other at one point, it will be a large growth of Christlike sympathy.

Now I assert confidently that the English working man is particularly open to sympathy. The working man may live in a poor dwelling; and after toiling all day in a coal pit, or cotton mill, or iron foundry, or dock, or chemical works, he may often look very rough and dirty. But after all, he is flesh and blood like ourselves. Beneath his outward roughness he has a heart and a conscience, a keen sense of justice, and a jealous recollection of his rights as a man and a Briton. He does not want to be patronized and flattered, any more than to be trampled on, scolded, or neglected; but he does like to be dealt with as a brother, in a friendly, kind, and sympathizing way. He wilt not be driven; he will do nothing for a cold, hard man, however clever he may be. But give him a Christian visitor to his home who really understands that it is the heart and not the coat which makes the man, and that the guinea's worth is in the gold, and not in the stamp upon it. Give him a visitor who will not only talk about Christ, but sit down in his house, and take him by the hand in a Christlike, familiar way. Give him a visitor, and specially a clergyman, who realizes that in Christ's holy religion there is no respect of persons, that rich and poor are "made of one blood," and need one and the same atoning blood, and that there is only one Saviour, and one Fountain for sin, and one heaven, both for employers and employed. Give him a clergyman who can weep with them that weep, and rejoice with them that rejoice, and feel a tender interest in the cares, and troubles, and births, and marriages, and deaths of the humblest dweller in his parish. Give the working man, I say, a clergyman of that kind, and, as a general rule, the working man will come to his church, and not be a communist or an infidel. Such a clergyman will not preach to empty benches.

How little, after all, do most people seem to realize the supreme importance of brotherly love and the absolute necessity of imitating that blessed Saviour who "went about doing good" to all, if we would prove ourselves His disciples! If ever there was a time when conduct like that of the good Samaritan in the parable was rare, it is the time in which we live. Selfish indifference to the wants of others is a painful characteristic of the age. Search the land in which we live, from the Isle of Wight to Berwick-on-Tweed, and from the Land's End to the North Foreland, and name, if you can, a single county or town in which the givers to good works are not a small minority, and in which philanthropic and religious agencies are not kept going, only and entirely, by painful begging and constant importunity. Go where you will, the report is always the same. Hospitals, missions at home and abroad, evangelistic and educational agencies, churches, chapels, and mission halls,—all are incessantly checked and hindered by want of support. Where are the Samaritans, we may well ask, in this land of Bibles and Testaments? Where are the Christians who live as if we are "all of one blood"? Where are the men who love their neighbours, and will help to provide for dying bodies and souls? Where are the people always ready and willing to give unasked, and without asking how much others have given? Millions are annually spent on deer forests, and moors, and hunting, and yachting, and racing, and gambling, and balls, and theatres, and dressing, and pictures, and furniture, and recreation. Little, comparatively, ridiculously little, is given or done for the cause of Christ. A miserable guinea subscription too often is the whole sum bestowed by some

Croesus on the bodies and souls of his fellow-men. The very first principles of giving seem lost and forgotten in many quarters. People must be bribed and tempted to contribute by bazaars, as children in badly-managed families are bribed and tempted to be good by sugar-plums! They must not be expected to give unless they get something in return! And all this goes on in a country where people call themselves Christians, and go to church, and glory in ornate ceremonials, and histrionic rituals, and what are called "hearty services," and profess to believe the parable of the Good Samaritan. I fear there will be a sad waking up at the last day.

Where, after all, to come to the root of the matter, where is that brotherly love which used to be the distinguishing mark of the primitive Christians? Where, amidst the din of controversy and furious strife of parties, where is the fruit of the Holy Spirit and the primary mark of spiritual regeneration? Where is that charity, without which we are no better than "sounding brass and tinkling cymbals"? Where is the charity which is the bond of perfectness? Where is that love by which our Lord declared all men should know His disciples, and which St. John said was the distinction between the children of God and the children of the devil? Where is it, indeed? Read in the newspapers the frightfully violent language of opposing politicians. Mark the hideous bitterness of controversial theologians, both in the press and on the platform. Observe the fiendish delight with which anonymous letter-writers endeavour to wound the feelings of opponents, and then to pour vitriol into the wound. Look at all this ghastly spectacle which any observing eye may see any day in England. And then remember that this is the country in which men are reading the New Testament and professing to follow Christ, and to believe that they are all of "one blood." Can anything more grossly inconsistent be conceived? Can anything be imagined more offensive to God? Truly, it is astonishing that such myriads should be so keen about Christian profession and external worship, and yet so utterly careless about the simplest elements of Christian practice. Where there is no love there is no spiritual life. Without brotherly love, although baptized and communicants, men are dead in trespasses and sins.

I shall wind up all I have to say on the point of duty by reminding my readers of the solemn words which St. Matthew records to have been spoken by our Lord in the twenty-fifth chapter of his Gospel. In the great and dreadful day of judgment, when the Son of man shall sit on the throne of His glory, there are some to whom He will say, "Depart, ye cursed, into everlasting fire, prepared for the devil and His angels: for I was an hungered, and ye gave Me no meat: I was thirsty, and ye gave Me no drink: I was a stranger, and ye took Me not in: naked, and ye clothed Me not; sick, and in prison, and ye visited Me not. Then shall they also answer Him, saying, Lord, when saw we Thee an hungered, or athirst, or a stranger, or naked, or sick, or in prison, and did not minister unto Thee? Then shall He answer them, saying, Verily I say unto you, Inasmuch as ye did it not to one of the least of these, ye did it not to Me" (Matt. 25:41-46).

I declare I know very few passages of Scripture more solemn and heart-searching than this. It is not charged against these unhappy lost souls, that they had committed murder, adultery, or theft, or that they had not been church-goers or communicants. Oh, no! nothing of the kind. They had simply done nothing at all. They had neglected love to others. They had not tried to lessen the misery, or increase the happiness, of this sin-burdened world. They had selfishly sat still, done no good, and had no eyes to see, or hearts to feel, for their brethren the members of Adam's great family. And so their end is everlasting punishment! If these words cannot set some people thinking when they look at the state of the masses in some of our large towns, nothing will.

And now I shall close this paper with three words of friendly advice, which I commend to the attention of all who read it. They are words in season for the days in which we live, and I am sure they are worth remembering.

(a) First and foremost, I charge you never to give up the old doctrine of the plenary inspiration of the whole Bible. Hold it fast, and never let it go. Let nothing tempt you to think that any part of the grand old volume is not inspired, or that any of its narratives, and especially in Genesis, are not to be believed. Once take up that ground, and you will find yourself on an inclined plane. Well will it be if you do not slip down into utter infidelity! Faith's difficulties no doubt are great; but the difficulties of scepticism are far greater.

(b) In the next place, I charge you never to give up the old doctrine of the blood of Christ, the complete satisfaction which that atoning blood made for sin, and the impossibility of being saved except by that blood. Let nothing tempt you to believe that it is enough to look at the example of Christ, or to receive the sacrament which Christ commanded to be received, and which many nowadays worship like an idol. When you come to your deathbed, you will want something more than an example and a sacrament. Take heed that you are found resting all your weight on Christ's substitution for you on the cross, and His atoning blood, or it will be better if you had never been born.

(c) Last but not least, I charge you never to neglect the duty of brotherly love, and practical, active, sympathetic kindness towards every one around you, whether high or low, or rich or poor. Try daily to do some good upon earth, and to leave the world a better world than it was when you were born. If you are really a child of God, strive to be like your Father and your great elder Brother in heaven. For Christ's sake, do not be content to have religion for yourself alone. Love, charity, kindness, and sympathy are the truest proofs that we are real members of Christ, genuine children of God, and rightful heirs of the kingdom of heaven.

Of "one blood" we were all born. In "one blood" we all need to be washed. To all partakers of Adam's "one blood" we are bound, if we love life, to be charitable, sympathizing, loving, and kind. The time is short. We are going, going, and shall soon be gone to a world where there is no evil to remedy, and no scope for works of mercy. Then for Christ's sake let us all try to do some good before we die, and to lessen the sorrows of this sin-burdened world.

CHAPTER VII[9]

John 7:37-38
"Let Any Man Come."

"In the last day, that great day of the feast, Jesus stood and cried, saying, If any man thirst, let him come unto Me, and drink. He that believeth on Me, as the Scripture hath said, out of his belly shall flow rivers of living water." —John 7:37-38

THE text which heads this paper contains one of those mighty sayings of Christ which deserve to be printed in letters of gold. All the stars in heaven are bright and beautiful; yet even a child can see that "one star differeth from another in glory" (1 Cor. 15:41). All

---

[9]The substance of great part of this paper was preached, as a sermon, under the dome of St. Paul's Cathedral, London, and in the nave of Chester Cathedral, in the year 1878.

Scripture is given by inspiration of God; but that heart must indeed be cold and dull which does not feel that some verses are particularly rich and full. Of such verses this text is one.

In order to see the whole force and beauty of the text, we must remember the place, the time, and occasion when it comes in.

The place, then, was Jerusalem, the metropolis of Judaism, and the stronghold of priests and scribes, of Pharisees and Sadducees.—The occasion was the feast of tabernacles, one of those great annual feasts when every Jew, if he could, went up to the temple, according to the law.—The time was "the last day of the feast," when all the ceremonies were drawing to a close, when the water drawn from the fountain of Siloam had been solemnly poured on the altar, and nothing remained for worshippers but to return home.

At this critical moment our Lord Jesus Christ "stood" forward on a prominent place, and spoke to the assembled crowds. I doubt not He read their hearts. He saw them going away with aching consciences and unsatisfied minds, having got nothing from their blind teachers the Pharisees and Sadducees, and carrying away nothing but a barren recollection of pompous forms. He saw and pitied them, and cried aloud, like a herald, "If any man thirst, let him come unto Me, and drink."—That this was all our Lord said on this memorable occasion I take leave to doubt. I suspect it is only the keynote of His address. But this, I believe, was the first sentence that fell from His lips: "If any man thirst, let him come unto Me." If any one wants living, satisfying water, let him come unto ME.

Let me remind my readers, in passing, that no prophet or Apostle ever took on himself to use such language as this. "Come with us," said Moses to Hobab (Num. 10:29); "Come to the waters," says Isaiah (Isa. 45:1); "Behold the Lamb," says John the Baptist (John 1:29); "Believe on the Lord Jesus Christ," says St. Paul (Acts 16:31). But no one except Jesus of Nazareth ever said, "Come to ME." That fact is very significant. He that said, "Come to Me," knew and felt, when He said it, that He was the Eternal Son of God, the promised Messiah, the Saviour of the world.

There are three points in this great saying of our Lord's to which I now propose to direct your attention.

I. You have a case supposed: "If any man thirst."

II. You have a remedy proposed: "Let him come unto Me, and drink."

III. You have a promise held out: "He that believeth on Me, as the Scripture hath said, out of his belly shall flow rivers of living water."

Each of these points concerns all into whose hands this paper may fall. On each of them I have somewhat to say.

I. In the first place, then, you have a case supposed. Our Lord says, "If any man thirst."

Bodily thirst is notoriously the most painful sensation to which the frame of mortal man is liable. Read the story of the miserable sufferers in the Black Hole at Calcutta.—Ask any one who has travelled over desert plains under a tropical sum—Hear what any old soldier will tell you is the chief want of the wounded on a battlefield.—Remember what the survivors of the crews of ships lost in mid-ocean, like The Cospatrick, go through. Mark the awful words of the rich man in the parable: "Send Lazarus that he may dip the tip of his finger in water to cool my tongue: for I am tormented in this flame" (Luke 16:24). The testimony is unvarying. There is nothing so terrible and hard to bear as thirst.

But if bodily thirst is so painful, how much more painful is thirst of soul! Physical suffering is not the worst part of eternal punishment. It is a light thing, even in this world, compared to the suffering of the mind and inward man. To see the value of our souls, and find out they are in danger of eternal ruin,—to feel the burden of unforgiven sin, and not to know where to turn for relief,—to have a conscience sick and ill at ease, and to be ignorant of the remedy,—to discover that we are dying, dying daily, and yet unprepared to meet God,—to have some clear view of our own guilt and wickedness, and yet to be in utter darkness about absolution,—this is the highest degree of pain,—the pain which drinks up soul and spirit, and pierces joints and marrow! And this, no doubt, is the thirst of which our Lord is speaking. It is thirst after pardon, forgiveness, absolution, and peace with God. It is the craving of a really awakened conscience, wanting satisfaction and not knowing where to find it, walking through dry places, and unable to get rest.

This is the thirst which the Jews felt, when Peter preached to them on the day of Pentecost. It is written that they were "pricked in their heart, and said, Men and brethren, what shall we do?" (Acts 2:37).

This is the thirst which the Philippian jailor felt, when he awoke to consciousness of his spiritual danger, and felt the earthquake making the prison reel under his feet. It is written that he "came trembling, and fell down before Paul and Silas, and brought them out, saying, Sirs, what must I do to be saved?" (Acts 16:30).

This is the thirst which many of the greatest servants of God seem to have felt, when light first broke in on their minds. Augustine seeking rest among the Manichean heretics and finding none,—Luther groping after truth among monks in Erfurt monastery,—John Bunyan agonizing amidst doubts and conflicts in his Elstow cottage,—George Whitefield groaning under self-imposed austerities, for want of clear teaching, when an undergraduate at Oxford,—all have left on record their experience. I believe they all knew what our Lord meant when He spoke of "thirst."

And surely, reader, it is not too much to say that all of us ought to know SOMETHING of this thirst, if not as much as Augustine, Luther, Bunyan, or Whitefield. Living as we do in a dying world,—knowing, as we must do, if we will confess it, that there is a world beyond the grave, and that after death comes the judgment,—feeling, as we must do in our better moments, what poor, weak, unstable, defective creatures we all are, and how unfit to meet God,—conscious as we must be in our inmost heart of hearts, that on our use of time depends our place in eternity,—we ought to feel and to realize something like "thirst" for a sense of peace with the living God. But alas, nothing proves so conclusively the fallen nature of man as the general, common want of spiritual appetite! For money, for power, for pleasure, for rank, for honour, for distinction,—for all these the vast majority are now intensely thirsting. To lead forlorn hopes, to dig for gold, to storm a breach, to try to hew a way through thick-ribbed ice to the North Pole,—for all these objects there is no lack of adventurers and volunteers. Fierce and Incensing is the competition for these corruptible crowns! But few indeed, by comparison, are those who thirst after eternal life. No wonder that the natural man is called in Scripture "dead," and "sleeping," and blind, and deaf. No wonder that he is said to need a second birth and a new creation. There is no surer symptom of mortification in the body than insensibility. There is no more painful sign of an unhealthy state of soul than an utter absence of spiritual thirst. Woe to that man of whom the Saviour can say, "Thou knowest not that thou art wretched, and miserable, and poor, and blind, and naked" (Rev. 3:17).

But who is there among the readers of this paper that feels the burden of sin, and longs for peace with God? Who is there that really feels the words of our Prayer Book Confession: "I have erred and strayed like a lost sheep,—there is no health in me,—I am a miserable offender"? Who is there that enters into the fulness of our Communion service, and can say with truth, "The remembrance of my sins is grievous, and the burden of them is intolerable"? You are the man that ought to thank God. A sense of sin, guilt, and poverty of soul, is the first stone laid by the Holy Ghost, when He builds a spiritual temple. He convinces of sin. Light was the first thing called into being in the material creation (Gen. 1:3). Light about our own state is the first work in the new creation. Thirsting soul, I say again, you are the person that ought to thank God. The kingdom of God is near you. It is not when we begin to feel good, but when we feel bad, that we take the first step towards heaven. Who taught thee that thou wast naked? Whence came this inward light? Who opened thine eyes and made thee see and feel? Know this day that flesh and blood hath not revealed these things unto thee, but our Father which is in heaven. Universities may confer degrees, and schools may impart knowledge of all the sciences, but they cannot make men feel sin. To realize our spiritual need, and feel true spiritual thirst, is the A B C in saving Christianity. It is a great saying of Elihu, in the book of Job, "God looketh upon men, and if any say, I have sinned, and perverted that which was right, and it profited me not; He will deliver his soul from death, and his life shall see the light" (Job 33:27-28). Let him that knows anything of spiritual "thirst" not be ashamed. Rather let him lift up his head, and begin to hope. Let him pray that God would carry on the work He has begun, and make him feel more.

II. Pass from the case supposed to the remedy proposed. "If any man thirst," says our blessed Lord Jesus Christ, "let him come unto Me, and drink."

There is a grand simplicity about this little sentence which cannot be too much admired. There is not a word in it of which the literal meaning is not plain to a child. Yet, simple as it appears, it is rich in spiritual meaning. Like the Koh-i-noor diamond, which you may carry between finger and thumb, it is of unspeakable value. It solves that mighty problem which all the philosophers of Greece and Rome could never solve,—"How can man have peace with God?" Place it in your memory side by side with six other golden sayings of your Lord:—"I am the bread of life: he that cometh unto Me shall never hunger; and he that believeth on ME shall never thirst."—"I am the Light of the world: he that followeth ME shall not walk in darkness, but shall have the light of life."—"I am the Door: by ME if any man enter in, he shall be saved."—"I am the Way, the Truth, and the Life: no man cometh unto the Father but by ME."—"Come unto Me, all ye that labour and are heavy-laden, and I will give you rest."—"Him that cometh to Me I will in no wise cast out."—Add to these six texts the one before you today. Get the whole seven by heart. Rivet them down in your mind, and never let them go. When your feet touch the cold river, on the bed of sickness and in the hour of death, you will find these seven texts above all price (John 6:35, 8:12, 10:9, 14:6; Matt. 11:28; John 6:37).

For what is the sum and substance of these simple words? It is this. Christ is that Fountain of living water which God has graciously provided for thirsting souls From Him, as out of the rock smitten by Moses, there flows an abundant stream for all who travel through the wilderness of this world. In Him, as our Redeemer and Substitute, crucified for our sins and raised again for our justification, there is an endless supply of all that men can need, pardon, absolution, mercy, grace, peace, rest, relief, comfort, and hope.

This rich provision Christ has bought for us at the price of His own precious blood. To open this wondrous fountain He suffered for sin, the just for the unjust, and bore our sins in His own body on the tree. He was made sin for us, who knew no sin, that we might be made the righteousness of God in Him (1 Pet. 2:24, 3:18; 2 Cor. 5:21). And now He is sealed and appointed to be the Reliever of all who are labouring and heavy-laden, and the

Giver of living water to all who thirst. It is His office to receive sinners. It is His pleasure to give them pardon, life, and peace. And the words of the text are a proclamation He makes to all mankind,—"If any man thirst, let him come unto Me, and drink."

Let every reader of this paper remember that the efficacy of a medicine depends in great measure on the manner in which it is used. The best prescription of the best physician is useless if we refuse to follow the directions which accompany it. Suffer the word of exhortation, while I offer some caution and advice about the fountain of living water.

(a) He that thirsts and wants relief must come to Christ Himself. He must not be content with coming to His Church and His ordinances, or to the assemblies of His people for prayer and praise. He must not stop short even at His holy table, or rest satisfied with privately opening his heart to His ordained ministers. Oh, no! he that is content with only drinking these waters "shall thirst again" (John 4:13). He must go higher, further, much further than this. He must have personal dealings with Christ Himself: all else in religion is worthless without Him. The King's palace, the attendant servants, the richly furnished banqueting-house, the very banquet itself, all are nothing unless we speak with the King. His hand alone can take the burden off our backs and make us feel free. The hand of man may take the stone from the grave and show the dead; but none but Jesus can say to the dead, "Come forth, and live" (John 11:41-43). We must deal directly with Christ.

(b) Again: he that thirsts and wants relief from Christ must actually come to Him. It is not enough to wish, and talk, and mean, and intend, and resolve, and hope. Hell, that awful reality, is truly said to be paved with good intentions. Thousands are yearly lost in this fashion, and perish miserably just outside the harbour. Meaning and intending they live; meaning and intending they die. Oh, no! we must "arise and come!" If the prodigal son had been content with saying, "How many hired servants of my father have bread enough and to spare, and I perish with hunger! I hope some day to return home," he might have remained for ever among the swine. It was when he AROSE AND CAME to his father that his father ran to meet him, and said, "Bring forth the best robe, and put it on him.... Let us eat and be merry" (Luke 15:20-23). Like him, we must not only "come to ourselves," and think, but we must actually come to the High Priest, to Christ. We must come to the Physician.

(c) Once again: he that thirsts and wants to come to Christ must remember that SIMPLE FAITH IS THE ONE THING REQUIRED. By all means let him come with a penitent, broken, and contrite heart; but let him not dream of resting on that for acceptance. Faith is the only hand that can carry the living water to our lips. Faith is the hinge on which all turns in the matter of our justification. It is written again and again, that "whosoever believeth shall not perish, but have eternal life" (John 3:15-16). "To him that worketh not, but believeth on Him that justifieth the ungodly, his faith is counted for righteousness" (Rom. 4:5). Happy is he that can lay hold on the principle laid down in that matchless hymn,—

> *"Just as I am: without one plea,*
> *But that Thy blood was shed for me,*
> *And that Thou bidst me come to Thee—*
> *O Lamb of God, I come."*

How simple this remedy for thirst appears! But oh, how hard it is to persuade some persons to receive it! Tell them to do some great thing, to mortify their bodies, to go on pilgrimage, to give all their goods to feed the poor, and so to merit salvation, and they will try to do as they are bid. Tell them to throw overboard all idea of merit, working, or doing, and to come to Christ as empty sinners, with nothing in their hands, and, like Naaman, they are ready to turn away in disdain (2 Kings 5:12). Human nature is always the same in every age. There are still some people just like the Jews, and some like the Greeks. To the Jews Christ crucified is still a stumbling-block, and to the Greeks foolishness. Their succession, at any rate, has never ceased! Never did our Lord say a truer word than that which He spoke to the proud scribes in the Sanhedrim, "And ye WILL NOT come unto Me, that ye might have life" (John 5:40).

But, simple as this remedy for thirst appears, it is the only cure for man's spiritual disease, and the only bridge from earth to heaven. Kings and their subjects, preachers and hearers, masters and servants, high and low, rich and poor, learned and unlearned, all must alike drink of this water of life, and drink in the same way. For eighteen centuries men have laboured to find some other medicine for weary consciences; but they have laboured in vain. Thousands, after blistering their hands, and growing grey in hewing out "broken cisterns, which can hold no water" (Jer. 2:13), have been obliged to come back at last to the old Fountain, and have confessed in their latest moment that here, in Christ alone, is true peace.

And simple as the old remedy for thirst may appear, it is the root of the inward life of all God's greatest servants in all ages. What have the saints and martyrs been in every era of Church history, but men who came to Christ daily by faith, and found His flesh meat indeed and His blood drink indeed? (John 6:55). What have they all been but men who lived the life of faith in the Son of God, and drank daily out of the fulness there is in Him? (Gal. 2:20). Here, at all events, the truest and best Christians, who have made a mark on the world, have been of one mind. Holy Fathers and Reformers, holy Anglican divines and Puritans, holy Episcopalians and Nonconformists, have all in their best moments borne uniform testimony to the value of the Fountain of life. Separated and contentious as they may sometimes have been in their lives, in their deaths they have not been divided. In their last struggle with the King of Terrors they have simply clung to the cross of Christ, and gloried in nothing but the "precious blood," and the Fountain open for all sin and uncleanness.

How thankful we ought to be that we live in a land where the great remedy for spiritual thirst is known,—in a land of open Bibles, preached gospel, and abundant means of grace,—in a land where the efficacy of Christ's sacrifice is still proclaimed, with more or less fulness, in 20,000 pulpits every Sunday. We do not realize the value of our privileges. The very familiarity of the manna makes us think little of it, just as Israel loathed "the light bread" in the wilderness (Num. 21:5). But turn to the pages of a heathen philosopher like the incomparable Plato, and see how he moped after light like one blindfold, and wearied himself to find the door. The humblest peasant who grasps the four "comfortable words" of our beautiful Communion service, in the Prayer Book, knows more of the way of peace with God than the Athenian sage.—Turn to the accounts which trustworthy travellers and missionaries give of the state of the heathen who have never heard the gospel. Read of the human sacrifices in Africa, and the ghastly self-imposed tortures of the devotees of Hindostan, and remember they are all the result of an unquenched "thirst" and a blind and unsatisfied desire to get near to God. And then learn to be thankful that your lot is cast in a land like your own.

Alas, I fear God has a controversy with us for our un-thankfulness! Cold indeed, and dead, must that heart be which can study the condition of Africa, China, and Hindostan, and not thank God that he lives in Christian England.

III. I turn, in the last place, to the promise held met to all who come to Christ. "He that believeth on Me, as the Scripture hath said, out of his belly shall flow rivers of living water."

The subject of Scripture promises is a vast and most interesting one. I doubt whether it receives the attention which it deserves in the present day. Clarke's Scripture Promises, I suspect, is an old book, which is far less studied than it was in the days of our fathers. Few Christians realize the number, and length, and breadth, and depth, and height, and variety of the precious "shalls" and "wills" laid up in the Bible for the special benefit and encouragement of all who will use them.

Yet promise lies at the bottom of nearly all the transactions of man with man in the affairs of this life. The vast majority of Adam's children in every civilized country are acting every day on the faith of promises. The labourer on the land works hard from Monday morning to Saturday night, because he believes that at the end of the week he shall receive his promised wages. The soldier enlists in the army, and the sailor enters his name on the ship's books in the navy, in the full confidence that those under whom they serve will at some future time give them their promised pay. The humblest maid-servant in a family works on from day to day at her appointed duties, in the belief that her mistress will give her the promised wages. In the business of great cities, among merchants, and bankers, and tradesmen, nothing could be done without incessant faith in promises. Every man of sense knows that cheques, and bills, and promissory notes, are the only means by which the immense majority of mercantile affairs can possibly be carried on. Men of business are compelled to act by faith and not by sight. They believe promises, and expect to be believed themselves. In short, promises, and faith in promises, and actions springing from faith in promises, are the backbone of nine-tenths of all the dealings of man with his fellow-creatures throughout Christendom.

Now promises in like manner, in the religion of the Bible, are one Hand means by which God is pleased to approach the soul of man. The careful student of Scripture cannot fail to observe that God is continually holding out inducements to man to listen to Him, obey Him, and serve Him; and undertaking to do great things, if man will only attend and believe. In short, as St. Peter says, "There are given to us exceeding great and precious promises" (2 Pet. 1:4). He who has mercifully caused all Holy Scripture to be written for our learning, has shown His perfect knowledge of human nature, by spreading over the book a perfect wealth of promises, suitable to every kind of experience and every condition of life. He seems to say, "Would you know what I undertake to do for you? Do you want to hear my terms? Take up the Bible and read."

But there is one grand difference between the promises of Adam's children and the promises of God, which ought never to be forgotten. The promises of man are not sure to be fulfilled. With the best wishes and intentions, he cannot always keep his word. Disease and death may step in like an armed man, and take away from this world him that promises. War, or pestilence, or famine, or failure of crops, or hurricanes, may strip him of his property, and make it impossible for him to fulfil his engagements. The promises of God, on the contrary, are certain to be kept. He is almighty: nothing can prevent His doing what He has said. He never changes: He is always "of one mind;" and with Him there is "no variableness or shadow of turning" (Job 23:13; Jas. 1:17). He will always keep His word. There is one thing which, as a little girl once told her teacher, to her surprise, God cannot do: "It is impossible for God to lie" (Heb. 6:18). The most unlikely and improbable things, when God has once said He will do them, have always come to pass. The destruction of the old world by a flood, and the preservation of Noah in the Ark, the birth of Isaac, the deliverance of Israel from Egypt, the raising of David to the throne of Saul, the miraculous birth of Christ, the resurrection of Christ, the scattering of the Jews all over the earth, and their continued preservation as a distinct people, who could imagine events more unlikely and improbable than these? Yet God said they should be, and in due time they all came to pass. In short, with God it is just as easy to do a thing as to say it. Whatever He promises, He is certain to perform.

Concerning the variety and riches of Scripture promises, far more might be said than it is possible to say in a short paper like this. Their name is legion. The subject is almost inexhaustible. There is hardly a step in man's life, from childhood to old age, hardly any position in which man can be placed, for which the Bible has not held out encouragement to every one who desires to do right in the sight of God. There are "shalls" and "wills" in God's treasury for every condition. About God's infinite mercy and compassion, about His readiness to receive all who repent and believe, about His willingness to forgive, pardon, and absolve the chief of sinners,—about His power to change hearts and alter our corrupt nature,—about the encouragements to pray, and hear the gospel, and draw near to the throne of grace, about strength for duty, comfort in trouble, guidance in perplexity, help in sickness, consolation in death, support under bereavement, happiness beyond the grave, reward in glory,—about all these things there is an abundant supply of promises in the Word. No one can form an idea of its abundance unless he carefully searches the Scriptures, keeping the subject steadily in view. If any one doubts it, I can only say, "Come and see." Like the Queen of Sheba at Solomon's court, you will soon say, "The half was not told me" (1 Kings 10:7).

The promise of our Lord Jesus Christ, which heads this paper, is somewhat peculiar. It is singularly rich in encouragement to all who feel spiritual thirst, and come to Him for relief, and therefore it deserves peculiar attention. Most of our Lord's promises refer specially to the benefit of the person to whom they are addressed. The promise before us takes a far wider range: it seems to refer to many others beside those to whom He spoke. For what says He?—"He that believeth on Me, as the Scripture hath said" (and everywhere teaches), "out of his belly shall flow rivers of living water. But this spake He of the Spirit, which they that believe on Him should receive." Figurative, undoubtedly, are these words,—figurative, like the earlier words of the sentence, figurative, like "thirst" and "drinking." But all the figures of Scripture contain great truths; and what the figure before us was meant to convey I will now try to show.

(1) For one thing, then, I believe our Lord meant that he who comes to Him by faith shall receive an abundant supply of everything that he can desire for the relief of his own soul's wants. The Spirit shall convey to him such an abiding sense of pardon, peace, and hope, that it shall be in his inward man like a well-spring never dry. He shall feel so satisfied with "the things of Christ," which the Spirit shall show him (John 16:15), that he shall rest from spiritual anxiety about death, judgment, and eternity. He may have his seasons of darkness and doubt, through his own infirmities or the temptations of the devil. But, speaking generally, when he has once come to Christ by faith he shall find in his heart of hearts an unfailing fountain of consolation. This, let us understand, is the first thing which the promise before us contains. "Only come to Me, poor anxious soul," our Lord

seems to say,—"Only come to Me, and thy spiritual anxiety shall be relieved. I will place in thy heart, by the power of the Holy Spirit, such a sense of pardon and peace, through my atonement and intercession, that thou shalt never completely thirst again. Thou mayest have thy doubts, and fears, and conflicts, while thou art in the body. But once having come to Me, and taken Me for thy Saviour, thou shalt never feel thyself entirely hopeless. The condition of thine inward man shall be so thoroughly changed, that thou shalt feel as if there was within thee an ever-flowing spring of water."

What shall we say to these things? I declare my own belief, that whenever a man or woman really comes to Christ by faith, he finds this promise fulfilled. He may possibly be weak in grace, and have many misgivings about his own condition. He may possibly not dare to say that he is converted, justified, sanctified, and meet for the inheritance of the saints in light. But for all that, I am bold to say the humblest and feeblest believer in Christ has got something within him which he would not part with, though he may not yet fully understand it. And what is that "something"? It is just that "river of living water" which begins to run in the heart of every child of Adam as soon as he comes to Christ and drinks. In this sense I believe this wonderful promise of Christ is always fulfilled.

(2) But is this all that is contained in the promise which heads this paper? By no means. There yet remains much behind. There is more to follow. I believe our Lord meant us to understand that he who comes to Him by faith shall not only have an abundant supply of everything which he needs for his own soul, but shall also become a source of blessing to the souls of others. The Spirit who dwells in him shall make him a fountain of good to his fellow-men, so that at the last day there shall be found to have flowed from him "rivers of living water."

This is a most important part of our Lord's promise, and opens up a subject which is seldom realized and grasped by many Christians. But it is one of deep interest, and deserves far more attention than it receives. I believe it to be a truth of God. I believe that just as "no man liveth unto himself" (Rom. 14:7), so also no man is converted only for himself; and that the conversion of one man or woman always leads on, in God's wonderful providence, to the conversion of others. I do not say for a moment that all believers know it. I think it far more likely that many live and die in the faith, who are not aware that they have done good to any soul. But I believe the resurrection morning and the judgment day, when the secret history of all Christians is revealed, will prove that the full meaning of the promise before us has never failed. I doubt if there will be a believer who will not have been to some one or other a "river of living water,"—a channel through whom the Spirit has conveyed saving grace. Even the penitent thief, short as his time was after he repented, has been a source of blessing to thousands of souls!

(a) Some believers are "rivers of living water" while they live. Their words, their conversation, their preaching, their teaching, are all means by which the water of life has flowed into the hearts of their fellow-men. Such, for example, were the Apostles, who wrote no Epistles and only preached the word. Such were Luther, and Whitefield, and Wesley, and Berridge, and Rowlands, and thousands of others of whom I cannot now speak particularly.

(b) Some believers are "rivers of living water" when they die. Their courage in facing the King of Terrors, their boldness in the most painful sufferings, their unswerving faithfulness to Christ's truth even at the stake, their manifest peace on the edge of the grave,—all this has set thousands thinking, and led hundreds to repent and believe. Such, for example, were the primitive martyrs, whom the Roman emperors persecuted. Such were John Huss, and Jerome of Prague. Such were Cranmer, Ridley, Latimer, Hooper, and the noble army of Marian martyrs. The work that they did at their deaths, like Samson, was far greater than the work done in their lives.

(c) Some believers are "rivers of living water" long after they die. They do good by their books and writings in every part of the world, long after the hands which held the pen are mouldering in the dust. Such men were Bunyan, and Baxter, and Owen, and George Herbert, and Robert M'Cheyne. These blessed servants of God do more good probably by their books at this moment, than they did by their tongues when they were alive. "Being dead, they yet speak" (Heb. 11:4).

(d) Finally, there are some believers who are "rivers of living water" by the beauty of their daily conduct and behaviour. There are many quiet, gentle, consistent Christians, who make no show and no noise in the world, and yet insensibly exercise a deep influence for good on all around them. They "win without the Word" (1 Pet. 3:1). Their love, their kindness, their sweet temper, their patience, their unselfishness, tell silently on a wide circle, and sow seeds of thought and self-inquiry in many minds. It was a fine testimony of an old lady who died in great peace,—saying that under God she owed her salvation to Mr. Whitefield:—"It was not any sermon that he preached; it was not anything that he ever said to me. It was the beautiful consistency and kindness of his daily life, in the house where he was staying, when I was a little girl. I said to myself, if I ever have any religion, Mr. Whitefield's God shall be my God."

I charge every reader of this paper to lay hold on this view of our Lord's promise, and never forget it. Think not for a moment that your own soul is the only soul that will be saved, if you come to Christ by faith and follow Him. Think of the blessedness of being a "river of living water" to others. Who can tell that you may not be the means of bringing many others to Christ? Live, and act, and speak, and pray, and work, keeping this continually in view. I knew a family, consisting of a father, mother, and ten children, in which true religion began with one of the daughters; and when it began she stood alone, and all the rest of the family were in the world. And yet, before she died, she saw both her parents and all her brothers and sisters converted to God, and all this, humanly speaking, began from her influence! Surely, in the face of this, we need not doubt, that a believer may be to others a "river of living water." Conversions may not be in your time, and you may die without seeing them. But never doubt that conversion generally leads to conversions, and that few go to heaven alone. When Grimshaw, of Haworth, the apostle of the north, died, he left his son graceless and godless. Afterwards the son was converted, never having forgotten his father's advice and example. And his last words were, "What will my old father say when he sees me in heaven?" Let us take courage and hope on, believing Christ's promise.

(1) And now, before we part, let me ask every one who reads this paper a plain question. Do you know anything of spiritual thirst? Have you ever felt any-tiring of genuine deep concern about your soul?—I fear that many know nothing about it. I have learned, by the painful experience of the third of a century, that people may go on for years attending God's house, and yet never feel their sins, or desire to be saved. The cares of this world, the love of pleasure, the "lust of other things," choke the good seed every Sunday, and make it unfruitful. They come to church with hearts as cold as the stone pavement on which they walk. They go away as thoughtless and unmoved as the old marble busts which look down on them from the monuments on the walls. Well, it may be so; but I do not yet despair of any one, so long as he is alive. That grand old bell in St.

Paul's Cathedral, London, which has struck the hours for so many years, is seldom heard by many citizens during the business hours of the day. The roar and din of traffic in the streets have a strange power to deaden its sound, and prevent men hearing it. But when the daily work is over, and desks are locked, and doors are closed, and books are put away, and quiet reigns in the great city, the case is altered. As the old bell strikes eleven, and twelve, and one, and two, and three at night, thousands hear it who never heard it during the day. And so I hope it will be with many a one in the matter of his soul. Now, in the plenitude of health and strength, in the hurry and whirl of business, I fear the voice of your conscience is often stifled, and you cannot hear it. But the day may come when the great bell of conscience will make itself heard, whether you like it or not. The time may come when, laid aside in quietness, and obliged by illness to sit still, you may be forced to look within, and consider your soul's concerns. And then, when the great bell of awakened conscience is sounding in your ears, I trust that many a man who reads this paper may hear the voice of God and repent, may learn to thirst, and learn to come to Christ for relief. Yes! I pray God you may yet be taught to feel before it be too late!

(2) But do you feel anything at this very moment? Is your conscience awake and working? Are you sensible of spiritual thirst, and longing for relief? Then hear the invitation which I bring you in my Master's name this day: If any man, "no matter who he may be,"—if any man, high or low, rich or poor, learned or unlearned,—"if any man thirst, let him come to Christ, and drink." Hear and accept that invitation without delay. Wait for nothing. Wait for nobody. Who can tell that you may not wait for "a convenient season" till it be too late! The hand of a living Redeemer is now held out from heaven; but it may be withdrawn. The Fountain is open now; but it may soon be closed for ever. "If any man thirst, let him come and drink" without delay. Though you have been a great sinner, and have resisted warnings, counsel, and sermons, yet come.—Though you have sinned against light and knowledge, against a father's advice, and a mother's tears, though you have lived for years without a Sabbath, and without prayer, yet come.—Say not that you know not how to come, that you do not understand what it is to believe, that you must wait for more light. Will a tired man say, that he is too tired to lie down? or a drowning man, that he knows not how to lay hold on the hand stretched out to help him? or the shipwrecked sailor, with a lifeboat alongside the stranded hulk, that he knows not how to jump in? Oh, cast away these vain excuses! Arise, and come! The door is not shut. The fountain is not yet closed. The Lord Jesus invites you. It is enough that you feel thirst, and desire to be saved. Come: come to Christ without delay. Who ever came to the fountain for sin and found it dry? Who ever went unsatisfied away?

(3) But have you come to Christ already and found relief? Then come nearer, nearer still. The closer your communion with Christ, the more comfort you will fed. The more you daily live by the side of the Fountain, the more you shall feel in yourself "a well of water springing up into everlasting life" (John 4:14). You shall not only be blessed yourself, but be a source of blessing to others.

In this evil world you may not perhaps feel all the sensible comfort you could desire. But remember you cannot have two heavens. Perfect happiness is yet to come. The devil is not yet bound. There is "a good time coming" for all who feel their sins and come to Christ, and commit their thirsting souls to His keeping. When He comes again, they will be completely satisfied.

Note[10]

THERE is a passage in an old writer which throws so much light on some points mentioned in this paper, that I make no excuse for giving it to the reader in its entirety. It comes from a work which is little known and less read. It has done me good, and I think it may do good to others.

"When a man is awakened, and brought to that, that all must be brought to, or to worse, 'What shall I do to be saved;' (Acts 16:30-31), we have the apostolic answer to it: 'Believe on the Lord Jesus Christ, and thou shalt be saved, and thy house.' This answer is so old that with many it seems out of date. But it is still, and will ever be, fresh, and new, and savoury, and the only resolution of this grand case of conscience, as long as conscience and the world lasts. No wit or art of man will ever find a crack or flaw in it, or devise another or a better answer; nor can any but this alone heal rightly the wound of an awakened conscience.

"Let us set this man to seek resolution and relief in this case of some masters in our Israel. According to their principles they must say to him, 'Repent, and mourn for your known sins, and leave them and loathe them; and God will have mercy on you.' 'Alas!' (saith the poor man), 'my heart is hard, and I cannot repent aright: yea, I find my heart more hard and vile than when I was secure in sin.' If you speak to this man of qualifications for Christ, he knows nothing of them; if of sincere obedience, his answer is native and ready: 'Obedience is the work of a living man, and sincerity is only in a renewed soul.' Sincere obedience is therefore as impossible to a dead, unrenewed sinner, as perfect obedience is. Why should not the right answer be given to the awakened sinner: 'Believe on the Lord Jesus Christ, and you shall be saved'? Tell him what Christ is, what He hath done and suffered to obtain eternal redemption for sinners, and that according to the will of God and his Father. Give him a plain downright narrative of the gospel salvation wrought out by the Son of God; tell him the history and mystery of the gospel plainly. It may be the Holy Ghost will work faith thereby, as He did in those first-fruits of the Gentiles (Acts 10:44).

"If he ask, What warrant he hath to believe on Jesus Christ? tell him, that he hath utter, indispensable necessity for it; for without believing on Him, he must perish eternally. Tell him that he hath God's gracious offer of Christ and all His redemption; with a promise that upon accepting the offer by faith, Christ, and salvation with Him, is his. Tell him that he hath God's express commandment (1 John 3:23), to believe on Christ's name; and that he should make conscience of obeying it, as well as any command in the moral law. Tell him of Christ's ability and goodwill to save; that no man was ever rejected by Him that cast himself upon Him; that desperate cases are the glorious triumphs of His art of saving. Tell him, that there is no midst (or medium) between faith and unbelief; that there is no excuse for neglecting the one, and continuing in the other; that believing on the Lord Jesus for salvation is more pleasing to God than all obedience to His law; and that unbelief is the most provoking to God, and the most damning to man, of all sins. Against the greatness of his sins, the curse of the law, and the severity of God as Judge, there is no relief to be held forth to him, but the free and boundless grace of God in the merit of Christ's satisfaction by the sacrifice of Himself.

"If he should say, What is it to believe on Jesus Christ? as to this, I find no such question in the Word: but that all did some way understand the notion of it; the Jews that

---

[10]From Robert Tralli's Works, 1696. Vol. i. 266-269.

did not believe on Him (John 6:28-30); the chief priests and Pharisees (John 7:48); the blind man (John 9:35). When Christ asked him, Believest thou on the Son of God? he answered, Who is he, Lord, that I may believe on Him? Immediately, when Christ had told him (John 9:37), he saith not, What is it to believe on Him? but, Lord, I believe; and worshipped Him: and so both professed and acted faith in Him. So the father of the lunatic (Mark 9:23-24), and the eunuch (Acts 8:37). They all, both Christ's enemies and His disciples, knew that faith in Him was a believing that the man Jesus of Nazareth was the Son of God, the Messiah, and Saviour of the world, so as to receive and look for salvation in His name (Acts 9:12). This was the common report, published by Christ and His Apostles and disciples; and known by all that heard it.

"If he yet ask, What he is to believe? you tell him, that he is not called to believe that he is in Christ, and that his sins are pardoned, and he a justified man; but that he is to believe God's record concerning Christ (1 John 5:10-12). And this record is, that God giveth (that is, offereth) to us eternal life in His Son Jesus Christ; and that all that with the heart believe this report, and rest their souls on these glad tidings, shall be saved (Rom. 10:9-11). And thus he is to believe, that he may be justified (Gal. 2:16).

"If he still say that this believing is hard, this is a good doubt, but easily resolved. It bespeaks a man deeply humbled. Anybody may see his own impotence to obey the law of God fully; but few find the difficulty of believing. For his relief and resolution ask him, What it is he finds makes believing difficult to him? Is it unwillingness to be justified and saved? Is it unwillingness to be so saved by Jesus Christ, to the praise of God's grace in Him, and to the voiding of all boasting in himself? This he will surely deny. Is it a distrust of the truth of the gospel record? This he dare not own. Is it a doubt of Christ's ability or goodwill to save? This is to contradict the testimony of God in the gospel. Is it because he doubts of an interest in Christ and his redemption? You tell him that believing on Christ makes up the interest in Him.

"If he say that he cannot believe on Jesus Christ because of the difficulty of the acting this faith, and that a Divine power is needful to draw it forth, which he finds not, you must tell him that believing in Jesus Christ is no work, but a resting on Jesus Christ. You must tell him that this pretence is as unreasonable as if a man, wearied with a journey and not able to go one step further, should argue, 'I am so tired, that I am not able to lie down,' when indeed he can neither stand nor go. The poor wearied sinner can never believe on Jesus Christ till he finds he can do nothing for himself; and in his first believing doth always apply himself to Christ for salvation, as a man hopeless and helpless in himself. And by such reasonings with him from the gospel, the Lord will (as He hath often done) convey faith and joy and peace by believing."

CHAPTER VIII[11]

1 John 5:4-5
Victory.

"For whatsoever is born of God overcometh the world: and this is the victory that overcometh the world, even our faith. Who is he that overcometh the world, but he that believeth that Jesus is the Son of God." —1 John 5:4-5

IT ought to be our practice, if we have any religion, to examine the state of our souls from time to time, and to find out whether we are "right in the sight of God" (Acts 8:21).

Are we true Christians? Are we likely to go to heaven when we die? Are we born again,—born of the Spirit,—born of God? These are searching questions, which imperatively demand an answer; and the text which heads this paper will help us to give that answer. If we are born of God, we shall have one great mark of character, we shall" overcome the world."

In opening up this subject, there are three points to which I propose to invite attention in this paper.

I. In the first place, let us consider the name by which St. John describes a true Christian. He calls him six times over, in his First Epistle, a man "born of God," and once, "begotten of God."

II. In the second place, let us consider the special mark which St. John supplies of a man born of God. He says that he "overcomes the world."

III. In the last place, let us consider the secret of the true Christian's victory over the world. He says, "This is the victory that overcometh the world, even our faith."

Let me clear the way by expressing an earnest hope that no reader will turn away from the subject before us, under the idea that it is a controversial one. I doubt whether any doctrine of the Bible has suffered so much from impatient dislike of controversy as that which is contained in the phrase, "Born of God." Yet that phrase contains a great foundation verity of Christianity, which can never be neglected without damage. Deep down, below strifes and contentions about the effect of baptism, and the meaning of liturgical services, there lies in those three words one of the primary rocks of the everlasting gospel, even the inward work of the Holy Ghost on the soul of man. The atoning work of Christ FOR us, and the sanctifying work of the Holy Ghost WITHIN US, are the two corner-stones of saving religion Surely a truth which the last writer of the New Testament brings forward no less than seven times in the five chapters of one Epistle,—a truth which he binds up seven times with some of the distinguishing characteristics of the Christian man,—such a truth ought not to be disliked or timidly passed by. Surely it may be handled profitably without entering upon debatable ground. I shall attempt so to handle it in this paper.

I. First and foremost, I ask my readers to notice the name by which St. John describes a true Christian. Here, and in five other places, he speaks of him as one "born of God."

Let us briefly analyze this rich and wonderful expression. The natural birth of any child of man, in the humblest rank of life, is an important event. It is the bringing into being of a creature who will outlive sun, moon, stars, and earth, and may one day develop

---

[11] The substance of this paper was originally preached as a sermon in St. Mary's Church, Cambridge, when I was select preacher, in 1879.

a character which shall shake the world. How much more important must spiritual birth be! How much must lie beneath that figurative phrase, "Born of God!"

(a) To be "born of God" is to be the SUBJECT OF AN INWARD CHANGE of heart, so complete, that it is like passing into a new existence. It is the introduction into the human soul of a seed from heaven, a new principle, a Divine nature, a new will. Certainly it is no outward bodily alteration; but it is no less certain that it is an entire alteration of the inward man. It adds no new faculties to our minds; but it gives an entirely new bent and bias to our old ones. The tastes and opinions of one "born of God," his views of sin, of the world, of the Bible, of God, and of Christ, are so thoroughly new, that he is to all intents and purposes what St. Paul calls "a new creature." In fact, as the Church Catechism truly says, it is "a death unto sin and a new birth unto righteousness."

(b) To be "born of God" is a change which is THE PECULIAR GIFT OF THE LORD JESUS CHRIST to all His believing people. It is He who plants in their hearts the Spirit of adoption, whereby they cry, Abba Father, and makes them members of His mystical body, and sons and daughters of the Lord Almighty (Rom. 8:15). It is written: "He quickeneth whom He will." "As the Father hath life in Himself, so hath He given to the Son to have life in Himself" (John 5:21-26). In short, as the first chapter of St. John teaches, so it will be as long as the world stands: "To as many as received Him He gave power to become the sons of God, even to them that believe on His name; which were born not of blood, nor of the will of the flesh, nor of the will of man, but of God" (John 1:12-13).

(c) To be "born of God" is a change which unquestionably is VERY MYSTERIOUS. The Lord Jesus Christ Himself tells us that in well-known words: "The wind bloweth where it listeth, and thou hearest the sound thereof, but canst not tell whence it cometh, and whither it goeth; so is every one that is born of the Spirit" (John 3:8). But we must all confess there are a thousand things in the natural world around us which we cannot explain, and yet believe. We cannot explain how our wills act daily on our members, and make them move, or rest, at our discretion; yet no one ever thinks of disputing the fact. The wisest philosopher cannot tell us the origin of physical life. What right, then, have we to complain because we cannot comprehend the beginning of spiritual life in him that is "born of God"?

(d) But to be "born of God" is a change which WILL ALWAYS BE SEEN AND FELT. I do not say that he who is the subject of it will invariably understand his own feelings. On the contrary, those feelings are often a cause of much anxiety, conflict, and inward strife. Nor do I say that a person "born of God" will always become at once an established Christian, a Christian in whose life and ways nothing weak and defective can be observed by others. But this I do say, the Holy Ghost never works in a person's soul without producing some perceptible results in character and conduct. The true grace of God is like light and fire: it cannot be hid; it is never idle; it never sleeps. I can find no such thing as "dormant" grace in Scripture. It is written, "Whosoever is born of God doth not commit sin; for His seed remaineth in him: and he cannot sin, because he is born of God" (1 John 3:9).

(e) To crown all, to be born of God is a thing which is of ABSOLUTE NECESSITY to our salvation. Without it we can neither know God rightly and serve Him acceptably in the life that now is, nor dwell with God comfortably in the life that is to come. There are two things which are indispensably needful before any child of Adam can be saved One is the forgiveness of his sins through the blood of Christ: the other is the renewal of his heart by the Spirit of Christ. Without the forgiveness we have no title to heaven: without the renewed heart we could not enjoy heaven. These two things are never separate. Every forgiven man is also a renewed man, and every renewed man is also a forgiven man. There are two standing maxims of the gospel which should never be forgotten: one is, "He that believeth not the Son shall not see life;" the other is, "If any man have not the Spirit of Christ, he is none of His" (John 3:36; Rom. 8:9). Quaint, but most true, is the old saying: "Once born, die twice, and die for ever; twice born, never die, and live for ever." Without a natural birth we should never have lived and moved on earth: without a spiritual birth we shall never live and dwell in heaven. It is written, "Except a man be born again, he cannot see the kingdom of God" (John 3:3).

And now, before I pass away from the name which St. John gives in this text to the true Christian, let us not forget to ask ourselves what we know experimentally about being "born of God." Let us search and try our hearts with honest self-examination, and seek to find out whether there is any real work of the Holy Ghost in our inward man. Far be it from me to encourage the slightest approach to hypocrisy, self-conceit, and fanaticism. Nor do I want any one to look for that angelic perfection in himself on earth, which will only be found in heaven. All I say is, let us never be content with the "outward and visible signs" of Christianity, unless we also know something of "inward and spiritual grace." All I ask, and I think I have a right to ask, is, that we should often take this First Epistle of St. John in our hands, and try to find out by its light whether we are "born of God."

One more thing let me add, which I dare not leave unsaid. Let us never be ashamed, in a day of abounding heresy, to contend earnestly for the Godhead and personality of the Holy Ghost, and the reality of His work on souls. Just as we clasp to our hearts the doctrine of the Trinity, and the proper Deity of our Lord Jesus Christ, as great foundation verities of the gospel, so let us grasp tightly the truth about God the Holy Ghost. Let us ever give Him in our religion the place and dignity which Scripture assigns to Him. Wherever in the providence of God we may be called to worship, let our first inquiry be, "Where is the Lamb?" and our second, "Where is the Holy Ghost?" We know there have been many martyrs for Jesus Christ and the true doctrine of justification. "A day may come," said a remarkable saint, "when there will need to be martyrs for the Holy Ghost, and His work within the soul." Happy is he who can say with heart, as well as lips, the familiar words of our venerable Church Catechism,—"I believe in God the Father, who hath made me and all the world: I believe in God the Son, who hath redeemed me and all mankind: I believe in God the Holy Ghost, who sanctifieth me, and all the elect people of God."

II. The second thing I will now ask my readers to notice in my text is, the special mark which St. John supplies of the man who is a true Christian. He says, "Whatsoever is born of God overcometh the world." In short, to use the words of that holy man Bishop Wilson, Bishop of Sodor and Man, the Apostle teaches that "the only certain proof of regeneration is victory."

We are all apt to flatter ourselves, that if we are duly enrolled members of that great ecclesiastical corporation the Church of England, our souls cannot be in much danger. We secretly stifle the voice of conscience with the comfortable thought, "I am a Churchman; why should I be afraid?"

Yet common sense and a little reflection might remind us that there are no privileges without corresponding responsibilities. Before we repose in self-satisfied confidence on our Church membership, we shall do well to ask ourselves whether we bear in our characters the marks of living membership of Christ's mystical body. Do we know anything of renouncing the devil and all his works, and crucifying the flesh with its affections and lusts? And, to bring this matter to a point, as it is set before us in our text, do we know anything of "overcoming the world"?

Of the three great spiritual enemies of man, it is hard to say which does most harm to the soul. The last day alone will settle that point. But I venture boldly to say, that at no former period has "the world" been so dangerous, and so successful in injuring Christ's Church, as it is just now. Every age is said to have its own peculiar epidemic disease. I suspect that "worldliness" is the peculiar plague of Christendom in our own era. That same love of the world's good things and good opinion,—that same dread of the world's opposition and blame,—which proved so fatal to Judas Iscariot, and Demas, and many more in the beginning of the gospel,—each is just as powerful in the nineteenth century as it was in the first, and a hundred times more. Even in days of persecution, under heathen emperors, these spiritual enemies slew their thousands, and in days of ease, and luxury, and free thought, like our own, they slay their tens of thousands. The subtle influence of the world, nowadays, seems to infect the very air we breathe. It creeps into families like an angel of light, and leads myriads captive, who never know that they are slaves. The enormous increase of English wealth, and consequent power of self-indulgence, and the immense growth of a passionate taste for recreations and amusements of all kinds; the startling rise and progress of a so-called liberality of opinion, which refuses to say anybody is wrong, whatever he does, and loudly asserts that, as in the days of the Judges, every one should think and do what is right in his own eyes, and never be checked, mall these strange phenomena of our age give the world an amazing additional power, and make it doubly needful for Christ's ministers to cry aloud, "Beware of the world!"

In the face of this aggravated danger, we must never forget that the word of the living God changes not. "Love not the world,"—"Be not conformed to this world,"—"The friendship of the world is enmity with God,"—these mighty sayings of God's statute-book remain still unrepealed (1 John 2:15; Rom. 12:2; Jas. 4:4). The true Christian strives daily to obey them, and proves the vitality of his religion by his obedience. It is as true now as it was eighteen hundred years ago, that the man "born of God" will be a man who, more or less, resists and overcomes the world. Such a man does not "overcome" by retiring into a corner, and becoming a monk or a hermit, but by boldly meeting his foes and conquering them. He does not refuse to fill his place in society, and do his duty in that position to which God has called him. But though "in" the world, he is not "of" the world. He uses it, but does not abuse it. He knows when to say No, when to refuse compliance, when to halt, when to say, "Hitherto have I gone, but I go no further." He is not wholly absorbed either in the business or the pleasures of life, as if they were the sum total of existence. Even in innocent things he keeps the rein on his tastes and inclinations, and does not let them run away with him. He does not live as if life was made up of recreation, or money-getting, or politics, or scientific pursuits, and as if there were no life to come. Everywhere, and in every condition, in public and in private, in business or in amusements, he carries himself like a "citizen of a better country," and as one who is not entirely dependent on temporal things. Like the noble Roman ambassador before Pyrrhus[12], he is alike unmoved by the elephant or by the gold. You will neither bribe him, nor frighten him, nor allure him into neglecting his soul. This is one way in which the true Christian proves the reality of his Christianity. This is the way in which the man "born of God" overcomes the world.

---

[12] The incorruptible Gaius Fabricius Luscinus.

I am fully aware that, at first sight, the things I have just said may appear "hard sayings." The standard of true Christianity which I have just raised may seem extravagant, and extreme, and unattainable in this life. I grant most freely that to "overcome" in the fashion I have described needs a constant fight and struggle, and that all such fighting is naturally unpleasant to flesh and blood. It is disagreeable to find ourselves standing alone every now and then, and running counter to the opinions of all around us. We do not like to appear narrow-minded, and exclusive, and uncharitable, and ungenial, and ill-natured, and out of harmony with our fellows. We naturally love ease and popularity, and hate collisions in religion, and if we hear we cannot be true Christians without all this fighting and warring, we are tempted to say to ourselves, "I will give it up in despair." I speak from bitter experience. I have known and felt all this myself.

To all who are tempted in this way,—and none, I believe, are so much tempted as the young,—to all who are disposed to shrink back from any effort to overcome the world, as a thing impossible, rote all such I offer a few words of friendly exhortation. Before you turn your back on the enemy, and openly confess that he is too strong for you,—before you bow down to the strong man, and let him place his foot on your neck, let me put you in remembrance of some things which, perhaps, you are forgetting.

Is not the world, then, one of the three great foes which you were solemnly bound at baptism to resist? Was it for nothing that these words were read, "We sign him with the sign of the cross, in token that hereafter he shall not be ashamed to confess the faith of Christ crucified, and manfully to fight under His banner against sin, THE WORLD, and the devil, and to continue Christ's soldier and servant unto his life's end"? And is it really come to this, that you mean to renounce your obligations, and retire from your Master's service, to desert your colours, to slink away to the rear, and refuse to fight?

Again, is it not true that myriads of men and women, no stronger than yourself, have fought this battle with the world, and won it? Think of the mighty hosts of Christian soldiers who have walked in the narrow way in the last eighteen centuries, and proved more than conquerors. The same Divine Captain, the same armour, the same helps and aids by which they overcame, are ready for you. Surely if they got the victory, you may hope to do the same.

Again, is it not true that this fight with the world is a thing of absolute necessity? Does not our Master say, "Whosoever doth not bear his cross, and come after Me, cannot be My disciple"? (Luke 14:27). "I came not to send peace on earth, but a sword" (Matt. 10:34). Here, at any rate, we cannot remain neutral, and sit still. Such a line of conduct may be possible in the strife of nations, but it is utterly impossible in that conflict which concerns the soul. The boasted policy of non-interference, the masterly inactivity" which pleases so many statesmen, the plan of keeping quiet and letting things alone,—all this will never do in the Christian warfare. To be at peace with the world, the flesh, and the devil, is to be at enmity with God, and in the broad way that leadeth to destruction. We have no choice or option. The promises to the Seven Churches in Revelation are only "to him that overcometh." We must fight or be lost. We must conquer or die eternally. We must put on the whole armour of God. "He that hath no sword, let him sell his garment and buy one" (Eph. 6:11; Luke 22:36).

Surely, in the face of such considerations as these, I may well charge and entreat all who are inclined to make peace with the world, and not resist it, to awake to a sense of their danger. Awake and cast aside the chains which indolence or love of popularity are gradually weaving round you. Awake before it is too late,—before repeated worldly acts have formed habits, and habits have crystallized into character, and you have become a helpless slave. When men on every side are volunteering for war, and ready to go forth to battle for a corruptible crown, stand up and resolve to do it for one that is incorruptible. The world is not so strong an enemy as you think, if you will only meet it boldly, and use the right weapons. The fancied difficulties will vanish, or melt away like snow, as you approach them. The lions you now dread will prove chained. Hundreds could tell you that they served the world for years, and found at last that its rewards were hollow and unreal, and its so-called good things could neither satisfy nor save. Cardinal Wolsey's dying words are only the language of ten thousand hearts at this minute,—

> *"Vain pomp and glory of this world, I hate ye:*
> *I feel my heart is opened.—*
> *Had I but serv'd my God with half the zeal*
> *I serv'd my king, He would not, in mine age,*
> *Have left me naked to mine enemies."*

But who, on the other hand, ever fought God's battle manfully against the world and failed to find a rich reward? No doubt the experience of Christian pilgrims is very various. Not all have "an abundant entrance" into the kingdom, and some are "saved so as by fire" (2 Pet. 1:11; 1 Cor. 3:15). But none, I am persuaded, have such joy and peace in believing, and travel to the celestial city with such light hearts, as those who come out boldly, and overcome the love and fear of the world. Such men the King of kings delights to honour while they live; and when they die, their testimony is that of old Bunyan's hero, Valiant,— "I am going to my Father's house; and though with great difficulty I have got hither, yet now I do not repent me of all the troubles I have been at to arrive where I am."

III. The third and last thing which I shall ask you to notice in this text is, the secret of the true Christian's victory over the world. St. John reveals that secret to us twice over, as if he would emphasize his meaning, and make it unmistakable: "This is the victory that overcometh the world, even our FAITH. Who is he that overcometh the world, but he that BELIEVETH that Jesus is the Son of God?"

Simplicity is a distinguishing characteristic of many of God's handiworks. "How beautifully simple!" has often been the philosopher's cry, on finding out some great secret of nature. Simplicity is the striking feature of the principle by which the man "born of God" overcomes the world. Perhaps he hardly understands it himself. But he is what he is, and does what he does, acts as he acts, behaves as he behaves, for one simple reason, he BELIEVES. He realizes the existence of unseen objects, compared to which the frowns or smiles, the favour or blame of the world, are trifles light as air. God, and heaven, and judgment, and eternity, are not "words and names" with him, but vast and substantial realities; and the faith of them makes everything else look shadowy and unreal. But, towering far above all other objects, he sees by faith an unseen Saviour, who loved him, gave Himself for him, paid his debt to God with His own precious blood, went to the grave for him, rose again, and appears in heaven for him as his Advocate with the Father. SEEING HIM, he feels constrained to love Him first and foremost, to set his chief affection on things above, not on things on the earth, and to live not for himself, but for Him who died for him. SEEING HIM, he fears not to face the world's displeasure, and fights on with a firm confidence that he will be "more than conqueror." In short, it is the expulsive power of a new principle, a living faith in an unseen God and an unseen Jesus, that minimizes the difficulties of a true Christian, drives away the fear of man, and overcomes the world.

This is the principle that made the Apostles what they were after the day of Pentecost. When Peter and John stood before the Council, and spoke in such fashion that all men marvelled at their boldness, their vivid faith saw One higher than Annas and Caiaphas and their companions, who would never forsake them. When Saul, converted and renewed, gave up all his brilliant prospects among his own nation, to become a preacher of the gospel he had once despised, he saw far away, by faith, One that was invisible, who could give him a hundredfold more in this present life, and in the world to come life everlasting. These all overcame by FAITH.

This is the principle which made the primitive Christians hold fast their religion even to death, unshaken by the fiercest persecution of heathen emperors. They were often unlearned and ignorant men, and saw many things through a glass darkly. But their so-called "obstinacy" astonished even philosophers like Pliny.

For centuries there were never wanting men like Polycarp and Ignatius, who were ready to die rather than to deny Christ. Fines, and prisons, and torture, and fire, and sword failed to crush the spirit of the noble army of martyrs. The whole power of imperial Rome, with her legions, proved unable to stamp out the religion which began with a few fishermen and publicans in Palestine. They overcame by FAITH.

This is the principle that made our own Reformers in the sixteenth century endure hardships even unto death, rather than withdraw their protest against the Church of Rome. Many of them, no doubt, like Rogers, and Philpot, and Bradford, might have enjoyed rich preferments and died quietly in their beds, if they would only have recanted. But they chose rather to suffer affliction, and strong in faith, died at the stake. This was the principle that made the rank and file of our English martyrs in the same age—labourers, artisans, and apprentices—yield their bodies to be burned. Poor and uneducated as they were, they were rich in faith; and if they could not speak for Christ, they could die for Him. These all overcame by BELIEVING.

But time would fail me if I brought forward all the evidence that might be adduced on this subject. Let us look at our own age. Let us consider the men who have made the greatest mark on the world for Christ's cause in the last hundred years. Let us remember how clergymen like Whitefield, and Wesley, and Romaine, and Venn stood alone in their day and generation, and revived English religion, in the face of opposition, slander, ridicule, and real persecution from nine-tenths of the professing Christians in our land. Let us remember how men like William Wilberforce, and Havelock, and Henry Lawrence, and Hedley Vicars, and George Moore, the Christian merchant, have witnessed for Christ in the most difficult positions, and displayed Christ's banner even in the House of Commons, in the camp, at the regimental mess table, or in the counting-house in the city. Let us remember how these noble servants of God were neither frightened nor laughed out of their religion, and won the respect even of their adversaries. These all had one principle. "Give me," said that strange dictator who rode rough-shod over England's Church and Crown in the seventeenth century, "Give me men that have a principle." These Christian soldiers of our own day had a principle, and that ruling principle was faith in an unseen God and Saviour. By this faith they lived, and walked, and fought the good fight, and overcame.

Does any one who reads this paper desire to live the life of a true Christian, and overcome the world? Let him begin by seeking to have the principle of victory within.

Without this, all outward show of spirituality is utterly worthless. There is many a worldly heart under a monk's cowl. Faith, inward faith, is the one thing needful. Let him begin by praying for FAITH. It is the gift of God, and a gift which those who ask shall never ask in vain. The fountain of faith is not yet dry. The mine is not exhausted. He who is called the "Author of faith" is the same yesterday, today, and for ever; and waits to be entreated (Heb. 12:2). Without faith you will never war a good warfare, never set down your foot firmly, never make progress on the ice of this slippery world. You must believe if you would do. If men do nothing in religion, and sit still like uninterested spectators of a show, it is simply because they do not believe. Faith is the first step towards heaven.

Would any one who reads this paper fight the Christian battle with constantly increasing success and prosperity? Then let him pray daily for a continual growth of faith. Let him abide in Christ, get closer to Christ, tighten his hold on Christ every day that he lives. Let him never forget the prayer of the disciples, "Lord, increase our faith." Let him watch jealously over his faith, and never let its fire burn low. According to the degree of his faith will be the measure of his peace, his strength, and his victory over the world.

(a) And now let us leave the whole subject with the solemn self-inquiry, "What do we know of that great test of religion which this text supplies? What do we know of overcoming the world? Where are we? What are we doing? Whose are we, and whom do we serve? Are we overcoming or being overcome?" Alas, it is a sorrowful fact, that many know not whether they are Christ's freemen or the world's slaves! The fetters of the world are often invisible. We are dragged downward insensibly, and are like one who sleeps in a boat, and knows not that he is drifting, gently drifting, towards the falls. There is no slavery so bad as that which is unfelt. There are no chains so really heavy as those which are unseen. Wise is that petition in our matchless Litany: "From all the deceits of the world, good Lord, deliver us."

I press this inquiry in all affection on my younger readers. You are just at that generous and unsuspecting age when the world seems least dangerous and most inviting, and it stands to reason you are most likely to be ensnared and overcome. Experience alone can make you see the enemy in his true colours. When you have as many grey hairs on your heads as I have, you will place a very different estimate on the good things, or the praise or the hatred of this world. But, even now, remember my caution: "If you love your souls, hold the world at arm's length. Beware of the world."

(b) Reader, you and I meet over this paper for once in our lives, and are parting in all probability to meet no more. You are perhaps launching forth on the waves of this troublesome world. My heart's desire and prayer to God is, that you may have a prosperous voyage, and be found at length in the safe haven of eternal life. But, oh, take heed that you are well equipped for the stormy waters you have to cross, and see that you have a compass to steer by, that you can depend on, and a pilot who will not fail! Beware of making shipwreck by conformity to the world. Alas, how many put to sea in gallant trim, with colours flying, and brilliant prospects, and are lost at last with all on board! They seem at first to begin with Moses, and Daniel, and the saints in Nero's household; but they end at last with Balaam, and Demas, and Lot's wife! Oh, remember the pilot and the compass! No compass like the Bible. No pilot like Christ!

Take the advice I give you, as a friend, this day. Ask the Lord Jesus Christ to come and dwell in your heart by faith, and to "deliver you from this present evil world" (Gal. 1:4). Ask Him to pour out His promised Spirit on you, and to make you willing to bear His easy yoke without further delay, and to resist the world. Strive, in the strength of

Christ, to get the victory over the world, whatever it may cost you. Be ashamed of being a slave, however gilded the chains may be. Be ashamed of the mark of the collar. Resolve to play the man and be free. Liberty is the greatest of blessings, and deserves the greatest struggles. Well said the Jewish rabbis in ancient days, "If the sea were ink, and the earth parchment, it would never serve to describe the praises of liberty." For freedom's sake, Greeks, and Romans, and Germans, and Poles, and Swiss, and Scotchmen, and Englishmen, have often cheerfully fought to the bitter end, and laid down their lives. Surely, if men have made such sacrifices for the freedom of their bodies, it is a disgrace to professing Christians if they will not fight for the liberty of their souls. This day, I repeat, resolve in the strength of Christ, that you will fight the good fight against the world; and not only fight, but overcome. "If the Son shall make you free, you shall be free indeed" (John 8:36).

(c) Finally, let us all remember that the Christian soldier's best time is yet to come. Here, in this world, we are often "sore and hindered" in our warfare. There are many hard things to be done and borne. Them are wounds and bruises; there are watchings and fatigues; there are reverses and disappointments. But the end of all things is at hand. For those who "overcome" there will be a conqueror's crown.

In the warfare of this world, the muster on the morning after a victory is often a sorrowful sight. I pity the man who could look at Miss Thompson's famous picture of *The Roll Call* without deep emotion. Even when peace is proclaimed, the return of victorious regiments is an occasion of very mingled feelings. That man must have had a cold heart who could see the Guards march back into London after the Crimean war without a sigh or a tear.

Thanks be to God, the review day of Christ's victorious army will be a very different thing. There will be none missing in that day. It will be a meeting without regret. It will be "a morning without clouds" and tears It will make rich amends for all we have suffered in resisting and overcoming the world.

He who saw our gracious Queen distributing the Victoria Cross at the Horse Guards during the Russian war might well be stirred and moved at the sight. But he who saw her come down from her seat to meet a wounded officer who could not walk, and, with her own royal hands, pin his decoration on his breast, will probably remember it as long as he lives.

But, after all, it was nothing compared to the transactions of that great day, when the Captain of our salvation and His victorious soldiers shall at length meet face to face. What tongue can tell the happiness of that time when we shall lay aside our armour, and "say to the sword, Rest, and be still!" What mind can conceive the blessedness of that hour when we shall see the King in His beauty, and hear these words, "Well done, good and faithful servant and soldier, enter thou into the joy of thy Lord"? For that glorious day let us wait patiently, for it cannot be far off. In the hope of it let us work, and watch, and pray, and fight on, and resist the world. And let us never forget our Captain's words: "In the world ye shall have tribulation: but be of good cheer; I have overcome the world" (John 16:33).

CHAPTER IX[13]

Acts 17:16-17
Athens.

"Now, while Paul waited for them at Athens, his spirit was stirred in him, when he saw the city wholly given to idolatry. Therefore disputed he in the synagogue with the Jews, and with the devout persons, and in the market daily with them that met with him." —Acts 17:16-17.

PERHAPS the reader of this paper lives in a town or city, and sees more of bricks and mortar than of green fields. Perhaps you have some relative or friend living in a town, about whom you naturally feel a deep interest. In either case, the verses of Scripture which head tiffs page demand your best attention. Give me that attention for a few short minutes while I try to show you the lessons which the passage contains.

You see face to face, in the verses before you, no common city and no common man.

The city is the famous city Athens,—Athens, renowned to this very day for its statesmen, philosophers, historians, poets, painters, and architects,—Athens, the eye of ancient Greece, as ancient Greece was the eye of the heathen world.

The man is the great Apostle of the Gentiles, St. Paul, St. Paul, the most laborious and successful minister and missionary the world has ever seen,—St. Paul, who by pen and tongue has left a deeper mark on mankind than any born of woman, except his Divine Master.

Athens and St. Paul, the great servant of Christ, and the great stronghold of old heathenism—are brought before us face to face. The result is told us: the interview is carefully described. The subject, I venture to think, is eminently suited to the times in which we live, and to the circumstances of many a dweller in London, Liverpool, Manchester, and other great English towns in the present day.

Without further preface, I ask you to observe three things in this passage:—

I. What St. Paul saw at Athens.
II. What St. Paul FELT at Athens.
III. What St. Paul DID at Athens.

I. First, then, What did St. Paul SEE at Athens?

The answer of the text is clear and unmistakable. He saw a "city wholly given to idolatry." Idols met his eyes in every street. The temples of idol gods and goddesses occupied every prominent position. The magnificent statue of Minerva, at least forty feet high, according to Pliny, towered above the Acropolis, and caught the eye from every point. A vast system of idol-worship overspread the whole place, and thrust itself everywhere on his notice. The ancient writer Pausanias expressly says, that "the Athenians surpassed all states in the attention which they paid to the worship of the gods." In short, the city, as the marginal reading says, was "full of idols."

And yet this city, I would have you remember, was probably the most favourable specimen of a heathen city which St. Paul could have seen. In proportion to its size, it very likely contained the most learned, civilized, philosophical, highly educated, artistic, intellectual population on the face of the globe. But what was it in a religious point of view? The city of wise men like Socrates and Plato,—the city of Solon, and Pericles, and

---

[13]This paper contains the substance of a sermon preached at St. Mary's, Oxford, before the University, in 1880.

Demosthenes,—the city of AEschylus, Sophocles, Euripides, and Thucydides,—the city of mind, and intellect, and art, and taste,—this city was "wholly given to idolatry." If the true God was unknown at Athens, what must He have been in the darker places of the earth? If the eye of Greece was so spiritually dim, what must have been the condition of such places as Babylon, Ephesus, Tyre, Alexandria, Corinth, and even of Rome? If men were so far gone from the light in a green tree, what must they have been in the dry?

What shall we say to these things? What are the conclusions to which we are irresistibly drawn by them?

Ought we not to learn, for one thing, the absolute need of a Divine revelation, and of teaching from heaven? Leave man without a Bible, and he will have a religion of some kind, for human nature, corrupt as it is, must have a God. But it will be a religion without light, or peace, or hope.

"The world by wisdom knew not God" (1 Cor. 1:21). Old Athens is a standing lesson which we shall do well to observe. It is vain to suppose that nature, unaided by revelation, will ever lead fallen man to nature's God. Without a Bible, the Athenian bowed down to stocks and stones, and worshipped the work of his own hands. Place a heathen philosopher, a Stoic or an Epicurean,—by the side of an open grave, and ask him about a world to come, and he could have told you nothing certain, satisfactory, or peace-giving.

Ought we not to learn, for another thing, that the highest intellectual training is no security against utter darkness in religion? We cannot doubt that mind and reason were highly educated at Athens, if anywhere in the heathen world. The students of Greek philosophy were not unlearned and ignorant men. They were well versed in logic, ethics, rhetoric, history, and poetry. But all this mental discipline did not prevent their city being a "city wholly given to idolatry." And are we to be told in the nineteenth century, that reading, writing, arithmetic, mathematics, history, languages, and physical science, without a knowledge of the Scriptures, are sufficient to constitute education? God forbid! We have not so learned Christ. It may please some men to idolize intellectual power, and to speak highly of the debt which the world owes to the Greek mind. One thing, at any rate, is abundantly clear. Without the knowledge which the Holy Ghost revealed to the Hebrew nation, old Greece would have left the world buried in dark idolatry. A follower of Socrates or Plato might have talked well and eloquently on many subjects, but he could have never answered the jailor's question, "What must I do to be saved?" (Acts 16:30). He could never have said in his last hour, "O death, where is thy sting? O grave, where is thy victory?"

Ought we not to learn, for another thing, that the highest excellence in the material arts is no preservative against the grossest superstition? The perfection of Athenian architecture and sculpture is a great and undeniable fact. The eyes of St. Paul at Athens beheld many a "thing of beauty" which is still "a joy for ever" to artistic minds. And yet the men who conceived and executed the splendid buildings of Athens were utterly ignorant of the one true God. The world nowadays is well-nigh drunk with self conceit about our so-called progress in arts and sciences. Men talk and write of machinery and manufactures, as if nothing were impossible. But let it never be forgotten that the highest art or mechanical skill is consistent with a state of spiritual death in religion. Athens, the city of Phidias, was a "city wholly given to idolatry." An Athenian sculptor might have designed a matchless tomb, but he could not have wiped a single tear from a mourner's eye.

These things ought not to be forgotten. They ought to be carefully pondered. They suit the times in which we live. We have fallen on a sceptical and an unbelieving age. We meet on every side with doubts and questionings about the truth and value of revelation. "Is not reason alone sufficient?" "Is the Bible really needful to make men wise unto salvation?" "Has not man a light within, a verifying power, able to guide him to truth and God?" Such are the inquiries which fall thick as hail around us. Such are the speculations which disquiet many unstable minds.

One plain answer is an appeal to facts. The remains of heathen Egypt, Greece, and Rome shall speak for us. They are preserved by God's providence to this very day as monuments of what intellect and reason can do without revelation. The minds which designed the temples of Luxor and Carnac, or the Parthenon or Coliseum, were not the minds of fools. The builders who executed their designs did better and more lasting work than any contractor can do in modern times. The men who conceived the sculptured friezes, which we know as the Elgin Marbles, were trained and intellectual to the highest degree. And yet in religion these men were darkness itself (Eph. 5:8). The sight which St. Paul saw at Athens is an unanswerable proof that man knows nothing which can do his soul good without a Divine revelation.

II. I ask you to notice, in the second place, what St. Paul FELT at Athens. He saw a "city wholly given to idolatry." How did the sight affect him? What did he feel?

It is instructive to observe how the same sight affects different people. Place two men on the same spot; let them stand side by side; let the same objects be presented to their eyes. The emotions called forth in the one man will often be wholly different from those called forth in the other. The thoughts which will be wakened up and brought to birth will often be as far as the poles asunder.

A mere artist visiting Athens for the first time would doubtless have been absorbed in the beauty of its buildings. A statesman or orator would have called up the memory of Pericles or Demosthenes. A literary man would have thought of Thucydides and Sophocles and Plato. A merchant would have gazed on the Piraeus, its harbour, and the sea. But an Apostle of Christ had far higher thoughts. One thing, above all others, swallowed up his attention, and made all else look small. That one thing was the spiritual condition of the Athenian people, the state of their souls. The great Apostle of the Gentiles was eminently a man of one thing. Like his Divine Master, he was always thinking of his "Father's business" (Luke 2:49). He stood at Athens, and thought of nothing so much as Athenian souls. Like Moses, Phinehas, and Elijah, "his spirit was stirred within him when he saw the city wholly given to idolatry."

Of all sights on earth, I know none so impressive, none so calculated to arouse thought in a reflecting mind, as the sight of a great city. The daily intercourse of man with man, which a city naturally produces, seems to sharpen intellect, and stimulate mental activity to an extent which dwellers in rural parishes, or other solitary places, cannot realize. Rightly or wrongly, the inhabitant of a city thinks twice as much, and twice as quickly, as the inhabitant of a rural village. It is the city "where Satan's seat is" (Rev. 2:13). It is the city where evil of every kind is most rapidly conceived, sown, ripened, and brought to maturity.—It is the city where the young man, leaving home, and launching into life, becomes soonest hardened, and conscience-seared by daily familiarity with the sight of sin.—It is the city where sensuality, intemperance, and worldly amusements of the vilest kind flourish most rankly, and find a congenial atmosphere.—It is the city where ungodliness and irreligion meet with the greatest encouragement, and the unhappy

Sabbath-breaker, or neglecter of all means of grace, can fortify himself behind the example of others, and enjoy the miserable comfort of feeling that "he does not stand alone!"—It is the city which is the chosen home of every form of superstition, ceremonialism, enthusiasm, and fanaticism in religion.—It is the city which is the hotbed of every kind of false philosophy, of Stoicism, Epicureanism, Agnosticism, Secularism, Scepticism, Positivism, Infidelity, and Atheism.—It is the city where that greatest of modern inventions, the printing-press, that mighty power for good and evil, is ever working with unsleeping activity, and pouring forth new matter for thought.—It is the city where the daffy newspapers are continually supplying food for minds, and moulding and guiding public opinion.—It is the city which is the centre of all national business. The banks, the law-courts, the Stock Exchange, the Parliament or Assembly, are all bound up with the city.—It is the city which, by magnetic influence, draws together the rank and fashion of the land, and gives the tone to the tastes and ways of society.—It is the city which practically controls the destiny of a nation. Scattered millions, in rural districts, without habitual concert or contact, are powerless before the thousands who dwell side by side and exchange thought every day. It is the towns which govern a land. I pity the man who could stand on the top of St. Paul's Cathedral, and look down on London without some emotion, and not reflect that he sees the heart whose pulsations are felt over the whole civilized globe. And shall I wonder for a moment that the sight of Athens "stirred the spirit" of such a man as the great Apostle of the Gentiles? I cannot wonder at all. It was just the sight which was likely to move the heart of the converted man of Tarsus, the man who wrote the Epistle to the Romans, and had seen Jesus Christ face to face.

He was stirred with holy compassion. It moved his heart to see so many myriads perishing for lack of knowledge, without God, without Christ, having no hope, travelling in the broad road which leadeth to destruction.

He was stirred with holy sorrow. It moved his heart to see so much talent misapplied. Here were hands capable of excellent works, and minds capable of noble conceptions. And yet the God who gave life and breath and power was not glorified.

He was stirred with holy indignation against sin and the devil. He saw the god of this world blinding the eyes of multitudes of his fellow-men, and leading them captive at his will. He saw the natural corruption of man infecting the population of a vast city like one common disease, and an utter absence of any spiritual medicine, antidote, or remedy.

He was stirred with holy zeal for His Master's glory. He saw the "strong man armed" keeping a house which was not lawfully his, and shutting out the rightful possessor. He saw his Divine Master unknown and unrecognised by His own creatures, and idols receiving the homage due to the King of kings.

Reader, these feelings which stirred the Apostle are a leading characteristic of a man born of the Spirit. Do you know anything of them? Where there is true grace, there will always be tender concern for the souls of others. Where there is true sonship to God, there will always be zeal for the Father's glory. It is written of the ungodly, that they not only commit things worthy of death, but "have pleasure in them that do them" (Rom. 1:32). It may be said with equal truth of the godly, that they not only mourn over sin in their own hearts, but mourn over sin in others.

Hear what is written of Lot in Sodom: "He vexed his soul from day to day with their unlawful deeds" (2 Pet. 2:8). Hear what is written of David: "Rivers of water run down mine eyes, because they keep not Thy law" (Psalms 119:136). Hear what is written of the godly in Ezekiel's time: "They sigh and cry for all the abominations that be done in the midst of the land" (Ezek. 9:4). Hear what is written of our Lord and Saviour Himself: "He beheld the city, and wept over it" (Luke 19:41). Surely it may be laid down as one of the first principles of Scriptural religion, that he who can behold sin without sorrowful feelings has not the mind of the Spirit. This is one of those things in which the children of God are manifest, and are distinguished from the children of the devil.

I call the special attention of my readers to this point. The times demand that we look it fully in the face. The feelings with which we regard sin, heathenism, and irreligion are a subject of vast importance in the present day.

I ask you, first, to look outside our own country, and consider the state of the heathen world. At least six hundred millions of immortal beings are at this moment sunk in ignorance, superstition, and idolatry. They live and die without God, without Christ, and without hope. In sickness and sorrow they have no comfort. In old age and death they have no life beyond the grave. Of the true way of peace through a Redeemer, of God's love in Christ, of free grace, of complete absolution from guilt, of a resurrection to life eternal, they have no knowledge. For long weary centuries they have been waiting for the tardy movements of the Church of Christ, while Christians have been asleep, or wasting their energies on useless controversies, and squabbling and wrangling about forms and ceremonies. Is not this a sight which ought to "stir the spirit?"

I ask you, next, to turn back to our own land, and consider the state of our great cities There are districts in our great metropolis, in Liverpool, in Manchester, in Birmingham, in the Black Country, where Christianity seems practically unknown. Examine the religious condition of East London, or of Southwark, or Lambeth. Walk through the north end of Liverpool on Saturday evening, or Sunday, or on a Bank Holiday, and see how Sabbath-breaking, intemperance, and general ungodliness appear to rule and reign uncontrolled. "When the strong man armed keepeth his palace, his goods are in peace" (Luke 11:21). And then remember that this state of things exists in a professedly Christian country, in a land where there is an Established Church, and within a few hours of Oxford and Cambridge! Once more I say, ought not these things to "stir" our hearts?

It is a sorrowful fact, that there is around us in the present day a generation of men who regard heathenism, infidelity, and irreligion with apathy, coolness, and indifference? They care nothing for Christian missions either at home or abroad. They see no necessity for them. They take no interest in the Evangelistic work of any Church or society. They treat all alike with undisguised contempt. They despise Exeter Hall They never give subscriptions. They never attend meetings. They never read a missionary report. They seem to think that every man shall be saved by his own law or sect, if he is only sincere; and that one religion is as good as another, if those who profess it are only in earnest. They are fond of decrying and running down all spiritual machinery or missionary operations. They are constantly asserting that modern missions at home or abroad do nothing, and that those who support them are little better than weak enthusiasts. Judging by their language, they appear to think that the world receives no benefit from missions and aggressive Christian movements, and that it would be a better way to leave the world alone What shall we say to these men? They meet us on every side. They are to be heard in every society. To sit by, and sneer, and criticise, and do nothing, this is apparently their delight and vocation. What shall we say to them?

Let us tell them plainly, if they will only hear us, that they are utterly opposed to the Apostle St. Paul. Let us show them that mighty model of a Christian missionary walking the streets of Athens, and "stirred" in spirit at the sight of a "city wholly given to idolatry."

Let us ask them why they do not feel as he felt, about the idolatry of China and Hindustan, of Africa and the South Seas, or about the semi-heathen districts of London, Liverpool, Manchester, Birmingham, and the Black Country. Let us ask them whether 1800 years have made any difference in the nature of God, the necessities of fallen man, the sinfulness of idol-worship, and the duty of Christians. We shall ask in vain for a reasonable answer: we shall get none. Sneers at our weakness are no argument against our principles. Jests at our infirmities and failures are no proof that our aims are wrong. Yes; they may have the wit and wisdom of this world upon their side; but the eternal principles of the New Testament are written clearly, plainly, and unmistakably. So long as the Bible is the Bible, charity to souls is one of the first of Christian graces, and it is a solemn duty to feel for the souls of the heathen, and of all unconverted people. He who knows nothing of this feeling has yet to become a learner in Christ's school. He who despises this feeling is not a successor of St. Paul, but a follower of him who said, "Am I my brother's keeper?"—even of Cain.

III. I ask my readers to observe, in the last place, what St. Paul DID at Athens. What he saw you have heard; what he felt you have been told; but how did he act?

He did something. He was not the man to stand still, and "confer with flesh and blood" in the face of a city full of idols. He might have reasoned with himself that he stood alone, that he was a Jew by birth, that he was a stranger in a strange land,—that he had to oppose the rooted prejudices and old associations of learned men, that to attack the old religion of a whole city was to beard a lion in his den, that the doctrines of the gospel were little likely to be effective on minds steeped in Greek philosophy. But none of these thoughts seem to have crossed the mind of St. Paul. He saw souls perishing; he felt that life was short, and time passing away; he had confidence in the power of his Master's message to meet every man's soul; he had received mercy himself, and knew not how to hold his peace. He acted at once; and what his hand found to do, he did with his might. Oh that we had more men of action in these days!

And he did what he did with holy wisdom as well as holy boldness. He commenced aggressive measures alone, and waited not for companions and helpers. But he commenced them with consummate skill, and in a manner most likely to obtain a footing for the gospel. First, we are told, he disputed "with the Jews" in the synagogue, and the "devout persons" or proselytes who attended the Jewish worship. Afterwards he went on to "dispute," or hold discussions, "in the market daily with them that met with him." He advanced step by step like an experienced general. Here, as elsewhere, St. Paul is a model to us: he combined fiery zeal and boldness with judicious tact and sanctified common sense. Oh that we had more men of wisdom in these days!

But what did the Apostle teach? What was the grand subject which he argued, and reasoned out, and discussed, both with Jew and Greek, in synagogue and street? That he exposed the folly of idolatry to the ignorant multitudes,—that he showed the true nature of God to the worshippers of images made with hands,—that he asserted the nearness of God to us all, and the certainty of a solemn reckoning with God at the judgment day, to Epicureans and Stoics,—these are facts which we have recorded fully in his address on Mars' Hill.

But is there nothing more than this to be learnt about the Apostle's dealings with the idolatrous city? Is there nothing more distinctive and peculiar to Christianity which St. Paul brought forward at Athens? There is indeed more. There is a sentence in the 18th verse of the chapter we are looking at, which ought to be written in letters of gold,—a sentence which ought to silence for ever the impudent assertion, which some have dared to make, that the great Apostle of the Gentiles was sometimes content to be a mere teacher of deism or natural theology! We are told in the 18th verse that one thing which arrested the attention of the Athenians was the fact, that St. Paul "preached Jesus and the resurrection."

Jesus and the resurrection! What a mine of matter that sentence contained! What a complete summary of the Christian faith might be drawn from those words! That they are only meant to be a summary, I have no doubt. I pity those who would cramp and pare down their meaning, and interpret them as nothing more than Christ's prophetical office and example. I think it incredible that the very Apostle who a few days after went to Corinth, "determined to know nothing but Christ crucified," or the doctrine of the cross, would keep back the cross from Athenian ears. I believe that "Jesus and the resurrection" is a sentence which stands for the whole gospel. The Founder's name, and one of the foundation facts of the gospel, stand before us for the whole of Christianity.

What, then, does this sentence mean? What are we to understand St. Paul preached?

(a) St. Paul at Athens preached the person of the Lord Jesus,—His divinity, His incarnation, His mission into the world to save sinners, His life, and death, and ascension up to heaven, His character, His teaching, His amazing love to the souls of men.

(b) St. Paul at Athens preached the work of the Lord Jesus,—His sacrifice upon the cross, His vicarious satisfaction for sin, His substitution as the just for the unjust, the full redemption He has procured for all, and specially effected for all who believe, the complete victory He has obtained for lost man over sin, death, and hell.

(c) St. Paul at Athens preached the offices of the Lord Jesus, has the one Mediator between God and all mankind, as the great Physician for all sin-sick souls, as the Rest-giver and Peace-maker for all heavy-laden hearts, as the Friend of the friendless, the High Priest and Advocate of all who commit their souls into His hands, the Ransom-payer of captives, the Light and Guide of all wandering from God.

(d) St. Paul at Athens preached the terms which the Lord Jesus had commanded His servants to proclaim to all the world;—His readiness and willingness to receive at once the chief of sinners; His ability to save to the uttermost all who come unto God by Him; the full, present, and immediate forgiveness which He offers to all who believe; the complete cleansing in His blood from all manner of sin; faith, or simple trust of heart, the one thing required of all who feel their sins and desire to be saved; entire justification without works, or doing, or deeds of law for all who believe.

(e) Last, but not least, St. Paul preached at Athens the resurrection of the Lord Jesus. He preached it as the miraculous fact on which Jesus Himself staked the whole credibility of His mission, and as a fact proved by such abounding evidence that no caviller at miracles has ever yet honestly dared to meets—He preached it as a fact, which was the very top-stone of the whole work of redemption, proving that what Christ undertook He fully accomplished, that the ransom was accepted, the atonement completed, and the prison doors thrown open for ever.—He preached it as a fact, proving beyond doubt the possibility and certainty of our own resurrection in the flesh, and settling for ever the great question, "Can God raise the dead?"

These things and many like them, I cannot doubt, St. Paul preached at Athens. I cannot for one moment suppose that he taught one thing at one place and one at another. The Holy Ghost supplies the substance of his preaching in that rich sentence, "Jesus and the resurrection." The same Holy Ghost has told us fully how he handled these subjects at

Antioch in Pisidia, at Philippi, at Corinth, and Ephesus. The Acts and the Epistles speak out on this point with no uncertain sound. I believe that "Jesus and the resurrection" means,—Jesus and the redemption He effected by His death and rising from the grave, His atoning blood, His cross, His substitution, His mediation, His triumphant entrance into heaven, and the consequent full and complete salvation of all sinners who believe in Him. This is the doctrine St. Paul preached. This is the work St. Paul did when he was at Athens.

Now, have we nothing to learn from these doings of the great Apostle of the Gentiles? There are lessons of deep importance to which I venture briefly to invite the attention of all who read this paper. I say briefly. I only throw them out, as seeds for private thought.

(a) Learn, for one thing, a doctrinal lesson from St. Paul's doings at Athens. The grand subject of our teaching, in every place, ought to be Jesus Christ. However learned or however unlearned, however high-born or however humble our audience, Christ crucified—Christ—Christ—Christ—crucified, rising, interceding, redeeming, pardoning, receiving, saving—Christ must be the grand theme of our teaching. We shall never mend this gospel. We shall never find any other subject which will do so much good. We must sow as St. Paul sowed, if we would reap as St. Paul reaped.

(b) Learn, for another thing, a practical lesson from St. Paul's doings at Athens. We must never be afraid to stand alone and be solitary witnesses for Christ, if need be, alone in a vast ungodly parish, in our own land,—alone in East London, in Liverpool, in Manchester,—alone in Delhi, or Benares, or Pekin,—it matters not. We need not hold our peace, if God's truth be on our side. One Paul at Athens, one Athanasius against the world, one Wycliffe against a host of Romish prelates, one Luther at Worms, these, these, are lighthouses before our eyes. God sees not as man sees. We must not stand still to count heads and number the people. One man, with Christ in his heart and the Bible in his hands, is stronger than a myriad of idolaters.

(c) Learn for another thing, the importance, let me rather say the necessity, of asserting boldly the supernatural element as an essential part of the Christian religion. I need not tell many who read these pages that unbelievers and sceptics abound in these days, who make a dead set at the miracles of the Bible, and are incessantly trying to throw them overboard as useless lumber, or to prove by ingenious explanations that they are fables and no miracles at all: Let us never be afraid to resist such teaching steadily, and to take our stand by the side of St. Paul. Like him, let us point to the resurrection of Christ, and confidently challenge all fair and reasonable men to refute the evidence by which it is supported. The enemies of supernatural religion have never refuted that evidence, and they never will. If Christ was not raised from the dead, the conduct and teaching of the Apostles after He left the world is an unsolved problem and a perfect mystery, which no man in his senses can account for. But if, as we believe, the resurrection of Christ is an undeniable fact which cannot be disproved, the whole fabric of sceptical arguments against supernatural religion is undermined, and must fall to the ground. The stupendous miracle of the resurrection of Christ once admitted, it is sheer nonsense to tell us that any other smaller miracle in the Bible is incredible or impossible.

(d) Learn, for one thing more, a lesson of encouragement to faith from St. Paul's doings at Athens. If we preach the gospel, we may preach with perfect confidence that it will do good. That solitary Jew of Tarsus who stood up alone on Mars' Hill appeared at the time to do little or nothing. He passed on his way, and seemed to have made a failure. The Stoics and Epicureans probably laughed and sneered as if the day was their own. But that solitary Jew was lighting a candle that has never since been put out. The Word that he proclaimed in Athens grew and multiplied, and became a great tree. That little leaven ultimately leavened the whole of Greece. The gospel that Paul preached triumphed over idolatry. The empty Parthenon stands, to this day, a proof that Athenian theology is dead and gone. Yes; if we sow good seed, we may sow it in tears, but we shall yet "come again with joy, bringing our sheaves with us" (Ps. 126:6).

I draw towards a conclusion. I pass from the consideration of what St. Paul saw, and felt, and did at Athens, to points of practical importance. I ask every reader of this paper what ought we to see, to feel, and to do?

(1) What ought we to see? It is an age of sightseeing and excitement. "The eye is not satisfied with seeing" (Eccles. 1:8). The world is mad after running to and fro, and the increase of knowledge. The wealth, the arts, the inventions of man are continually gathering myriads into great Exhibitions. Thousands and tens of thousands are annually rushing about and gazing at the work of men's hands.

But ought not the Christian to look at the map of the world? Ought not the man who believes the Bible to gaze with solemn thoughts on the vast spaces in that map which are yet spiritually black, dead, and without the gospel? Ought not our eyes to look at the fact that half the population of the earth is yet ignorant of God and Christ, and yet sitting still in sin and idolatry, and that myriads of our own fellow-countrymen in our great cities are practically little better than heathen, because Christians do so little for souls?

The eyes of God see these things, and our eyes ought to see them too.

(2) What aught we to feel? Our hearts, if they are right in the sight of God, ought to be affected by the sight of irreligion and heathenism. Many indeed are the feelings which the aspect of the world ought to call up in our hearts.

Thankfulness we ought to feel for our own countless privileges. Little indeed do the bulk of English people know the amount of their own daily unpaid debt to Christianity. Well would it be for some if they could be compelled to dwell for a few weeks every year in a heathen land.

Shame and humiliation we ought to feel when we reflect how little the Church of England has done for the spread of Christianity hitherto. God has indeed done great things for us since the days when Cranmer, Ridley, and Latimer went to the stake,—has preserved us through many trials, has enriched us with many blessings. But how little return we have made Him! How few of our 15,000 parishes do anything worthy of the cause of missions at home or abroad! How little zeal some congregations show for the salvation of souls! These things ought not so to be!

Compassion we ought to feel when we think of the wretched state of unconverted souls, and the misery of all men and women who live and die without Christ. No poverty like this poverty! No disease like this disease! No slavery like this slavery! No death like this, death in idolatry, irreligion, and sin! Well may we ask ourselves, Where is the mind of Christ, if we do not feel for the lost? I lay it down boldly, as a great principle, that the Christianity which does not make a man feel for the state of unconverted people is not the Christianity which came down from heaven 1800 years ago, and is embalmed in the New Testament. It is a mere empty name. It is not the Christianity of St. Paul.

(3) Finally, what ought we to do? This, after all, is the point to which I want to bring your mind. Seeing and feeling are well; but doing is the life of religion. Passive impressions which do not lead to action have a tendency to harden the conscience, and do us positive harm. What ought we to do? We ought to do much more than we have ever done yet. We might all probably do more. The honour of the gospel, the state of the

missionary field abroad, the condition of our overgrown cities at home, all call upon us to do more.

Need we stand still, and be ashamed of the weapons of our warfare? Is the gospel, the old Evangelical creed, unequal to the wants of our day? I assert boldly that we have no cause to be ashamed of the gospel at all. It is not worn out. It is not effete. It is not behind the times. We want nothing new, nothing added to the gospel, nothing taken away. We want nothing but "the old paths," the old truths fully, boldly, affectionately proclaimed. Only preach the gospel fully, the same gospel which St. Paul preached, and it is still "the power of God unto salvation to every one that believeth," and nothing else called religion has any real power at all (Rom. 1:16.)

Need we stand still and be ashamed of the results of preaching the gospel? Shall we hang down our heads, and complain that "the faith once delivered to the saints" has lost its power, and does no good? We have no cause to be ashamed at all. I am bold to say that no religious teaching on earth can point to any results worth mentioning except that which is called doctrinal, dogmatic theology. What deliverance on earth have all the modern schools—which scorn dogmatic teaching—what deliverance have they wrought? What overgrown and semi-heathen parishes in the metropolis, in our great seaports, our manufacturing towns, our colliery districts, have they evangelized and civilized? What New Zealand, what Red River, what Sierra-Leone, what Tinnevelly can the high-sounding systems of this latter-day point to as a fruit of their system? No! if the question, "What is truth?" is to be solved by reference to results and fruits, the religion of the New Testament, the religion whose principles are summarized, condensed, and embalmed in our Articles, Creeds, and Prayer Book, has no cause to be ashamed.

What can we do now bug humble ourselves for the past, and endeavour, by God's help, to do more for time to come? Let us open our eyes more, and see. Let us open our hearts more, and feel. Let us stir up ourselves to do more work ruby self-denying gifts, by zealous co-operation, by bold advocacy, by fervent prayer. Let us do something worthy of our cause. The cause for which Jesus left heaven and came down to earth deserves the best that we can do.

And now, let me close this paper by returning to the thought with which it began. Perhaps your lot is cast in a city or town. The population of our rural districts is annually decreasing. The dwellers in towns are rapidly outnumbering the dwellers in country parishes. If you are a dweller in a town, accept the parting words of advice which I am about to offer. Give me, your best attention while I speak to you about your soul.

(1) Remember, for one thing, that you are placed in a position of peculiar spiritual danger. From the days of Babel downwards, wherever Adam's children have been assembled in large numbers, they have always drawn one another to the utmost extremities of sin and wickedness. The great towns have always been Satan's seat. It is the town where the young man sees abounding examples of ungodliness; and, if he is determined to live in sin, will always find plenty of companions. It is the town where the theatre and the casino, the dancing room and the drinking bar, are continually crowded. It is the town where the love of money, or the love of amusement, or the love of sensual indulgence, lead captive myriads of slaves. It is the town where a man will always find hundreds to encourage him in breaking the Sabbath, despising the means of grace, neglecting the Bible, leaving off the habit of prayer. Reader, consider these things. If you live in a town, take care. Know your danger. Feel your weakness and sinfulness. Flee to Christ, and

commit your soul to His keeping. Ask Him to hold you up, and you will be safe. Stand on your guard. Resist the devil Watch and pray.

(2) Remember, on the other hand, if you live in a town, you will probably have some special helps which you cannot always find in the country. There are few English towns in which you will not find a few faithful servants of Christ, who will gladly assist you and aid you in your journey towards heaven. Few indeed are the English towns in which you will not find some minister who preaches the gospel, and some pilgrims in the narrow way who are ready to welcome any addition to their number.

Reader, be of good courage, and never give way to the despairing thought that it is impossible to serve Christ in a town. Think rather that with God nothing is impossible. Think of the long list of witnesses who have carried the cross, and been faithful unto death in the midst of the greatest temptations. Think of Daniel and the three children in Babylon. Think of the saints in Nero's household at Rome. Think of the multitudes of believers at Corinth and Ephesus and Antioch in the days of the Apostles. It is not place but grace that makes the Christian. The holiest and most useful servants of God who have ever lived were not hermits in the wilderness but dwellers in towns.

Remember these things, and be of good cheer. Your lot may be cast in a city like Athens, "wholly given to idolatry." You may have to stand alone in the bank, the counting-house, the place of business, or the shop.

But you are not really alone, if Christ is with you. Be strong in the Lord, and in the power of His might. Be bold, thorough, decided, and patient. The day will come when you will find that even hi a great city a man may be a happy, useful Christian, respected while he lives, and honoured when he dies.

CHAPTER X[14]

Acts 26:24-29
Portraits.

"And as he thus spake for himself, Festus said with a loud voice, Paul, thou art beside thyself; much learning doth make thee mad.

"But he said, I am not mad, most noble Festus; but speak forth the words of truth and soberness. For the king knoweth of these things, before whom also I speak freely: for I am persuaded that none of these things are hidden from him; for this thing was not done in a corner. King Agrippa, believest thou the prophets? I know that thou believest.

"Then Agrippa said unto Paul, Almost thou persuadest me to be a Christian.

"And Paul said, I would to God, that not only thou, but also all that hear me this day, were both almost and altogether such as I am, except these bounds." —Acts 26:24-29.

THERE is a collection of pictures in London called the National Portrait Gallery. It contains the likenesses of nearly all the great men who have made a mark in English history. It is well worth seeing. But I doubt whether it contains three portraits which deserve a more attentive study than the three which I am going to show you in this paper.

---

[14]This paper contains the substance of a sermon, preached in April 1881 which is also known as, "Three Pictures! And which is mine?"

One striking feature of the Bible is the rich variety of its contents. That grand old Book, which for eighteen centuries has baffled the attacks of unfriendly critics, is not only a storehouse of doctrine, precept, history, poetry, and prophecy. The Holy Ghost has also given us a series of lifelike portraits of human nature, in all its various aspects, which deserve our attentive study. Who does not know that we often learn more from patterns and examples than from abstract statements?

The well-known piece of Scripture which heads this paper supplies an admirable illustration of my meaning. It forms the conclusion of the chapter in which the Apostle St. Paul makes a defence of himself before the Roman governor Festus and the Jewish king Agrippa. Three pictures of three very different men hang before us. They are types of three classes of men who are to be seen among us at this very day. Their succession has never ceased. In spite of changing fashions, scientific discoveries, and political reforms, the inward heart of man in every age is always the same. Come and let us stand before these three pictures, as we would stand before the painting of a Gainsborough, a Reynolds, or a Romney, and see what we may learn.

I. Let us look, first, at Festus, the Roman governor. This is the man who abruptly broke in upon St. Paul's address, exclaiming, "Paul, thou art beside thyself; much learning doth make thee mad."

Festus, no doubt, was a heathen, ignorant of any religion except the idolatrous temple-worship, which in the time of the Apostles overspread the civilized world. From the language he addressed to Agrippa in a preceding chapter, he seems to have been profoundly ignorant both of Judaism and Christianity. He spoke of "questions of their own superstition, and of one Jesus, which was dead, whom Paul affirmed to be alive" (Acts 25:19). Most probably, like many a proud Roman in the declining age of the Roman Empire, he regarded all religions with secret contempt, as all equally false, or equally true, and all alike unworthy of the notice of a great man. As for a Jew talking of showing "light to the Gentiles," the very idea was ridiculous! To keep in with the world, to have the favour of man, to care nothing for anything but the things seen, to please "my lord" Augustus,—this was probably the whole religion of Porcius Festus.

Now, are there many among us like Festus? Yes! I fear there are tens of thousands. They are to be found in every rank and class of society. They walk in our streets. They travel with us in railway carriages. They meet us in the daily intercourse of the world. They fill the various relations of life respectably. They are often good men of business, and eminent in the professions they have chosen. They discharge the various duties of their positions with credit, and leave a good name behind them, when their place is empty. But, like Festus, they have no religion!

These are they who seem to live as if they had no souls. From January to December, they appear neither to think, nor feel, nor see, nor know anything about a life to come. It forms no part of their schemes, and plans, and calculations. They live as if they had nothing to attend to but the body,—nothing to do but to eat, and drink, and sleep, and dress, and get money, and spend money,—and no world to provide for except the world which we see with our eyes.

These are they who seldom, if ever, use any means of grace, whether public or private. Praying and Bible-reading, and secret communion with God, are things which they despise and let alone. They may be very well for the aged, the sick, and the dying; for the clergy, the monk, and the nun; but not for them! If ever they attend a place of worship, it is only as a matter of form, to appear respectable; and too often they never attend except on the occasion of some great public ceremony, or at a wedding, or a funeral.

These are they who profess their inability to understand anything like zeal or earnestness about religion. They regard the Societies, the Institutions, the literature, the Evangelistic efforts of Christians, at home or abroad, with sublime contempt. Their maxim is to let everybody alone. The comparative claims of Church and Dissent, the strife of parties within our pale, the debates of Convocations, Congresses, and Diocesan Conferences, are all alike matters of indifference to them. They look coldly at them from a distance, like the philosopher described by the Latin poet Lucretius, and regard them as the childish struggles of weak folks, unworthy of the notice of a cultivated mind. And if such subjects are ever brought up in their company, they brush them away with some satirical remark, or some oft-repeated old smart saying of scepticism.

Will any one deny that there are multitudes of people around us such as I have tried to describe,—kind people, perhaps, moral people, good-natured people, easy to get on with, unless you get on the subject of religion? It is impossible to deny it. Their name is "legion," for they are many. The tendency of these latter days to make an idol of intellect,—the desire to be independent and to think for yourself, the disposition to worship private judgment, to exalt your own isolated opinion, and to deem it finer and cleverer to go wrong with a few than right with a crowd, all this helps to swell the ranks of the followers of Festus. I fear he is the type of a large class.

Such people are a melancholy sight. They often remind me of some grand old ruin, like Melrose or Bolton Abbey, where enough remains of beauteous arches, and columns, and towers, and traceried windows to show what the building once was, and what it might have been now if God had not left it. But now all is cold, and silent, and gloomy, and suggestive of decay, because the Master of the house, the Lord of life, is not there. Just so it is with many of the followers of Festus. You often feel, when you observe their intellectual power, their gifts of speech, their taste, their energy of character, "what men these might be if God had His rightful place in their souls!" But without God all is wrong. Alas, for the crushing power of unbelief and pride, when they get complete mastery of a mall, and reign over him uncontrolled! No wonder that Scripture describes unconverted man as "blind,—sleeping, beside himself,—and dead."

Is Festus reading this paper today? I am afraid not! Religious tracts and books, like Sunday services and sermons, are not in his line. On Sundays, Festus probably reads the newspaper, or looks over his worldly accounts, or visits his friends, or goes a journey, and secretly wishes an English Sunday was more like a Continental one, and the theatres and museums were open. On week-days, Festus is constantly employed in business, or politics, or, recreations, or killing time in the trifling pursuits of modem society; and he lives like a butterfly, as thoughtless as if there were no such thing as death, or judgment, or eternity. Oh, no: Festus is not the man to read this paper!

But is a man like Festus in a hopeless condition, and beyond the reach of mercy? No, indeed! I thank God he is not. He has yet got a conscience at the bottom of his character, which, however much seared, is not quite dead,—a conscience which, like the great bell of St. Paul's at midnight, when the roar of city business is over, will sometimes make itself heard. Like Felix, and Herod, and Ahab, and Pharaoh, the followers of Festus have their times of visitation; and, unlike them, they sometimes awake before it is too late, and become different men. There are seasons in their lives when they are driven in upon themselves, and feel "the powers of the world to come," and find that mortal man cannot get on without God. Sickness, and solitude, and disappointments, and losses of money, and deaths of loved ones, can sometimes make the proudest hearts bow down, and confess that the "grasshopper is a burden." Manasseh is not the only one who "in time of affliction" turned to God, and began to pray. Yes! I have long felt that we must never despair of any one. The age of spiritual miracles is not past. With Christ and the Holy Ghost nothing is impossible. The last day will show that there were some who began with Festus and were like him, but at last turned round, repented, and ended with St. Paul. While there is life we must hope, and pray for others.

II. Let us now turn to a very different picture. Let us look at King Agrippa. This is the man who was so much struck by St. Paul's address that he said, "Almost thou persuadest me to be a Christian."

"Almost." Let me dwell for a moment on that expression. I am well aware that many think our Authorized English Version of the Bible is in fault here, and fails to give the true meaning of the original Greek. They assert that the phrase would be more correctly rendered, "In a short time," or "with weak and feeble argument thou art persuading me." I am bold to say that I cannot accept the view of these critics, though I admit that the phrase is rather obscure. But in questions like these I dare not call any man master. I hold with several excellent commentators, both ancient and modern,[15] that the translation given in our Authorized Version is right and correct. I am fortified in my belief by the fact that this is the view of one who thought, and spoke, and wrote in the language of the New Testament—I mean the famous Greek Father Chrysostom. And last, but not least, no other view appears to me to harmonize with the exclamation of the Apostle St. Paul in the verse which follows. "Almost!" he seems to say, taking up Agrippa's words. "I want thee to be not almost, but altogether a Christian." On these grounds I stand by our Old Version.

Agrippa, whose picture now demands our attention, was in many respects very unlike Festus. Of Jewish extraction, and brought up among Jews, if not of pure Jewish blood, he was thoroughly familiar with many things of which the Roman governor was utterly ignorant. He knew and "believed the prophets." He must have understood many things in St. Paul's address, which were mere "words and names" and raving fancies to his companion in the place of hearing. He had a secret inward conviction that the man before him had truth on his side. He saw, and felt, and was moved, and affected, and conscience-stricken, and had inward wishes and longing desires. But he could get no further. He saw; but he had not courage to act. He felt; but he had not the will to move. He was not far from the kingdom of God; but he halted outside. He neither condemned nor ridiculed Christianity; but, like a man who is paralyzed, he could only look at it and examine it, and had not strength of mind to lay hold on it and receive it into his heart.

Now, are there many professing Christians like Agrippa? I fear there is only one answer to that question. They are an exceeding great army, a multitude which it is difficult to number. They are to be found in our churches, and are pretty regular attendants on all means of grace. They have no doubt of the truth of the Bible. They have not the slightest objection to the doctrines of the gospel. They know the difference between sound and unsound teaching. They admire the lives of holy people. They read good books, and give money to good objects. But, unhappily, they never seem to get beyond a certain point in their religion. They never come out boldly on Christ's side, never take up the cross, never confess Christ before men, never give up petty inconsistencies. They often tell you that

---

[15] Luther, Beza, Grotius, Poole, Bengel, Stier, and Dean Howson.

they "mean, and intend, and hope, and purpose" some day to be more decided Christians. They know they are not quite what they ought to be at present, and they hope one day to be different. But the "convenient season" never seems to come. Meaning and intending they go on, and meaning and intending they go off the stage. Meaning and intending they live, and meaning and intending, too oft, they die,—kind, good-natured, respectable people; not enemies, but friends to St. Paul, but, like Agrippa, "almost Christians."

How is it, you may well ask, that men can go so far in religion, and yet go no further? How is it that they can see so much, and know so much, and yet not follow the light they have to the "perfect day"? How is it that intellect and reason and conscience can make such progress towards Christianity, and yet heart and will can lag behind?

The answers to these questions are soon given. The fear of man keeps back some. They have a cowardly dread of being laughed at, mocked, and despised, if they become decided Christians. They dare not risk the loss of man's good opinion. Like many of the Jewish rulers in our Lord's time, they "love the praise of men more than the praise of God" (John 12:43). The love of the world keeps back others. They know that decided religion entails separation from some of the fashionable amusements and modes of spending time, which are common in the world. They cannot make up their minds to this separation. They shrink from their baptismal vow to "renounce the pomps and vanities of this world." Like Lot's wife, they would like to be delivered from the wrath of God; but, like her, they must "look back" (Gen. 19:26). A certain subtle form of self-righteousness keeps back many. They take comfort in the secret thought that, at any rate, they are not so bad as Festus. They are not like some people they know: they do not despise religion. They go to church. They admire earnest men like St. Paul Surely they will not be lost on account of a few inconsistencies!—The morbid dread of being party-spirited keeps back many, and especially young men. They are oppressed with the idea that they cannot take a decided line in religion without committing themselves to some particular "school of thought." This is what they do not want to do. They forget that the case of Agrippa is not one of doctrine, but of conduct, and that decided action about duty is the surest way to obtain light about doctrinal truth. "If any man will do God's will, he shall know of the doctrine" (John 7:17). Some secret sin, I fear, keeps back not a few. They know in their own hearts that they are clinging to something which is wrong in God's sight. There is a Herodias, or a Drusilla, or a Bernice, or an Achan's wedge of gold somewhere, in their private history, which will not bear the light of day. They cannot part with this darling. They cannot cut off the right hand, or pluck out the right eye, and so they cannot become disciples. Alas! for these excuses. Weighed in the balance, they are worthless and vain. Alas! for those who rest in them. Except they awake, and cast off their chains, they will make shipwreck for ever.

Is Agrippa reading this paper today? Are there any like him whose eyes are on this page? Take a kindly warning from a minister of Christ, and try to realize that you are in a very dangerous position. Wishing, and feeling, and meaning, and intending, do not make up saving religion. They are but painted corks, which may enable you to float on the surface for a time, and keep your head above water, but they will not prevent you being carried down the stream, and being at last swept over a worse fall than that of Niagara And, after all, you are not happy. You know too much of religion to be happy in the world: you are too much mixed up with the world to get any comfort from your religion. In short, you are neither happy in the world nor out of the world. Awake to a sense of your danger and your folly. Resolve by God's help to become decided. Draw the sword, and cast away the scabbard. "If you have no sword, sell your garment and buy one" (Luke 22:36). Burn your ships, and march straight forward. Do not merely look at the ark, and admire it; but enter in, before the door is shut and the flood begins. One thing, at any rate, may be laid down as an axiom in the elements of religion: An "almost" Christian is neither a safe nor a happy man.

III. Let us turn now to the last picture of the three. Let us look at the man whom Festus thought "beside himself," and by whom Agrippa was "almost persuaded to be a Christian." Let us look at St. Paul. This is the man who boldly said," I would to God, that not only thou, but all that hear me this day, were both almost and altogether such as I am, except these bonds." He wished his hearers no chains or imprisonment, such as he was suffering when he spoke. But he did wish them to be of one mind with him about the one thing needful; and to share his peace, his hope, his solid comfort, his expectations.

"Altogether such as I am." A weighty and memorable saying! It is the language of one who is thoroughly convinced and persuaded that he is in the right. He has cast overboard all doubts and hesitations. He holds the truth with the firm grasp of both hands, and not with finger and thumb. It is the language of the man who wrote in one place, "I know whom I have believed, and that He is able to keep that which I have committed to Him against that day."—And in another place, "I am persuaded that neither death, nor life, nor angels, nor principalities, nor powers, nor things present, nor things to come, nor height, nor depth, nor any other creature, shall be able to separate us from the love of God, which is in Christ Jesus our Lord" (2 Tim. 1:12; Rom. 8:38-39).

(a) St. Paul was altogether convinced of the truth of the facts of Christianity. That the Lord Jesus Christ was actually "God manifest in the flesh,"—that He had proved His divinity by doing miracles which could not be denied,—that He had, finally, risen from the grave and ascended up into heaven, and was sitting at God's right hand as man's Saviour,—on all these points he had thoroughly made up his mind, and had not the slightest doubt of their credibility. On behalf of them he was willing to die.

(b) St. Paul was altogether convinced of the truth of the doctrines of Christianity. That we are all guilty sinners, and in danger of eternal ruin, that the grand object of Christ coming into the world was to make atonement for our sins, and to purchase redemption by suffering in our stead on the cross,—that all who repent and believe on Christ crucified are completely forgiven all sins,—and that there is no other way to peace with God and heaven after death, but faith in Christ,—all this he most stedfastly believed. To teach these doctrines was his one object from his conversion till his martyrdom.

(c) St. Paul was altogether convinced that he himself had been changed by the power of the Holy Spirit, and taught to live a new life,—that a holy life, devoted and consecrated to Christ, was the wisest, happiest life a man could live, that the favour of God was a thousand times better than the favour of man,—and that nothing was too much to do for Him who had loved him and given Himself for him. He ran his race ever "looking unto Jesus," and spending and being spent for Him (Heb. 12:2; 2 Cor. 5:15, 12:15).

(d) Last, but not least, St. Paul was altogether convinced of the reality of a world to come. The praise or favour of man, the rewards or punishments of this present world, were all as dross to him. He had before his eyes continually an inheritance incorruptible, and a crown of glory that would never fade away (Phil. 3:8; 2 Tim. 4:8). Of that crown he knew that nothing could deprive him. Festus might despise him, and think him "mad." The Roman emperor, to whom he was going, might order him to be beheaded or thrown to the lions. What matter? He was firmly persuaded that he had treasure laid up in heaven which neither Festus nor Caesar could touch, and which would be his to all eternity.

This is what St. Paul meant when he said "altogether such as I am." About the facts, doctrines, practice, and rewards to come of Christianity, he had a rooted, settled, firm conviction,—a conviction which he longed to see all men sharing. He was confident: he wanted others to enjoy the same confidence. He had no doubt or fear about the future state of his soul. He would fain have seen Festus, Agrippa, Bernice, and all around them, in the same happy condition.

Now, are there many in the present day like St. Paul? I do not of course mean, are there many inspired Apostles? But I do mean, is it common to meet Christians who are as thorough, as unhesitating, as full of assurance as he was? I fear there can only be one answer to this question. "Not many," whether rich or poor, high or low, "are called."— "Strait is the gate, and narrow is the way, that leadeth unto life, and few there be that find it" (1 Cor. 1:26; Matt. 7:14). Look where you please, search where you like in town or in country, there are few "altogether" Christians. Festus and Agrippa are everywhere: they meet us at every turn. But there are few thorough, wholehearted followers of St. Paul. Yet one thing is very certain. These few are the "salt of the earth," and the "light of the world" (Matt. 5:13-14). These few are the glory of the Church, and serve to keep it alive. Without them, the Church would be little better than a decaying carcass, a white-washed sepulchre, a lighthouse without light, a steam-engine without fire, a golden candlestick without a candle, a joy to the devil, and an offence to God.

These are the kind of men who shake the world, and leave an indelible mark behind them. Martin Luther, and John Wesley, and William Wilberforce were hated and lightly esteemed while they lived; but the work they did for Christ will never be forgotten. They were "altogether" Christians.

These are the kind of men who enjoy true happiness in their religion. Like Paul and Silas, they can sing in prison, and, like Peter, they can sleep quietly on the very edge of the grave (Acts 12:6, 16:25). Strong faith gives them an inward peace which makes them independent of earthly troubles, and compels even their enemies to wonder. Your lukewarm Laodicean Christians have little comfort in their religion. It is the "thorough" men who have great peace. The first Marian martyr, John Rogers, when he was going to be burned alive for Protestantism, is said to have walked to the stake in Smithfield as cheerfully as if he were going to his wedding. The outspoken, courageous words of old Latimer, before the faggots were lighted, in the day of his martyrdom, in Broad Street, Oxford, are not forgotten to this very day. "Courage! Brother Ridley," he cried to his fellow-sufferer; "we shall light a candle in England today, by God's grace, which shall never be put out." These men were "altogether" Christians.

He that would be safe and prepared to meet his God at a moment's notice, at evening, at cock-crowing, or in the morning,—he that would enjoy felt peace in his religion, peace unaffected by sicknesses, bereavements, bankruptcies, revolutions, and the last trumpet's sound,—he that would do good in his day and generation, and be a fountain of Christian influence to all around him, influence known and recognised long after he has been laid in his grave,—let that man remember what I tell him today, and never forget it. You must not be content to be an "almost" Christian, like Agrippa. You must strive, and labour, and agonize, and pray to be an "altogether" Christian, like St. Paul.

And now, let us leave these three pictures with self-inquiry and self-examination. The time is short. Our years are quickly passing away. The world is growing old. The great assize will soon begin. The Judge will soon appear. What are we? To whom are we like? Whose is this image and superscription upon us? Is it that of Festus, or of Agrippa, or of St. Paul?

Where are Festus and Agrippa now? We do not know. A veil is drawn over their subsequent history, and whether they died as they lived we cannot tell. But where is St. Paul, the "altogether" Christian? That question we can answer. He is "with Christ, which is far better" (Phil. 1:23). He is waiting for the resurrection of the just, in that paradise of rest where sin and Satan and sorrow can trouble him no more. He has fought the good fight. He has finished his course, he has kept the faith. A crown is laid up for him which he will receive in the great review day of the Lord's appearing (2 Tim. 4:7-8).

And, let us thank God, though St. Paul is dead and gone, the Saviour who made St. Paul what he was, and kept him to the end, still lives and never changes,—always able to save, always willing to receive. Let the time past suffice us, if we have trifled with our souls hitherto. Let us turn over a new leaf. Let us arise and begin with Christ, if we never began before. Let us go on with Christ to the end, if we have begun with Him already. With the grace of God, nothing is impossible. Who would have thought that Saul the Pharisee, the persecutor of Christians, would ever become the "altogether Christian" himself, would become the great Apostle of the Gentiles, and would turn the world upside down? While there is life there is hope. The follower of Festus and Agrippa may yet be converted, and live for years, and lie down in the grave at last an "altogether" Christian like St. Paul.

CHAPTER XI[16]

John 6:68
"To Whom?"

"Then Simon Peter answered Him, Lord, to whom shall we go?
Thou hast the words of eternal life." —John 6:68.

THE chapter containing the text which heads this page, is singularly rich in matter.

It begins, we must remember, with that well-known miracle, the feeding of five thousand men with five loaves and two fishes,—a miracle which some early writers call the greatest which Christ ever worked,—the only miracle which all the four Evangelists alike record,—a miracle which exhibited creative power.

It goes on to show us another miracle of hardly less striking character, the walking of Christ on the waters of the sea of Galilee,—a miracle which exhibited our Lord's power, when He thought fit, to suspend the so-called laws of nature. It was as easy for Him to walk on the water as it had been to create land and sea at the beginning.

The chapter then carries us on to that wonderful discourse in the synagogue of Capernaum, which St. John alone, of all the four Gospel writers, was inspired to give to the world. Christ, the true bread of life,—the privileges of all who come to Him and believe,—the deep mystery of Mary's, in the year 1880. It is now published with some omissions and alterations eating Christ's flesh and drinking Christ's blood, and the life

---

[16]The substance of these pages was originally preached at Oxford, 1879.

which that flesh and blood convey,—what a wealth of precious truth lies here! How great the debt which the Church owes to the fourth Gospel!

And, finally, as the chapter draws to a close, we have the noble outburst of the warm-hearted Apostle St. Peter,—"Lord, to whom shall we go? Thou hast the words of eternal life." In this remarkable verse there are three points to which I now propose to invite the attention of all into whose hands this paper may fall.

I. In the first place, I ask you to observe the occasion of these words being spoken. What made this fiery, impulsive disciple cry out, "To whom shall we go?" The verses which precede our text supply an answer. "From that time many went back, and walked no more with Him. Then said Jesus to the twelve, Will ye also go away?"

There you have recorded a melancholy and most instructive fact. Even from Christ Himself, who "spake as never man spake," and did works of matchless power, and lived as no one ever lived, holy, harmless, undefiled, and separate from sinners, even from Christ many, after following Him for a time, went away. Yes! many, not a few, many in the noontide blaze of miracles and sermons, such as earth had never seen or heard before, many turned away from Christ, left Him, deserted Him, gave up His blessed service, and went back,—some to Judaism, some to the world, and some, we may fear, to their sins. "If they did these things in a green tree, what may we expect in a dry?" If men could forsake Christ, we have no right to be surprised if His erring, weak ministers are forsaken also in these last days.

But why did these men go back? Some of them, probably, went back because they had not counted the cost, and "when tribulation or persecution arose because of the word" they were offended. Some of them went back because they had totally misunderstood the nature of our Lord's kingdom, and had dreamed only of temporal advantages and rewards. Most of them, however, it is very clear, went back because they could not receive the deep doctrine which had just been proclaimed,—I mean the doctrine that "eating Christ's flesh and drinking Christ's blood" are absolutely necessary to salvation. It is the old story. As it was in the beginning, so it will be to the end. There is nothing which the dark, natural heart of man dislikes so much as the so-called "blood theology." Cain turned away in his proud ignorance from the idea of vicarious sacrifice, and the Jews who fell away from our Lord, "went back" when they heard that they must "eat the flesh and drink the blood" of the Son of man.

But there is no denying the fact that these Jews who "went back" have never been without followers and imitators. Their succession, at any rate, has never ceased. Millions in every age have been admitted into the Church by baptism, and begun life as professing Christians, and then, on coming to man's estate, have turned their back altogether on Christ and Christianity. Instead of "continuing Christ's faithful soldiers and servants," they have become servants of sin, the world, and unbelief. The defection is continually going on: it is an old disease, and must not surprise us. The heart is always deceitful and desperately wicked; the devil is always busy, and seeking whom he may devour; the world is always ensnaring; the way of life is narrow, the enemies many, the friends few, the difficulties great, the cross heavy, the doctrine of the gospel offensive to the natural man. What thoughtful person need wonder that multitudes in every age go back from Christ? They are brought within the outward fold of the Church in childhood, and then, on coming to manhood, they throw off all religion, and perish miserably in the wilderness.

Yet I am bold to say that the disposition to go back from Christ was never so strong as it is in these days. Never were the objections to vital Christianity so many, so plausible, and so specious. For it is an age of free thought and liberty of action, an age of scientific inquiry, and determination to question and cress-examine ancient opinions, an age of greedy pursuit of pleasure and impatience of restraint, an age of idolatry of intellect, and extravagant admiration of so-called cleverness, an age of Athenian craving for novelty and constant love of change, an age when we see on all sides a bold but ever shifting scepticism, which at one time tells us that man is little better than an ape, and at another that he is little less than a god, an age when there is a morbid readiness to accept the shallowest arguments in favour of unbelief, and a simultaneous lazy unwillingness to investigate the great fundamental evidences of Divine revelation. And, worst of all, it is an age of spurious liberality, when, under the high-sounding phrases of "No party spirit! no bigotry!" and the like, men live and die without having any distinct opinions at all. In an age like this, can any thinking Christian wonder that departure from Christ is common? Let him cease to wonder, and not waste his time in complaints. Let him rather gird up his loins like a man, and do what he can to stay the plague. Let him set his feet down firmly in "the old paths," and remember that the defection he sees is only an old complaint in an aggravated form. Let him stand between the dead and living, and try to stop the mischief. Let him "cry aloud, and spare not." Let him say, "Stand to your colours; the battle of Christianity is not lost: will ye also go away?"

I dare believe that many young persons into whose hands this paper may fall are often sorely tempted to go back from Christ. You launch forth into the world, perhaps, from quiet homes, where the primary truths of Christianity were never called in question for a moment, to hear all sorts of strange theories broached, and strange opinions advanced, which contradict the old principles which you have been taught to believe. You find to your astonishment that free thought and free handling of sacred subjects have reached such a pitch that the very foundations of faith seem shaken. You discover to your amazement that cleverness and religion do not always go together, and that it is possible for the highest intellect to be ready to thrust God out of His own world. Who can wonder if this state of things is a rude shock to the tender faith of many young persons, and that, reeling under it, they are tempted to go back from Christ, and throw away Christianity altogether?

Now, if any one who reads this paper is tempted in this fashion, I entreat him for Christ's sake to be firm, to play the man, and resist the temptation. Try to realize that there is nothing new in the state of things which now perplexes you. It is nothing but the old disease which has always plagued and tried the Church in every age, even from the day when Satan said to Eve, "Ye shall not surely die." It is only the sifting process which God permits, in order to separate the wheat from the chaff, through which we must all pass. The world after all, with its pitfalls and snares for the soul, with its competitions and struggles, its failures and successes, its disappointments and its perplexities, its perpetual crop of crude theories and extreme views, its mental conflicts and anxieties, its extravagant free thought, and its equally extravagant superstition,—the world is a fiery furnace and ordeal, through which all believers must make up their minds to pass. The temptation to cast off your first faith and go back from Christ is sure to meet you sooner or later, as it has met millions before, in one form or another. To realize that in resisting it you are only resisting an old and often beaten enemy of the soul, is one half the battle.

And, as I ask you not to be surprised at the temptation to leave Christ, so also I entreat you not to be shaken by it. What though scores of men you know give way under the assault, cast off their Christian armour, neglect their Bibles, misuse their Sundays, and live practically without God in the world? What though clever men, promising men, the sons of parents who never dreamed of such things, forsake the banner under which they were enrolled, and become mere nothingarians, or believers in nothing? Let none of these things move you. Set your face as a flint towards Jerusalem. Set your foot down firmly in the old paths, the good and tried way to the celestial city.

What fruit have the deserters to show compared to the followers of Peter, James, and John? What increase of inward peace and outward usefulness? What rest of conscience? What comfort in trial? No! while many go away from Christ, do you cling to Him with purpose of heart. Cling to your old habits of daily prayer and daily Bible reading, and regular attendance on means of grace. Better a thousand times to be on Christ's side with a few, and be laughed at and despised for a season, than to have the praise of the many for a few short years, and then awake too late to find that without Christ you are without peace, or hope, or heaven.

II. In the second place, let us consider the question which Peter asked in reply to his Master's appeal, "Will ye also go away?" "Lord," cries the warm-hearted and impulsive Apostle. "Lord, to whom shall we go?" That question, no doubt, like hundreds in the Bible, was equivalent to a strong affirmation. "There is none beside Thee to whom we can go." It is like the saying of David, "Whom have I in heaven but Thee? and there is none on earth that I desire beside Thee" (Ps. 73:25).

When we think of the age when Peter lived, we cannot help feeling that he had abundant cause to ask that question. In his days, at the end of 4000 years, "the world by wisdom knew not God" (1 Cor. 1:21). Egypt, Assyria, Greece, and Rome, the very nations which attained the highest excellence in secular things, in the things of religion were sunk in gross darkness. The fellow-countrymen of matchless historians, tragedians, poets, orators, and architects, worshipped idols, and bowed down to the work of their own hands. The ablest philosophers of Greece and Rome groped after truth like blind men, and wearied themselves in vain to find the door. The whole earth was defiled with spiritual ignorance and immorality, and the wisest men could only confess their need of light, like the Greek philosopher Plato, and groan and sigh for a deliverer. Peter might well cry, "Lord, if we leave Thee, to whom shall we go?"

Where, indeed, could the Apostle have turned for peace of heart, for satisfaction of conscience, for hope in a world to come, if he had gone away from the synagogue of Capernaum with the deserters, and left Christ 1854 years ago! Would he have found what he wanted among the formal Pharisees, or the skeptical Sadducees, or the worldly Herodians, or the ascetic Essenes, or the philosophical schools of Athens, Alexandria, or Rome? Would Gamaliel, or Caiaphas, or Stoics, or Epicureans, or Platonists, have quenched his spiritual thirst, or fed his soul? It is waste of time to ask such questions. All these pretended fountains of knowledge had long been proved to be man-made cisterns, broken cisterns, which could hold no water. They satisfied no anxious mind. He that drank of these waters soon thirsted again.

But the question which Peter asked is one which true Christians may always ask boldly, when they are tempted to go away from Christ. At this very day, when men tell us that Christianity is an effete and worn-out thing, we may safely challenge them to show us anything better. They may ply us, if they will, with objections to revealed religion, and say many things to which we can offer no reply. But, after all, we may confidently defy them to show us "a more excellent way," and more solid ground than that which is occupied by the man who simply believes all the Bible, and follows Christ.

Grant for a moment, that in an hour of weakness we listen to the temptation to go away from Christ. Grant that we close our Bibles, reject all dogmas, and with a sublime contempt for the fossilized theology of our forefathers, content ourselves with a polished nothingarianism, or a few scraps of cold formality. In what respect shall we find that we have increased our happiness or usefulness? What solid thing shall we get to replace what we have left? Once turn your back on Christ, and where will you find peace for your conscience, strength for duty, power against temptation, comfort in trouble, support in the hour of death, hope in looking forward to the grave? You may well ask. Nothingarianism can give no answer. These things are only found by those who live the life of faith in a crucified and risen Christ.

To whom, indeed, shall we go for help, strength, and comfort, if we turn our backs on Christ? We live in a world of troubles, whether we like it or not. You can no more stave off and prevent them than king Canute could prevent the tide rising and rudely swelling round the royal chair. Our bodies are liable to a thousand ailments, and our hearts to a thousand sorrows. No creature on earth is so vulnerable, and so capable of intense physical as well as mental suffering, as man. Sickness, and death, and funerals, and partings, and separations, and losses, and failures, and disappointments, and private family trials, which no mortal eye sees, will break in upon us from time to time; and human nature imperatively demands help, help, help to meet them! Alas, where will thirsty, wailing human nature find such help if we leave Christ?

The plain truth is, that nothing but an almighty personal Friend will ever meet the legitimate wants of man's soul. Metaphysical notions, philosophical theories, abstract ideas, vague speculations about "the unseen, the infinite, the inner light," and so forth, may satisfy a select few for a time. But the vast majority of mankind, if they have any religion at all, will never be content with a religion which does not supply them with a Person to whom they may look and trust. It is just this craving after a person which gives the Mariolatry of Rome its curious power. And this principle once admitted, where will you find one so perfectly fitted to satisfy man as the Christ of the Bible? Look round the world, and point out, if you can, any object of faith fit to be compared with this blessed Son of God, set forth before our eyes in the Gospels. In face of a dying world we want positives and not negatives. "To whom shall we go, if we go away from Christ?"

Men may tell us, if they please, that our old fountain of living waters is drying up, and that the nineteenth century needs a new theology. But I fail to see evidence to confirm this assertion. I see multitudes of men and women all over the world, after 1800 years, continuing to drink at this fountain; and none who honestly stoop to drink, complain that their thirst is not relieved. And all this time, those who profess to despise the good old fountain can show us nothing whatever to take its place. The mental freedom and higher light they promise are as deceptive as the mirage of the African desert, and as unreal as a dream. A substitute for the old fountain exists nowhere but in man's imagination. He that leaves it will find that he must return, or perish of thirst. Perhaps some of my younger readers may secretly think that the difficulties of revealed religion are inexplicable, and are trying to persuade themselves that they know not "where to go" in these dark and cloudy days. I entreat them to consider that the difficulties of unbelief are far greater than the difficulties of faith. When men have said all they can to depreciate the old paths of the Bible, and draw you away from Christ,—when they have piled up the ancient, stale objections of various readings, doubtful authorship, inconsistent statements, and supposed incredible miracles, they can still offer no substitute for the Scripture, or answer the question, "To whom shall we go?" There still remains the great, broad fact that the leading evidences of revelation have never been overthrown, that we are weak creatures in a sorrowful world, and need a helping hand, which Christ alone holds out, and which millions for eighteen centuries have found, and are finding, sufficient. The great argument of probability is entirely on our side. Surely it is wiser to cling to Christ and Christianity, with all its alleged difficulties, than to launch on an ocean of uncertainties, and travel towards the grave hopeless, comfortless, and professing to know nothing at all about the unseen world.

And, after all, departure from Christ on account of the supposed hardness of certain doctrines will secure no immunity from mental conflicts. The problems of Christianity may seem great and deep; but the problems of unbelief are greater and deeper still And not the least problem is the impossibility of answering the question, "Shall I find elsewhere any real peace or rest of soul, if I leave Christ? To whom shall I go? Where in all the world shall I find a more excellent way than that of faith in Jesus? Where is the personal friend who will supply His place?" Give me a thousand times rather the old Evangelical Christianity, with all its difficult facts and doctrines, the incarnation, the atonement, the resurrection, the ascension, than the cold, barren creed of the Socinian or the Deist, or the cheerless negations of modern unbelief. Give me the religion of texts and hymns and simple faith, which satisfies thousands, rather than the dreary void of speculative philosophy, which thoroughly satisfies none.

III. Let us consider, lastly, the noble declaration which Simon Peter makes in our text: "Thou hast the words of eternal life."

I do not for a moment suppose that the Apostle fully grasped the meaning of the words which he here used. It would be inconsistent with all that we read of his knowledge, before our Lord's resurrection, to suppose that he did. It may well be doubted whether he meant more than this: "Thou art the true Messiah; Thou art the promised Prophet like unto Moses, of whom it is written, I will put My words in His mouth, and He shall speak unto them all that I shall command Him" (Deut. 18:18). I believe that well-known text was in Peter's mind, though he did not yet realize its wealth of meaning.

But of one thing we may be very sure. That expression "eternal life" must have been very familiar to him and all the twelve, while Jesus went in and out among them I suspect that there were few days when they did not hear it fall from His lips, and they caught it up if they did not fully understand it. In the brief record of our Lord's teaching, contained in the four Gospels, you have it twenty-five times. In St. John's Gospel alone it occurs seventeen times. In this very sixth chapter we read it five times over. No doubt it was ringing in Peter's ears when he spoke.

But though Peter "knew not what he said" that day, there came a day when his understanding was opened, after his Lord's resurrection, and he saw heights and depths in the "words of eternal life" which before the crucifixion he only saw "through a glass darkly." And we, in the full light of the Acts and Epistles, need feel no doubt whatever as to the things which this mighty phrase, which our Lord so often used, included.

Christ's words of eternal life were words about the nature of that life which He came into the world to proclaim, a life begum in the soul by faith while we live, and perfected in glory when we die.—They were words about the way in which this eternal life is provided for sinful man, even the way of His atoning death, as our Substitute, on the cross.—They were words about the terms on which this eternal life is made our own, if we feel our need of it, even the terms of simple faith. As Latimer said, it is but "believe and have."—They were words about "the training and discipline on the way to eternal life, which are so much needed by man and so richly provided, even the renewing and sanctifying grace of the Holy Ghost. They were words about the comforts and encouragements by the way, laid up for all who believe to life everlasting, even Christ's daily help, sympathy, and watchful care. All this and much more, of which I cannot nosy speak particularly, is contained in that little phrase, "Words of eternal life." No wonder that our Lord says in a certain place, "I am come that they might have life, and have it more abundantly." "I have given them the words that Thou gavest Me" (John 10:10, 17:8).

Let us consider for a moment what vast numbers of men and women, in these last eighteen centuries, have found these "words of eternal life" not merely "words," but solid realities. They have been persuaded of them, and embraced them, and found them meat and drink to their souls. We are compassed about with a great cloud of witnesses, who in the faith of these words have lived happy and useful lives, and died glorious deaths. Where is he that will dare to deny this? Where shall we find such lives and deaths without Christ?

It was faith in Christ's "words of eternal life" which made Peter and John stand up boldly before the Jewish council, and confess their Master without fear of consequences, saying, "There is none other name given under heaven among men whereby we can be saved" (Acts 4:12).

It was faith in Christ's "words of eternal life" which made Paul come out from Judaism, spend his life in preaching the gospel, and say on the brink of the grave, "I know whom I have believed, and that He is able to keep that which I have committed to Him against that day" (2 Tim. 1:12).

It was faith in Christ's "words of eternal life" which made Bishop Hooper go boldly to the stake at Gloucester, after saying, "Life is sweet, and death is bitter; but eternal life is more sweet, and eternal death more bitter."

It was faith in Christ's "words of eternal life" which made Nicholas Ridley and Hugh Latimer endure a fiery death in Broad Street, Oxford, rather than deny the principles of the Reformation.

It was faith in Christ's "words of eternal life" which made Henry Martyn turn his back on ease and distinction at Cambridge, go forth to a tropical climate, and die a solitary death as a missionary.

It was faith in Christ's "words of eternal life" which made that honourable woman, Catherine Tait, as recorded in a most touching biography, resign five children in five weeks to the grave, in the full assurance that Christ would keep His word, take care of them both in body and soul, and bring them with Him to meet her at the last day.

What a fearful contrast to such facts as these appears in the lives and deaths of those who turn their backs on Christ, and seek other masters! What fruits can the advocates of non-Christian theories, and ideas, and principles, point to with all their cleverness? What holy, loving, peaceful quietness of spirit have they exhibited? What victories have they won over darkness, immorality, superstition, and sin? What successful missions have they carried on? What seas have they crossed? What countries have they civilized or moralized? What neglected home populations have they improved? What self-denying labours have they gone through? What deliverance have they wrought in the earth? You may well ask; you will get no answer. No wonder our Lord said of false prophets, "By their fruits ye shall know them" (Matt. 7:15-16). It is only those who can say with Peter, "Thou hast the words of eternal life," who make a mark on mankind while they live, and say, "O death, where is thy sting?" when they die.

(a) In conclusion, I entreat every one who reads this paper to ask himself whether he is going away from Christ, like the Jews, or clinging boldly to Christ, like Peter. You live in dangerous days. There was a time when irreligion was scarcely respectable; but that time has long ceased to be. But even now Christ continues to knock at the door of your hearts, and asks you to ponder your ways and take heed what you do. "Will ye go away?" Dare to set up an assize in your heart of hearts, and look within. Resist the lazy Epicurean feeling which bids you never scrutinize your inward character. Depend on it, an hour will come when you will feel the need of a great Friend in heaven. Without Him you may live tolerably; without Him you will never comfortably die.

You may tell me, perhaps, that you do not really mean to forsake Christ, although you are not at present all that you ought to be. But there are some things in religion about which you cannot make up your mind, and are waiting for more light. Or you are working hard for some special object, and have not time just now, and hope, like Felix, for "a convenient season." But, oh! waiting, lingering soul, what is neglect of Christ's word, and ordinances, and day, but "going away from Christ"? Awake to see that you are on an inclined plane, and are gradually going downward. You are drifting, drifting daily, further, further away from God. Awake, and resolve, by God's help, to drift no more.

(b) But, next to having no religion at all, I entreat every reader of this paper to beware of a religion in which Christ has not His rightful place. Let us never try to satisfy ourselves with a little cheap, formal Christianity, taken up carelessly on Sunday morning, and laid aside at night, but not influencing us during the week. Such Christianity will neither give us peace in life, nor hope in death, nor power to resist temptation, nor comfort in trouble. Christ only has "the words of eternal life," and His words must be received, believed, embraced, and made the meat and drink of our souls. A Christianity without living, felt communion with Him, without grasp of the benefits of His blood and intercession, a Christianity without Christ's sacrifice and Christ's Priesthood, is a powerless, wearisome form.

(c) Let us, finally, "hold fast the profession of our faith without wavering," if we have reason to hope we are Christ's true servants. Let men laugh at us, and try to turn us away as much as they please. Let us calmly and humbly say to ourselves at such times: "After all, to whom can I go if I leave Christ?" I feel within that He has "words of eternal life." I see that thousands find them meat and drink to their souls. Where He goes, I will go; and where He lodges, I will lodge. In a dying world, I can see nothing better. I will cling to Christ and His words. They never failed any one who trusted them, and I believe they will not fail me.

CHAPTER XII

Heb. 4:14
Our Profession.

"Seeing then that we have a great High Priest, that is passed into the heavens, Jesus the Son of God, let us hold fast our profession." —Heb. 4:14.

A CAREFUL reader of the Epistle to the Hebrews can hardly fail to observe that the words "let us" are found no less than four times in the fourth chapter. In the first verse you will read, "let us fear,"—in the eleventh verse, "let us labour,"—in the fourteenth verse, "let us hold fast,"—and in the sixteenth verse, "let us come boldly to the throne of grace." We should take note of this.

Now why did the Apostle St. Paul write in this way? He did it because the Hebrew Christians, to whom he wrote, were a peculiar people, and occupied a peculiar position. They were not like Gentile converts, who had been brought up to worship idols, and had never received any revelation from God. The Jews were a people who had enjoyed the special favour of God for fifteen hundred years. All through that long period they had possessed the law of Moses, and an immense amount of spiritual light, which had not been given to any other nation on earth. These privileges had made them very sensitive and jealous at the idea of any change. They needed to be approached very gently and delicately, and to be addressed in a peculiar style. All this St. Paul, himself born a Jew, remembered well. He puts himself on a level with them, and says, "Let us,—I speak to myself as well as to you, lest I should offend you."

But this is not all. I might add that the Jewish Christians had very peculiar trials to undergo. I suspect they were far more persecuted and ill-used after their conversion than the Gentile Christians were. No doubt it was a hard thing for a Gentile to turn from idols. But it was a much harder thing for a Jew to profess that he was not content with the ceremonial law of Moses, and that he had found a better priest, and a better sacrifice, even Jesus of Nazareth, and the blood of the cross. This also St. Paul remembered well, and he cheers and encourages them by placing himself by their side, and saying, "Let us fear,"— "let us labour,"—"let us hold fast,"—"let us come boldly,"—"I am as you are, we are all in the same boat."

I shall confine myself in this paper to the text which heads it, and I shall try to answer three questions.

I. What is this profession of which St. Paul speaks?

II. Why does St. Paul say, "Let us hold fast"?

III. What is the grand encouragement which St. Paul gives us to "hold fast"?

Before I go any further, I ask my readers to remember that the things we are about to consider were written by inspiration of the Holy Ghost for the benefit of the whole Church of Christ in every age down to the end of the world. They were meant to be used by all true Christians in England, and by all classes, whether high or low, rich or poor, in London, or Liverpool, or in any part of the earth. The Epistle to the Hebrews is not an old worn-out letter which only suits the Jews of eighteen centuries ago. It is meant for you and me.

We all need to be exhorted to "hold fast our profession."

I. Let us begin by considering what is meant by "our profession."

When St. Paul uses this expression, there can be little doubt about his meaning. He meant that public "profession" of faith in Christ and obedience to Him, which every person made when he became a member of the Christian Church. In the days of the Apostle, when a man or woman left Judaism or heathenism, and received Christ as a Saviour, he declared himself a Christian by certain acts. He did it by being publicly baptized, by joining the company of those who had been baptized already, by publicly promising to give up idolatry and wickedness of all kinds, and by habitually taking part with the followers of Jesus of Nazareth in all their religious assemblies, their ways, and their practices. This is what St. Paul had in view when he wrote the words, "Let us hold fast our profession."

Profession in those days was a very serious matter, and entailed very serious consequences. It often brought on a man persecution, loss of property, imprisonment, and even death. The consequence was that few persons ever made a Christian profession in the early Church unless they were thoroughly in earnest, truly converted, and really believers. No doubt there were some exceptions. People like Ananias and Sapphira, and Simon Magus, and Demas, crept in and joined themselves to the disciples. But these were exceptional cases. As a general rule, it was not worth while for a man to profess Christianity if his heart was not entirely in his profession. It cost much. It brought on a man the risk of a vast amount of trouble, and brought in very little gain. The whole result was, that the proportion of sincere, right-hearted, and converted persons in the Church of the Apostle's days was far greater than it ever has been at any other period in the last eighteen centuries. There was a very deep meaning in St. Paul's words when he said, "Let us hold fast our profession."

In the days in which we live, "profession" is a very different thing. Millions of people profess and call themselves Christians, whom the Apostle would not have called Christians at all. Millions are annually baptized, and added to the rolls and registers of churches, who have little or no religion. Many of them live and die without ever attending a place of worship, and live very ungodly lives. Many more only go to a church or chapel occasionally, or once on Sunday at the most. Many others pass through life without ever becoming communicants, and live and die in the habitual neglect of that Holy Sacrament which the Lord commanded to be received. Most of these people are reckoned Christians while they live, and are buried with Christian burial when they die. But what would St. Paul have said of them? I fear there can be no doubt about the answer. He would have said they did not deserve to be reckoned members of any Church at all! He would not have addressed them as "saints and faithful brethren in Christ Jesus." He would not have called upon them to "hold fast their profession." He would have told them they had no profession to hold fast, and that they were "yet dead in trespasses and sins" (Eph. 2:1). All this is sorrowful and painful, but it is only too true. Let those deny it who dare.

Let us, however, thank God that there are not a few to be found in every part of Christendom who really are what they profess to be—true, sincere, earnest-minded, hearty, converted, believing Christians. Some of them, no doubt, belong to churches in which their souls get little help. Some of them have very imperfect knowledge, and hold the truth in solution, with a mixture of many defective views. But they have all certain common marks about them. They see the value of their souls, and really want to be saved. They feel the sinfulness of sin, and hate it, and fight with it, and long to be free from it. They see that Jesus Christ alone can save them, and that they ought to trust only in Him. They see that they ought to live holy and godly lives, and in their poor way they try to do it. They love their Bibles, and they pray, though both their reading and their praying are very defective. Some of them, in short, are in the highest standard of Christ's school, and are strong in knowledge, faith, and love. Others are only in the infants' room, and in everything are weak and poor. But in one point they are all one. Their hearts are right in the sight of God; they love Christ; their faces are set towards heaven, and they want to go there. These are those in the present day to whom I wish in this paper to apply St. Paul's exhortation, "Let us hold fast our profession." Let us cling to it, and not let it go.

Now I cannot forget that we meet thousands of persons in daily life who are always saying, "I make no profession of religion." They not only say it, but rather glory in saying it, as if it was a right, wise, and proper thing to say. They seem even to despise those who make a profession, and to regard them as hypocrites and impostors, or, at any rate, as weak and foolish people. If this paper happens to fall into the hands of any person of this kind, I have somewhat to say to him, and I invite his best attention.

I do not deny that there are many hypocrites in religion. There always were, and there always will be, as long as the world stands. As long as there is good gold and silver coin in the realm, so long there will be forging, coining, and counterfeit money. The very existence of bad coins is an indirect proof that there is something which it is worth while to imitate, and that there is such a thing as good current money in circulation. It is just the same with Christianity! The very fact that there are many false professors in the churches is an indirect proof that there are such persons as true-hearted and sound believers. It is one of Satan's favourite devices, in order to bring discredit on Christianity, to persuade some unhappy people to profess what they do not really believe. He tries to damage the cause of our Lord Jesus Christ in the world by sending out wolves in sheep's clothing, and by raising up men and women who talk the language of Canaan, and wear the coat of God's children, while they are inwardly rotten at heart. But these things do not justify a man in condemning all religious profession.

I tell those who boast that they make no profession, that they are only exhibiting their own sorrowful ignorance of Holy Scripture. The hypocrisy of some unhappy people must never prevent us doing our own duty, without caring what men may say or think of us. We must never be ashamed of showing ourselves boldly on Christ's side, by honouring His word, His day, and His ordinances, by speaking up for Christ's cause on all proper occasions, and by firmly refusing to conform to the sins and the follies of the children of this world. The words of our Lord Jesus Christ ought never to be forgotten: "Whosoever shall be ashamed of Me and of My words, of him shall the Son of man be ashamed when He shall come in His own glory, and in His Father's, and of the holy angels" (Luke 9:26). If we will not confess Christ upon earth, and openly profess that we are His servants, we must not expect that Christ will confess us in heaven at the last day.

In short, the very last thing that a man should be ashamed of is the "profession" of religion. There are many things unhappily of which most people seem not ashamed at all. Ill-temper, selfishness, want of charity, laziness, malice, backbiting, lying, slandering, intemperance, impurity, gambling, Sabbath-breaking,—all these are terribly common things among men, and of most of them people do not seem a bit ashamed, though they ought to be! They that habitually "do such things will not inherit the kingdom of God" (Gal. 5:21). But of Bible-reading, praying, holy living, and working for the good of bodies and souls, no one ever need be ashamed. These may be things which many laugh at, dislike, and despise, and have no taste for, but they are the very things with which God is well pleased. Once more, I repeat, whatever men may say, the very last thing of which we ought to be ashamed is our "profession" of faith in Christ, and obedience to Christ.

II. Let us, in the second place, consider, Why St. Paul says, "Let us hold fast our profession." The answer to this question is threefold, and demands the serious attention of all who hope that they are really sincere in their Christian profession.

(a) For one thing, OUR HEARTS are always weak and foolish, even after conversion. We may have passed from death to life, and be renewed in the spirit of our minds. We may see the value of our souls, as we once did not. We may have become new creatures; old things may have passed away, and all things may have become new. But believers must never forget that until they die they carry about with them a weak, foolish, and treacherous heart. The roots of all manner of evil are still within us, although cut down to the ground by the grace of the Holy Ghost. Whether we like to acknowledge it or not, there are within us, at our very best, latent dislike of trouble, secret desire to please man and keep in with the world, carelessness about our private Bible-reading and our prayers, envy and jealousy of others, laziness about doing good, selfishness and desire to have our own way, forgetfulness of the wishes of others, and want of watchfulness over our own besetting sins. All these things are often lying hid within us, and below the surface of our hearts. The holiest saint may find to his cost some day that they are all there alive, and ready to show themselves. No wonder that our Lord Jesus said to the three Apostles in the garden, "Watch and pray, lest ye enter into temptation. The spirit truly is ready, but the flesh is weak" (Mark 14:38). I have no doubt that St. Paul had the heart in view, when he wrote those words, "Hold fast."—"Let us therefore hold fast our profession."

(b) For another thing, the world is a source of immense danger to the Christian soul. From the day that we are converted, we are living in a most unhealthy atmosphere for religion. We live and move and have our being in the midst of a vast multitude of people who are utterly without vital Christianity. In every rank of life we meet with hundreds who, however moral and respectable, seem to care for nothing but such things as these,— What shall I eat? What shall I drink? What can I get? What can I spend? How shall I employ my time? What profit can I make? What amusement can I have? What pleasant company can I enjoy! As for God, and Christ, and the Holy Ghost, and the Bible, and prayer, and repentance, and faith, and holy living, and doing good in the world, and death, and resurrection, and judgment, and heaven and hell, they are subjects which never appear to come across them except in sickness, or at a funeral. Now to live constantly in the midst of such people, as a Christian must do, is sure to be a great trial to him, and requires constant watchfulness to prevent his getting harm. We are incessantly tempted to give way about little things, and to make compromises and concessions. We naturally dislike giving offence to others, and having frictions and collisions with relatives, friends, and neighbours. We do not like to be laughed at and ridiculed by the majority, and to feel that we are always in a minority in every company into which we go. I fear that too many are laughed out of heaven and laughed into hell. It is a true saying of Solomon, "The fear of man bringeth a snare" (Prov. 29:25). I once knew a brave sergeant of a cavalry regiment, who, after living to the age of fifty without any religion, became for the last few years of his life a decided Christian. He told me that when he first began to think about his soul, and to pray, some months passed away before he dare tell his wife that he said his prayers; and that he used to creep upstairs without his boots at evening, that his wife might not hear him, and find out what he was doing!

The plain truth is, that "the whole world lieth in wickedness" (1 John 5:19), and it is vain to ignore the danger that the world causes to the believer's soul. The spirit of the world, and the tone of the world, and the tastes of the world, and the air of the world, and the breath of the world, are continually about him every day that he lives, drawing him down and pulling him back. If he does not keep his faith in lively exercise, he is sure to catch infection, and take damage, like the travellers through the Campagna at Rome, who take a fever without being aware of it at the time. The most mischievous and unsanitary gas is that which our bodily senses do not detect. We have reason to pray continually for an increase of that faith of which St. John says, "that it gives us the victory over the world" (1 John 5:4). Happy, indeed, is that Christian who can be in the world and yet not of the world, who can do his duty in it, and yet not be conformed to it, who can pass through it unmoved by its smiles or its frowns, its flattery or its enmity, its open opposition or its playful ridicule, its sweets or its bitters, its gold or its sword! When I think what the world is, and see what harm it has done and is doing to souls, I do not wonder that St. Paul says, "Hold fast."—"Let us hold fast our profession."

(c) For one thing more, the devil is a constant enemy to the Christian's soul. That great, sleepless, and unwearied foe is always labouring to do us harm. It is his constant object to wound, hurt, vex, injure, or weaken, if he cannot kill and destroy. He is an unseen enemy who is always near us, "about our path, and about our bed," and spying out all our ways, prepared to suit his temptations to the special weak points of every man. He knows us far better than we know ourselves. He has been studying one book for 6000 years, the book of fallen human nature, and he is a spirit of almost boundless subtlety and cunning, and of boundless malice. The best of saints has little idea how many vile suggestions in his heart come from the devil, and what a restless adversary stands at his right hand.

This is he who tempted Eve at the beginning, and persuaded her that she might disobey God, eat the forbidden fruit and not die.—This is he who tempted David to number the people, and to cause the death of 70,000 of his subjects by pestilence in three days.—This is he who tried to tempt our Lord in the wilderness immediately after His baptism, and even quoted Scripture to gain his end.—This is he who opposed our Lord all throughout His three years' ministry, sometimes by possessing the bodies of unhappy men and women in a most mysterious manner, and at last by putting it into the heart of one of His Apostles to betray Him.—This is he who constantly opposed the Apostles after our Lord's ascension, and tried to stop the progress of the gospel.—This is he of whom St. Paul testifies that even "Satan is transformed into an angel of light," and that false teachers are his agents (2 Cor. 11:14).

Does any reader of this paper foolishly suppose that the devil is asleep, or dead, or less mischievous now than in old time? Nothing of the kind! He is still "walking about like a roaring lion, seeking whom he may devour." He is still "going to and fro in the earth, and walking up and down in it" (1 Pet. 5:8; Job 1:7). It is he who goes among heathen nations and persuades them to shed oceans of blood in the worship of idols, or murderous wars. It is he who goes to and fro amongst fallen Churches, persuading them to throw aside the Bible, and satisfy people with formal worship or grovelling superstitions.—It is he who walks up and down in Protestant countries, and stirs up party spirit, and bitter political strife, setting class against class, and subjects against rulers, in order to distract men's minds from better things.—It is he who is continually going to the ears of intellectual and highly educated men, persuading them that the old Bible is not true, and advising them to be content with Atheism, Theism, Agnosticism, Secularism, and a general contempt for the world to come. It is he, above all, who persuades foolish people that there is no such person as a devil, and no future judgment after death, and no hell. In all this fearful list of things I firmly believe that the devil lies at the bottom, and is the true root, reason, and cause. Can we suppose for a moment that he will let true Christians go quietly to heaven, and not tempt them by the way?

Away with the silly thought! We have need to pray against the devil, as well as against the world and the flesh. In the great trinity of enemies which the believer should daily remember, the devil perhaps is the greatest because he is the least seen. Nothing delights him so much (if, indeed, he can be delighted at all) as to injure a true Christian, and make him bring discredit on his religion. When I think of the devil, I do not wonder that St. Paul said, "Hold fast."—"Let us hold fast our profession."

Now I suspect that some reader of this paper may be secretly thinking that I am an alarmist, and that there is no need of such watchfulness, carefulness, and "holding fast." I ask such a person to turn with me to the Bible for a few moments, and to consider seriously what that blessed book teaches.

I ask him to remember that Judas Iscariot and Demas both began well, and made a good profession. One was a chosen Apostle of our Lord Jesus Christ, a constant companion of our blessed Saviour for three years. He walked with Him, talked with Him, heard His teaching, saw His miracles, and up to the very night before our Lord was crucified was never thought a worse man than Peter, James, or John. Yet this unhappy man at last let go his profession, betrayed his Master, came to a miserable end, and went to his own place.—The other man whom I named, Demas, was a chosen companion of the Apostle St. Paul, and professed to be of like mind with that eminent man of God. There can be little doubt that for some years he journeyed with him, helped him, and took part in his evangelistic labours. But how did it all end? He gave up his profession, and the last Epistle St. Paul wrote contains this melancholy record: "Demas has forsaken me, having loved this present world" (2 Tim. 4:10). We never hear of him again.

To every one who thinks I have dwelt too much on the Christian's dangers, I say this day, Remember Demas, remember Judas Iscariot, tighten your grasp, "hold fast your profession," and beware. We may appear to men to be very good Christians for a season, and yet prove at last to be stony-ground hearers, and destitute of a wedding garment.

But this is not all. I ask every believer to remember that if he does not "hold fast," he may pierce himself through with many sorrows, and bring great discredit on his character. We should never forget David's awful fall in the matter of the wife of Uriah, and Peter's thrice-repeated denial of his Master, and Cranmer's temporary cowardice, of which he so bitterly repented at last. Are we greater and stronger than they? "Let us not be high-minded, but fear." There is a godly fear which is of great use to the soul. It was the great Apostle of the Gentiles who wrote these words: "I keep under my body, and bring it into subjection; lest, after I have preached to others, I myself should be a castaway" (1 Cor. 9:27).

Does any Christian reader of these pages desire much happiness in his religion, and much joy and peace in believing? Let him take an old minister's advice this day, and "hold fast his profession." Let him resolve to be very thorough, very decided, very watchful, very careful about the state of his soul. The more boldly he shows his colours, and the more uncompromising and firm he is, the lighter will he find his heart, and the more sensibly will he feel the sun shining on his face. None are so happy in God's service as decided Christians. When John Rogers, the first martyr in Queen Mary's time, was being led to Smithfield to be burned, the French Ambassador reported that he looked as bright and cheerful as if he were going to his wedding.

Does any Christian reader of these pages desire much usefulness to others in his religion? Let me assure him that none do so much good in the long run of life, and leave such a mark on their generation, as those who "hold fast their profession" most tightly, and are most decided servants of Christ. Few men, perhaps, did more for the cause of the Protestant Reformation, and shook the power of Rome more completely in this country, than the two noble bishops who were burned back to back at one stake in Oxford, and would not let go their faith to save their lives. I need not say that I refer to Ridley and Latimer. The careless, thoughtless, irreligious world takes notice of such men, and is obliged to allow that there is something real and solid in their religion. The more light shines in our lives, the more good shall we do in the world. It is not for nothing that our

Lord says, in the Sermon on the Mount, "Let your light so shine before men, that they may see your good works, and glorify your Father which is in heaven" (Matt. 5:16).

Let us gather up all these things in our memories, and never forget them. Let it be a settled principle in our minds, that it is of immeasurable importance to our happiness and usefulness to "hold fast our profession," and to be always on our guard. Let us dismiss from our minds the crude modern idea that a believer has only got to sit still, and "yield himself" to God. Let us rather maintain the language of Scripture, and strive to "mortify the deeds of our body," to "crucify our flesh," to "cleanse ourselves from all filthiness of flesh and spirit," to wrestle, to fight, and live the soldier's life (Rom. 8:13; Gal. 5:24; 2 Cor. 7:1; Eph. 6:12; 1 Tim. 6:12; 2 Tim. 2:3). One might think that the account of the armour of God in the Epistle to the Ephesians ought to settle the question of our duty. But the plain truth is, men will persist in confounding two things that differ, that is justification and sanctification. In justification, the word to be addressed to man is, Believe, only believe. In sanctification, the word must be, Watch, pray, and fight. What God has divided, let us not mingle and confuse. I can find no words to express my own deep sense of the immense importance of "holding fast our profession."

III. In the last place, let us consider what encouragement there is to Christians to hold fast their profession.

The Apostle St. Paul was singularly fitted, both by grace and nature, to handle this subject. Of all the inspired writers in the New Testament, none seems to have been so thoroughly taught of God to deal with the conflicts of the human heart as St. Paul. None was better acquainted with the dangers, diseases, and remedies of the soul. The proof of this is to be seen in the seventh chapter of his Epistle to the Romans, and the fifth chapter of his Second Epistle to the Corinthians. Those two chapters ought to be frequently studied by every Christian who wishes to understand his own heart.

Now what is the ground of encouragement which St. Paul proposes? He tells us to "hold fast our profession," and not let it go, because "we have a great High Priest that is passed into the heavens, Jesus the Son of God."

That word "High Priest" would ring with power in the ears of a Jewish reader far more than it would in the ears of Gentile Christians. It would stir up in his mind the remembrance of many typical things in the service of the tabernacle and temple. It would make him recollect that the Jewish high priest was a kind of mediator between God and the people;—that he alone went once every year into the Holy of Holies on the day of atonement, and had access through the veil to the mercy-seat;—that he was a kind of daysman between the twelve tribes and God, to lay his hand on both (Job. 9:33);—that he was the chief minister over the house of God, who was intended "to have compassion on the ignorant and them that were out of the way" (Heb. 5:2). All these things would give the Jews some idea of what St. Paul meant when he said, "Let us hold fast," because we have got a great High Priest in heaven. The plain truth is, that the Christian is meant to understand that we have a mighty, living Friend in heaven, who not only died for us, but rose again, and after rising again took His seat at the right hand of God, to be our Advocate and Intercessor with the Father until He comes again. We are meant to understand that Christ not only died for us, but is alive for us, and actively working on our behalf at this very day. In short, the encouragement that St. Paul holds out to believers is, the living priesthood of Jesus Christ.

Is not this exactly what he meant when he told the Hebrews that Christ is "able to save them to the uttermost who come unto God by Him, because He ever liveth to make intercession for them" (Heb. 7:25)?—Is not this what he meant when he told the Romans, "If, when we were enemies, we were reconciled to God by the death of His Son, much more, being reconciled, we shall be saved by His life" (Rom. 5:10)?—Is not this what he meant when he wrote that glorious challenge, "Who is he that condemneth? It is Christ that died, yea, rather, that is risen again, who is even at the right hand of God, who also maketh intercession for us" (Rom. 8:34)? Here, in one word, is the believer's fountain of consolation. He is not only to look to a Saviour who died as his Substitute, and shed His blood for him, but to a Saviour who also after His resurrection took His seat at God's right hand, and lives there as his constant Intercessor and Priest.

Let us think for a moment what a wonderful and suitable High Priest is the High Priest of our profession, a million times superior to any high priest of the family of Aaron.

Jesus is a High Priest of almighty power, for He is very God of very God, never slumbering, never sleeping, never dying, and eternal. The Jewish high priests were "not suffered to continue by reason of death" (Heb. 7:23), but Christ being raised from the dead dieth no more. Our great High Priest never grows old, and never dies (Rom. 6:9).

Jesus is a High Priest who is perfect Man as well as perfect God. He knows what our bodies are, for He had a body Himself, and is acquainted with all its sinless weakness and pains. He knows what hunger, and thirst, and suffering are, for He lived for thirty-three years upon earth, and knows the physical nature of an infant, a child, a boy, a young man, and a man of full age. "He hath suffered Himself, being tempted" (Heb. 2:18).

Jesus is a High Priest of matchless sympathy. He can be "touched with the feeling of our infirmities" (Heb. 4:15). His heart was always overflowing with love, pity, and compassion while He was on earth. He wept at the grave of Lazarus. He wept over unbelieving Jerusalem. He had an ear ready to hear every cry for help, and was ever going about doing good to the sick and the afflicted. One of His last thoughts on the cross was one of care for His mother, and one of His first messages after His resurrection was one of "peace" to His poor fallen Apostles. And He is not changed. He has carried that wonderful heart up to heaven, and is ever watching the weakest lamb in His flock with merciful tenderness.

Jesus is a High Priest of perfect wisdom. He knows exactly what each of us is, and what each of us requires. "He will not suffer us to be tempted above that which we are able to bear" (1 Cor. 10:13), nor allow us to remain in the furnace of suffering one moment beyond the time that is required for our refining. He will give us strength according to our day, and grace according to our need. He knows the most secret feelings of our hearts, and understands the meaning of our feeblest prayers. He is not like Aaron, and Eli, and Abiathar, and Annas, and Caiaphas, an erring and imperfect high priest in dealing with those who come to Him, and spread out their petitions before Him. He never makes any mistakes.

I challenge every reader of this paper to tell me, if he can, what greater consolation and encouragement the soul of man can have than the possession of such a High Priest as this? We do not think enough of Him in these days. We talk of His death, and His sacrifice, and His blood, and His atonement, and His finished work on the cross; and no doubt we can never make too much of these glorious subjects. But we err greatly if we stop short here. We ought to look beyond the cross and the grave, to the life, the priesthood, and the constant intercession of Christ our Lord. Unless we do this, we have only a defective view of Christian doctrine. The consequences of neglecting this part of our Lord's offices are very serious, and have done great harm to the Church and the world.

Young men and women in all our churches, and generally speaking, all new believers, are taking immense damage for want of right teaching about the priestly office of Christ. They feel within themselves a daily craving after help, and grace, and strength, and guidance in running the race set before them along the narrow way of life. It does not satisfy them to hear that they ought to be always looking back to the cross and the atonement. There is something within them which whispers that they would like to have a living friend. Then comes the devil, and suggests that they ought to go to earthly priests, and make confession, and receive absolution, and keep up the habit of doing this continually. They are often all too ready to believe it, and foolishly try to supply the hunger of their souls by extravagantly frequent reception of the Lord's Supper, and submitting to the spiritual directorship of some clergyman.—All this is little better than religious opium-eating and dram-drinking. It soothes the heart for a little season, but does no real good, and often results in bringing souls into a state of morbid superstitious bondage. It is not the medicine which Scripture has provided. The truth which all believers, and especially young men and women in these days, have need to be told is the truth of Christ's life in heaven, and priestly intercession fox us. We need no earthly confessor, and no earthly priest. There is only one Priest to whom we ought to go with our daffy wants, even Jesus the Son of God. It is impossible to find one more mighty, more loving, more wise, more ready to help than He is. It is a wise saying of an old divine, that "the eyes of a believer ought to be fixed on Christ in all his dealings with God. The one eye is to be set on His oblation, and the other on His intercession." Let us never forget this. The true secret of holding fast our profession is to be continually exercising faith in the priestly office of Christ, and making use of it every day.

He that acts on this principle will find it possible to serve God and be a Christian in any position, however hard it may be. He need not suppose for a moment, that he cannot have true religion without retiring from the world, and going into a monastery, or living like a hermit in a cave. A young woman must not suppose that she cannot serve God in her own family, because of unconverted parents, brothers, and sisters, and that she must-go into some "Religious House;' so called, in company with a few like-minded women. All such ideas are senseless and unscriptural; they come from beneath, and not from above. At school or in college, in the army or the navy, in the bank or at the bar, in the merchant's house or on 'Change, it is possible for a man to serve God. As a daughter at home, or a teacher in a high school, or an assistant in a house of business, a woman can serve God, and must never give way to the cowardly thought that it is impossible. But how is it all to be done? Simply by living the life of faith in the Son of God, by continually looking back to Him on the cross, and to the fountain of His blood for daily pardon and peace of conscience, and by daily looking up to Him at the right hand of God interceding for us, and daily drawing from Him supplies of grace in this world of need. This is the sum of the whole matter. We have a great High Priest who is passed into the heavens, and through Him it is possible not only to begin, but to "hold fast" our profession.

I will now conclude this paper by addressing a few words of direct practical exhortation to every reader into whose hands it may happen to fall.

(a) Do you belong to that huge class of so-called Christians who make no profession of religion at all? Alas! it is a pity this class should be so large; but it is vain to shut our eyes to the fact that it is very large. These of whom I speak are not atheists or infidels; they would not for a moment like to be told they are not Christians. They go to places of worship, they think Christianity a very proper thing for baptisms, weddings, and funerals.

They say grace before and after dinner; they like their children to have some religion in their education. But they never seem to get any further; they shrink from making a "profession." It is useless to tell them to "hold fast," because they have nothing to hold.

I ask such persons, in all affection and kindness, to consider how unreasonable and inconsistent their position is. Most of them believe the Apostles' Creed. They believe there is a God, and a world to come after death, and a resurrection, and a judgment, and a life everlasting. But what can be more senseless than to believe all these vast realities, and yet to travel on towards the grave without any preparation for the great future? You will not deny that you will have to meet the Lord Jesus Christ, the Judge of all, when the last trumpet sounds, and you will stand before the great white throne. But where will you be in that awful day, if you have never professed faith, love, and obedience to that Judge during the time of your life upon earth? How can you possibly expect Him to confess and own you in that hour, if you have been afraid or ashamed to confess Him, and to declare yourself boldly upon His side, while you are upon earth?

Think of these things, I beseech you, and change your plan of life. Cast aside vain excuses and petty reasons for delay. Resolve by the grace of God to lay firm hold on Jesus Christ, and to enlist like a man under HIS banners. That blessed Saviour will receive you just as you are, however unworthy you may feel yourself. Wait for nothing, and wait for nobody. Begin to pray this very day, and to pray real, lively, fervent prayers, such as the penitent thief prayed upon the cross. Take down your long-neglected Bible, and begin to read it. Break off every known bad habit. Seek the company and friendship of thoroughgoing Christians. Give up going to places where your soul can get nothing but harm. In one word, begin to make "a profession," fearing neither the laughter nor the scorn of man. The word of the Lord Jesus is for you as well as another: "Him that cometh to Me I will in no wise cast out" (John 6:37). I have seen many people on their death-beds, but I never met with one who said he was sorry he had made a "profession" of religion.

(b) In the last place, do you belong to that much smaller class of persons who really profess Christian faith, and Christian obedience, and are trying, however weakly, to follow Christ in the midst of an evil world. I think I know something of what goes on in your hearts. You sometimes feel that you will never persevere to the end, and will be obliged some day to give up your profession. You are sometimes tempted to write bitter things against yourself, and to fancy you have got no grace at all. I am afraid there are myriads of true Christians in this condition, who go trembling and doubting toward heaven, with Despondency, and Much-Afraid, and Fearing in the Pilgrim's Progress, and fear they will never get to the Celestial City at all. But oddly enough, in spite of all their groans and doubts and fears, they do not turn back to the city from which they came (Heb. 11:15). They press on, though faint, yet pursuing, and, as John Wesley used to say of his people, "they end well."

Now, my advice to all such persons, if any of them are reading this paper, is very simple. Say every morning and evening of your life, "Lord, increase my faith." Cultivate the habit of fixing your eye more simply on Jesus Christ, and try to know more of the fulness there is laid up in Him for every one of His believing people. Do not be always boring down over the imperfections of your own heart, and dissecting your own besetting sins. Look up. Look more to your risen Head in heaven, and try to realize more than you do that the Lord Jesus not only died for you, but that He also rose again, and that He is ever living at God's right hand as your Priest, your Advocate, and your Almighty Friend. When the Apostle Peter "walked upon the waters to go to Jesus," he got on very well as long as his eye was fixed upon his Almighty Master and Saviour. But when he looked away to the winds and waves, and reasoned, and considered his own strength, and the weight of his body, he soon began to sink, and cried, "Lord, save me." No wonder that our gracious Lord, while grasping his hand and delivering him from a watery grave, said, "O thou of little faith, wherefore didst thou doubt?" Alas! many of us are very like Peter,— we look away from Jesus, and then our hearts faint, and we feel sinking (Matt. 14:28-31).

Think, last of all, how many millions of men and women like yourself have got safe home during the last eighteen hundred years. Like you, they have had their battles and their conflicts, their doubts and their fears. Some of them have had very little "joy and peace in believing," and were almost surprised when they woke up in Paradise. Some of them enjoyed full assurance, and strong consolation, and have entered the haven of eternal life, like a gallant ship in full sail. And who are these last that have done so? Those who have not only held their profession between finger and thumb, but have grasped it firmly with both hands, and have been ready to die for Christ, rather than not confess Him before men. Take courage, believer. The bolder and more decided you are, the more comfort you will have in Christ. You cannot have two heavens, one here, and the other hereafter. You are yet in the world, and you have a body, and there is always near you a busy devil. But great faith shall always have great peace. The happiest person in religion will always be that man or woman who can say, with a true heart, like St. Paul, "The life that I live in the flesh, I live by the faith of the Son of God, who loved me, and gave Himself for me." In myself I see nothing, but I keep ever looking to Jesus, and by His grace I hold fast my profession (Gal. 2:20).

And now I cannot leave this great and solemn subject without offering to all who read it a parting word of warning about the times in which we live. I will try to explain briefly what I mean.

I believe, then, that for three centuries there has not been an age in which it has been so needful to urge professing Christians to "hold fast" as it is at this time. No doubt there is plenty of religion of a certain sort in these days. There are many more attendants on public worship all over the land than there were thirty years ago. But it may well be doubted whether there is any increase of vital Christianity. I am greatly mistaken if there is not a growing tendency to "hold fast" nothing in religion, and a disposition to hold everything as loosely as possible. "Nothing fast! Everything loose!" seems the order of the day.

How is it in matters of faith and doctrine? It used to be thought important to hold clear and distinct views about such points as the inspiration of the Scriptures, the atonement, the work of the Spirit, the personality of the devil, the reality of future punishment. It is not thought so now. The old order of things has passed away. You may believe anything or nothing on these subjects, so long as you are earnest and sincere. Holding fast has given way to holding loose.

How is it in matters of worship and ritual? It used to be thought important to be content with the plain teaching of the Prayer Book. It is not thought so now. You must have the Lord's Table called an altar, and the sacrament called a sacrifice, without the slightest warrant in the Prayer Book, and a ceremonial fitted to these novel views. And then if you complain, you are told that you are very narrow and illiberal, and that a clergyman ought to be allowed to do and say and teach anything, if he is only earnest and sincere. Holding fast has given way to holding loose.

How is it in the matter of holy living? It used to be thought important to "renounce the pomps and vanity of this wicked world," and to keep clear of races, theatre-going, balls, card-playing, and the like. It is not thought so now. You may do anything and go anywhere you please, so long as you keep Lent, and occasionally attend early Communion? You must not be so very strict and particular! Once more I say, holding fast has given way to holding loose.

This state of things, to say the least, is not satisfactory. It is full of peril. It shows a condition of Christianity which, I am certain, would not have satisfied St. Paul or St. John. The world was not turned upside down by such vague, loose doctrine and practice eighteen centuries ago. The souls of men in the present day will never receive much benefit from such loose Christianity either in England or anywhere else. Decision in teaching and living is the only Christianity which God has blessed in the ages that are past, or will continue to bless in our own time. Loose, vague, misty, broad Christianity may avoid offence and please people in health and prosperity, but it will not convert souls, or supply solid comfort in the hour of sorrow or sickness, or on the bed of death.

The plain truth is, that "sincerity and earnestness" are becoming the idol of many English Christians in these latter days. People seem to think it matters little what opinions a man holds in religion, so long as he is "earnest and sincere;" and you are thought uncharitable if you doubt his soundness in the faith! Against this idolatry of mere "earnestness" I enter my solemn protest. I charge every reader of this paper to remember that God's written Word is the only rule of faith, and to believe nothing to be true and soul-saving in religion which cannot be proved by plain texts of Scripture. I entreat him to read the Bible, and make it his only test of truth and error, right and wrong. And for the last time I say, "Hold fast, and not loose,—hold fast your profession."

CHAPTER XIII

Matt. 8:11
Many.

"Many shall come from the east and west, and shall sit down with Abraham, Isaac, and Jacob in the kingdom of heaven." —Matt. 8:11.

THE words of Scripture which head this page were spoken by our Lord Jesus Christ. You may take them either as a prophecy or as a promise. In either point of view they are deeply interesting, and contain much food for thought.

Take the words as a prophecy, and remember that they are sure to be fulfilled The Bible contains many predictions of things most unlikely and improbable, which have yet proved true. Was it not said of Ishmael, the father of the Arabian race, that he was to be a "wild man, his hand against every man, and every man's hand against him"? (Gen. 16:12). We see the fulfilment of those words at this very day, when we look at the tribes in the Sudan, or observe the ways of the Bedouins.—Was it not said of Egypt that it was finally to become "the basest of kingdoms," and its inhabitants a people who could neither govern themselves nor be governed? (Ezek. 29:15). We see the fulfilment of those words at this very day along the whole valley of the Nile, and every statesman in Europe knows it to his sorrow. It will be just the same with the prophecy before our eyes. "Many shall sit down in the kingdom of heaven."

Take the words as a promise. It was spoken for the encouragement of the Apostles, and of all Christian ministers and teachers down to the present day. We are often tempted to think that preaching, and teaching, and visiting, and trying to bring souls to Christ does no good, and that our labour is all thrown away. But here is the promise of One who "cannot lie," and never failed to keep HIS word. He cheers us with a gracious sentence. He would have us not faint or give way to despair. Whatever we may think, and however little success we may see, there is a Scripture before us which cannot be broken, "Many shall sit down in the kingdom of heaven."

I. We have first in these words the number of those who shall be saved. Our Lord Jesus Christ declares that they shall be "many."

How strange that word "many" sounds! Will any be saved who are not born again, washed in Christ's blood, and sanctified by the Holy Ghost? Will any be saved (except infants) who have not repented of sin, believed on the Lord Jesus for forgiveness, and been made holy in heart? None, none, certainly none. If men and women can be saved without repentance, faith, and holiness, we may as well throw the Bible away, and give up Christianity altogether.

But are there many people of this kind to be seen in the world? Alas! there are very few. The believers whom we see and know are "a little flock." "Strait is the gate, and narrow is the way, which leadeth unto life, and few there be that find it" (Matt. 7:14). Few are to be seen in towns, and few in country parishes! Few among the rich, and few among the poor! Few among the old, and few among the young! Few among the learned, and few among the unlearned! Few in palaces, and few in cottages! It is an abiding sorrow with all true Christians that they meet so few with whom they can pray, and praise, and read the Bible, and talk of spiritual things. They often feel to stand alone. Many are the people who never go to any place of worship from the first day of January to the last day of December, and seem to live without God in the world. Few are the communicants in any congregation—a mere handful compared to those who never go to the Lord's table at all. Few are the men and women who do anything for the cause of Christ upon earth, or appear to care whether those around them are lost or saved. Can any one deny these things? Impossible! Yet here is our Lord Jesus Christ saying, "Many shall sit down in the kingdom of heaven."

Now, why did our Lord say so? He never made a mistake, and all that He says is true. Let me try to throw some light on this question.

(a) There shall be "many" when all are gathered together who have died in the Lord, from Abel, the first saint, down to the last who is found alive when the trumpet sounds, and the resurrection takes place. They shall be a "multitude which no man can number" (Rev. 7:9).

(b) There shall be "many" when all the infants who died before they knew good from evil, or their right hand from their left, are called from their little graves, and assembled. Few, probably, are aware what an enormous proportion of children never live for a year! They shall be "a multitude which no man can number."

(c) There shall be "many" when all the believers of every name, and nation, and people, and tongue, the Old Testament saints, like Enoch, and Noah, and Abraham, and Isaac, and Jacob, and Moses, and David, and the prophets,—the saints of the New Testament, like the Apostles, the saints among the primitive Christians, and the Reformers,—when all these are brought together, they will be "a multitude which no man can number."

(d) There will be "many" when the true Christians are gathered together, who are now scattered over the face of the globe, and not known either by the Church or the world. There are not a few who belong to no congregation, and are not numbered on any list of communicants, though their names are in the Lamb's book of life. Some of them live and die in great neglected parishes unknown and unvisited. Some of them get hold of the truth by hearing the gospel preached by missionaries at home or abroad; though the preacher has never known them, and they have never been formally enrolled in the list of converts. Some of them are soldiers and sailors, who stand alone in regiments and on-board ship, and are not understood by their companions. There are myriads of such persons, I believe, who live the life of faith, and love Christ, and are known to the Lord, though not known by men. These also will make a large addition to the "multitude which no man can number."

The plain truth is, that the family of God will be found at last much larger than most of us suppose it is. We look at the things, we see with our own eyes, and we forget how much there is going on in the world, in Europe, Asia, Africa, and America, which our eyes never see at all. The inner life of the vast majority of all around us is a hidden thing, of which we know nothing. We do not think of the ages that are past, and the countless millions who are now "dust and ashes," though each in his turn fell asleep in Christ, and was carried to Abraham's bosom. No doubt it is perfectly true, that "wide is the gate, and broad is the way, that leads to destruction, and many there be which go in thereat" (Matt. 7:13). It is fearful to think what an immense majority of all around us appear dead in sin, and utterly unprepared to meet God. But, for all that, we must not underrate the number of God's children. Even supposing they are in a minority, when judged by human estimate, they will still prove at last to be very many in the kingdom of glory, an enormous company, "a multitude which no man can number."

Is any reader of this paper disposed to laugh at religion, because those who profess it decidedly are few in number? Are you secretly inclined to despise those who read their Bibles, and make a conscience of keeping their Sundays holy, and trying to walk closely with God? Are you afraid of making a profession yourself, because you think there will be so few with you and so many against you, and you do not like to be singular, and stand alone? Alas! there have always been many like you! When Noah built the Ark, there were few with him, and many mocked at him; but he was found to be in the right at last. When the Jews were rebuilding the wall of Jerusalem after the return from Babylon, Sanballat and Tobiah scoffed at them, and said, "What do these feeble Jews?"—When the Lord Jesus Christ left the world, only a hundred and twenty disciples met together in the upper chamber in Jerusalem, while the friends of the unbelieving Pharisees, and scribes, and priests were numbered by tens of thousands. But the disciples were right, and their enemies were wrong.—When bloody Mary sat on the throne, and Latimer and Ridley were burnt at the stake, the friends of the gospel seemed very few, and their enemies were a great majority. Yet the Reformers were right, and their enemies were wrong.—Take care what you are doing! Beware of judging vital Christianity by the small number of those who seem to profess it. You may have the crowd with you now, and the laugh may be on your side. But a day is coming when you will open your eyes with amazement, and find out, perhaps too late, that the very people whom you despised were not few, but "many," a vast company, "a multitude which no man can number."

Is any reader of this paper disposed to be cast down and discouraged, because he loves Christ, and tries to serve Him, but finds himself almost entirely alone? Does your heart sometimes fail you, and your hands hang down, and your knees wax faint, because you so seldom meet any one whom you can pray with, and praise with, and read with, and talk with about Christ, and open your heart to without fear? Do you ever mourn in secret for want of company? Well, you are only drinking the cup which many have drunk before you. Abraham, and Isaac, and Jacob, and Joseph, and Moses, and Samuel, and David, and the prophets, and Paul, and John, and the Apostles were all people who stood very much alone. Do you expect to fare better than them? Take comfort, and have faith. There is more grace in the world than you can see, and more Christians travelling towards heaven than you are aware of. Elijah thought he stood alone, when there were "seven thousand in Israel who had not bowed the knee to Baal." Take comfort, and look forward. Your good time is coming. You will have plenty of company by and by. You will find many and not few in the kingdom of heaven, many to welcome you, many to rejoice and praise with many with whom you will spend a blessed eternity. How pleasant it is to meet a single saint now for a few short hours! How it cheers and refreshes us, like snow in summer or sunshine after clouds! What, then, will it be when we shall see an enormous company of saints, without a single unconverted sinner to spoil the harmony, all men and women of faith, and none unbelievers, all wheat and no chaff, "a multitude which no man can number"! Surely the "many" we shall see in heaven will make ample amends for the "few" that we now see upon earth.

II. We have, secondly, in our Lord Jesus Christ's words, the dwellings and position of those who shall be finally saved. It is written "that they shall come from the east and the west."

There can be little doubt that this expression is a proverbial one. It must not be taken literally, as if the saved were not to come from the north and south, but only from the rising and setting of the sun. We find the same expression in Psalm 103:12, where it is said, "As far as the east is from the west, so far hath He removed our transgressions from us." The meaning is simply this: The saved shall come from different places, from distant places, and from places where you would have thought it most unlikely they would be found.

(a) They will not all have belonged to one Church. There will be Episcopalians, and Presbyterians, and Independents, and Baptists, and Methodists, and Plymouth Brethren, and many other kinds of Christians whom I have neither space nor time to name. However much they may disagree and dispute now, they will have to agree at last. They will find to their amazement that the points upon which they were of one mind were a vast quantity, and the points on which they differed were very few. They will all be able to say with one heart, "Hallelujah! praise to Him who loved us, and washed us from our sins in His own blood!" And they will all be able to reply with one voice, "Amen, amen!" The anthem in heaven, said good George Whitefield, will be to all eternity, "What hath God wrought!" The points of earthly disagreement will have dropped off, and melted like snow in spring. The common teaching of the Holy Ghost will stand out clear and plain before every eye in heaven. At length there will be one real "Holy Catholic Church," without spot or blemish or any such thing, without quarrelling, controversy, or dissension, all wheat and no tares, all sound members and none unsound.

(b) They will come from various countries in every part of the globe, from Greenland's icy mountains, and the scorching regions of the tropics, from India and Australia, from America and from China, from New Zealand and the Islands of the Pacific Ocean, from Africa and from Mexico. Some will have laid their bones in solitary graves like Henry Martyn in Persia, with none to do them honour in their death. Some will have been buried at sea with a sailor's funeral. Some will have died the death of martyrs, and been burnt to ashes like our own Reformers. Some will have fallen victims to malignant climates, or heathen violence at missionary stations. And some will have died, like Moses, in places where no human eye saw them. But they shall all come together, and meet again in the kingdom of heaven. It matters little where we are buried, and how we are buried, and in what kind of a grave. China is just as near to heaven as England is, and the sea shall give up her dead at the same moment as the land. Our coffin, and our funeral, and the burial service, and the long procession of mourners, are all matters of very secondary importance. The one point we should aim to make sure, from whatever place we may come, is to be amongst those who "shall sit down in the kingdom of heaven."

(c) They shall come from utterly different ranks, classes, and professions. Heaven will be a place for servants as well as masters, for maids as well as mistresses, for poor as well as rich, for the unlearned as well as the learned, for tenants as well as landlords, for subjects as well as rulers, for the pauper as well as the Queen. There is no royal road to heaven, and there will be no class distinctions when we get there. At length there will be perfect equality, perfect fraternity, and perfect freedom. It will matter nothing whether we had much money on earth, or none at all. The only question will be, whether we have really repented of our sins, really believed on the Lord Jesus, and were really converted and sanctified people. There will be no preference given to those who have come from monasteries, nunneries, or hermits' caves. It is very likely that those who have done their duty in that state of life to which God called them, and have carried Christ's cross in the army or the navy, in Parliament or at the bar, in the bank or the merchant's office, behind the counter or at the bottom of a coal-pit, will be found in the first rank in the kingdom of heaven. It is not necessary to wear a peculiar dress, or to put on an austere countenance, and to retire from the world, in order to sit down in the kingdom of heaven.

(d) They shall come from most unlikely places, and from positions in which you would have thought the seed of eternal life could never have grown up in a soul. Saul, the young Pharisee, came from the feet of Gamaliel, and from persecuting Christians, and rose to be the great Apostle of the Gentiles, who turned the world upside down. Daniel lived in Babylon, and served God faithfully in the midst of idolatry and heathenism. Peter was once a fisherman on the sea of Galilee. Matthew was a public tax-gatherer, who spent his days in receiving custom. Luther and Latimer began life as devoted Papists, and ended life as devoted Protestants. John Bunyan, the author of the Pilgrim's Progress, was once a careless, thoughtless, swearing, bell-ringing young man, in a country village. George Whitefield served in a public-house at Gloucester, and spent his early days in cleaning pots and carrying out beer. John Newton, the author of well-known hymns and letters, was once the captain of a slave-ship on the coasts of Africa, and saw no harm in buying and selling human flesh and blood. All these truly "came from east and west," and seemed at one time in their lives the most unlikely people in the world to come to Christ, and "sit down in the kingdom of heaven." But they did come unmistakably, and they are an everlasting proof that our Lord Jesus Christ's words are strictly true. Men and women may "come from the east and west," and yet be found at last in the kingdom of eternal happiness and glory.

Let us learn never to despair of the salvation of any one as long as he lives. Fathers ought never to despair of prodigal sons. Mothers ought never to despair of self-willed, headstrong daughters. Husbands should never despair of wives, nor wives of husbands.

There is nothing impossible with God. The arm of grace is very long, and can reach those who seem very far off. The Holy Ghost can change any heart. The blood of Christ can cleanse away any sin. Let us pray on, and hope on for others, however unlikely their salvation may appear to be at present. We shall see many in heaven whom we never expected to see there. The last may yet prove first, and the first last. The famous Grimshaw, the Apostle of Yorkshire, when he died, left his only son unconverted, careless, thoughtless, and indifferent to religion. The day came when the young man's heart was changed, and he walked in the steps of his father. And when he lay upon his death-bed, one of his last words was, "What will my old father say when he sees me in heaven!"

Let us learn not to sorrow "as those who have no hope," when we part from friends who are true Christians, and part, perhaps, for ever. The separations and goodbyes of this world are probably some of its most painful things. When the family circle is broken up, when the old nest begins to lose its inmates, when the young man sets sail for Australia, New Zealand, or the Fiji Islands, with no hope of returning for ten or twelve years,—when these things take place, it is a sore trial to flesh and blood. I have witnessed scenes on the landing-stage at Liverpool, when the great steamships are about to start for America, which might bring tears to the eyes of the most cold-hearted stranger. The partings of this world are terrible things; but true faith in Christ, and the resurrection to eternal life through Him, takes the sting out of the worst of partings. It enables a believer to look beyond the things seen to the things unseen, to the coming of the Saviour, and our gathering together unto Him. Yes, it is a pleasant thing to remember, as the great ship moves away, and we wave our last adieus, "it is but a little time, and we shall see them all again to part no more." God's people shall come together from east and west, and we shall all meet at last "in the kingdom of heaven," and go out no more.

III. We have, thirdly, in our Lord Jesus Christ's words, the future portion and reward of those who shall be finally saved. It is written, "they shall sit down in the kingdom of heaven."

That expression, "sit down," is a very pleasant and comfortable one to my mind. Let us sift it, and examine it, and see what it contains. In the judgment day, believers shall STAND with boldness at the right hand of Christ, and say, "Who shall lay anything to the charge of God's elect? It is God that justifieth. Who is he that condemneth? It is Christ that died, yea rather, that is risen again, who is even at the right hand of God, who also maketh intercession for us" (Rom. 8:33-34). But when the judgment is passed and over, and the eternal kingdom begins, they shall "SIT DOWN."

(a) Sitting down implies a sense of confidence and being at home. If we were in the presence of a stern judge, or of a king clothed in awful majesty, we should not dare to sit down. But there will be nothing to make believers afraid in the kingdom of heaven. The sins of their past lives will not make them tremble and feel alarmed. However many, however great, and however black, they will all have been washed away in Christ's precious blood, and not one spot will remain. Completely justified, completely absolved, completely forgiven, completely "accepted in the Beloved," they will be counted righteous before God for the sake of Him who was "made sin for us, though He knew no sin" (2 Cor. 5:21). Though the sins of their lives "were as scarlet, they shall be made white as snow; and though red like crimson, they shall be as wool." Their sins will be "remembered no more," "sought for, and not found," "blotted out as a thick cloud," "cast behind God's back," "plunged in the depths of the sea." Believers will need no purgatory after they die. It is ignorance and unbelief to think so. Once joined to Christ by faith, they are complete in the sight of God the Father, and even the perfect angels shall see no spot in them. Surely they may well sit down, and feel at home! They may remember all the sins of their past lives, and be humbled at the recollection of them. But those sins will not make them afraid.

The sense of daily failure, weakness, imperfection, and inward conflict, will no longer mar their peace. At last their sanctification will be completed. The war within shall come to a perfect end. Their old besetting sins and infirmities will have dropped off, and melted away. At length they shall be able to serve God without weariness, and attend on Him without distraction, and not be obliged to cry continually, "Wretched man that I am, who shall deliver me from the body of this death?" (Rom. 7:24). Who can tell the blessedness of all this while we are yet in the body? Here in this world we do not realize the completeness of our justification, and "groan, being burdened," by reason of our imperfect sanctification. Our best endeavours after holiness are accompanied by a sorrowful consciousness of daily failure. But when "the old man" is at last entirely dead, and the flesh no longer lusts against the spirit,—when there is an end of indwelling sin, and the world and the devil can no longer tempt us,—then at last we shall understand what God has prepared for them that love Him. We shall "sit down in the kingdom of heaven."

(b) But this is not all. Sitting down implies rest, and a complete cessation of work, and toil, and conflict. There is a rest that remaineth for the people of God. Here in this life we are never still. The Word of God tells us, that the Christian must "walk," and "run," and "work," and "labour," and "fight," and "groan," and "carry the cross," and wear the "armour," and stand like a sentinel on guard in an enemy's land. It is not till we enter the kingdom of heaven that we must expect to "sit down." Work for Christ, no doubt, is pleasant, and even in this life brings a rich reward,—the reward of a happy conscience, a reward which the mere politician, or merchant, or man of pleasure can never reap, because they only seek a corruptible crown. "They that drink of these waters shall thirst again." But even the Christian's work is exhausting to flesh and blood; and so long as we dwell in a mortal body, work and weariness will go together. The very sight of sin in others, which we cannot check, is a daffy trial to our souls. No doubt the fight of faith is a "good fight," but there never can be fighting without wounds, and pain, and fatigue. The very armour the Christian is bid to put on is heavy. The helmet and the breastplate, the shield and the sword, without which we cannot overcome the devil, can never be worn without constant exertion.

Surely it will be a blessed time when our enemies will all be slain, and we can lay aside our armour in safety, and "sit down in the kingdom of heaven."

In the meantime let us never forget that the time is short. Even the devil knows that, and "has great wrath because he has but a short time" (Rev. 12:12). Let us work on, and fight on, in full assurance of hope, with the blessed recollection that it shall not be for ever. When the great battle of Waterloo was raging, and the event of the day seemed to tremble in the balance, it is said that the Duke of Wellington kept calmly turning his eyes to the left, in the confident expectation that in a little time his Prussian allies would appear, and his victory would be sure. Let this kind of hope animate our souls when we are bearing the labour and heat of the day. Our King is soon coming, and when He comes we shall "sit down," and toil and fight no more.

IV. The fourth and last thing which the words of our Lord Jesus Christ contain is, the company which those who are finally saved shall enjoy for ever.

Now, company is one great secret of happiness. Man is by nature a social being. It is a rare exception indeed to find any one who likes to be always alone. A palace filled with untold wealth and luxuries, would at last be little better than a prison if we lived in it entirely alone. A cottage with congenial companions is a happier dwelling-place than a royal castle with no one to speak to, no one to listen to, no one to exchange mind with, nothing to converse with, but ends own poor heart. We all want some one to live with and love, and the dweller in a solitary island, like Robinson Crusoe, is never satisfied, if he is a real man. Our blessed Lord, who formed man out of the dust of the earth, and made him what he is, knows that perfectly well When, therefore, He describes the future portion of His believing people, He takes care to tell us what kind of company they shall have in the kingdom of heaven. He says that the saved shall "sit down with Abraham, Isaac, and Jacob" in the world to come.

Now what does that expression mean? Let us look at it, analyse it, and see what it contains.

The companions of the saved in the eternal world shall be all the believers who have ever lived on earth, from the beginning to the end. The old soldiers, the old pilgrims, the old servants of Christ, the old members of Christ's family, all, in a word, who have lived by faith and served Christ, and walked with God, these shall form the company in which the saved shall spend an endless existence.

They shall see all the old worthies of whom they read in the Old Testament,—the patriarchs, the prophets, and the holy kings, who looked forward to the coming of Christ, but died without seeing Him. They shall see the New Testament saints, the Apostles, and the holy men and women who saw Christ face to face. They shall see the early Fathers who died for the truth, and were thrown to the lions, or beheaded under the persecution of the Roman emperors. They shall see the gallant Reformers who revived the gospel out of the dust on the Continent, and unstopped the wells of living water which Rome had filled up with rubbish. They shall see the blessed martyrs of our own land who brought about the glorious Protestant Reformation, and gave the Bible to our countrymen in the English tongue, and cheerfully died at the stake for the cause of the gospel. They shall see the holy men of the last century, Whitefield, and Wesley, Romaine, and their companions, who, in the face of bitter opposition, revived religion in the Church of England. Above all, they shall see their own friends who fell asleep in Christ, and whom they once followed to their graves, with many tears, and see them with the comfortable thought that they shall part no more. Surely the thought of such companionship as this should cheer us as we travel on the narrow way! It is a good thing yet to come.

There is little happiness in company unless there is entire sympathy and congeniality of taste. It is one of the heaviest trials of a true Christian upon earth, that he meets so few people who are entirely of one mind with him about religion. How often in society he finds himself obliged to hold his tongue and say nothing, and to hear and see many things which make his heart ache, and send him back to his own home heavy and depressed! It is a rare privilege to meet two or three occasionally to whom he can open his heart, and with whom he can speak freely, without fear of giving offence or being misunderstood. But there will be an end of this state of things in the kingdom of heaven. Those who are saved will find none there who have not been led by the same Spirit, and gone through the same experience as themselves. There will not be a man or woman there who has not felt deeply the burden of sin, mourned over it, confessed it, fought with it, and tried to crucify it. There will not be a man or woman there who has not fled to Christ by faith, cast the whole weight of his soul upon Him, and rejoiced in Him as his Redeemer. There will not be a man or woman there who has not delighted in the Word of God, poured out his soul in prayer at the throne of grace, and striven to live a holy life. In a word, there will be none there who have not known something of repentance toward God, faith toward our Lord Jesus Christ, and holiness of life and conversation. It is pleasant to meet a few people of this kind on earth as we travel along the narrow way that leads to heaven. It refreshes us like a brook by the way, and is like a little peep within the veil. But what will it be when we see "a multitude, which no man can number," of saints completely delivered from all sin, and not one single unconverted person among them to mar the harmony!

What shall it be when we shall meet our own believing friends once more, at last made perfect, and find that their besetting sins, and our own besetting sins, have all passed away, and there is nothing left in us but grace without corruption! Yet all this is to come when we pass within the veil. The inhabitants are not to be a mixed multitude, unable to understand one another. They are all to be of one heart and of one mind. We are not to sit down amidst ignorant, godless, and unconverted people, but "with Abraham, Isaac, and Jacob in the kingdom of heaven." Heaven itself would be no heaven if all sorts of characters got there, as some people falsely teach. There could be no order and no happiness in such a heaven. There must be "meetness for the inheritance of the saints in light" (Col. 1:12).

(1) And now, reader, before you lay down this paper, ask yourself whether you shall be found among the many who shall "sit down in the kingdom of heaven." The question demands an answer. I charge you to give your soul no rest until you can answer it in a satisfactory way. Time is passing quickly away, and the world is growing old. The signs of the times ought to set us all thinking. "The distress of nations with perplexity" seems to increase every year. The wisdom of statesmen seems utterly unable to prevent wars and confusion in every direction. The progress of art, and science, and civilization appear entirely powerless to prevent the existence of enormous moral evils. Nothing will ever cure the diseases of human nature but the return of the Great Physician, the Prince of Peace, the second coming of Jesus Christ Himself. And when He comes, shall you be found among the "many" who shall "sit down with Abraham, Isaac, and Jacob in the kingdom of heaven"?

Why should you not be found among the many? I know no reason except your own want of will, or your own indolence and laziness, or your own determined love of sin and the world. An open door is before you: why not enter into it? The Lord Jesus Christ is able and ready to save you: why not commit your soul to Him, and lay hold on the hand which He holds out from heaven? I repeat that I know no reason why you should not be found amongst the "many" at the last day.

You fancy there is time enough, and no need of hurry or immediate decision. You had better take care what you are saying. It is not given to all men and women to live to threescore years and ten, and then die quietly in their beds. The notice to quit this mortal body sometimes comes very suddenly, and men and women are summoned to go forth in a moment into the unseen world. You had better use time while you have it, and not make shipwreck on that miserable rock, "a convenient season."

Are you afraid that people will laugh at you, and mock you, if you begin to care for your soul, and to seek a place in the kingdom of heaven? Cast the cowardly feeling behind your back, and resolve never to be ashamed of religion. Alas! there are too many who will find at last that they were laughed out of heaven, and laughed into hell. Fear not the reproach of man, who at most can only injure your body. Fear Him who is able to destroy both soul and body in hell. Lay hold boldly on Christ, and He will give you the victory over all that you now fear. He that enabled the Apostle Peter, who once ran away and denied his Master, to stand firm as a rock before the Jewish Council, and at length to die for the gospel, is still living at the right hand of God, and is able to save to the uttermost all who come to God by Him, and to make you more than conqueror.

Do you think that you will not be happy if you seek to have your soul saved, and to sit down in the kingdom of heaven? Cast aside the unworthy thought as a lying suggestion of the devil. There are no people so truly happy as true Christians. Whatever a sneering world may please to say, they have meat to eat which the world knows not, and inward comforts which the world cannot understand. There is no gloominess in true religion, and no religion in looking gloomy, sour, or austere. In spite of cross and conflict, the true Christian has an inward peace compared to which the world has nothing to give; for it is a peace which trouble, bereavement, sickness, and death itself cannot take away. The words of the Master are strictly true, "Peace I leave with you, My peace I give unto you: not as the world giveth, give I unto you. Let not your heart be troubled, neither let it be afraid" (John 14:27). If men and women want to be truly happy, they should strive to be amongst those who "shall sit down in the kingdom of heaven."

(2) Last, but not least, let me wind up all by offering a word of exhortation and encouragement to those who have reason to hope that they are among the many who shall sit down in the kingdom of heaven.

Would you have much joy and peace in believing? Try to do all the good you can in the world. There is always much to be done, and few to do it. There are always many living and dying in ignorance and sin, and no one goes near them, and tries to save their souls. We live in days when there is much talk about High Churchism, and Low Churchism, and Broad Churchism, and Ritualism, and Rationalism, and Scepticism, but little real Christian work done to mend the evils of the times! If all the Communicants in all our churches laid themselves out to go among those who are without God in the world, with the Bible in their hands, and Christlike loving sympathy in their hearts, they would soon be far happier than they are now, and the face of society would soon be changed. Idleness is one great cause of the low spirits of which so many complain. Too many, far too many Christians, seem quite content to go to heaven alone, and to care nothing about bringing others into the kingdom of God.

If you try to do good in the right way, you never need doubt that good will be done. Many a Sunday-school teacher comes home on Sunday night with a heavy heart, and fancies that his or her labour is all in vain. Many a visitor returns from his rounds, and thinks he is producing no effect. Many a minister comes down from his pulpit desponding and cast down, imagining that his preaching is to no purpose. But all this is disgraceful unbelief. There is often far more going on in hearts and consciences than we see. "He that goeth forth weeping, but sowing precious seed, shall come again with joy at the last day, and bring his sheaves with him" (Ps. 126:6). There are more being converted and saved than we suppose. "Many shall sit down in the kingdom of heaven" whom we never expected to see there when we died. Let us read on, and pray on, and visit on, and speak on, and tell of Christ to every one whom we can get at. If we are only "stedfast, unmovable, always abounding in the work of the Lord," we shall find, to our amazement, that our labour was not in vain in the Lord (1 Cor. 15:58).

But if we try to do good, we must always cultivate patience. We cannot have two heavens: a heaven here, and a heaven hereafter. The battle is not yet over. The harvest-time is not yet come. The devil is not yet bound. The time when our Lord's promise shall be fulfilled is not yet arrived. But it will arrive before long. When our gracious Queen at the end of the Crimean war came forward in front of the Horse Guards, and with her own royal hands gave the Victoria Cross to the gallant soldiers who had earned it, that public honour made rich amends for all that those soldiers had gone through. Balaklava, and Inkerman, and the hardships of the trenches were all forgotten for the time, and seemed comparatively small things. What, then, will be the joy when the Captain of our salvation shall gather His faithful soldiers round Him, and give to each one a crown of glory that fadeth not away! Surely we may well wait in patience for that day. It is coming, and will surely come at last. Remembering that day, let us cast behind us doubts and unbelief, and set our faces steadily towards Jerusalem. "The night is far spent, and the day is at hand" (Rom. 13:12). Not one word of the blessed promise before us shall fail: "Many shall come from the east and the west, and shall sit down with Abraham, Isaac, and Jacob, in the kingdom of heaven."

CHAPTER XIV[17]

2 Sam. 23:4-5
Without Clouds.

"He shall be as the light of the morning, when the sun rises, even a morning without clouds; as the tender grass springeth out of the earth by clear shining after rain. Although my house be not so with God; yet He hath made with me an everlasting covenant, ordered in all things, and sure: for this is all my salvation, and all my desire, although He make it not to grow." —2 Sam. 23:4-5.

THE text which heads this page is taken from a chapter which ought to be very interesting to every Christian. It begins with the touching expression, "These be the last words of David."

Whether that means, "these are the last words which David ever spoke by inspiration as a Psalmist," or "these are among the last sayings of David before his death," signifies little. In either point of view, the phrase suggests many thoughts.

It contains the experience of an old servant of God who had many ups and downs in his life. It is the old soldier remembering his campaigns. It is the old traveller looking back on his journeys.

I. Let us first consider David's humbling cotillion.

He looks forward with a prophetic eye to the future coming of the Messiah, the promised Saviour, the seed of Abraham, and the seed of David. He looks forward to the Advent of a glorious kingdom in which there shall be no wickedness, and righteousness shall be the universal character of all the subjects. He looks forward to the final gathering of a perfect family in which there shall be no unsound members, no defects, no sin, no sorrow, no deaths, no tears. And he says, the light of that kingdom shall be "as the light of the morning when the sun riseth, even a morning without clouds."

---

[17]The substance of this paper was delivered as an address at the opening of the Chapel of the Turner Memorial Home of Rest, the Dingle, Liverpool, October 16th, 1885.

But then he turns to his own family, and sorrowfully says, "My house is not so with God." It is not perfect, it is not free from sin, and it has blots and blemishes of many kinds. It has cost me many tears. It is not so as I could wish, and so as I have vainly tried to make it.

Poor David might well say this! If ever there was a man whose house was full of trials, and whose life was full of sorrows, that man was David. Trials from the envy of his own brethren,—trials from the unjust persecution of Saul, retrials from his own servants, such as Joab and Ahithophel,—trials from a wife, even that Michal who once loved him so much,—trials from his children, such as Absalom, Amnon, and Adonijah,—trials from his own subjects, who at one time forgot all he had done, and drove him out of Jerusalem by rebellion,—trials of all kinds, wave upon wave, were continually breaking on David to the very end of his days. Some of the worst of these trials, no doubt, were the just consequences of his own sins, and the wise chastisement of a loving Father. But we must have hard hearts if we do not feel that David was indeed "a man of sorrows."

But is not this the experience of many of God's noblest saints and dearest children? What careful reader of the Bible can fail to see that Adam, and Noah, and Abraham, and Isaac, and Jacob, and Joseph, and Moses, and Samuel, were all men of many sorrows, and that those sorrows chiefly arose out of their own homes?

The plain truth is, that home trials are one of the many means by which God sanctifies and purifies His believing people. By them He keeps us humble. By them He draws us to Himself. By them He sends us to our Bibles. By them He teaches us to pray. By them He shows us our need of Christ. By them He weans us from the world. By them He prepares us for "a city which hath foundations," in which there will be no disappointments, no tears, and no sin. It is no special mark of God's favour when Christians have no trials. They are spiritual medicines, which poor fallen human nature absolutely needs. King Solomon's course was one of unbroken peace and prosperity. But it may well be doubted whether this was good for his soul.

Before we leave this part of our subject, let us learn some practical lessons.

(a) Let us learn that parents cannot give grace to their children, or masters to their servants. We may use all means, but we cannot command success. We may teach, but we cannot convert. We may show those around us the bread and water of life, but we cannot make them eat and drink it. We may point out the way to eternal life, but we cannot make others walk in it. "It is the Spirit that quickeneth." Life is that one thing which the cleverest man of science cannot create or impart. It comes "not of blood, nor of the will of man" (John 1:13). To give life is the grand prerogative of God.

(b) Let us learn not to expect too much from anybody or anything in this fallen world. One great secret of unhappiness is the habit of indulging in exaggerated expectations. From money, from marriage, from business, from houses, from children, from worldly honours, from political success, men are constantly expecting what they never find; and the great majority die disappointed. Happy is he who has learned to say at all times, "My soul, wait thou only upon God; my expectation is from Him" (Ps. 62:5).

(c) Let us learn not to be surprised or fret when trials come. It is a wise saying of Job, "Man is born to trouble as the sparks fly upward" (Job 5:7). Some, no doubt, have a larger cup of sorrows to drink than others. But few live long without troubles or cares of some kind. The greater our affections the deeper are our afflictions, and the more we love the more we have to weep. The only certain thing to be predicted about the babe lying in his cradle is this,—if he grows up, he will have many troubles, and at last he will die.

(d) Let us learn, lastly, that God knows far better than we do what is the best time for taking away from us those whom we love. The deaths of some of David's children were painfully remarkable, both as to age, manner, and circumstances. When David's little infant lay sick, David thought he would have liked the child to live, and he fasted and mourned till all was over. Yet, when the last breath was drawn, he said, with strong assurance of seeing the child again, "I shall go to him, but he shall not return to me" (2 Sam. 12:23). But when, on the contrary, Absalom died in battle—Absalom the beautiful Absalom the darling of his heart—but Absalom who died in open sin against God and his father, what did David say then? Hear his hopeless cry, "O Absalom, my son, my son, would God I had died for thee!" (2 Sam. 18:33). Alas! we none of us know when it is best for ourselves, our children, and our friends to die. We should pray to be able to say, "My times are in Thy hands," let it be when Thou wilt, where Thou wilt, and how Thou wilt (Ps. 31:15).

II. Let us consider, secondly, what was the source of David's present comfort in life. He says, "Though my house is not as I could wish, and is the cause of much sorrow, God has made with me an everlasting covenant, ordered in all things, and sure." And then he adds, "This is all my salvation, and all my desire."

Now this word "covenant" is a deep and mysterious thing, when applied to anything that God does. We can understand what a covenant is between man and man. It is an agreement between two persons, by which they bind themselves to fulfil certain conditions and do certain things. But who can fully understand a covenant made by the Eternal God? It is something far above us and out of sight. It is a phrase by which He is graciously pleased to accommodate Himself to our poor weak faculties, but at best we can only grasp a little of it.

The covenant of God to which David refers as his comfort must mean that everlasting agreement or counsel between the Three Persons of the Blessed Trinity which has existed from all eternity for the benefit of all the living members of Christ.

It is a mysterious and ineffable arrangement whereby all things necessary for the salvation of our souls, our present peace, and our final glory, are fully and completely provided, and all this by the joint work of God the Father, God the Son, and God the Holy Ghost. The redeeming work of God the Son by dying as our Substitute on the cross,—the drawing work of God the Father by choosing and drawing us to the Son,—and the sanctifying work of the Holy Ghost in awakening, quickening, and renewing our fallen nature,—are all contained in this covenant, besides everything that the soul of the believer needs between grace and glory.

Of this covenant, the Second Person of the Trinity is the Mediator (Heb. 12:24). Through Him all the blessings and privileges of the covenant are conveyed to every one of His believing members. And when the Bible speaks of God making a covenant with man, as in the words of David, it means with man in Christ as a member and part of the Son. They are His mystical body, and He is their Head, and through the Head all the blessings of the eternal covenant are conveyed to the body. Christ, in one word, is "the Surety of the covenant," and through Him believers receive its benefits. This is the great covenant which David had in view.

True Christians would do well to think about this covenant, remember it, and roll the burden of their souls upon it far more than they do. There is unspeakable consolation in the thought that the salvation of our souls has been provided for from all eternity, and is not a mere affair of yesterday. Our names have long been in the Lamb's book of life. Our pardon and peace of conscience through Christ's blood, our strength for duty, our comfort in trial, our power to fight Christ's battles, were all arranged for us from endless ages, and long before we were born. Here upon earth we pray, and read, and fight, and struggle, and groan, and weep, and are often sore and hindered in our journey. But we ought to remember that an Almighty eye has long been upon us, and that we have been the subjects of divine provision though we knew it not.

Above all, Christians should never forget that the everlasting covenant is "ordered in all things and sure." The least things in our daily life are working together for good, though we may not see it at the time. The very hairs of our head are all numbered, and not a sparrow falls to the ground without our Father. There is no luck or chance in anything that happens to us. The least events in our life are parts of an everlasting scheme or plan in which God has foreseen and arranged everything for the good of our souls.

Let us all try to cultivate the habit of remembering the everlasting covenant. It is a doctrine full of strong consolation, if it is properly used. It was not meant to destroy our responsibility. It is widely different from Mohammedan fatalism. It is specially intended to be a refreshing cordial for practical use in a world full of sorrow and trial. We ought to remember, amid the many sorrows and disappointments of life, that "what we know not now, we shall know hereafter." There is a meaning and a "needs be" in every bitter cup that we have to drink, and a wise cause for every loss and bereavement under which we mourn.

After all, how little we know! We are like children who look at a half-finished building, and have not the least idea what it will look like when it is completed. They see masses of stone, and brick, and rubbish, and timber, and mortar, and scaffolding, and dirt, and all in apparent confusion. But the architect who designed the building sees order in all, and quietly looks forward with joy to the day when the whole building will be finished, and the scaffolding removed and taken away. It is even so with us. We cannot grasp the meaning of many a providence in our lives, and are tempted to think that all around us is confusion. But we should try to remember that the great Architect in heaven is always doing wisely and well, and that we are always being "led by the right way to a city of habitation" (Ps. 107:7). The resurrection morning will explain all. It is a quaint but wise saying of an old divine, that "true faith has blight eyes, and can see even in the dark."

It is recorded of Barnard Gilpin, a Reformer who lived in the days of the Marian martyrdoms, and was called the Apostle of the North, that he was famous for never murmuring or complaining, whatever happened to him. In the worst and blackest times he used to be always saying, "It is all in God's everlasting covenant, and must be for good." Towards the close of Queen Mary's reign, he was suddenly summoned to come up from Durham to London, to be tried for heresy, and in all probability, like Ridley and Latimer, to be burned. The good man quietly obeyed the summons, and said to his mourning friends, "It is in the covenant, and must be for good." On his journey from Durham to London, his horse fell, and his leg was broken, and he was laid up at a roadside inn. Once more he was asked, "What do you think of this?" Again he replied, "It is all in the covenant, and must be for good." And so it turned out. Weeks and weeks passed away before his leg was healed, and he was able to resume his journey. But during those weeks the unhappy Queen Mary died, the persecutions were stopped, and the worthy old Reformer returned to his northern home rejoicing. "Did I not tell you," he said to his friends, "that all was working together for good?"

Well would it be for us if we had something of Barnard Gilpin's faith, and could make practical use of the everlasting covenant as he did. Happy is the Christian who can say from his heart these words,—

> *"I know not the way I am going,*
>   *But well do I know my Guide;*
> *With a childlike trust I give my hand*
>   *To the mighty Friend by my side.*
> *The only thing that I say to Him,*
>   *As He takes it, is—'Hold it fast;*
> *Suffer me not to lose my way,*
>   *And bring me home at last.'"*

III. Let us consider, lastly, what was King David's hope for the future. That hope, beyond doubt, was the glorious advent of the Messiah at the end of the world, and the setting up of a kingdom of righteousness, at the final "restitution of all things" (Acts 3:21).

Of course king David's views of this kingdom were dim and vague compared to those which are within reach of every intelligent reader of the New Testament. He was not ignorant of the coming of Messiah to suffer, for he speaks of it in the 22nd Psalm. But he saw far behind it the coming of Messiah to reign, and his eager faith overleaped the interval between the two Advents. That his mind was fixed upon the promise, that the "seed of the woman should" one day completely "bruise the serpent's head," and that the curse should be taken off the earth, and the effects of Adam's fall completely removed, I feel no doubt at all. The Church of Christ would have done well if she had walked in David's steps, and given as much attention to the Second Advent as David did.

The figures and comparisons which David uses in speaking of the advent and future kingdom of the Messiah are singularly beautiful, and admirably fitted to exhibit the benefits which it will bring to the Church and the earth. The Second Advent of Christ shall be "as the light of the morning when the sun riseth, even a morning without clouds; as the tender grass springing out of the earth by clear shining after rain." Those words deserve a thousand thoughts. Who can look around him, and consider the state of the world in which we live, and not be obliged to confess that clouds and darkness are now on every side? "The whole creation groaneth and travaileth in pain" (Rom. 8:22). Look where we will, we see confusion, quarrels, wars between nations, helplessness of statesmen, discontent and grumbling of the lower classes, excessive luxury among the rich, extreme poverty among the poor, intemperance, impurity, dishonesty, swindling, lying, cheating, covetousness, heathenism, superstition, formality among Christians, decay of vital religion,—these are the things which we see continually over the whole globe, in Europe, Asia, Africa, and America. These are the things which defile the face of creation, and prove that the devil is "the prince of this world," and the kingdom of God is not yet come. These are clouds indeed, which often hide the sun from our eyes.

But there is a good time coming, which David saw far distant, when this state of things shall be completely changed. There is a kingdom coming, in which holiness shall be the rule, and sin shall have no place at all.

Who can look around him in his own neighbourhood, and fail to see within a mile of his own house that the consequences of sin lie heavily on earth, and that sorrow and trouble abound? Sickness, and pain, and death come to all classes, and spare none, whether rich or poor. The young often die before the old, and the children before the parents. Bodily suffering of the most fearful description, and incurable disease, make the existence of many miserable. Widowhood, and childlessness, and solitariness, tempt many to feel weary of life, though everything which money can obtain is within their reach. Family quarrels, and envies, and jealousies break up the peace of many a household, and are a worm at the root of many a rich man's happiness. Who can deny that all these things are to be seen on every side of us? There are many clouds now.

Will nothing end this state of things? Is creation to go on groaning and travailing for ever after this fashion? Thanks be to God, the Second Advent of Christ supplies an answer to these questions. The Lord Jesus Christ has not yet finished His work on behalf of man. He will come again one day (and perhaps very soon) to set up a glorious kingdom, in which the consequences of sin shall have no place at all. It is a kingdom in which there shall be no pain and no disease, in which "the inhabitant shall no more say, I am sick" (Isa. 33:24). It is a kingdom in which there shall be no partings, no moves, no changes, and no good-byes. It is a kingdom in which there shall be no deaths, no funerals, no tears, and no mourning worn. It is a kingdom in which there shall be no quarrels, no losses, no crosses, no disappointments, no wicked children, no bad servants, no faithless friends. When the last trumpet shall sound, and the dead shall be raised incorruptible, there will be a grand gathering together of all God's people, and when we awake up after our Lord's likeness we shall be satisfied (Ps. 17:15). Where is the Christian heart that does not long for this state of things to begin? Well may we take up the last prayer in the Book of Revelation, and often cry, "Come quickly, Lord Jesus" (Rev. 22:20).

(a) And now, have we troubles? Where is the man or woman on earth who can say, "I have none"? Let us take them all to the Lord Jesus Christ. None can comfort like Him. He who died on the cross to purchase forgiveness for our sins, is sitting at the right hand of God with a heart full of love and sympathy. He knows what sorrow is, for He lived thirty-three years in this sinful world, and suffered Himself being tempted, and saw suffering every day. And He has not forgotten it. When He ascended into heaven, to sit at the right hand of the Father, He took a perfect human heart with Him. "He can be touched with the feeling of our infirmities" (Heb. 4:15). He can feel. Almost His last thought upon the cross was for His own mother, and He cares for weeping and bereaved mothers still.

He would have us never forget that our departed friends in Christ are not lost, but only gone before. We shall see them again in the day of gathering together, for "them that sleep in Jesus will God bring with Him" (1 Thess. 4:14). We shall see them in renewed bodies, and know them again, but better, more beautiful, more happy than we ever saw them on earth. Best of all, we shall see them with the comfortable feeling that we meet to part no more.

(b) Have we troubles? Let us never forget the everlasting covenant to which old David clung to the end of his days. It is still in full force. It is not cancelled. It is the property of every believer in Jesus, whether rich or poor, just as much as it was the property of the son of Jesse. Let us never give way to a fretting, murmuring, complaining spirit. Let us firmly believe at the worst of times, that every step in our lives is ordered by the Lord, with perfect wisdom and perfect love, and that we shall see it all at last. Let us not doubt that He is always doing all things well. He is good in giving, and equally good in taking away.

(c) Finally, have we troubles? Let us never forget that one of the best of remedies and most soothing medicines is to try to do good to others, and to be useful. Let us lay ourselves out to make the sorrow less and the joy greater in this sin-burdened world. There is always some good to be done within a few yards of our own doors. Let every Christian strive to do it, and to relieve either bodies or minds.

> *"To comfort and to bless,*
> *To find a balm for woe,*
> *To tend the lone and fatherless,*
> *Is angel's work below."*

Selfish feeding on our own troubles, and lazy poring over our sorrows, are one secret of the melancholy misery in which many spend their lives. If we trust in Jesus Christ's blood, let us remember His example. He ever "went about doing good" (Acts 10:38). He came not to be ministered unto, but to minister, as well as to give His life a ransom for many. Let us try to be like Him. Let us walk in the steps of the good Samaritan, and give help wherever help is really needed. Even a kind word spoken in season is often a mighty blessing. That Old Testament promise is not yet worn out: "Blessed is the man that provideth for the sick and needy; the Lord shall deliver him in the time of trouble" (Ps. 41:1, Prayer-book version).

CHAPTER XV

Canticles 4:12
The Lord's Garden.

THE Lord Jesus Christ has a garden. It is the company of all who are true believers in Him. They are His garden.

Viewed in one light, believers are Jesus Christ's spouse. They are all joined to Him by art everlasting covenant that cannot be broken; wedded to Him by the marriage of faith; taken by Him to be His for ever, with all their debts and liabilities, with all their faults and imperfections. Their old name is gone, they have no name but that of their Bridegroom. God the Father regards them as one with His dear Son. Satan can lay no charge against them. They are the Lamb's wife: "My Beloved is mine, and I am His" (Cant. 2:16).

Viewed in another light, believers are Christ's sister. They are like to Him in many things. They have His Spirit; they love what He loves, and hate what He hates; they count all His members brethren; through Him they have the spirit of adoption, and can say of God, "He is my Father." Faint indeed is their resemblance to their elder Brother! And still they are like.

Viewed in a third light, believers are Christ's garden. Let us see how and in what way.

I. Jesus calls His people a garden, because they are altogether different firm the men of the world. The world is a wilderness: it brings forth little but thorns and thistles; it is fruitful in nought but sin. The children of this world are an untilled wilderness in God's sight. With all their arts and sciences, intellect and skill, eloquence and statesmanship, poetry and refinement,—with all this they are a wilderness, barren of repentance, faith, holiness, and obedience to God. The Lord looks down from heaven, and where He sees no grace, there the Lord can see nothing but a "wilderness" state of things. The Lord Jesus Christ's believing people are the green spot of the earth; the oasis amidst barren deserts; they are His garden.

He calls His people a garden, because they are sweet and beautiful to His mind. He looks on the world, and it grieves Him to the heart: He looks on the little flock of His believing people, and is well pleased. He sees in them the fruit of His travail, and is satisfied. He rejoices in spirit when He sees the kingdom revealed to babes, though the wise and prudent receive it not. As in the day of Noah's sacrifice, He smells a sweet odour and is refreshed. It is very wonderful, very mysterious! Believers are vile in their own eyes, and feel themselves miserable sinners; yet Jesus says, "Thou art all fair,—sweet is thy voice,—thy countenance is comely,—beautiful as Tirzah, comely as Jerusalem, fair as the moon, and clear as the sun" (Cant. 1:15, 4:7, 2:14, 6:10, etc.). Oh, the depths! It sounds incomprehensible and almost incredible; but it is true.

He calls His people a garden, because He delights to walk among them. He sees the children of this world, but He mingles not with them. His eyes are on all their ways, but He does not come down to talk with them, as He did to Abraham, like a man with his friend.

On the other hand, He loves to walk among His candle, sticks, and see whether the light burns brightly. He loves to be present in the assemblies of His saints, and to come in and sup with them, and they with Him. He loves to come with His Father, and make His abode with His disciples; and wheresoever two or three are gathered in His name, there is He. He loves to come into His garden and eat His pleasant fruits; to go down to the beds of spices, and gather lilies; to see whether the vine flourishes, and the tender grape appears, and the pomegranates bud forth (Cant. 7:12). In short, He holds peculiar communion with His people, and deals familiarly with them, as He does not with the world.

He calls His people a garden, because they are useful, and bear fruit and flowers. Where is the real use of the children of this world? Of what value are they, while they continue unconverted? They are unprofitable tenants and worthless cumberers of the ground. They bring no glory to the Lord that bought them; they fulfil not their part in creation; they stand alone in the world of created beings, not doing the work for which their Maker meant them. The heavens declare the glory of God,—the trees, the corn, the grass, the flowers, the streams, the birds speak forth His praise,—but the man of the world does nothing to show that he cares for God, or serves God, or loves God, or feels grateful for Christ's redeeming death.

The Lord's people are not so. They bring Him some revenue of glory. They bear some little fruit, and are not altogether barren and unprofitable servants. Compared to the world, they are a garden.

II. The Lord's garden has a distinctive peculiarity about it. It is a garden inclosed.

There is an inclosure round believers; or else they never would be saved. This is the secret of their safety. It is not their faithfulness, their strength, or their love, it is the wall around them which prevents their being lost. They are a "garden inclosed."

They are inclosed by God the Father's everlasting election. Long before they were born,—long before the foundations of the world, God knew them, chose them, and appointed them to obtain salvation by Jesus Christ. The children of this world do not like to hear this doctrine proclaimed. It humbles man, and leaves him no room to boast. But whether it is abused or not, the doctrine of election is true. It is the corner-stone of the believer's foundation, that he was chosen in Christ before the world began. Who can rightly estimate the strength of this inclosure?

They are inclosed by the special love of God the Son. The Lord Jesus is the Saviour of all men, but He is specially the Saviour of them that believe. He has power over all flesh, but He gives eternal life to them that are specially given to Him, in a way that He does to none others. He shed HIS blood on the cross for all, but He only washes those who have part in Him. He invites all, but He quickens whom He will, and brings them to glory. He prays for them: He prays not for the world. He intercedes for them, that they may be kept from evil, that they may be sanctified by the truth, that their faith fail not. Who can fully describe the blessedness of this inclosure?

They are inclosed by the effectual working of God the Holy Ghost. The Spirit of Christ calls them out from the world, and separates them as effectually as if a wall were built between them and it. He puts in them new hearts, new minds, new tastes, new desires, new sorrows, new joys, new wishes, new pleasures, new longings. He gives them new eyes, new ears, new affections, new opinions. He makes them new creatures; they are born again, and with a new birth they begin a new existence. Mighty indeed is the transforming power of the Holy Spirit! The believer and the world are completely put asunder, and everlastingly separated. You may place a believer and an unbeliever together, marry them, join them under one roof, but you cannot unite them any more into one piece. The one is part of the "garden inclosed," and the other is not. Effectual calling is a barrier that cannot be broken.

Who can tell the comfort of this threefold wall of inclosure! Believers are inclosed by election, inclosed by washing and intercession, inclosed by calling and regeneration. Great is the consolation of these threefold bands of love around us, the love of God the Father, the love of God the Son, the love of God the Holy Ghost! A threefold cord is not easily broken.

Does any reader suppose for a moment that all this was not needed? I believe that nothing short of this threefold inclosure could save the Lord's garden from utter ruin. Without election, intercession, and regeneration, there is not one soul who would get to heaven. The wild boar out of the wood would break in and devour; the roaring lion would come in and trample all under his feet. The devil would soon lay the Lord's garden level with the ground.

Blessed be God for this, that we are "a garden inclosed!" Blessed be God, our final safety hangs not on anything of our own,—not on our graces and feelings,—not on our degree of sanctification,—not on our perseverance in well-doing,—not on our love,—not on our growth in grace,—not on our prayers and Bible-readings,—not even on our faith. It hangs on nothing else but the work of Father, Son, and Holy Ghost. If this three-fold work inclose us, who shall overthrow our hope? If God be for us, who can be against us?

Adam had a heart free from sin. Adam was strong in innocency, and undefiled by contact with bad examples and corrupt neighbours. Adam was on vantage ground, a thousand times higher than we now occupy; and yet Adam fell before temptation. There was no inclosure round him, no wall to keep Satan out, no barrier round the first flower of the Lord's garden;—and see how Adam fell!

Let believers open their sleepy eyes, and try to understand the value of their privileges! This is the most blessed part of the Lord's garden. It is a "garden inclosed." I believe if there was no election, there would be no salvation. I never saw a man who would be saved if it depended in any wise on himself. Let us all thank the Lord Jesus, every day, and thank Him from our hearts, that His people are a chosen and guarded people, and that His garden is nothing less than "a garden inclosed."

III. The Lord's garden is not empty: it is always full of flowers. It has had many in time past, it has many at the time present. Believers are the flowers that fill the Lord's garden.

I will mention two things about the flowers in the garden of the Lord Jesus. In some things they are all exactly like one another. In some things they are as various and diverse as the flowers in the gardens of this world.

(a) In some things they are all alike.

(1) They have all been transplanted. Not one of the Lord's flowers grew naturally in His garden. They were all born children of wrath, even as others. No man is born with grace in his heart. Every believer among the Lord's people was at one time at enmity with Him, and in a state of condemnation. It was the grace of God that first called him out of the world. It was the Spirit of Christ who made him what he is, and planted him in the garden of the Lord. In this the Lord's people are all alike: they are all transplanted flowers.

(2) The Lord's flowers are all alike in their root. In outward things they may differ, but underneath they are all the same. They are all rooted and grounded on Jesus Christ. Believers may worship in different places, and belong to different churches, but their foundation is the same,—the cross and the blood.

(3) The Lord's flowers are all at their beginning weak. They do not come to full maturity at once. They are at first like new-born babes, tender and delicate, and needing to be fed with milk, and not with strong meat. They are soon checked and thrown back. All begin in this way.

(4) The Lord's flowers all need the light of the sun. Flowers cannot live without light. Believers cannot live comfortably unless they see much of the face of Jesus Christ. To be ever looking on Him, feeding on Him, communing with Him,—this is the hidden spring of the life of God in man's soul.

(5) The Lord's flowers all need the dews of the Spirit. Flowers wither without moisture. Believers need daily, hourly, to be renewed by the Holy Ghost in the spirit of their minds. We cannot Live on old grace, if we would be fresh, living, real Christians. We must be daily more filled with the Spirit. Every chamber in the inward temple must be filled.

(6) The Lord's flowers are all in danger of weeds. Flower-beds need constant weeding. Believers need daily to search and see that they do not let besetting sins grow on undisturbed. These are the things that choke the actings of grace, and chill the influences of the Spirit. All are in peril of this; all should beware.

(7) The Lord's flowers all require pruning and digging. Flowers left alone soon dwindle and grow small. No careful gardener leaves his roses alone all the year round. Just so believers need stirring, shaking, mortifying, or else they become sleepy, and incline like Lot to settle down by Sodom. And if they are slow about the work of pruning, God will often take it in hand for them.

(8) The Lord's flowers all grow. None but hypocrites and wolves in sheep's clothing, and painted Christians, stand still True believers are never long the same. It is their desire to go on from grace to grace, strength to strength, knowledge to knowledge, faith to faith, holiness to holiness. Visit a border of the Lord's garden after two or three years' absence, and you will see this. If you see it not, you may well suppose there is a worm at the root. Life grows; but death stands still and decays.

(b) But while the Lord's flowers are all alike in some things, they are various and diverse in others, even as the flowers in our own gardens. Let us consider this point a little.

Believers have many things in common, one Lord, one faith, one baptism of the Spirit, one hope, one foundation, one reverence for the Word, one delight in prayer, one newness of heart. And yet there are some things in which they are not one. Their general experience is the same, and their title to heaven the same: and yet there are varieties in their specific experience. There are shades of diversity in their views and feeling. They are not so altogether and completely one that they can quite understand each other in all things, at all times, and in all points. Very important is it to bear this in mind! Believers are one in genus, but not one in species, one in great principles, not one in all particulars, one in reception of the whole truth, not one in the proportion they give to the parts of truth, one in the root, but not one in the flower, one in the part that only the Lord Jesus sees, not one in the part that is seen of the world.

You cannot understand your brother or sister in some things. You could not do as they do, speak as they speak, act as they act, laugh as they laugh, admire what they admire. Oh, be not hasty to condemn them! Make them not offenders for a word. Set them not down in a low place because they and you have little sympathy, few harmonizing and responding strings in your hearts,—because you soon come to a standstill in communing with them, and discover that they and you have only a limited extent of ground in common! Write it down on the tablets of your heart, that there are many schools, orders, classes, diversities of Christians. You may all be in the Lord's garden, and be united on grand doctrines; and yet for all that, the Lord's garden is made up of various sorts of flowers. All His flowers are useful: none must be despised. And yet His garden contains widely different sorts.

(1) Some that grow in the Lord's garden are like the flowers which are brilliant and showy in colour, but not sweet. You see them afar off, and they attract the world's eye, and their tints are beautiful, but you can say no more.

These are frequently the public Christians,—the popular preachers,—the speakers on platforms,—the lions of listening companies,—the people talked of, and pointed at, and run after. Such persons are the tulips, and sunflowers, and peonies, and dahlias of the Lord's garden, wonderful, gaudy, bright and glorious in their way, but not sweet.

(2) Some are like those flowers which make no show at all, and yet are the sweetest.

These are the Christians whom the world never hears of; they rather shrink from public observation. They hold on the even tenor of their way, and pass silently on towards home; but they sweeten all around them.

These are they that are rare and hard to find: but the better they are known, the more they are loved. Ask their true character in their own homes, and in their families,—ask husbands, wives, children, servants, their character, and you will soon discover that not a tenth part of their beauty and excellence is known by the world. The nearer you go, the more perfume will these dwellers in the Lord's garden give out. These are the Lord's violets,—valued by only few, but to those who know them, oh, how sweet!

(3) Some in the Lord's garden are like those flowers which cannot live in cold weather.

These are the Christians who have but a little strength, who faint in the day of adversity, who only flourish when everything around them is smooth and warm. A cold wind of trial, and unexpected frost of affliction, nips them and cuts them down. But the Lord Jesus is very merciful; He will not suffer them to be tempted above what they can endure. He plants them in sheltered and sunny places of His garden. He protects them and hedges them round by strong plants, to break the cold. Let no man despise them. They are the Lord's flowers, beautiful in their place and in their way.

(4) Some in the Lord's garden are like those hardy flowers which flower even in winter.

These are those rough Christians who never seem to feel any trials; whom nothing, either of opposition or affliction, appears to move. Doubtless there is not that softness and sweetness about them that we admire in others. We miss that lovable delicacy which in some people is such an unexplainable charm. They chill us sometimes by their rudeness and want of sympathy when compared to many we know. And yet let no man despise them. They are the crocuses in the garden of the Lord, beautiful in their place and way, and valuable in their own season.

(5) Some in the Lord's garden are never so sweet as after rain.

These are the Christians who show most grace under trial and affliction. In the day of sunshine and prosperity they become careless: they need the shower "of some sorrow to come down on them to make their full excellency appear. There is more beauty of holiness about their tears than about their smiles: they are more like Jesus when they weep than when they laugh. These are the roses of the Lord's garden: lovely and sweet and beautiful at all times, but never so much so as after rain.

(6) Some in the Lord's garden are never so sweet as at night.

These are the believers who need constant trial to keep them close to the throne of grace. They cannot bear the sunshine of prosperity: they become careless in prayer, sleepy about the Word, listless about heaven, too fond of nestling with some Benjamin in the corner of this world. Such persons the Lord Jesus often keeps under a cloud, to preserve them in a right frame. He sends wave after wave, trouble after trouble, to make them sit like Mary at His feet, and be near the cross. It is the very darkness they are obliged to walk in which makes them so sweet.

(7) Some in the Lord's garden are never so sweet as when crushed.

These are the Christians whose reality comes out most under some tremendous and uncommon judgment. The winds and storms of heavy affliction roll over them, and then, to the astonishment of the world, the spices flow out. I once saw a young woman who had lain on a bed six years in a garret, with a spinal complaint, helpless, motionless, cut off from everything that could make this world enjoyable. But she belonged to the garden of Jesus: she was not alone, for He was with her. You would have thought she would have been gloomy; she was all brightness. You would have expected her to be sorrowful; she was ever rejoicing. You would suppose she was weak and needed comfort; she was strong and able to comfort others. You would fancy she must have felt dark; she seemed to me all light. You would imagine her countenance was grave; it was full of calm smiles, and the gushing forth of inward peace. You would have pardoned her almost if she had murmured; she breathed of nothing but perfect happiness and content. The crushed flowers in the Lord's garden are sometimes exceeding sweet!

(8) Some of the flowers in the Lord's garden are never fully valued till they are dead.

These are those humble believers who, like Dorcas, are full of good works and active love towards others. These are those unostentatious ones who dislike profession and publicity, and love to go about, like their Lord and Master, doing good to souls,—visiting the fatherless and the widows, pouring in balm on wounds which this heartless world neither knows nor cares for, ministering to the friendless, helping the destitute, preaching the gospel not to silk and velvet, but to the poor.

These are not noticed by this generation: but the Lord Jesus knows them, and His Father also. When they are dead and gone, their work and labour of love all comes out. It is written with a diamond on the hearts of those they have assisted: it cannot be hid. They speak being dead, though they were silent when living. We know their worth when gone, if we did not while we had them with us. The tears of those who have been fed in soul or body by their hand tell forth to the wondering world that some have gone home whose place cannot easily be supplied, and that a gap is made which it will be hard to fill up. These shall never have that wretched epitaph, "Departed without being desired." These are the lavender in the Lord's garden, never so much appreciated and admired as when cut off and dead.

And now let me wind up with a few words of practical application.

There is one thing about the Lord's garden, which I see nothing like in this world.

The flowers of this world all die, and wither and lose their sweetness, and decay, and come to nothing at last. The fairest flowers are not really everlasting. The oldest and strongest of nature's children comes to an end.

It is not so with the Lord's flowers. The children of grace can never die. They may sleep for a season; they may be taken away when they have served their generation, and done their work. The Lord is continually coming down to His garden and "gathering lilies," laying flowers in His bosom one after the other; but the Lord's flowers shall all rise again.

When the Lord comes again the second time, He shall bring His people with Him. His flowers shall live once more, more bright, more sweet, more lovely, more beautiful, more glorious, more pure, more shining, more fair. They shall have a glorious body like their Lord's, and shall flourish for ever in the courts of our God.

(1) Reader, are you in the Lord's garden, or are you in the wilderness of this world?

You must be in one or the other. You must take your choice. Which have you chosen, and which do you choose now? The Lord Jesus would fain transplant you.

He strives with you by His Spirit. He would fain add you to the number of His beloved ones. He knocks at the door of your heart by word and by providence. He whispers to your conscience, "Awake, arise, repent, be converted, and come away!"

Oh, turn not away from Him that speaketh! Resist not the Holy Ghost. Choose not your place in the wilderness, but in the garden. Awake, arise, and turn away from the world.

(2) Reader! the wilderness or the garden! Which will you have?

If the wilderness, you will have your own way, run wild, grow to waste, bring forth fruit and flowers to yourself, become a barren, unprofitable, useless plant, live unloved and unlovable to yourself, and at last be gathered in the bundle with the tares, and burned!

If the garden,—you will not have your own way. But you will have what is far better, you will have God and Christ for your own. You will be cultivated, watered, tended, moved, pruned, trained by the Lord Jesus Himself; and at last your name shall be found in the bundle of life.

CHAPTER XVI

Prov. 22:6
The Duties Of Parents.

"Train up a child in the way he should go; and when he is old,
he will not depart from it."—Prov. 22:6.

I SUPPOSE that most professing Christians are acquainted with the text at the head of this page. The sound of it is probably familiar to your ears, like an old tune. It is likely you have heard it, or read it, talked of it, or quoted it, many a time. Is it not so?

But, after all, how little is the substance of this text regarded! The doctrine it contains appears scarcely known, the duty it puts before us seems fearfully seldom practised. Reader, do I not speak the truth?

It cannot be said that the subject is a new one. The world is old, and we have the experience of nearly six thousand years to help us. We live in days when there is a mighty zeal for education in every quarter. We hear of new schools rising on all sides. We are told of new systems, and "new books for the young, of every sort and description. And still for all this, the vast majority of children are manifestly not trained in the way they should go, for when they grow up to man's estate, they do not walk with God.

Now how shall we account for this state of things? The plain truth is, the Lord's commandment in our text is not regarded; and therefore the Lord's promise in our text is not fulfilled.

Reader, these things may well give rise to great searchings of heart. Suffer then a word of exhortation from a minister, about the right training of children. Believe me, the subject is one that should come home to every conscience, and make every one ask himself the question, "Am I in this matter doing what I can?"

It is a subject that concerns almost all. There is hardly a household that it does not touch. Parents, nurses, teachers, godfathers, godmothers, uncles, aunts, brothers, sisters,—all have an interest in it. Few can be found, I think, who might not influence some parent in the management of his family, or affect the training of some child by suggestion or advice. All of us, I suspect, can do something here, either directly or indirectly, and I wish to stir up all to bear this in remembrance.

It is a subject, too, on which all concerned are in great danger of coming short of their duty. This is pre-eminently a point in which men can see the faults of their neighbours more clearly than their own. They will often bring up their children in the very path which they have denounced to their friends as unsafe. They will see motes in other men's families, and overlook beams in their own. They will be quick sighted as eagles in detecting mistakes abroad, and yet blind as bats to fatal errors which are daily going on at home. They will be wise about their brother's house, but foolish about their own flesh and blood. Here, if anywhere, we have need to suspect our own judgment. This, too, you will do well to bear in mind.[18]

---

[18] As a minister, I cannot help remarking that there is hardly any subject about which people seem so tenacious as they are about their children. I have sometimes been perfectly astonished at the slowness of sensible Christian parents to allow that their own children are in fault, or deserve blame. There are not a few persons to whom I would far rather speak about their own sins, than tell them their children had done anything wrong.

Come now, and let me place before you a few hints about right training. God the Father, God the Son, God the Holy Ghost bless them, and make them words in season to you all Reject them not because they are blunt and simple; despise them not because they contain nothing new. Be very sure, if you would train children for heaven, they are hints that ought not to be lightly set aside.

I. First, then, if you would train your children rightly, train them in the way they should go, and not in the way that they would.

Remember children are born with a decided bias towards evil, and therefore if you let them choose for themselves, they are certain to choose wrong.

The mother cannot tell what her tender infant may grow up to be,—tall or short, weak or strong, wise or foolish: he may be any of these things or not,—it is all uncertain. But one thing the mother can say with certainty: he will have a corrupt and sinful heart. It is natural to us to do wrong. "Foolishness," says Solomon, "is bound in the heart of a child" (Prov. 22:15). "A child left to himself bringeth his mother to shame" (Prov. 29:15). Our hearts are like the earth on which we tread; let it alone, and it is sure to bear weeds.

If, then, you would deal wisely with your child, you must not leave him to the guidance of his own will. Think for him, judge for him, act for him, just as you would for one weak and blind; but for pity's sake, give him not up to his own wayward tastes and inclinations. It must not be his likings and wishes that are consulted. He knows not yet what is good for his mind and soul, any more than what is good for his body. You do not let him decide what he shall eat, and what he shall drink, and how he shall be clothed. Be consistent, and deal with his mind in like manner. Train him in the way that is scriptural and right, and not in the way that he fancies.

If you cannot make up your mind to this first principle of Christian training, it is useless for you to read any further. Self-will is almost the first thing that appears in a child's mind; and it must be your first step to resist it.

II. Train up your child with all tenderness, affection, and patience.

I do not mean that you are to spoil him, but I do mean that you should let him see that you love him.

Love should be the silver thread that runs through all your conduct. Kindness, gentleness, long-suffering, forbearance, patience, sympathy, a willingness to enter into childish troubles, a readiness to take part in childish joys,—these are the cords by which a child may be led most easily,—these are the clues you must follow if you would find the way to his heart.

Few are to be found, even among grown-up people, who are not more easy to draw than to drive. There is that in all our minds which rises in arms against compulsion; we set up our backs and stiffen our necks at the very idea of a forced obedience. We are like young horses in the hand of a breaker: handle them kindly, and make much of them, and by and by you may guide them with thread; use them roughly and violently, and it will be many a month before you get the mastery of them at all.

Now children's minds are cast in much the same mould as our own. Sternness and severity of manner chill them and throw them back. It shuts up their hearts, and you will weary yourself to find the door.

But let them only see that you have an affectionate feeling towards them,—that you are really desirous to make them happy, and do them good,—that if you punish them, it is intended for their profit, and that, like the pelican, you would give your heart's blood to nourish their souls; let them see this, I say, and they will soon be all your own. But they must be wooed with kindness, if their attention is ever to be won.

And surely reason itself might teach us this lesson. Children are weak and tender creatures, and, as such, they need patient and considerate treatment. We must handle them delicately, like frail machines, lest by rough fingering we do more harm than good. They are like young plants, and need gentle watering,—often, but little at a time.

We must not expect all things at once. We must remember what children are, and teach them as they are able to bear. Their minds are like a lump of metal—not to be forged and made useful at once, but only by a succession of little blows. Their understandings are like narrow-necked vessels we must pour in the wine of knowledge gradually, or much of it will be spilled and lost. "Line upon line, and precept upon precept, here a little and there a little," must be our rule. The whetstone does its work slowly, but frequent rubbing will bring the scythe to a fine edge. Truly there is need of patience in training a child, but without it nothing can be done.

Nothing will compensate for the absence of this tenderness and love. A minister may speak the truth as it is in Jesus, clearly, forcibly, unanswerably; but if he does not speak it in love, few souls will be won. Just so you must set before your children their duty,—command, threaten, punish, reason,—but if affection be wanting in your treatment, your labour will be all in vain.

Love is one grand secret of successful training. Anger and harshness may frighten, but they will not persuade the child that you are right; and if he sees you often out of temper, you will soon cease to have his respect. A father who speaks to his son as Saul did to Jonathan (1 Sam. 20:30), need not expect to retain his influence over that son's mind.

Try hard to keep up a hold on your child's affections. It is a dangerous thing to make your children afraid of you. Anything is almost better than reserve and constraint between your child and yourself; and this will come in with fear. Fear puts an end to openness of manner;—fear leads to concealment;—fear sows the seed of much hypocrisy, and leads to many a lie. There is a mine of truth in the Apostle's words to the Colossians: "Fathers, provoke not your children to anger, lest they be discouraged" (Col. 3:21). Let not the advice it contains be overlooked.

III. Train your children with an abiding persuasion ca your mind that much depends upon you.

Grace is the strongest of all principles. See what a revolution grace effects when it comes into the heart of an old sinner,—how it overturns the strongholds of Satan,—how it casts down mountains, fills up valleys,—makes crooked things straight,—and new creates the whole man. Truly nothing is impossible to grace.

Nature, too, is very strong. See how it struggles against the things of the kingdom of God,—how it fights against every attempt to be more holy,—how it keeps up an unceasing warfare within us to the last hour of life. Nature indeed is strong.

But after nature and grace, undoubtedly, there is nothing more powerful than education. Early habits (if I may so speak) are everything with us, under God. We are made what we are by training. Our character takes the form of that mould into which our first years are cast.[19]

---

[19]"He has seen but little of life who does not discern everywhere the effect of education on men's opinions and habits of thinking. The children bring out of the nursery that which displays itself

We depend, in a vast measure, on those who bring us up. We get from them a colour, a taste, a bias which cling to us more or less all our lives. We catch the language of our nurses and mothers, and learn to speak it almost insensibly, and unquestionably we catch something of their manners, ways, and mind at the same time. Time only will show, I suspect, how much we all owe to early impressions, and how many things in us may be traced up to seeds sown in the days of our very infancy, by those who were about us. A very learned Englishman, Mr. Locke, has gone so far as to say: "That of all the men we meet with, nine parts out of ten are what they are, good or bad, useful or not, according to their education."

And all this is one of God's merciful arrangements. He gives your children a mind that will receive impressions like moist clay. He gives them a disposition at the starting-point of life to believe what you tell them, and to take for granted what you advise them, and to trust your word rather than a stranger's. He gives you, in short, a golden opportunity of doing them good. See that the opportunity be not neglected, and thrown away. Once let slip, it is gone for ever.

Beware of that miserable delusion into which some have fallen, that parents can do nothing for their children, that you must leave them alone, wait for grace, and sit still. These persons have wishes for their children in Balaam's fashion,—they would like them to die the death of the righteous man, but they do nothing to make them live his life. They desire much, and have nothing. And the devil rejoices to see such reasoning, just as he always does over anything which seems to excuse indolence, or to encourage neglect of means.

I know that you cannot convert your child. I know well that they who are born again are born, not of the will of man, but of God. But I know also that God says expressly, "Train up a child in the way he should go," and that He never laid a command on man which He would not give man grace to perform. And I know, too, that our duty is not to stand still and dispute, but to go forward and obey. It is just in the going forward that God will meet us. The path of obedience is the way in which He gives the blessing. We have only to do as the servants were commanded at the marriage feast in Cana, to fill the water-pots with water, and we may safely leave it to the Lord to turn that water into wine.

IV. Train with this thought continually before your eyes—that the soul of your child is the first thing to be considered.

Precious, no doubt, are these little ones in your eyes; but if you love them, think often of their souls. No interest should weigh with you so much as their eternal interests. No part of them should be so dear to you as that part which will never die. The world, with all its glory, shall pass away; the hills shall melt; the heavens shall be wrapped together as a scroll; the sun shall cease to shine. But the spirit which dwells in those little creatures, whom you love so well, shall outlive them all, and whether in happiness or misery (to speak as a man) will depend on you.

This is the thought that should be uppermost on your mind in all you do for your children. In every step you take about them, in every plan, and scheme, and arrangement that concerns them, do not leave out that mighty question, "How will this affect their souls?"

Soul love is the soul of all love. To pet and pamper and indulge your child, as if this world was all he had to look to, and this life the only season for happiness—to do this is

---

throughout their lives." —Cecil.

not true love, but cruelty. It is treating him like some beast of the earth, which has but one world to look to, and nothing after death. It is hiding from him that grand truth, which he ought to be made to learn from his very infancy, that the chief end of his life is the salvation of his soul.

A true Christian must be no slave to fashion, if he would train his child for heaven. He must not be content to do things merely because they are the custom of the world; to teach them and instruct them in certain ways, merely because it is usual; to allow them to read books of a questionable sort, merely because everybody else reads them; to let them form habits of a doubtful tendency, merely because they are the habits of the day. He must train with an eye to his children's souls. He must not be ashamed to hear his training called singular and strange. What if it is? The time is short,—the fashion of this world passeth away. He that has trained his children for heaven, rather than for earth, for God, rather than for man, he is the parent that will be called wise at last.

V. Train your child to a knowledge of the Bible.

You cannot make your children love the Bible, I allow. None but the Holy Ghost can give us a heart to delight in the Word. But you can make your children acquainted with the Bible; and be sure they cannot be acquainted with that blessed book too soon, or too well.

A thorough knowledge of the Bible is the foundation of all clear views of religion. He that is well-grounded in it will not generally be found a wavier, and carried about by every wind of new doctrine. Any system of training which does not make a knowledge of Scripture the first thing is unsafe and unsound.

You have need to be careful on this point just now, for the devil is abroad, and error abounds. Some are to be found amongst us who give the Church the honour due to Jesus Christ. Some are to be found who make the sacraments saviours and passports to eternal life. And some are to be found in like manner who honour a catechism more than the Bible, or fill the minds of their children with miserable little story-books, instead of the Scripture of truth. But if you love your children, let the simple Bible be everything in the training of their souls; and let all other books go down and take the second place.

Care not so much for their being mighty in the catechism, as for their being mighty in the Scriptures. This is the training, believe me, that God will honour. The Psalmist says of Him, "Thou hast magnified Thy Word above all Thy name" (Ps. 138:2); and I think that He gives an especial blessing to all who try to magnify it among men.

See that your children read the Bible reverently. Train them to look on it, not as the word of men, but as it is in truth, the Word of God, written by the Holy Ghost Himself, all true, all profitable, and able to make us wise unto salvation, through faith which is in Christ Jesus.

See that they read it regularly. Train them to regard it as their soul's daily food, as a thing essential to their soul's daily health. I know well you cannot make this anything more than a form; but there is no telling the amount of sin which a mere form may indirectly restrain.

See that they read it all. You need not shrink from bringing any doctrine before them. You need not fancy that the leading doctrines of Christianity are things which children cannot understand. Children understand far more of the Bible than we are apt to suppose.

Tell them of sin, its guilt, its consequences, its power, its vileness: you will find they can comprehend something of this.

Tell them of the Lord Jesus Christ, and His work for our salvation,—the atonement, the cross, the blood, the sacrifice, the intercession: you will discover there is something not beyond them in all this.

Tell them of the work of the Holy Spirit in man's heart, how He changes, and renews, and sanctifies, and purifies: you will soon see they can go along with you in some measure in this. In short, I suspect we have no idea how much a little child can take in of the length and breadth of the glorious gospel They see far more of these things than we suppose.[20]

Fill their minds with Scripture. Let the Word dwell in them richly. Give them the Bible, the whole Bible, even while they are young.

VI. Train them to a habit of prayer.

Prayer is the very life-breath of true religion. It is one of the first evidences that a man is born again. "Behold," said the Lord of Saul, in the day he sent Ananias to him, "Behold, he prayeth" (Acts 9:11). He had begun to pray, and that was proof enough.

Prayer was the distinguishing mark of the Lord's people in the day that there began to be a separation between them and the world. "Then began men to call upon the name of the Lord" (Gen. 4:26).

Prayer is the peculiarity of all real Christians now. They pray,—for they tell God their wants, their feelings, their desires, their fears; and mean what they say. The nominal Christian may repeat prayers, and good prayers too, but he goes no further.

Prayer is the turning-point in a man's soul. Our ministry is unprofitable, and our labour is vain, till you are brought to your knees. Till then, we have no hope about you.

Prayer is one great secret of spiritual prosperity. When there is much private communion with God, your soul will grow like the grass after rain; when there is little, all will be at a standstill, you will barely keep your soul alive. Show me a growing Christian, a going forward Christian, a strong Christian, a flourishing Christian, and sure am I, he is one that speaks often with his Lord. He asks much, and he has much. He tells Jesus everything, and so he always knows how to act.

Prayer is the mightiest engine God has placed in our hands. It is the best weapon to use in every difficulty, and the surest remedy in every trouble. It is the key that unlocks the treasury of promises, and the hand that draws forth grace and help in time of need. It is the silver trumpet God commands us to sound in all our necessity, and it is the cry He has promised always to attend to, even as a loving mother to the voice of her child.

Prayer is the simplest means that man can use in coming to God. It is within reach of all,—the sick, the aged, the infirm, the paralytic, the blind, the poor, the unlearned,—all can pray. It avails you nothing to plead want of memory, and want of learning, and want of books, and want of scholarship in this matter. So long as you have a tongue to tell your soul's state, you may and ought to pray. Those words, "Ye have not, because ye ask not" (Jas. 4:2), will be a fearful condemnation to many in the day of judgment.

Parents, if you love your children, do all that lies in your power to train them up to a habit of prayer. Show them how to begin. Tell them what to say. Encourage them to persevere. Remind them if they become careless and slack about it. Let it not be your fault, at any rate, if they never call on the name of the Lord.

---

[20] As to the age when the religious instruction of a child should begin, no general rule can he laid down. The mind seems to open in some children much more quickly than in others. We seldom begin too early. There are wonderful examples on record of what a child can attain to, even at three years old.

This, remember, is the first step in religion which a child is able to take. Long before he can read, you can teach him to kneel by his mother's side, and repeat the simple words of prayer and praise which she puts in his mouth. And as the first steps in any undertaking are always the most important, so is the manner in which your children's prayers are prayed, a point which deserves your closest attention. Few seem to know how much depends on this. You must beware lest they get into a way of saying them in a hasty, careless, and irreverent manner. You must beware of giving up the oversight of this matter to servants and nurses, or of trusting too much to your children doing it when left to themselves. I cannot praise that mother who never looks after this most important part of her child's daily life herself. Surely if there be any habit which your own hand and eye should help in forming, it is the habit of prayer. Believe me, if you never hear your children pray yourself, you are much to blame. You are little wiser than the bird described in Job, "which leaveth her eggs in the earth, and warmeth them in the dust, and forgetteth that the foot may crush them, or that the wild beast may break them. She is hardened against her young ones, as though they were not hers: her labour is in vain without fear" (Job 39:14-16).

Prayer is, of all habits, the one which we recollect the longest. Many a grey-headed man could tell you how his mother used to make him pray in the days of his childhood. Other things have passed away from his mind perhaps. The church where he was taken to worship, the minister whom he heard preach, the companions who used to play with him,—all these, it may be, have passed from his memory, and left no mark behind. But you will often find it is far different with his first prayers. He will often be able to tell you where he knelt, and what he was taught to say, and even how his mother looked all the while. It will come up as fresh before his mind's eye as if it was but yesterday.

Reader, if you love your children, I charge you, do not let the seed-time of a prayerful habit pass away unimproved. If you train your children to anything, train them, at least, to a habit of prayer.

VII. Train them to habits of diligence, and regularity about public means of grace.

Tell them of the duty and privilege of going to the house of God, and joining in the prayers of the congregation. Tell them that wherever the Lord's people are gathered together, there the Lord Jesus is present in an especial manner, and that those who absent themselves must expect, like the Apostle Thomas, to miss a blessing. Tell them of the importance of hearing the Word preached, and that it is God's ordinance for converting, sanctifying, and building up the souls of men. Tell them how the Apostle Paul enjoins us not "to forsake the assembling of ourselves together, as the manner of some is" (Heb. 10:25); but to exhort one another, to stir one another up to it, and so much the more as we see the great day approaching.

I call it a sad sight in a church when nobody comes up to the Lord's table but the elderly people, and the young men and the young women all turn away. But I call it a sadder sight still when no children are to be seen in a church, excepting those who come to the Sunday School, and are obliged to attend. Let none of this guilt lie at your doors. There are many boys and girls in every parish, besides those who come to school, and you who are their parents and friends should see to it that they come with you to church.

Do not allow them to grow up with a habit of making vain excuses for not coming. Give them plainly to understand, that so long as they are under your roof it is the rule of your house for every one in health to honour the Lord's house upon the Lord's day, and that you reckon the Sabbath-breaker to be a murderer of his own soul.

See to it too, if it can be so arranged, that your children go with you to church, and sit near you when they are there. To go to church is one thing, but to behave well at church is quite another. And believe me, there is no security for good behaviour like that of having them under your own eye.

The minds of young people are easily drawn aside, and their attention lost, and every possible means should be used to counteract this. I do not like to see them coming to church by themselves, they often get into bad company by the way, and so learn more evil on the Lord's day than in all the rest of the week. Neither do I like to see what I call "a young people's corner" in a church. They often catch habits of inattention and irreverence there, which it takes years to unlearn, if ever they are unlearned at all. What I like to see is a whole family sitting together, old and young, side by side,—men, women, and children, serving God according to their households.

But there are some who say that it is useless to urge children to attend means of grace, because they cannot understand them.

I would not have you listen to such reasoning. I find no such doctrine in the Old Testament. When Moses goes before Pharaoh (Ex. 10:9), I observe he says, "We will go with our young and with our old, with our sons and with our daughters: for we must hold a feast unto the Lord." When Joshua read the law (Josh. 8:35), I observe, "There was not a word which Joshua read not before all the congregation of Israel, with the women and the little ones, and the strangers that were conversant among them." "Thrice in the year," says Ex. 34:23, "shall all your men-children appear before the Lord God, the God of Israel." And when I turn to the New Testament, I find children mentioned there as partaking in public acts of religion as well as in the Old. When Paul was leaving the disciples at Tyre for the last time, I find it said (Acts 21:5), "They all brought us on our way, with wives and children, till we were out of the city: and we kneeled down on the shore, and prayed."

Samuel, in the days of his childhood, appears to have ministered unto the Lord some time before he really knew Him. "Samuel did not yet know the Lord, neither was the word of the Lord yet revealed unto him" (1 Sam. 3:7). The Apostles themselves do not seem to have understood all that our Lord said at the time that it was spoken: "These things understood not His disciples at the first: but when Jesus was glorified, then remembered they that these things were written of Him" (John 12:16).

Parents, comfort your minds with these examples. Be not cast down because your children see not the full value of the means of grace now. Only train them up to a habit of regular attendance. Set it before their minds as a high, holy, and solemn duty, and believe me, the day will very likely come when they will bless you for your deed.

VIII. Train them to a habit of faith.

I mean by this, you should train them up to believe what you say. You should try to make them feel confidence in your judgment, and respect your opinions, as better than their own. You should accustom them to think that, when you say a thing is bad for them, it must be bad, and when you say it is good for them, it must be good; that your knowledge, in short, is better than their own, and that they may rely implicitly on your word. Teach them to feel that what they know not now, they will probably know hereafter, and to be satisfied there is a reason and a needs-be for everything you require them to do.

Who indeed can describe the blessedness of a real spirit of faith? Or rather, who can tell the misery that unbelief has brought upon the world? Unbelief made Eve eat the forbidden fruit,—she doubted the truth of God's word: "Ye shall surely die." Unbelief made the old world reject Noah's warning, and so perish in sin. Unbelief kept Israel in the wilderness,—it was the bar that kept them from entering the promised land. Unbelief made the Jews crucify the Lord of glow,—they believed not the voice of Moses and the prophets, though read to them every day. And unbelief is the reigning sin of man's heart down to this very hour,—unbelief in God's promises,—unbelief in God's threatenings,—unbelief in our own sinfulness,—unbelief in our own danger,—unbelief in everything that runs counter to the pride and worldliness of our evil hearts. Reader, you train your children to little purpose if you do not train them to a habit of implicit faith,—faith in their parents' word, confidence that what their parents say must be right.

I have heard it said by some, that you should require nothing of children which they cannot understand: that you should explain and give a reason for everything you desire them to do. I warn you solemnly against such a notion. I tell you plainly, I think it an unsound and rotten principle. No doubt it is absurd to make a mystery of everything you do, and there are many things which it is well to explain to children, in order that they may see that they are reasonable and wise. But to bring them up with the idea that they must take nothing on trust, that they, with their weak and imperfect understandings, must have the "why" and the "wherefore" made clear to them at every step they take,—this is indeed a fearful mistake, and likely to have the worst effect on their minds.

Reason with your child if you are so disposed, at certain times, but never forget to keep him in mind (if you really love him) that he is but a child after all,—that he thinks as a child, he understands as a child, and therefore must not expect to know the reason of everything at once.

Set before him the example of Isaac, in the day when Abraham took him to offer him on Mount Moriah (Gen. 22). He asked his father that single question, "Where is the lamb for a burnt-offering?" and he got no answer but this, "God will provide Himself a lamb." How, or where, or whence, or in what manner, or by what means,—all this Isaac was not told; but the answer was enough. He believed that it would be well, because his father said so, and he was content.

Tell your children, too, that we must all be learners in our beginnings,—that there is an alphabet to be mastered in every kind of knowledge, that the best horse in the world had need once to be broken,—that a day will come when they will see the wisdom of all your training. But in the meantime if you say a thing is right, it must be enough for them,—they must believe you, and be content.

Parents, if any point in training is important, it is this. I charge you by the affection you have to your children, use every means to train them up to a habit of faith.

IX. Train, them to a habit of obedience.

This is an object which is worth any labour to attain. No habit, I suspect, has such an influence over our lives as this. Parents, determine to make your children obey you, though it may cost you much trouble, and cost them many tears. Let there be no questioning, and reasoning, and disputing, and delaying, and answering again. When you give them a command, let them see plainly that you will have it done.

Obedience is the only reality. It is faith visible, faith acting, and faith incarnate. It is the test of real discipleship among the Lord's people. "Ye are My friends if ye do whatsoever I command you" (John 15:14). It ought to be the mark of well-trained children, that they do whatsoever their parents command them. Where, indeed, is the honour which the fifth commandment enjoins, if fathers and mothers are not obeyed cheerfully, willingly, and at once?

Early obedience has all Scripture on its side. It is in Abraham's praise, not merely he will train, his family, but "he will command his children, and his household after him" (Gen. 18:19). It is said of the Lord Jesus Christ Himself, that when "He was young He was subject to Mary and Joseph" (Luke 2:51). Observe how implicitly Joseph obeyed the order of his father Jacob (Gen. 37:13). See how Isaiah speaks of it as an evil thing, when "the child shall behave himself proudly against the ancient" (Isa. 3:5). Mark how the Apostle Paul names disobedience to parents as one of the bad signs of the latter days (2 Tim. 3:2). Mark how he singles out this grace of requiring obedience as one that should adorn a Christian minister: "a bishop must be one that ruleth well his own house, having his children in subjection with all gravity." And again, "Let the deacons rule their children and their own houses well" (1 Tim. 3:4-12). And again, an elder must be one "having faithful children, children not accused of riot, or unruly" (Tit. 1:6).

Parents, do you wish to see your children happy? Take care, then, that you train them to obey when they are spoken to,—to do as they are bid. Believe me, we are not made for entire independence, we are not fit for it. Even Christ's freemen have a yoke to wear, they "serve the Lord Christ" (Col. 3:24). Children cannot learn too soon that this is a world in which we are not all intended to rule, and that we are never in our right place until we know how to obey our betters. Teach them to obey while young, or else they will be fretting against God all their lives long, and wear themselves out with the vain idea of being independent of His control.

Reader, this hint is only too much needed. You will see many in this day who allow their children to choose and think for themselves long before they are able, and even make excuses for their disobedience, as if it were a thing not to be blamed. To my eyes, a parent always yielding, and a child always having its own way, are a most painful sight;—painful, because I see God's appointed order of things inverted and turned upside down;—painful, because I feel sure the consequence to that child's character in the end will be self-will, pride, and self-conceit. You must not wonder that men refuse to obey their Father which is in heaven, if you allow them, when children, to disobey their father who is upon earth.

Parents, if you love your children, let obedience be a motto and a watchword continually before their eyes.

X. Train them to a habit of always speaking the truth.

Truth-speaking is far less common in the world than at first sight we are disposed to think. The whole truth, and nothing but the truth, is a golden rule which many would do well to bear in mind. Lying and prevarication are old sins. The devil was the father of them,—he deceived Eve by a bold lie, and ever since the fall it is a sin against which all the children of Eve have need to be on their guard.

Only think how much falsehood and deceit there is in the world! How much exaggeration! How many additions are made to a simple story! How many things left out, if it does not serve the speaker's interest to tell them! How few there are about us of whom we can say, we put unhesitating trust in their word! Verily the ancient Persians were wise in their generation: it was a leading point with them in educating their children, that they should learn to speak the truth. What an awful proof it is of man's natural sinfulness, that it should be needful to name such a point at all!

Reader, I would have you remark how often God is spoken of in the Old Testament as the God of truth. Truth seems to be especially set before us as a leading feature in the character of Him with whom we have to do. He never swerves from the straight line. He abhors lying and hypocrisy. Try to keep this continually before your children's minds. Press upon them at all times, that less than the truth is a lie; that evasion, excuse-making, and exaggeration are all halfway houses towards what is false, and ought to be avoided. Encourage them in any circumstances to be straightforward, and, whatever it may cost them, to speak the truth.

I press this subject on your attention, not merely for the sake of your children's character in the world,—though I might dwell much on this,—I urge it rather for your own comfort and assistance in all your dealings with them. You will find it a mighty help indeed, to be able always to trust their word. It will go far to prevent that habit of concealment, which so unhappily prevails sometimes among children. Openness and straightforwardness depend much upon a parent's treatment of this matter in the days of our infancy.

XI. Train them to a habit of always redeeming the time.

Idleness is the devil's best friend. It is the surest way to give him an opportunity of doing us harm. An idle mind is like an open door, and if Satan does not enter in himself by it, it is certain he will throw in something to raise bad thoughts in our souls.

No created being was ever meant to be idle. Service and work is the appointed portion of every creature of God. The angels in heaven work,—they are the Lord's ministering servants, ever doing His will. Adam, in Paradise, had work, he was appointed to dress the garden of Eden, and to keep it. The redeemed saints in glory will have work,—"They rest not day and night," singing praise and glory to Him who bought them. And man, weak, sinful man, must have something to do, or else his soul will soon get into an unhealthy state. We must have our hands filled, and our minds occupied with something, or else our imaginations will soon ferment and breed mischief.

And what is true of us, is true of our children too. Alas, indeed, for the man that has nothing to do! The Jews thought idleness a positive sin: it was a law of theirs that every man should bring up his son to some useful trade,—and they were right. They knew the heart of man better than some of us appear to do.

Idleness made Sodom what she was. "This was the iniquity of thy sister Sodom, pride, fulness of bread, and abundance of idleness was in her" (Ezek. 16:49). Idleness had much to do with David's awful sin with the wife of Uriah.—I see in 2 Sam. 11 that Joab went out to war against Ammon, "but David tarried still at Jerusalem." Was not that idle? And then it was that he saw Bathsheba,—and the next step we read of is his tremendous and miserable fall.

Verily, I believe that idleness has led to more sin than almost any other habit that could be named. I suspect it is the mother of many a work of the flesh, the mother of adultery, fornication, drunkenness, and many other deeds of darkness that I have not time to name. Let your own conscience say whether I do not speak the truth. You were idle, and at once the devil knocked at the door and came in.

And indeed I do not wonder;—everything in the world around us seems to teach the same lesson. It is the still water which becomes stagnant and impure: the running, moving streams are always clear. If you have steam machinery, you must work it, or it soon gets out of order. If you have a horse, you must exercise him; he is never so well as when he has regular work. If you would have good bodily health yourself, you must take exercise. If you always sit still, your body is sure at length to complain. And just so is it with the soul. The active moving mind is a hard mark for the devil to shoot at. Try to be always full of useful employment, and thus your enemy will find it difficult to get room to sow tares.

Reader, I ask you to set these things before the minds of your children. Teach them the value of time, and try to make them learn the habit of using it well. It pains me to see children idling over what they have in hand, whatever it may be. I love to see them active and industrious, and giving their whole heart to all they do; giving their whole heart to lessons, when they have to learn;—giving their whole heart even to their amusements, when they go to play.

But if you love them well, let idleness be counted a sin in your family.

XII. Train them with a constant fear of over-indulgence.

This is the one point of all on which you have most need to be on your guard. It is natural to be tender and affectionate towards your own flesh and blood, and it is the excess of this very tenderness and affection which you have to fear. Take heed that it does not make you blind to your children's faults, and deaf to all advice about them. Take heed lest it make you overlook bad conduct, rather than have the pain of inflicting punishment and correction.

I know well that punishment and correction are disagreeable things. Nothing is more unpleasant than giving pain to those we love, and calling forth their tears. But so long as hearts are what hearts are, it is vain to suppose, as a general rule, that children can ever be brought up without correction.

Spoiling is a very expressive word, and sadly full of meaning. Now it is the shortest way to spoil children to let them have their own way,—to allow them to do wrong and not to punish them for it. Believe me, you must not do it, whatever pain it may cost you unless you wish to ruin your children's souls.

You cannot say that Scripture does not speak expressly on this subject: "He that spareth his rod, hateth his son; but he that loveth him, chasteneth him betimes" (Prov. 13:24). "Chasten thy son while there is hope, and let not thy soul spare for his crying" (Prov. 19:18). "Foolishness is bound in the heart of a child: but the rod of correction shall drive it from him" (Prov. 22:15). "Withhold not correction from the child, for if thou beatest him with the rod he shall not die. Thou shalt beat him with the rod, and deliver his soul from hell" (Prov. 23:13-14). "The rod and reproof give wisdom: but a child left to himself bringeth his mother to shame." "Correct thy son, and he shall give thee rest, yea, he shall give delight to thy soul" (Prov. 29:15-17).

How strong and forcible are these texts! How melancholy is the fact, that in many Christian families they seem almost unknown! Their children need reproof, but it is hardly ever given; they need correction, but it is hardly ever employed. And yet this book of Proverbs is not obsolete and unfit for Christians. It is given by inspiration of God, and profitable. It is given for our learning, even as the Epistles to the Romans and Ephesians. Surely the believer who brings up his children without attention to its counsel is making himself wise above that which is written, and greatly errs.

Fathers and mothers, I tell you plainly, if you never punish your children when they are in fault, you are doing them a grievous wrong. I warn you, this is the rock on which the saints of God, in every age, have only too frequently made shipwreck. I would fain persuade you to be wise in time, and keep clear of it. See it in Eli's case. His sons Hophni and Phinehas "made themselves vile, and he restrained them not." He gave them no more than a tame and lukewarm reproof, when he ought to have rebuked them sharply. In one word, He honoured his sons above God. And what was the end of these things? He lived to hear of the death of both his sons in battle, and his own grey hairs were brought down with sorrow to the grave (1 Sam. 2:22-29, 3:13).

See, too, the case of David. Who can read without pain the history of his children, and their sins? Amnon's incest, Absalom's murder and proud rebellion,—Adonijah's scheming ambition: truly these were grievous wounds for the man after God's own heart to receive from his own house. But was there no fault on his side? I fear there can be no doubt there was. I find a clue to it all in the account of Adonijah in 1 Kings 1:6, "HIS father had not displeased him at any time in saying, Why hast thou done so?" There was the foundation of all the mischief. David was an over-indulgent father, father who let his children have their own way, and he reaped according as he had sown.

Parents, I beseech you, for your children's sake, beware of over-indulgence. I call on you to remember, it is your first duty to consult their real interests, and not their fancies and likings;—to train them, not to humour them;—to profit, not merely to please.

You must not give way to every wish and caprice of your child's mind, however much you may love him. You must not let him suppose his will is to be everything, and that he has only to desire a thing and it will be done. Do not, I pray you, make your children idols, lest God should take them away, and break your idol, just to convince you of your folly.

Learn to say "No" to your children. Show them that you are able to refuse whatever you think is not fit for them. Show them that you are ready to punish disobedience, and that when you speak of punishment, you are not only ready to threaten, but also to perform. Do not threaten too much.[21] Threatened folks, and threatened faults, live long. Punish seldom, but really and in good earnest, frequent and slight punishment is a wretched system indeed.[22]

Beware of letting small faults pass unnoticed under the idea "it is a little one." There are no little things in training children; all are important. Little weeds need plucking up as much as any. Leave them alone, and they will soon be great.

Reader, if there be any point which deserves your attention, believe me, it is this one. It is one that will give you trouble, I know. But if you do not take trouble with your children when they are young, they will give you trouble when they are old. Choose which you prefer.

XIII. Train them remembering continually how God trains His children.

The Bible tells us that God has an elect people, a family in this world. All poor sinners who have been convinced of sin, and fled to Jesus for peace, make up that family. All of us who really believe on Christ for salvation are its members.

Now God the Father is ever training the members of this family for their everlasting abode with Him in heaven. He acts as a husbandman pruning his vines, that they may bear more fruit. He knows the character of each of us, our besetting sins, our weaknesses, our peculiar infirmities, our special wants. He knows our works and where we dwell, who are our companions in life, and what are our trials, what our temptations, and what are our

---

[21] Some parents and nurses have a way of saying, "Naughty child," to a boy or girl on every slight occasion, and often without good cause. It is a very foolish habit. Words of blame should never be used without real reason.

[22] As to the best way of punishing a child, no general rule can be laid down. The characters of children are so exceedingly different, that what would be a severe punishment to one child, would be no punishment at all to another. I only beg to enter my decided protest against the modern notion that no child ought ever to be whipped. Doubtless some parents use bodily correction far too much, and far too violently; but many others, I fear, use it far too little.

privileges. He knows all these things, and is ever ordering all for our good. He allots to each of us, in His providence, the very things we need, in order to bear the most fruit, as much of sunshine as we can stand, and as much of rain, as much of bitter things as we can bear, and as much of sweet. Reader, if you would train your children wisely, mark well how God the Father trains His. He doeth all things well; the plan which He adopts must be right.

See, then, how many things there are which God withholds from His children. Few could be found, I suspect, among them who have not had desires which He has never been pleased to fulfil. There has often been some one thing they wanted to attain, and yet there has always been some barrier to prevent attainment. It has been just as if God was placing it above our reach, and saying, "This is not good for you; this must not be." Moses desired exceedingly to cross over Jordan, and see the goodly land of promise; but you will remember his desire was never granted.

See, too, how often God leads His people by ways which seem dark and mysterious to our eyes. We cannot see the meaning of all His dealings with us; we cannot see the reasonableness of the path in which our feet are treading. Sometimes so many trials have assailed us,—so many difficulties encompassed us, that we have not been able to discover the needs-be of it all. It has been just as if our Father was taking us by the hand into a dark place and saying, "Ask no questions, but follow Me." There was a direct road from Egypt to Canaan, yet Israel was not led into it; but round, through the wilderness. And this seemed hard at the time. "The soul of the people," we are told, "was much discouraged because of the way" (Exod. 13:17; Num. 21:4).

See, also, how often God chastens His people with trial and affliction. He sends them crosses and disappointments; He lays them low with sickness; He strips them of property and friends; He changes them from one position to another; He visits them with things most hard to flesh and blood; and some of us have well-nigh fainted under the burdens laid upon us. We have felt pressed beyond strength, and have been almost ready to murmur at the hand which chastened us. Paul the Apostle had a thorn in the flesh appointed him, some bitter bodily trial, no doubt, though we know not exactly what it was. But this we know, he besought the Lord thrice that it might be removed; yet it was not taken away (2 Cor. 12:8-9).

Now, reader, notwithstanding all these things, did you ever hear of a single child of God who thought his Father did not treat him wisely? No, I am sure you never did. God's children would always tell you, in the long run, it was a blessed thing they did not have their own way, and that God had done far better for them than they could have done for themselves. Yes! And they could tell you, too, that God's dealings had provided more happiness for them than they ever would have obtained themselves, and that His way, however dark at times, was the way of pleasantness and the path of peace.

I ask you to lay to heart the lesson which God's dealings with His people is meant to teach you. Fear not to withhold from your child anything you think will do him harm, whatever his own wishes may be. This is God's plan.

Hesitate not to lay on him commands, of which he may not at present see the wisdom, and to guide him in ways which may not now seem reasonable to his mind. This is God's plan.

Shrink not from chastising and correcting him whenever you see his soul's health requires it, however painful it may be to your feelings; and remember medicines for the mind must not be rejected because they are bitter. This is God's plan.

And be not afraid, above all, that such a plan of training will make your child unhappy. I warn you against this delusion. Depend on it, there is no surer road to unhappiness than always having our own way. To have our wills checked and denied is a blessed thing for us; it makes us value enjoyments when they come. To be indulged perpetually is the way to be made selfish; and selfish people and spoiled children, believe me, are seldom happy.

Reader, be not wiser than God; train your children as He trains His.

XIV. Train them remembering continually the influence of your own example.

Instruction, and advice, and commands will profit little, unless they are backed up by the pattern of your own life. Your children will never believe you are in earnest, and really wish them to obey you, so long as your actions contradict your counsel. Archbishop Tillotson made a wise remark when he said, "To give children good instruction, and a bad example, is but beckoning to them with the head to show them the way to heaven, while we take them by the hand and lead them in the way to hell."

We little know the force and power of example. No one of us can live to himself in this world; we are always influencing those around us, in one way or another, either for good or for evil, either for God or for sin.—They see our ways, they mark our conduct, they observe our behaviour, and what they see us practise, that they may fairly suppose we think right. And never, I believe, does example tell so powerfully as it does in the case of parents and children.

Fathers and mothers, do not forget that children learn more by the eye than they do by the ear. No school will make such deep marks on character as home. The best of schoolmasters will not imprint on their minds as much as they will pick up at your fireside. Imitation is a far stronger principle with children than memory. What they see has a much stronger effect on their minds than what they are told.

Take care, then, what you do before a child. It is a true proverb, "Who sins before a child, sins double." Strive rather to be a living epistle of Christ, such as your families can read, and that plainly too. Be an example of reverence for the Word of God, reverence in prayer, reverence for means of grace, reverence for the Lord's day.—Be an example in words, in temper, in diligence, in temperance, in faith, in charity, in kindness, in humility. Think not your children will practise what they do not see you do. You are their model picture, and they will copy what you are. Your reasoning and your lecturing, your wise commands and your good advice; all this they may not understand, but they can understand your life.

Children are very quick observers; very quick in seeing through some kinds of hypocrisy, very quick in finding out what you really think and feel, very quick in adopting all your ways and opinions. You will often find as the father is, so is the son.

Remember the word that the conqueror Caesar always used to his soldiers in a battle. He did not say "Go forward," but "Come." So it must be with you in training your children. They will seldom learn habits which they see you despise, or walk in paths in which you do not walk yourself. He that preaches to his children what he does not practise, is working a work that never goes forward. It is like the fabled web of Penelope of old, who wove all day, and unwove all night. Even so, the parent who tries to train without setting a good example is building with one hand, and pulling down with the other.

XV. Train them remembering continually the power of sin. I name this shortly, in order to guard you against unscriptural expectations.

You must not expect to find your children's minds a sheet of pure white paper, and to have no trouble if you only use right means. I warn you plainly you will find no such thing. It is painful to see how much corruption and evil there is in a young child's heart, and how soon it begins to bear fruit. Violent tempers, self-will, pride, envy, sullenness, passion, idleness, selfishness, deceit, cunning, falsehood, hypocrisy, a terrible aptness to learn what is bad, a painful slowness to learn what is good, a readiness to pretend anything in order to gain their own ends,—all these things, or some of them, you must be prepared to see, even in your own flesh and blood. In little ways they will creep out at a very early age; it is almost startling to observe how naturally they seem to spring up. Children require no schooling to learn to sin.

But you must not be discouraged and cast down by what you see. You must not think it a strange and unusual thing, that little hearts can be so full of sin. It is the only portion which our father Adam left us; it is that fallen nature with which we come into the world; it is that inheritance which belongs to us all. Let it rather make you more diligent in using every means which seem most likely, by God's blessing, to counteract the mischief. Let it make you more and more careful, so far as in you lies, to keep your children out of the way of temptation.

Never listen to those who tell you your children are good, and well brought up, and can be trusted. Think rather that their hearts are always inflammable as tinder. At their very best, they only want a spark to set their corruptions alight. Parents are seldom too cautious. Remember the natural depravity of your children, and take care.

XVI. Train them remembering continually the promises of Scripture.

I name this also shortly, in order to guard you against discouragement.

You have a plain promise on your side, "Train up your child in the way he should go, and when he is old he shall not depart from it" (Prov. 22:6). Think what it is to have a promise like this. Promises were the only lamp of hope which cheered the hearts of the patriarchs before the Bible was written. Enoch, Noah, Abraham, Isaac, Jacob, Joseph,—all lived on a few promises, and prospered in their souls. Promises are the cordials which in every age have supported and strengthened the believer. He that has got a plain text upon his side need never be cast down. Fathers and mothers, when your hearts are failing, and ready to halt, look at the word of this text, and take comfort.

Think who it is that promises. It is not the word of a man, who may lie or repent; it is the word of the King of kings, who never changes. Hath He said a thing, and shall He not do it? Or hath He spoken, and shall He not make it good? Neither is anything too hard for Him to perform. The things that are impossible with men are possible with God. Reader, if we get not the benefit of the promise we are dwelling upon, the fault is not in Him, but in ourselves.

Think, too, what the promise contains, before you refuse to take comfort from it. It speaks of a certain time when good training shall especially bear fruit,—"when a child is old." Surely there is comfort in this. You may not see with your own eyes the result of careful training, but you know not what blessed fruits may not spring from it, long after you are dead and gone. It is not God's way to give everything at once. "Afterward" is the time when He often chooses to work, both in the things of nature and in the things of grace. "Afterward" is the season when affliction bears the peaceable fruit of righteousness (Heb. 12:11). "Afterward" was the time when the son who refused to work in his father's vineyard repented and went (Matt. 21:29). And "afterward" is the time to which parents must look forward if they see not success at once,—you must sow in hope and plant in hope.

"Cast thy bread upon the waters," saith the Spirit, "for thou shalt find it after many days" (Eccles. 11:1). Many children, I doubt not, shall rise up in the day of judgment, and bless their parents for good training, who never gave any signs of having profited by it during their parents' lives. Go forward then in faith, and be sure that your labour shall not be altogether thrown away. Three times did Elijah stretch himself upon the widow's child before it revived. Take example from him, and persevere.

XVII. Train them, lastly, with continual prayer for a blessing on all you do.

Without the blessing of the Lord, your best endeavours will do no good. He has the hearts of all men in His hands, and except He touch the hearts of your children by His Spirit, you will weary yourself to no purpose. Water, therefore, the seed you sow on their minds with unceasing prayer. The Lord is far more willing to hear than we to pray; far more ready to give blessings than we to ask them;—but He loves to be entreated for them. And I set this matter of prayer before you, as the top-stone and seal of all you do. I suspect the child of many prayers is seldom cast away.

Look upon your children as Jacob did on his; he tells Esau they are "the children which God hath graciously given thy servant" (Gen. 33:5). Look on them as Joseph did on his; he told his father, "They are the sons whom God hath given me" (Gen. 48:9). Count them with the Psalmist to be "an heritage and reward from the Lord" (Ps. 127:3). And then ask the Lord, with a holy boldness, to be gracious and merciful to His own gifts. Mark how Abraham intercedes for Ishmael, because he loved him, "Oh that Ishmael might live before thee" (Gen. 17:18). See how Manoah speaks to the angel about Samson, "How shall we order the child, and how shall we do unto him?" (Judg. 13:12). Observe how tenderly Job cared for his children's souls, "He offered burnt-offerings according to the number of them all, for he said, It may be my sons have sinned, and cursed God in their hearts. Thus did Job continually" (Job 1:5). Parents, if you love your children, go and do likewise. You cannot name their names before the mercy-seat too often.

And now, reader, in conclusion, let me once more press upon you the necessity and importance of using every single means in your power, if you would train children for heaven.

I know well that God is a sovereign God, and doeth all things according to the counsel of His own will. I know that Rehoboam was the son of Solomon, and Manasseh the son of Hezekiah, and that you do not always see godly parents having a godly seed. But I know also that God is a God who works by means, and sure am I, if you make light of such means as I have mentioned, your children are not likely to turn out well.

Fathers and mothers, you may take your children to be baptized, and have them enrolled in the ranks of Christ's Church;—you may get godly sponsors to answer for them, and help you by their prayers;—you may send them to the best of schools, and give them Bibles and Prayer Books, and fill them with head knowledge:-but if all this time there is no regular training at home, I tell you plainly, I fear it will go hard in the end with your children's souls. Home is the place where habits are formed;—home is the place where the foundations of character are laid;—home gives the bias to our tastes, and likings, and opinions. See then, I pray you, that there be careful training at home. Happy indeed is the man who can say, as Bolton did upon his dying bed, to his children, "I do believe not one of you will dare to meet me before the tribunal of Christ in an unregenerate state."

Fathers and mothers, I charge you solemnly before God and the Lord Jesus Christ, take every pains to train your children in the way they should go. I charge you not merely for the sake of your children's souls; I charge you for the sake of your own future comfort and peace. Truly it is your interest so to do. Truly your own happiness in great measure depends on it. Children have ever been the bow from which the sharpest arrows have pierced man's heart. Children have mixed the bitterest cups that man has ever had to drink. Children have caused the saddest tears that man has ever had to shed. Adam could tell you so; Jacob could tell you so; David could tell you so. There are no sorrows on earth like those which children have brought upon their parents. Oh! take heed, lest your own neglect should lay up misery for you in your old age. Take heed, lest you weep under the ill-treatment of a thankless child, in the days when your eye is dim, and your natural force abated.

If ever you wish your children to be the restorers of your life, and the nourishers of your old age, if you would have them blessings and not curses, joys and not sorrows, Judahs and not Reubens, Ruths and not Orpahs, if you would not, like Noah, be ashamed of their deeds, and, like Rebekah, be made weary of your life by them: if this be your wish, remember my advice betimes, train them while young in the right way.

And as for me, I will conclude by putting up my prayer to God for all who read this paper, that you may all be taught of God to feel the value of your own souls. This is one reason why baptism is too often a mere form, and Christian training despised and disregarded. Too often parents feel not for themselves, and so they feel not for their children. They do not realize the tremendous difference between a state of nature and a state of grace, and therefore they are content to let them alone.

Now the Lord teach you all that sin is that abominable thing which God hateth. Then, I know you will mourn over the sins of your children, and strive to pluck them out as brands from the fire.

The Lord teach you all how precious Christ is, and what a mighty and complete work He hath done for our salvation. Then, I feel confident you will use every means to bring your children to Jesus, that they may live through Him.

The Lord teach you all your need of the Holy Spirit, to renew, sanctify, and quicken your souls. Then, I feel sure you will urge your children to pray for Him without ceasing, and never rest till He has come down into their hearts with power, and made them new creatures.

The Lord grant this, and then I have a good hope that you will indeed train up your children well,—train well for this life, and train well for the life to come; train well for earth, and train well for heaven; train them for God, for Christ, and for eternity.

CHAPTER XVII[23]

Phil. 1:1
The Rights And Duties Of Lay Churchmen.

"Paul and Timotheus, the servants of Jesus Christ, to all the saints in Christ Jesus which are at Philippi, with the bishops and deacons." —Phil. 1:1.

THIS opening verse of St. Paul's Epistle to the Philippians is a very remarkable text of Scripture. I suspect it receives far less attention from Bible readers than it deserves. Like the gold of California, men have walked over it for centuries, and have not observed

---

[23]The substance of this was originally preached in Winchester Cathedral on April 2, 1886.

what was under their feet. In fact, if some Anglican divines had stood at the Apostle's elbow when he wrote this verse, I believe they would have hinted that he had made a mistake.

Now what do I mean by all this? What is the remarkable point to which I refer? The point on which I place my finger is St. Paul's mention of "the saints" before the "bishops and deacons." He places the laity before the clergy when he addresses the Philippian Church. He puts the body of the baptized in the front rank, and the ministers in the rear.

There is no room for dispute about the various readings of manuscripts in this case. Here, at any rate, the Revised Version does not touch the language of the text.

It was unmistakably given by inspiration of God, and written for our learning. As such, I see in it the germ of a great truth, which demands special notice in the present day. In short, it opens up the grave subject of the rights and duties of the lay members of a Christian Church.

There are three questions which I propose to examine in this paper:—

I. What was the position of the lay members of a Church in the days of the Apostles?

II. What has been the position of the laity of the Church of England for the last 200 years?

III. What ought we to aim at, in the matter of the laity, in order to strengthen and reform the Established Church of England?

I approach the whole subject with a deep sense of its delicacy and difficulty. I disclaim the slightest sympathy with those revolutionary counsellors who want us to throw overboard Creeds and Articles and Formularies, and turn the Church into a Pantheon, in the vain hope of buying off invaders. I desire nothing but scriptural and reasonable reforms, and I know no reform so likely to strengthen the Church of England as that of placing her laity in their rightful position. One of the best modes of promoting effective Church defence in this day is to promote wise Church reform.

I. What, then, was the position of the lay members of Churches in the days of the Apostles? Let us imagine ourselves paying a visit to the baptized communities at Rome, or Corinth, or Ephesus, or Thessalonica, or Jerusalem, and let us see what we should have found, and what Scripture teaches about them. In this, as in many other matters, we have a right to ask, "What light can we get from the New Testament?"

This is an inquiry which deserves special attention, and I am much mistaken if the result does not astonish some persons, and make them open their eyes.

I say then, without hesitation, that you will not find a single text in the New Testament in which the ordained ministers alone are ever called "the Church," or ever act for the Church without the laity uniting and co-operating in their action.

Are the deacons appointed? The twelve recommend it, but "the whole multitude" choose (Acts 6:5). Is a council held to consider whether the heathen converts should be circumcised, and keep the ceremonial law? The decision arrived at is said to come from "the apostles, and elders, and brethren," with "the whole Church" (Acts 15:22-23).—Are inspired Epistles written by St. Paul to particular Churches? In eight cases they are addressed to "the Church, the saints, the faithful brethren"—and in only one case (the Epistle to the Philippians) is there any mention of "bishops and deacons" in the opening address. Does St. Paul send instructions to the Church about the Lord's Supper, and about speaking with tongues? He sends them to "them that are sanctified in Christ Jesus" not to the ministers.—Is discipline exercised against an unsound member? I find St. Paul giving directions to the saints at Corinth, without mentioning the ministry: "Put away from among yourselves that wicked person" (1 Cor. 5:13).—Is a man "overtaken in a fault" to be restored to communion? St. Paul tells those who are "spiritual" among the Galatians to do it, and does not refer it to their ministers. (Gal. 6:1).—Is an Epistle written to the Christian Hebrews? Not a word is said about "rulers" until you come to the last chapter. Does St. James write a General Epistle? He addresses the "twelve tribes," and only names "teachers" in the third chapter. Does St. Peter write a General Epistle? He writes to the whole body of the elect, and says nothing to the "elders" till he arrives at the last chapter, and even then he is careful to remind them that they are not "lords over God's heritage." As for the Second Epistle of St. Peter, and the Epistles of St. John and St. Jude, they never touch the subject of the ministry at all.

Now let no one mistake me. That there was to be a distinct order of men to minister to the Church is, to my eyes, most plainly taught in the New Testament. St. Paul, we are told, "ordained elders in every Church" (Acts 14:23). See 1 Cor. 12:28; Eph. 4:11; 1st and 2nd Epistles to Timothy; and Titus. But that "the Church" in any city or country meant especially the laity, and the ministers were only regarded as the "servants of the Church" (2 Cor. 4:5), seems to me as clear as the sun at noon-day. As for a Church in which the clergy acted alone, settled everything, decided everything, judged everything, and managed everything, and the laity had no voice at all, I cannot find the ghost of the shadow of such a thing in the Acts or Epistles of the New Testament. On the contrary, while St. Paul tells the Thessalonians to "esteem their ministers very highly," it is to the laity, and not the clergy, that he addresses the words, "Warn them that are unruly, comfort the feeble-minded, support the weak" (1 Thess. 5:13-14). I trust that Churchmen who remember the Sixth Article of our English Church will not fail to observe this.

Before I go any further in this paper, I think it right to say a few words in self-defence, to prevent possible misunderstanding. If any one supposes that I wish to exalt and exaggerate the position of the laity at the expense of the clergy, and that I think lightly of the ministerial office, he is totally mistaken. In a deep sense of the value of the Christian ministry, as an ordinance of Christ, and a necessity in a fallen world, I give place to no man. But I dare not overstep scriptural limits in this matter. I cannot refrain from saying that a sacerdotal ministry, a mediatorial ministry, an infallible ministry, a ministry of men who by virtue of episcopal ordination have any monopoly of knowledge, or any special ability to settle disputed questions of faith or ritual such a ministry, in my judgment, is an innovation of man, and utterly without warrant of Holy Scripture. It is a ministry which has been borrowed from the typical system of the Jewish Church, and has no place in the present dispensation. The Christian minister is a teacher, an ambassador, a messenger, a watchman, a witness, a shepherd, a steward, and is expressly authorized by the Epistles to Timothy and Titus, where his duties are clearly laid down. But there is a conspicuous absence of New Testament proof that he is a sacrificing priest.

In saying this I do not stand alone. The learned Bishop of Durham, in his exhaustive work on Philippians, uses the following language:—

"The kingdom of Christ has no sacerdotal system. It interposes no sacrificial tribe or class between God and man by whose entreaties alone God is reconciled and man forgiven. Each individual member holds personal communion with the Divine Head. To Him immediately he is responsible, and from Him directly he obtains pardon and draws strength" (p. 174, ed. 3).

Again, he says: "The sacerdotal title is never once conferred on the ministers of the Church. The only priests under the gospel, designated as such under the New Testament, are the saints, the members of the Christian brotherhood" (p. 132, ed. 3).

This is sound speech, which cannot be condemned.

First published in 1868, it has stood the test of eighteen years' criticism, and its principles remain unanswered and unanswerable. To these principles I firmly adhere, and I press them on the consideration of all English Churchmen in the present day.

I leave the subject of the lay members of the apostolic Churches at this point, and commend it to the attention of all who read this paper. It is my conviction that the prominent position occupied by the laity in these primitive communities was one grand secret of their undeniable strength, growth, prosperity, and success. There were no sleeping partners in those days. Every member of the ecclesiastical body worked. Every one felt bound to do something. All the baptized members, whether men or women, if we may judge from the 16th chapter of the Epistle to the Romans, took a direct active interest in the welfare and progress of the whole ecclesiastical body. They were not tame, ignorant sheep, led hither and thither at the beck of an autocratic shepherd. The best regiment in an army is that in which officers and privates take an equal interest in the efficiency of the whole corps. It is the ferment in which the officers trust the privates and the privates trust the officers, as they did when they fought through that eventful night at Rorke's Drift in the Zulu war. It is the regiment in which every private is intelligent, and behaves as if the success of the campaign depended on him. It is the regiment in which every private knows his duty, and is honourably proud of his profession, and would fight to the last for the colours, even if every officer fell Such a regiment was a primitive Church in apostolic days. It had its officers, its bishops, and deacons. It had orders, due subordination, and discipline. But the mainspring and backbone of its strength lay in the zeal, intelligence, and activity of its laity. Oh that we had something of the same sort in the organization of the Church of England!

II. The second thing which I propose to do is to examine the position of the laity of the Church of England during the last two centuries and at the present day.

Let us begin with a definition. When we talk of the laity of our Established Church, what do we mean? We mean, of course, all within her pale who are not ordained to any ministerial office. We mean the people of the Church, in contradistinction to the clergy. How immensely important a body they are, it is needless to say. It would be a waste of time to dwell long on such a point. Without the lay members, a Church can hardly be said to exist. No doubt the old saying is true, "Ubi tres, ibi ecclesia." But a general without an army, a colonel without a regiment, or a ship captain without a crew, are not more useless and helpless than a Church consisting of clergy without laity. In the Church of England, at any rate, there is at present no lack of laymen. There are probably 500 laymen in proportion to each clergyman. In point of numbers alone, therefore, apart from all other considerations, the laity are a most important part of the Church of England. Now I contend that the position of our lay Churchmen at this moment falls very short of the New Testament standards, and is therefore very unsatisfactory. I hold it to be a canon and axiom of the Christian faith, that the nearer a Church can get to the pattern of Scripture the better she is, and the farther she gets away from it the worse. It is vain to deny that in the actual working machinery and administration of our Church, in its arrangements, plans, schemes, and normal organization, the lay members have comparatively no place at all! Do the bishops meet in solemn conclave at Lambeth Palace to consider the state of our Zion?

There is no place for the laity.—Does Convocation hold its annual debates? There is no representation of the laity.—Does the bishop of a diocese make his annual arrangements for the work of his See? Has he any difficult problem to solve about discipline or the best mode of dealing with some criminous clerk? He has no council of laymen.—Has a vacant living or incumbency to be filled up? The appointment is made without the slightest regard to the opinion of the parishioners. I state simple facts. I defy any one to deny their correctness.

Of course I shall be reminded that the laity are represented in our Church by the churchwardens, who are elected every Easter, and summoned annually to the visitation of the archdeacon or bishop. I have not forgotten this at all. I only ask, in reply, whether churchwardens are not, as a rule, appointed with very little regard to spiritual qualifications? I ask whether their annual attendance at visitations is not ordinarily a mere ceremony and form? How many churchwardens know anything about a visitation, except that they go to a certain town, hear a charge about some dry subject which very possibly they do not understand, perhaps dine with the other churchwardens, and then go home? How many churchwardens accept office with the least idea of taking a constant active interest in all the Church's affairs? How many of them are expected to know anything about the Church's doctrines, ceremonies, government, difficulties, schemes, or plans? They are often most excellent men, and capable of doing excellent service. But practically little or nothing is expected of them, and little or nothing except secular and financial business is ever given them to do. The man who thinks that the office of churchwarden completely fulfils the New Testament idea of the laity's position in a Church must have taken leave of his common sense. That there are exceptional churchwardens who really do great things for the Church I am well aware. But they are such brilliant exceptions that they only prove the truth of my rule. If all churchwardens would do their duty always, as some churchwardens do their duty sometimes, the Church of England would be a far stronger Church than it is.

Of course I shall be reminded again that lay Churchmen occupy a prominent place in Church confesses and conferences, and fill a very useful position on the committees of religious societies. I am quite aware of this, but it is entirely beside the question. All these are purely voluntary agencies, which form no part of the Church's authorized and normal machinery. It is the organized system of the Church that I am looking at, and not the gratuitous service of exceptional lay volunteers.

But some one, again, will remind me that the House of Commons represents the laity of the Church of England. Surely the less we say about that the better! The man who talks in this way must have read history to very little purpose, or has been asleep for 200 years. We are not living in 1686, but in 1888. The pleasant old theory that Church and State are co-extensive and identical has long since vanished into thin air, and is a thing of the past. The House of Commons is a powerful body, no doubt, and "monarch of all it surveys." But it is no longer an assembly of none but "Churchmen." Moreover, it is notorious that there is no subject the House of Commons "cares so little to discuss as religion, and that there are no religious interests which fare so badly in its hands as those of the Church of England.

But unhappily this is not all. There is something more behind. The laity of our Church are not where they ought to be in the direct work of Christ, and the furtherance of Christianity in the land. A mischievous habit of leaving all religion to the parson of the parish has overspread the country, and the bulk of lay Churchmen seem to think that they have nothing to do with the Church but to receive the benefit of her means of grace, while they contribute nothing in the way of personal active exertion to promote her efficiency. The vast majority of church-goers appear to suppose that when they have gone to church on Sunday, and have been at the Lord's Supper, they have done their duty, and are not under the slightest obligation to warn, to teach, to rebuke, to edify others, to promote works of charity, to assist evangelization, or to raise a finger in checking sin, and advancing Christ's cause in the world. Their only idea is to be perpetually receiving, but never doing anything at all. They have taken their seats in the right train, and are only to sit quiet, while the clerical engine draws them to heaven, perhaps half asleep. If an Ephesian or Philippian or Thessalonian lay Churchman were to rise from the dead and see how little work lay Churchmen do for the English Church, he would not believe his eyes. The difference between the primitive type of a lay Churchman and the English type is the difference between light and darkness, black and white. The one used to be awake and alive, and always about his Master's business. The other is too often asleep practically, and torpid, and idle, and content to leave the religion of the parish in the hands of the parson. Each is baptized. Each uses means of grace. Each hears sermons, and professes himself a Christian. But the Churchmanship of the one is utterly unlike that of the other. When this is the case—and who will deny it?—there must be something painfully wrong in our organization. If the Philippian lay Churchman was right, the English lay Churchman cannot be right. We are weighed in the balances and found wanting. The very language in common use is a plain proof that there is something sadly wrong. The "Church" now-a-days means the "clergy;" and when some young man proposes to be ordained, his friends tell you that he is "going into the Church," as if he had not been in the Church long ago!

With every desire to make the best of our Church and its constitution, I cannot avoid the conclusion that in the matter of the laity its system is at present defective and infra-scriptural. I cannot reconcile the position of the English lay Episcopalian in 1888 with that of his brother in any apostolic Church eighteen centuries ago. I cannot make the two things square. To my eyes, it seems that in the regular working of the Church of England, almost everything is left in the hands of the clergy, and hardly anything is assigned to the laity! The clergy settle everything! The Clergy manage everything! The clergy arrange everything! The laity are practically allowed neither voice, nor place, nor opinion, nor power, and must accept whatever the clergy decide for them. In all this there is no intentional slight. Not the smallest reflection is implied on the trustworthiness and ability of the laity. But from one cause or another they are left out in the cold, passive recipients and not active members, in a huge ecclesiastical corporation,—sleeping partners, and not working agents in an unwieldy and ill-managed concern. In short, in the normal action of the Church of England, lay Churchmen have been left on a siding. Like soldiers not wanted, they have fallen out of the ranks, retired to the rear, and sunk out of sight.

Now, what is the true cause of this anomalous state of things? It is one which may easily be detected. The position of the English laity is neither more nor less than a rag and remnant of Popery. It is part of that "damnosa haereditas" which Rome has bequeathed to our Church, and which has never been completely purged away. Our Reformers themselves were not perfect men, and the characteristic jealousy of Queen Elizabeth prevented their perfecting the work of the English Reformation. Among other blots which they left on the face of our Church, I must sorrowfully admit that neglect of the interests of the laity was not the least one. To make the clergy mediators between Christ and man,—to exalt them far above the laity, and put all ecclesiastical power into their hands,—to clothe them with sacerdotal authority, and regard them as infallible guides in all Church matters,—this has always been an essential element of the Romish system. This element our Reformers, no doubt, ought to have corrected by giving more power to the laity, as John Knox did in Scotland. They omitted to do so, either from want of time or from want of royal permission. The unhappy fruit of the omission has been that gradually the chief authority in our Church matters has fallen almost entirely into the hands of the clergy, and the laity have been left without their due rights and powers. The effect at the present day is that the English laity are far below the position they ought to occupy, and the English clergy are far above theirs. Both parties, in short, are in the wrong place.

What are the consequences of this unsatisfactory state of things? They are precisely what might be expected—evil and only evil. Departure from the mind of God, even in the least things, is always sure to bear bitter fruit. Lifted above their due position, the English clergy have always been inclined to sacerdotalism, priestism, self-conceit, and an overweening estimate of their own privileges and powers. Fallen below their due position, the English laity, with occasional brilliant exceptions, have taken little interest in Church matters, and have been too ready to leave everything ecclesiastical to be managed by the clergy. In the meantime, for three centuries the Established Church of England has suffered great and almost irremediable damage.

Seldom considered, seldom consulted, seldom trusted with power, seldom invested with authority, the English lay Churchman, as a rule, is ignorant, indifferent, or apathetic about Church questions. How few laymen know anything about Church work in their own diocese! How few care one jot for Convocation! How few could tell you, if their lives depended on it, who are the proctors of their diocese! How few understand the meaning of the great doctrinal controversies by which their Church is almost rent asunder! How few exhibit as much personal interest or anxiety about them, as a Roman spectator would have exhibited about the fight of a couple of gladiators in the arena of the Coliseum! How few could tell you anything more than this, "that there is some squabble among the parsons; and they don't pretend to understand it!"—This is a melancholy picture; but I fear it is a sadly correct one. And yet who can wonder? The English laity have never yet had their rightful position in the management of the Church of England.

You may lay it down as an infallible rule, that the best way to make a man feel an interest in a business is to make him a "part of the concern." The rule applies to ecclesiastical corporations as well as to commercial ones. The Scotch Presbyterians, the English Nonconformists, the American Episcopalians, the Colonial Episcopalians, all realize the importance of this principle, and take care to carry it out. The Church of England alone has lost sight of this principle altogether. The laity have never been properly employed, or trusted, or considered, or called forward, or consulted, or placed in position, or armed with authority, as they ought to have been. The consequence is that, as a body, they neither know, nor care, nor feel, nor understand, nor think, nor read, nor exercise their minds, nor trouble their heads much, about Church affairs. The system under which this state of things has grown up is a gigantic mistake. The sooner it is cut up by the roots and turned upside down the better. If we want to remove one grand cause of our Church's present weakness, we must completely alter the position of the laity. On this point, if on no other, there is great need of Church reform.

III. Let us, in the last place, consider our own immediate duty. What ought we to aim at, in the matter of the laity, in order to strengthen the Established Church of England?

When I speak of aims, I shall have to come to practical details, and I shall not shrink from saying precisely what I mean. Grant for a moment that we have at length discovered that our lay Churchmen are not in their rightful position.—What is the remedy for the evil? What is the change that is required? What ought to be done?

The answers that some men make to these questions are so puerile, weak, and inadequate, that I am almost ashamed to name them. They tell us coolly that the laity may become lay-agents and Scripture-readers, though even this at one time, I remember, was thought a shocking innovation. They may even exhort and give little addresses—may teach Sunday schools and be parochial visitors—may manage Reformatories and Houses of Refuge—may attend Committees, and superintend Church finance. My reply is, that all such suggestions are ridiculously below the mark, and show woeful ignorance of the Church's need. I marvel that sensible men can have the face to make them. Oh, mighty condescension! Oh, wondrous liberality! We will let laymen do rough work which could not be clone at all without them, and which they have no need to ask the clergy's leave to do! If this is all that people mean when they talk of enlisting "lay co-operation," I am sorry for them. Such doctoring will not heal the wounds of our Zion. Such reforms will not win back the lukewarm sympathies of our laity, and make them the right arm of the Church of England.

The reform I plead for in the position of our laity is something far deeper, higher, wider, broader, more thorough, more complete. I plead for the general recognition of the mighty principle, that nothing ought to be done in the Church without the laity, in things great or in things small. I contend that the laity ought to have a part, and voice, and hand, and vote, in everything that the Church says and does, except ordaining and ministering in the congregation. I contend that the voice of the Church of England ought to be not merely the voice of the bishops and presbyters, but the voice of the laity as well, and that no Church action should ever be taken, and no expression of Church opinion ever put forth, in which the laity have not an equal share with the clergy. Such a reform would be a return to New Testament principles. Such a reform would increase a hundredfold the strength of the Church of England. What the details of such a reform ought to be, I will now proceed to explain.

(a) The unit with which we ought to begin, if we would raise the position of lay Churchmen to the standard of the apostolic times, beyond doubt, the parish. From one end of the land to the other we should try to establish the great principle, that every clergyman shall continually consult his lay parishioners.

If he does not like to have anything so stiff and formal-sounding as a "parochial council," let him at any rate often confer with his churchwardens, sidesmen, and communicants about his work. Especially let him do nothing in the way of changing times and modes of worship, nothing in the matter of new ceremonials, new decorations, new gestures, new postures, without first taking counsel with his lay-people. The church is theirs, and not his; he is their servant, and they are not his: they have surely a right to be consulted. Who can tell the amount of offence that might be prevented if clergymen always acted in this way? No people, I believe, are more reasonable than lay Churchmen, if they are only approached and treated in a reasonable way. Above all, let every parochial incumbent make a point of teaching every communicant that he is an integral part of the Church of England, and is bound to do all that he can for its welfare,—to visit, to teach, to warn, to exhort, to edify, to help, to advise, to comfort, to support, to evangelize; to awaken the sleeping, to lead on the inquiring, to build up the saints, to promote repentance, faith, and holiness everywhere, according to his gifts, time, and opportunity. He should educate his people to see that they must give up the lazy modern plan of leaving everything to the parson, and must be active agents instead of sleeping partners. On this point, I grieve to say, the Methodists and Dissenters beat Churchmen hollow. With them, every new member is a new home missionary in their cause. Never will things go well with the Church of England until every individual member realizes that he has a duty to do to his Church, and keeps that duty continually in view.

I begin purposely with this point. I am certain it is a vital one, and lies at the root of the whole subject which we are considering. Best of all, it is a reform which may be commenced at once, and needs no Act of Parliament to start it. It needs nothing but a determination on the part of the rectors, vicars, and perpetual curates of England to bring the matter before the communicants of their respective parishes, and to incite them to come forward and do their duty. They have the matter, I believe, in the hollow of their hands. The laity, I believe, would respond to the invitation, if they once realized that the health of the Church was at stake, and that there was work for them to do. In truth, it is our day of visitation. In our Established Church it will never do to try to man the walls with officers, and let the rank and file sit idle in their barracks. Clergy and laity must learn to work together. We must have not only an apostolical succession of ministers, but an apostolical succession of laymen, if our Church is to stand much longer.

(b) The next point which demands our attention, if we want to raise the laity of the Church to a scriptural position, is the absolute necessity of giving every parish and congregation some voice and vote in the appointment of its ministers. I make no apology for taking up this defect in our present system, because it is directly handled in the Church Patronage Bill which is being brought before Parliament. I own that I care little for some of the provisions of that Bill, and I doubt much if they would work well, supposing they passed the fiery ordeal of Lords' and Commons' Committees. But there is one clause in the proposed measure which is most praiseworthy, and I hail it with deep satisfaction. I refer to the clause which would enable the inhabitants of any parish to offer objections to a clergy man being placed over them, for a certain time after his name is made known. I regard this as emphatically a move in the right direction. I am not anxious to see patronage concentrated in one set of hands. Much less am I anxious to see clergymen elected entirely by the parishioners or congregation. But I do think that the people should have some voice in the appointment of ministers, and that they should not be left to the mercy of an incompetent patron, and not allowed to make any objection to his choice. We all know that a si quis must be read before an ordination, and I contend that a si quis should be required in every case before an Institution.

Our present system of appointment to livings entirely ignores the laity, and often proves a grievous abuse. Clergymen are constantly thrust upon unwilling parishes and disgusted congregations, who are entirely unfit for their position, and the people are obliged to submit. The parishioners are consequently driven away from church, and the Establishment suffers irreparable damage. It is high time to give up this system. Let every patron be required to send the name of the clergyman whom he wishes to nominate to a vacant living, to the churchwardens, one month before he presents the name to the bishop. Let the name of the proposed new incumbent be publicly read out in church like banns, and affixed to the church doors, on three or four Sundays consecutively, and let any one be invited to object if he can. Let the objector be obliged to satisfy the bishop and his council that there are good reasons, whether doctrinal or practical, for his objections, and let the bishop and his council have power, if satisfied, to refuse the patron's nominee. Of course such a safeguard as this might often be ineffectual. The objections to the nominee may often be frivolous or incapable of proof. But at any rate a principle would be established. The laity of a parish could no longer complain that they are perpetually handed over to new parsons without having the slightest voice in the transaction. One right the laity even now possess, I remind them, which I heartily wish they would exercise more frequently than they do. They may effectually prevent young men being ordained who are unfit for orders, by objecting when the si quis is read. Well would it be for the Church of England if the laity in this matter would always do their duty!

(c) The third and last reform in the position of the laity which we should aim to obtain, is the admission of lay Churchmen to their rightful place in the administration and management of the whole Church. I entirely agree with two of my Right Rev. Brethren, that we greatly want a National Church Council, composed of bishops, presbyters, and laymen.

Such a council ought not to possess any legislative powers, or to interfere in the slightest degree with the prerogative of the Crown or the Royal supremacy. There ought, therefore, to be no great difficulty in obtaining legal powers for its formation, and it ought not to be regarded with jealousy when formed. Its main object should be to bring the clergy and the laity face to face, and to enable them to consider all matters affecting the Church's welfare, and, if necessary, to bring them under the notice of Parliament. Its main advantage would be, that when it brought anything before Parliament which required legislation, it would be able to say, "Here is a matter about which the clergy and laity of the Established Church are agreed. In the name of that Church we ask you to take it up, and make it the law of the land."

I am afraid it is vain to hope for any large measure of Convocation reform. Ancient and venerable as the Synods of Canterbury and York undoubtedly are, I think no one will say that they truly represent the Church of England. Even if they adequately represented the clergy, it is certain that they do not represent the laity. This alone is an immense and intolerable defect, and completely prevents the laity, as a rule, taking any interest in the proceedings of Convocation. They feel that they are left out in the cold, and have neither voice, nor vote, nor place, nor part in the discussions, either at Westminster or York, even when the subjects discussed concern themselves most intimately. We need not wonder that they do not like this. According to the word of God, they are "the Church" as much as the clergy. They have quite as much at stake in the Church's welfare. They are often as well educated, as intelligent, as well-informed, as spiritually-minded, as able to discern "things that differ" in religion, as any clerk, man. The words of the judicious Hooker are worth remembering: "Till it be proved that some special law of Christ hath for ever annexed unto the clergy alone the power to make ecclesiastical laws, we are to hold it a thing most consonant with equity and reason, that no ecclesiastical laws be made in a Christian commonwealth, without consent as well of the laity as of the clergy." (Hooker, Book viii. chap. 6.) The simple fact that the lay people have at present neither voice nor place in the English Convocation, is enough to show that it is an institution totally unsuited to the age, and behind the times.

Of course I do not forget that a house of laymen has been called into existence in the province of Canterbury, with the express purpose of acting as a consultative body, and an assistant to Convocation, and it has been resolved to form a similar house of laymen at York. No doubt the formation of these two bodies is a great step in the right direction. It is a public acknowledgment that the time has come when lay Churchmen must be asked to take a more active interest in the affairs of the Established Church, and that their past torpid position, as sleeping partners in the great ecclesiastical concern, can no longer be maintained. For this tardy recognition of the rights and duties of laymen I am very thankful. A great principle has been established, and I trust the clock will never be put back.

But though I lay no claims to infallibility of judgement, I must respectfully express a doubt whether these new Houses of Laymen meet the wants of the day, and are anything more than a temporary makeshift. I might say something about the extreme difficulty of getting a really representative House of Laymen to meet at York! But I will not dwell on this. I will only point out three objections which appear to me not easily answered.

(a) In the first place, these Houses of Laymen will have no legal status, unless they are formally authorized by the Crown and Parliament, and will be nothing more than voluntary debating societies. Convocation, on the contrary, is one of the oldest legal institutions in the realm. How these two bodies are to work together under these conditions is not very clear. It is an attempt to unite iron and clay. It is sewing a new patch on an old garment.

(b) In the second place, the mode of forming, composing, and electing these Houses of Laymen appears at present far from satisfactory. If they are to consist of laymen elected by the various diocesan conferences, they certainly will not be a fair representation of the laity of the Church of England. For one thing, the constitution of diocesan conferences is not uniform, and differs widely in different dioceses of England and Wales. For another thing, it is notorious that in most dioceses very few lay Churchmen attend a diocesan conference, and most of them ignore it altogether.

(c) Last, but not least, it does not seem quite clear what these Houses of Laymen are to be allowed to discuss. The idea which has been propounded, that they are never to open their mouths about "questions of faith and doctrine," is to my mind most objectionable. It is unreasonable to suppose that intelligent English laymen, men of light and leading and intellectual power, will ever submit to be practically muzzled, and forbidden to speak of any but temporal matters.

Such prohibition, in my opinion, is sure to lead ultimately to friction and collision. If you call in the laity to aid in the administration of the Church, you must trust them, and give them liberty of speech.

It is very possible that answers may be found to these objections, though at present I fail to see them. I am thankful for the avowed expression of a desire to call in the help of the laity, and make use of their opinion on Church matters. But I have a firm conviction that no movement in this direction will ever do much good, until we have a real National Council, composed of the 30 bishops, and some 60 presbyters, and 120 laymen, elected from the 30 dioceses of England and Wales, and including laymen of the middle class, as well as of the upper ranks of society. But I believe that the best and ablest lay Churchmen will never join a mere voluntary assembly, in which their discussions and decisions would be utterly destitute of any authority, and their resolutions would carry no weight.

Above all, we want a Council in which bishops, presbyters, and laymen, shall sit together and consider subjects face to face. The clergy would then have an opportunity of finding out what public opinion is, and discovering that they are not infallible. The laity would have an opportunity of showing the clergy what is really going on in the world, and introducing practical business-like wisdom into their councils. This plan would be of immense advantage to all parties.

I leave the rights and duties of lay Churchmen at this point. I have no time to pursue the subject further. I am conscious that I have advanced opinions which are distasteful to some minds, and startling because of their novelty. But I have yet to learn that the reform in the position of the laity which I have suggested is not most desirable in the abstract, and most imperatively demanded by the times. Between Liberationists, Romanists, and Agnostics, the good ship of the Church is on a lee shore, and the breakers are in sight. Clergy and laity must co-operate, if the ship is to be saved. It is no time to prophesy smooth things, and look through telescopes with blind eyes, and cry "Peace, peace! Let us sit still."

(a) "Sacrilegious reform!" some will cry. They think it downright wicked to let the laity have anything to do with spiritual matters. They wish them to be nothing but Gibeonites, hewers of wood and drawers of water for the clergy. They talk gravely about Dathan, and Abiram, and Uzzah putting his hand to the ark, and Uzziah taking on himself to burn incense in the temple. To such men I reply, "Look at the Irish Church, and learn wisdom." If Disestablishment comes,—and many far-sighted men say it is sure to come at last,—you will be obliged to cast yourselves on the aid of the laity, whether you like it or not. Even if it does not come, you will never be really strong, unless you place the laity in their rightful position. As to the vague talk about sacrilege, it is all nonsense. Touch the idea with the Ithuriel spear of Scripture, and it will vanish away.

(b) But "it is a dangerous reform," some men will cry. "The laity will take the reins into their hands, and lord it over the consciences of the clergy." Such fears are simply ridiculous. There is far more real danger in letting the laity sit idle, and giving them no active interest in the Church's affairs. I have a better opinion of the laity than these alarmists have. The new ecclesiastical machinery may work awkwardly at first, like a new steam-engine, when its joints are stiff, and its bearings hot. The laity may not understand at first what they have to do. But give them time, give them time. Show them that you trust them, and make them see what is wanted, and I have no doubt the laity would soon settle down in their place, and work with a will. Remember how admirably the Irish laity set their house in order after Disestablishment, and have more faith in English laymen.

(c) "But it is a useless reform," some men will finally cry. "The laity are unfit to advise bishops, or sit in Church councils, or give an opinion about the fitness of incumbents." I do not believe it for one moment. The lay members of our Church may not be critics of Greek or Hebrew, or deep theologians, compared to many of the clergy. But many of them have quite as much grace, and quite as much knowledge of the English Bible. Above all, they have, as a rule, much more common sense than the clergy. No man can be ignorant of that who knows how our best laymen conduct themselves on the committees of our great religious Societies. The observation of Lord Clarendon about the clerical body is, alas! only too true. After long experience, he declared his conviction that "clergymen understand the least, and take the worst measure of human affairs of all mankind that can write or read." I fear, if he lived in the present day, he would not give us, as a body, a much better character. Nothing, I firmly believe, would be such an advantage to the Church as to leaven all its action with a judicious mixture of the lay element. The true cause of half the Church's mistakes in these latter days has been the absence of the laity from their rightful place.

The greatest peril of the Established Church in this day consists in the favourite policy of total inaction which pleases so many, and their inability to see that we are in danger. "A little more sleep! a little more slumber! Why cannot you let things alone?" This is the reply continually made when Church reforms are spoken of, and pressed on men's attention. "Why should we fear?" they cry. "There is no real danger." Will any one tell me there is no inward danger, when the real presence, and the Romish confessional, and ecclesiastical lawlessness, and Home Rule, are quietly tolerated on one side, and the atonement, and Christ's divinity, and the inspiration of Scripture, and the reality of miracles, are coolly thrown overboard on the other? Will any one tell me there is no outward danger, when infidels, Papists, and Dissenters are hungering and thirsting after the destruction of the Establishment, and compassing sea and land to accomplish their ends?—What! no danger, when myriads of our working classes never enter the walls of our Church, and would not raise a finger to keep her alive, while by household suffrage they have got all power into their hands! What! no danger, when the Irish Church has been disestablished, the Act of Union has been trampled under foot, Protestant endowments have been handed over to Papists, the thin edge of the wedge for severing Church and State has been let in, and the statesman who did all this is still alive, and thought by many to be infallible. No danger, indeed! I can find no words to express my astonishment that men say so. But, alas! there are never wanting men who, having eyes see not, and having ears hear not, and who will not understand.

The Established Church of England is in danger. There is no mistake about it. This is the one broad, sweeping reason why I advocate Church reforms. There is a "handwriting on the wall," flashing luridly from the other side of St. George's Channel, which needs no Daniel to interpret it. There is a current setting in towards the Disestablishment of all National Churches, and we are already in it. We are gradually drifting downwards, though many perceive it not; but those who look at the old landmarks cannot fail to see that we move. We shall soon be in the rapids. A few, a very few years, and, unless we exert ourselves, we shall be over the falls. The English public seems drunk with the grand idea of "free trade" in everything, in religion as well as in commerce, in churches as well as in corn. A portion of the daily press is constantly harping on the subject. And shall we sit still and refuse to set our house in order? I, for one, say, God forbid! Shall we wait till we are turned out into the street and obliged to reform ourselves in the midst of a hurricane of confusion? I, for one, say, God forbid! The experienced general tells us that it is madness to change front in the face of an enemy. If we believe that danger is impending over the Church Establishment, let us not wait till the storm bursts. Let us gird up our loins while we can, and attempt Church reforms.

1. I now commend the whole subject to the prayerful attention of the clergy. "Consider what I say, and the Lord give you understanding in all things." Oh that I could blow a trumpet in the ear of every rector and vicar in England, and awaken him to a sense of the Church's danger! The horizon is very black. I believe it is our time of visitation. It is no time to fold our arms and sit still. Is our Church going to live or die? If we would defend her, we must "set in order the things that are wanting," and aim at Church reforms.

2. I commend the whole subject to the minds of all thoughtful lay Churchmen. I invite you to assist us in maintaining the Church of our forefathers, the old Protestant Church of England, and to come forward and take up your rightful place and position. It is your best policy to do so. Except clergy and laity close their ranks and work shoulder to shoulder, we shall never hold the fort, and win the day. It would be your happiness to do so. You

would find a rich reward for your soul in activity for Christ's cause in this sinful world, and being general fellow-helpers with your clergy. Think what an immense blessing one single layman like Lord Shaftesbury may be to the land in which he lives. Think what England might be if we had a hundred more lay Churchmen like him. You would soon find out the enormous luxury of doing good, and being useful to your fellow-creatures. Just now you would give new life to the Church of England, render her, by God's blessing, invincible by her foes, and hand her down to your children's children, "Fair as the moon, clear as the sun, and terrible as an army with banners" (Cant. 6:10).

Note

I commend to all readers of this sermon the following extract from a leading article in the Guardian newspaper of January 5, 1870. From such a quarter, testimony to the importance of the "Position of Laity" is doubly valuable:—

"We have shown, we trust, that we are far from insensible to the dangers that might possibly arise from the admission of the laity to a larger degree of authority and influence than they now enjoy in the Anglican communion as known within these isles. Let us now glance for a moment at the strength of the case on behalf of the claims being urged by the laity.

"Under the patriarchal system, the regale and the pontifical were united. The head of the family was at once king and priest; and the idea that some sacrifices could only be offered by a king was so widely spread that Athens, after becoming a democracy, retained for this end a King-Archon, and Rome in like manner a Rex Sacrificulus. This union is to some extent still preserved in Thibet, in China, and in most countries under Mahometans rule. In Palestine we know that the two authorities were dissevered; the royalty ultimately falling to Judah, and the priesthood to Levi. Subsequently we read of Saul, Uzzah, and Uzziah being punished for usurpation of offices not intrusted to their care. Yet, when we reflect on the great pains bestowed by David in the matter of ritual, on the deposition of Abiathar by Solomon, on the action of pious monarchs such as Josiah and Hezekiah, and on the position of Zerubbabel and his descendants after the captivity, it must surely be acknowledged that the lay influence under the Mosaic dispensation was immense. One of the famous Jesuit commentators (either a Lapide or Maldonatus) does not hesitate to admit that in the Jewish polity the State was superior to the Church. In the time of our Lord at least one-third of the Sanhedrim consisted of laymen.

"When we turn to the infant Church Catholic, almost the earliest step taken by the community is one involving the action of the laity. The seven deacons were chosen by the whole multitude. And if various readings cause some difficulty respecting the Council of Jerusalem, yet the confirmation of its decision by the whole Church is a recorded fact. Evidence of the continuation of a line of thought and action consistent with these commencements is supplied by Dr. Moberly from the works of great and saintly doctors, a Cyprian and a Chrysostom, and from the Acts of early councils held at Carthage, at Eliberis, at Toledo, and among our own Anglo-Saxon ancestors. At the Councils of Pisa and of Constance, a prominent place was assigned to Canonists and other doctors of law who were simple laymen. Moreover, the great universities of Europe, though lay corporations, having received from the Church as well as from the State commissions to teach theology, were constantly appealed to for opinions both on questions relating to the faith and on cases of conscience. The reference concerning the lawfulness of Henry VIII's marriage to these famous bodies is the best known instance in our history, but it is by no means a solitary one. In the fourteenth century, such judgments, especially those proceeding from the University of Paris, had been very numerous; and so much weight was attached to them that they almost supplied the place (says Palmer) of the judgments of Provincial Synods.

"Nor have the laity achieved merely small things in the way of theology. It is true, as might have been expected, that the formation of dogma, necessitated by heresy, has been for the most part the work of bishops and presbyters, an Athanasius, a Leo, an Augustine. But not only have masterly apologies for the faith and works of Christian literature proceeded in great numbers from laic pens, but laymen have also, at certain times and places, shown themselves superior in their zeal for purity of doctrine to that portion of the Church which, as a rule, constitutes Ecclesia docens. A notable example occurs in the history of Arianism. Certain bishops of semi-Arian tendencies found it impossible to infuse into the laity of their flocks the heretical poison which they themselves had imbibed. It was a layman, too, who first called attention to the heresy of Nestorius. In our own time, the lay members of ecclesiastical Conventions in the United States have not unfrequently exhibited a more moderate and conservative tone than their clerical brethren."

CHAPTER XVIII

John 3:3; 2 Cor. 5:17
Questions About Regeneration.

THE paper which begins at this page is intended to supply information to all Churchmen who are puzzled and perplexed about baptismal regeneration. That famous doctrine is so widely held, and so confidently declared to be true, that I think it desirable to discuss the whole subject under the simple form of questions and answers. I wish to show those whose minds are in a state of suspense, that Churchmen who hold that baptism and regeneration do not always go together, have a great deal more of reason, logic, Scripture, and the Prayer Book on their side than is commonly supposed. Their views, at any rate, ought not to be regarded, as they too often are, with supercilious and unreasoning contempt. I venture, therefore, to think that the arguments contained in this paper deserve respectful consideration.

1. What is regeneration?

It is that complete change of heart and character which the Holy Spirit works in a person when he becomes a real Christian. The Church Catechism calls it "a death unto sin, and a new birth unto righteousness." It is the same thing as being "born again," or "born of God," or "born of the Spirit," "Except a man be born again" means "except a man be regenerate." "If any man be in Christ, he is a new creature;" that is, he is "born again, or regenerate" (John 3:3; 2 Cor. 5:17).

2. But are not all professing Christians real Christians?

Certainly not. Thousands, unhappily, are only Christians in name, and have nothing of real Christianity either in their hearts or lives. Just as St. Paul said, "He is not a Jew, which is one outwardly" (Rom. 2:28); so he would have said, "He is not a Christian, which is one outwardly." Just as he said, "He is a Jew, which is one inwardly;" so he would have said, "He is a Christian, which is one inwardly." In short, real Christians are regenerate, and merely nominal Christians are not.

3. But how are we to know whether we are regenerate or not? Is it a thing we can possibly find out before we die?

Regeneration may always be known by the fruits and effects it produces on a person's life and character. It is always attended by certain marks, evidences, effects, results, and consequences. Every regenerate person has these marks more or less distinctly, and he that has them not is not regenerate. A regeneration which produces no effects, bears no fruit, and cannot be seen in a person's life, is a regeneration never mentioned in Scripture.

4. What are the marks and evidences of regeneration? They are laid down for us so clearly and plainly in the First Epistle of St. John, that he who runs may read them. It is written there, "Whosoever is born of God doth not commit sin;" "Whosoever believeth that Jesus is the Christ is born of God;" "Every one that doeth righteousness is born of Him;" "Every one that loveth is born of God;" "Whatsoever is born of God overcometh the world;" "He that is begotten of God keepeth himself" (1 John 3:9, 5:1, 2:29, 4:7, 5:4, 5:18). If plain English words have any meaning, these texts mean that he who has these marks is "born again" or "regenerate," and he who has them not is not regenerate.

5. Have all regenerate persons these marks of regeneration in the same degree of depth, strength, clearness, and distinctness?

Most certainly not. There is a wide difference between the highest and lowest measure of grace possessed by those who are "born again." There are real and true Christians who are only "babes" in spiritual attainments, and there are others who are "strong," and vigorous, and able to do great things for Christ (1 John 2:12-14). The Scripture speaks of little faith and great faith, of little strength and great strength. One thing only is certain,— every regenerate person has more or less the marks of regeneration, and he who has none of them is not born again (Matt. 14:31, 15:28; Rev. 3:8; Rom. 15:1).

6. But are not all baptized persons regenerate, and does not regeneration always accompany baptism?

Certainly not. Myriads of baptized persons have not a single Scriptural mark of regeneration about them, and never had in their lives. They know nothing whatever of "a death unto sin, and a new birth unto righteousness." On the contrary, they too often live in sin, and are enemies of all righteousness. To say that such persons are "regenerate" on account of their baptism, is to say that which seems flatly contrary to the First Epistle of St. John. The Church Catechism says that baptism contains two parts,—the outward and visible sign, and the inward and spiritual grace But the Catechism nowhere says that the sign and the grace always go together.

7. But does not the Baptismal Service of the Church Prayer Book say of every baptized child, "This child is regenerate," and does it not tell us to thank God that it hath "pleased Him to regenerate the infant"? What can this mean? How can it be explained?

The Baptismal Service uses these expressions in the charitable supposition that those who use the Service, and bring their children to be baptized, are really what they profess to be. As Bishop Carleton says, "All this is the charity of the Church; and what more can you make of it?" As Bishop Downame says, "We are to distinguish between the judgment of charity and the judgment of certainty."

8. But is this explanation of the language of the Baptismal Service honest, natural, and just? Is it the real meaning which ought to be put on the words?

It is the only meaning which is consistent with the whole spirit of the Prayer Book. From first to last the Prayer Book charitably assumes that all who use it are real, thorough Christians. This is the only sense in which the Burial Service can be interpreted. This is the only sense in which we can teach children the Church Catechism. We bid them say, "The Holy Ghost sanctifieth me and all the elect people of God." Yet no man in his senses would say that all children who say the Catechism are really "sanctified" or really "elect," because they use these words.

9. But ought we not to believe that all who use Christ's ordinances receive a blessing as a matter of course?

Certainly not. The benefit of Christ's ordinances depends entirely on the spirit and manner in which they are used. The Scripture expressly says that a man may receive the Lord's Supper "unworthily," and eat and drink "to his own condemnation." The Articles of the Church of England declare that in such only as receive sacraments "rightly, worthily, and with faith," they have a wholesome effect and operation. They do not convey grace as a matter of course, "ex opere operato," in the same way that a medicine acts on the body. The famous Hooker teaches that "all receive not the grace of God which receive the sacraments of His grace." To maintain that every child who is baptized with water is at once regenerated and born again, appears to turn the sacrament of baptism into a mere form, and to contradict both Scripture and the Thirty-nine Articles.

10. But do not all infants receive baptism worthily, since they offer no obstacle to the grace of baptism? and are they not consequently all regenerated, as a matter of course, the moment they are baptized?

Certainly not. No infant is of itself worthy to receive grace, because, as the Catechism says, it is "born in sin and a child of wrath." It can only be received into the Church, and baptized on the faith and profession of its parents or sponsors. No true missionary thinks of baptizing heathen children without friends or sponsors. The Church Catechism asks the question, "Why are infants baptized?" But it does not give as an answer, "Because they offer no obstacle to grace,"—but "because they promise repentance and faith by their Sureties." Let us always remember that an infant has no title to baptism but the profession of its Sureties. Surely when these Sureties know nothing of repentance or faith, or of what they are promising, common sense points out that the infant is not likely to get any inward benefit from the sacrament. In plain words, if parents or sponsors bring an infant to baptism in utter ignorance, without faith or prayer or knowledge, it is monstrous to suppose that this infant must, nevertheless, receive regeneration. At this rate, it would matter nothing in what way sacraments are used, whether with ignorance or with knowledge, and it would signify nothing whether those who use them were godly or ungodly; the children of believing and of unbelieving parents would receive precisely the same benefit from baptism! Such a conclusion seems unreasonable and absurd.

11. But does not St. Paul say in his Epistles that Christians are "buried with Christ in baptism" and that baptized persons have "put on Christ"? (Gal. 3:27; Col. 2:12).

No doubt St. Paul says so. But the persons of whom he said this were not baptized in infancy, but when they were grown up, and in days too when faith and baptism were so closely connected, that as soon as a man believed he confessed his faith publicly by baptism. But there is not a single passage in the New Testament which describes at length the effect of baptism on an infant, nor a single text which says that all infants are born again, or regenerated, or buried with Christ in baptism. As Canon Mozley says, "Scripture nowhere asserts, either explicitly or implicitly, the regeneration of infants in baptism" (Mozley's Baptismal Controversy, p. 34). Besides this, we are expressly told that Simon the sorcerer, after his baptism, had "no part" in Christ, and his "heart was not right in the sight of God." Simon, therefore, could not have been regenerated, or born again in baptism (Acts 8:21).

12. But does not Peter say, "Baptism doth also save us"? and if it saves us, must it not also regenerate us? (1 Pet. 3:21).

No doubt St. Peter says so. But those who quote this text should not stop at the words "save us," but read carefully on to the end of the sentence. They will then see that St. Peter distinctly fences and guards his statement, by saying that the baptism which "saves" is not the mere outward application of water to the body, but the baptism which is accompanied by the "answer of a good conscience toward God." Moreover, it is a curious fact that St. Peter, who uses the expression "baptism saves," is the very same Apostle who told Simon after baptism that he was "in the bond of iniquity," and his "heart was not right in the sight of God" (Acts 8:21).

13. But does not our Lord Jesus Christ say to Nicodemus, "Except a man be born of water and the Spirit, he cannot enter into the kingdom of God"? (John 3:3). Does not this mean that all who are baptized with water are regenerate?

Certainly not. It proves nothing of the kind. The utmost that can be made of this famous and often quoted text is, that it shows the necessity of being "born of water and the Spirit" if we would be saved. But it does not say that all who are baptized, or "born of water," are at the same time "born of the Spirit." It may prove that there is a connection sometimes between baptism and regeneration, but it does not supply the slightest proof that an invariable connection always exists.

14. But may it not be true that all baptized persons receive the grace of spiritual regeneration in baptism, and that many of them afterwards lose it?

There is no plain warrant for such a statement in the Bible. St. Peter says expressly, that we are "born again, not of corruptible seed, but of incorruptible" (1 Pet. 1:23). The Seventeenth Article of our Church speaks of grace as a thing that cannot be lost: "They that be endowed with so excellent a benefit of God, walk religiously in good works,—and at length attain to everlasting felicity." It is very dishonouring to the mighty inward work of the Holy Ghost to suppose that it can be so continually lost and trampled under foot. Moreover, myriads of baptized persons from their very earliest infancy never give the slightest evidence of having any grace to lose, and are not one bit better, as boys and girls, than the unbaptized children of Quakers and Baptists. No wonder that Robert Abbott, Bishop of Salisbury in 1615, asks the question, "If there be that cure that they speak of in the baptized, how is it that there is so little effect or token thereof?"

15. But may it not be true that all baptized persons receive the grace of regeneration in baptism, and that it remains within them like a dormant seed, alive, though at present beaching no fruit?

Certainly not. The Apostle St. John expressly forbids us to suppose that there can be such a thing as dormant or sleeping grace. He says, "Whosoever is born of God does not commit sin, for his seed remaineth in him, and he cannot sin because he is born of God" (1 John 3:9). This witness is true. When there can be light which cannot be seen, and fire without heat, then, and not till then, there may be grace that is dormant and inactive. The well-known words, "Stir up the gift of God that is in thee," are far too often addressed to the baptized. Yet common sense will tell any one who refers to his Bible that these words were not used at all about the effects of baptism, but about the gifts of ministers (2 Tim. 1:6).

16. But do not the early Fathers hold that all baptized persons are necessarily regenerated in baptism? and have not many great and learned divines in every age maintained the same opinion?

The Fathers used very extravagant language about both the sacraments, and are not safe guides on this point. Moreover, they often contradict themselves and one another. The divines who deny that regeneration always accompanies baptism are as worthy of attention, and as learned and wise, as any divines who ever held baptismal regeneration. It is sufficient to say that Archbishops Cranmer, Whitgift, Usher, and Leighton, Bishops Latimer, Ridley, Jewell, Davenant, Carleten, Hopkins, and Robert Abbott, have left distinct evidence that they did not consider the grace of spiritual regeneration to be necessarily and invariably tied to baptism. After all, in questions like these we must call no man Master. It matters little what man says. What saith the Scripture?

17. But does not this view of regeneration, according to which many baptized persons are not regenerate at all, and receive no benefit whatever from their baptism, do great dishonour to one of Christ's sacraments, and tend to bring it into contempt?

Not at all. The truth is exactly the other way. To say that infant baptism confers grace mechanically, as a chemical solution produces an effect on a photographic plate, and that if water and certain words are used by a thoughtless, careless clergyman over the child of thoughtless, ignorant parents, the child is at once born again,—to say, furthermore, that an immense spiritual effect is produced by baptism when no effect whatever can be seen,—all this, to many thinking persons, seems calculated to degrade baptism! It tends to make observers suppose that baptism is useless, or that regeneration means nothing at all. He that would do honour to baptism should maintain that it is a high and holy ordinance, which, like every ordinance appointed by Christ, ought not to be touched without solemn reverence; and that no blessing can be expected unless it is used with heart, and knowledge, and faith, and prayer, and followed by godly training of the child baptized. Above all, he should maintain that when baptism does good, the good will be seen in the life and ways of the baptized. Those who do not feel satisfied about this matter will do well to study attentively the strong language which God uses about His own ordinances, when used formally and carelessly, in the prophet Isaiah (Isa. 1:11-12).

What did the prophet mean when he wrote these words: "To what purpose is the multitude of your sacrifices unto Me? saith the Lord.—I delight not in the blood of bullocks or of lambs"? He evidently meant that God's own ordinances may be made perfectly useless by man's misuse of them.

18. But may we not believe that regeneration means nothing more than a change of state, and does not mean a moral and spiritual change at all? May we not believe that it is a mere ecclesiastical word, signifying nothing more than admission to a state of Church privilege? And may we not then say that every person baptized is regenerated in baptism?

Of course we may say and believe anything we please in a free country like England, and this idea of an ecclesiastical regeneration cuts the knot of some difficulties, and has always satisfied some minds. But it is an insuperable difficulty that the word "regeneration" is never once used in this sense in the New Testament. Moreover, the parallel expression "born of God," in St. John's First Epistle, most certainly means a great deal more than being admitted into a state of ecclesiastical privilege! To say, for instance, "Whosoever is baptized doth not commit sin,—and overcometh the world," would be ridiculous, because untrue.—Moreover, the Church Catechism distinctly teaches that the inward and spiritual grace in baptism is not a mere ecclesiastical change, but "a death unto sin and a new birth unto righteousness." Moreover, the Homily for Whitsunday expressly describes regeneration as an inward and spiritual change. One thing is very certain: no unlearned reader of the Bible ever seems to understand how a person can be "regenerate" and yet not saved. The poor and simple-minded cannot take in the idea of ecclesiastical regeneration!

19. But is it not more kind, and liberal, and charitable, to assume that all baptized persons are regenerate, and to address them as such?

Most certainly not. On the contrary, it is calculated to lull conscience into a fatal security. It is likely to feed sloth, check self-examination, and encourage an easy, self-satisfied condition of soul. No religious statement is kind and charitable which is not strictly true. To keep back any part of God's truth, in order to appear kind, is not only a mistake but a sin. The way to do good is to warn people plainly, that they must not suppose they are regenerate because they are baptized. They must be told to examine themselves whether they are "born again," and not to believe they are regenerate, except they have the scriptural marks of regeneration.

20. But is it really necessary to attach such importance to this doctrine of regeneration? Is it not sufficient to teach people that they must be "good," and go to church, and be "in earnest," and do their duty, and that then they will get to heaven, somehow, at last, without telling them in this positive dogmatic way, they must be "born again"?

The answer to these questions is short and simple. Christians have no rule of religious faith and practice except the Bible. If the Bible is true, regeneration is absolutely necessary to salvation. It is written, "Except a man be born again, he cannot see the kingdom of God;" "Ye must be born again;"—"Except ye be converted and become as little children, ye shall in no wise enter the kingdom of heaven" (John 3:3-8; Matt. 18:3). It is possible for people to enter heaven and be saved, like the penitent thief, without baptism; but no one can be saved and go to heaven without regeneration. The penitent thief, though not baptized, was "born again." Regeneration, therefore, is a doctrine of primary and first-rate importance.

21. But if these things are true, and no one can be saved without regeneration, are there not many professing Christians who are in a very dangerous position? Are not those who are without the marks of being "born again" in imminent peril of being lost for ever?

Of course they are. But this is exactly what the Bible teaches from first to last about them. It is written, "Wide is the gate and broad is the way that leadeth to destruction, and many there be which go in thereat." It is written again, "Many walk of whom I tell you weeping, that they are the enemies of the cross of Christ, whose end is destruction" (Matt. 7:13; Phil. 3:18). It is the most miserable part of many people's religious condition, that they fancy they will go to heaven because they are baptized and go to church, while in reality, not being regenerate, they are on the road to eternal ruin.

22. Can ministers of the Church of Christ give regenerating grace to their people?

Most certainly not. St. John expressly says that those who are born of God are born, "not of blood, nor of the will of the flesh, nor of the will of man, but of God" (John 1:13). "It is the Spirit that quickeneth." Paul may plant, and Apollos may water; but God only can "give the increase" (John 6:63; 1 Cor. 3:7). Ministers, like John the Baptist, can baptize with water, but Christ alone can "baptize with the Holy Ghost" (Mark 1:8). To give spiritual life, as well as physical life, is the peculiar prerogative of God. Man can neither give it to himself, nor to another.

23. But supposing these things are true, what aught those unhappy persons to do who have no marks of regeneration about them, and feel that they are not born again? Are they to sit still in hopeless despair?

The Bible gives a simple answer to that question. If a man really feels his need of regeneration and desires it, he must seek Christ, the fountain of life, and cry mightily to Him. He must ask Him who baptizes with the Holy Ghost to baptize his heart, and to give him grace. It is written, "To as many as received Him, He gave power to become the sons of God" (John 1:12). He must pray for a new heart. It is written, "Your Father will give the Holy Spirit to them that ask Him" (Luke 11:13). He must seek life diligently in the use of God's Word. It is written that "faith cometh by hearing."—"Of his own will begat he us with the Word of truth" (Rom. 10:17; James 1:18). No man ever sought grace honestly in this way, and sought in vain. He that will not take the trouble to seek in this fashion does not really desire regeneration, and is not in earnest about his soul.

24. But supposing a person finds in himself some reason to hope that he really is born again, and has the true marks of regeneration, what is he to do? Is he to sit still, and take no more trouble about his soul?

Certainly not. He must strive daily to "grow in grace and in the knowledge of Christ" (2 Pet. 3:18). He must seek to deepen and strengthen the work of the Holy Spirit within him, by diligently exercising the grace he has received. He must "cleanse himself from all filthiness of flesh and spirit, perfecting holiness in the fear of God" (2 Cor. 7:1). He must endeavour to "abide in Christ" more closely, and to live the life of faith in the Son of God. He that thinks he is regenerate, and does not feel a continual desire to be more holy and more like Christ every year he lives, is in a very unsatisfactory and unhealthy state of soul (John 15:4-5; Gal. 2:20; 2 Pet. 1:5-10).

25. Have Evangelical Churchmen who hold the views of regeneration maintained in this paper any cause to be ashamed of their opinions?

None whatever. They can safely defy any one to prove that their views are not in harmony with Scripture, with the Thirty-nine Articles, with the Prayer Book, with the Catechism, with the Homilies, and with the writings of many of the best divines in the Church of England. Those who occupy such a position as this have no cause to be ashamed. The last day will prove who is right. To the judgment of that day we may safely and confidently appeal.

I conclude this paper with one general remark about the great principle on which the "Book of Common Prayer" was at first compiled. It is one which runs throughout the Liturgy from end to end. The mischief which has arisen, and the false teaching which has flowed from gross ignorance or neglect of this principle, are simply incalculable. Let me show what it is.

The principle of the Prayer Book is to suppose all members of the Church to be in reality what they are in profession, to be true believers in Christ, to be sanctified by the Holy Ghost. The Prayer Book takes the highest standard of what a Christian ought to be, and is all through worded accordingly. The minister addresses those who assemble together for public worship as believers. The people who use the words the Liturgy puts into their mouths are supposed to be believers. But those who drew up the Prayer Book never meant to assert that all who were members of the Church of England were actually and really true Christians! On the contrary, they tell us expressly in the Articles, that "in the visible Church the evil be ever mingled with the good." But they held that if forms of devotion were drawn up at all, they must be drawn up on the supposition that those who used them were real Christians, and not false ones. And in so doing I think they were quite right. A Liturgy for unbelievers and unconverted men would be absurd, and practically useless. The part of the congregation for whom it was meant would care little or nothing for any Liturgy at all. The holy and believing part of the congregation would find its language entirely unsuited to them, and beneath their wants.

How any one can fail to see this principle running through the Prayer-book Services, is one of those things which I must frankly say I fail to understand. It is quite certain that St. Paul wrote his Epistles in the New Testament to the Churches upon this principle. He constantly addresses their members as "saints" and "elect," and as having grace, and faith, and hope, and love, though it is evident that some of them had no grace at all! I am firmly convinced that the compilers of our Prayer Book drew up its Services upon the same lines, the lines of charitable supposition; and it is on this principle alone that the book can be interpreted, and especially on the subject of Baptism and Regeneration.[24]

CHAPTER XIX

Tit. 2:6
Thoughts For Young Men.

WHEN St. Paul wrote his Epistle to Titus about his duty as a minister, he mentioned young men as a class requiring particular attention. After speaking of aged men and aged women, and young women, he adds this pithy advice, "Young men likewise exhort to be sober-minded" (Tit. 2:6). I am going to follow the Apostle's advice. I propose to offer a few words of friendly exhortation to young men.

I am growing old myself, but there are few things I remember so well as the days of my youth. I have a most distinct recollection of the joys and the sorrows, the hopes and the fears, the temptations and the difficulties, the mistaken judgments and the misplaced affections, the errors and the aspirations, which surround and accompany a young man's life. If I can only say something to keep some young man in the right way, and preserve him from faults and sins, which may mar his prospects both for time and eternity, I shall be very thankful.

There are four things which I propose to do:—

I. I will mention some general reasons why young men need exhorting.

II. I will notice some special dangers against which young men need to be warned.

III. I will give some general counsels which I entreat young men to receive.

IV. I will set down some special rules of conduct which I strongly advise young men to follow.

On each of these four points I have something to say, and I pray to God that what I say may do good to some soul.

I. Reasons for exhorting Young Men.

In the first place, What are the general reasons why young men need peculiar exhortation? I will mention several of them in order.

---

[24]Those who wish to study this subject more deeply are advised to read Canon Faber's Primitive Doctrine of Regeneration, 8vo. Dean Goode on The Effects of Infant Baptism, 8vo. Canon Mozley on Baptismal Regeneration, 8vo. Canon Mozley on The Baptismal Controversy, 8vo.

(1) For one thing, there is the painful fact that there are few young men anywhere who seem to have any religion. I speak without respect of persons; I say it of all. High or low, rich or poor, gentle or simple, learned or unlearned, in town or in country,—it makes no matter. I tremble to observe how few young men are led by the Spirit,—how few are in that narrow way which leads to life,—how few are setting their affections upon things above,—how few are taking up the cross, and following Christ. I say it with all sorrow, but I believe, as in God's sight, I am saying nothing more than the truth.

Young men, you form a large and most important class in the population of this country; but where, and in what condition, are your immortal souls? Alas, whatever way we turn for an answer, the report will be one and the same!

Let us ask any faithful minister of the gospel, and mark what he will tell us. How many unmarried young people can he reckon up who come to the Lord's Supper? Who are the most backward about means of grace,—the most irregular about Sunday services,—the most difficult to draw to weekly lectures and prayer meetings,—the most inattentive under preaching at all times? Which part of his congregation fills him with most anxiety? Who are the Reubens for whom he has the deepest "searchings of heart"? Who in his flock are the hardest to manage,—who require the most frequent warnings and rebukes,—who occasion him the greatest uneasiness and sorrow,—who keep him most constantly in fear for their souls, and seem most hopeless? Depend on it, his answer will always be, "The Young Men!"

Let us ask the parents in any parish throughout England, and see what they will generally say. Who in their families give them most pain and trouble? Who need the most watchfulness, and most often vex and disappoint them? Who are the first to be led away from what is right, and the last to remember cautions and good advice? Who are the most difficult to keep in order and bounds? Who most frequently break out into open sin, disgrace the name they bear, make their friends unhappy, embitter the old age of their relations, and bring down grey hairs with sorrow to the grave? Depend on it, the answer will generally be, "The Young Men!"

Let us ask the magistrates and officers of justice, and mark what they will reply. Who go to public-houses and beer-shops most? Who are the greatest Sabbath-breakers? Who make up riotous mobs and seditious meetings? Who are oftenest taken up for drunkenness, breaches of the peace, fighting, poaching, stealing, assaults, and the like? Who fill the gaols, and penitentiaries, and convict ships? Who are the class which requires the most incessant watching and looking after? Depend on it, they will at once point to the same quarter,—they will say, "The Young Men."

Let us turn to the upper classes, and mark the report we shall get from them. In one family the sons are always wasting time, health, and money, in the selfish pursuit of pleasure. In another, the sons will follow no profession, and fritter away the most precious years of their life in doing nothing. In another, they take up a profession as a mere form, but pay no attention to its duties. In another, they are always forming wrong connections, gambling, getting into debt, associating with bad companions, keeping their friends in a constant fever of anxiety. Alas, rank, and title, and wealth, and education, do not prevent these things! Anxious fathers, and heart-broken mothers, and sorrowing sisters, could tell sad tales about them, if the truth were known. Many a family, with everything this world can give, numbers among its connections some name that is never named,—or only named with regret and shame,—some son, some brother, some cousin, some nephew,— who will have his own way, and is a grief to all who know him.

There is seldom a rich family which has not got some thorn in its side, some blot in its page of happiness, some constant source of pain and anxiety;—and often, far too often, is not this the true cause, "The Young Men"?

What shall we say to these things? These are facts,—plain staring facts,—facts which meet us on every side,—facts which cannot be denied. How dreadful this is! How dreadful the thought, that every time I meet a young man, I meet one who is in all probability an enemy of God,—travelling in the broad way which leads to destruction,—unfit for heaven! Surely, with such facts before me, you will not wonder that I exhort you,—you must allow there is a cause.

(2) For another thing, death and judgment are before young men, even as others, and they nearly all seem to forget it.

Young men, it is appointed unto you once to die; and however strong and healthy you may be now, the day of your death is perhaps very near. I see young people sick as well as old. I bury youthful corpses as well as aged. I read the names of persons no older than yourselves in every churchyard. I learn from books that, excepting infancy and old age, more die between thirteen and twenty-three than at any other season of life. And yet you live as if you were sure at present not to die at all.

Are you thinking you will mind these things tomorrow? Remember the words of Solomon: "Boast not thyself of tomorrow; for thou knowest not what a day may bring forth" (Prov. 27:1). "Serious things tomorrow," said a heathen,[25] to one who warned him of coming danger; but his tomorrow never came. Tomorrow is the devil's day, but today is God's. Satan cares not how spiritual your intentions may be, and how holy your resolutions, if only they are fixed for tomorrow. Oh, give not place to the devil in this matter! Answer him, "No: Satan! It shall be today, today." All men do not live to be patriarchs, like Isaac and Jacob. Many children die before their fathers. David had to mourn the death of his two finest sons; Job lost all his ten children in one day. Your lot may be like one of theirs, and when death summons, it will be vain to talk of tomorrow,—you must go at once.

Are you thinking you will have a convenient season to mind these things by and by? So thought Felix and the Athenians to whom Paul preached; but it never came. Hell is paved with such fancies. Better make sure work while you can. Leave nothing unsettled that is eternal. Run no risk when your soul is at stake. Believe me, the salvation of a soul is no easy matter. All need a "great" salvation, whether young or old; all need to be born again, all need to be washed in Christ's blood,—all need to be sanctified by the Spirit. Happy is that man who does not leave these things uncertain, but never rests till he has the witness of the Spirit within him, telling him that he is a child of God.

Young men, your time is short. Your days are but a span long,—a shadow, a vapour,—a tale that is soon told. Your bodies are not brass. "Even the young men," says Isaiah, "shall utterly fall" (Isa. 40:30). Your health may be taken from you in a moment:—it only needs a fall, a fever, an inflammation, a broken blood-vessel,—and the worm would soon feed upon you. There is but a step between any one of you and death. This night your soul might be required of you. You are fast going the way of all the earth,—you will soon be gone. Your life is all uncertainty,—your death and judgment are perfectly sure. You too must hear the Archangel's trumpet, and go forth to stand before the great white throne of judgement,—you too must obey that summons, which Jerome says was

---

[25] Archias the Theban.

always fining in his ears: "Arise, ye dead, and come to judgment." "Surely I come quickly," is the language of the Judge Himself. I cannot, dare not, will not let you alone.

Oh that you would all take to heart the words of the Preacher: "Rejoice, O young man, in thy youth, and let thy heart cheer thee in the days of thy youth, and walk in the ways of thine heart, and in the sight of thine eyes; but know thou, that for all these things God will bring thee into judgment" (Eccles. 11:9). Wonderful, that with such a prospect, any man can be careless and unconcerned! Surely none are so mad as those who are content to live unprepared to die. Surely the unbelief of men is the most amazing thing in the world. Well may the clearest prophecy in the Bible begin with these words, "Who hath believed our report?" (Isa. 53:1). Well may the Lord Jesus say, "When the Son of man cometh, shall He find faith on the earth?" (Luke 18:8). Young men, I fear lest this be the report of many of you in the courts above: "They will not believe" I fear lest you be hurried out of the world, and awake to find out, too late, that death and judgment are realities. I fear all this, and therefore I exhort you.

(3) For another thing, what young men will be, in all probability depends on what they are now, and they seem to forget this.

Youth is the seed-time of full age,—the moulding season in the little space of human life,—the turning-point in the history of man's mind.

By the shoot we judge of the tree,—by the blossoms we judge of the fruit,—by the spring we judge of the harvest,—by the morning we judge of the day,—and by the character of the young man, we may generally judge what he will be when he grows up.

Young men, be not deceived. Think not you can, at will, serve lusts and pleasures in your beginning, and then go and serve God with ease at your latter end. Think not you can live with Esau, and then die with Jacob. It is a mockery to deal with God and your souls in such a fashion. It is an awful mockery to suppose you can give the flower of your strength to the world and the devil, and then put off the King of kings with the scraps and leavings of your hearts, the wreck and remnant of your powers. It is an awful mockery, and you may find to your cost the thing cannot be done.

I daresay you are reckoning on a late repentance. You know not what you are doing. You are reckoning without God. Repentance and faith are the gifts of God, and gifts that He often withholds, when they have been long offered in vain. I grant you true repentance is never too late, but I warn you at the same time, late repentance is seldom true. I grant you, one penitent thief was converted in his last hours, that no man might despair; but I warn you, only one was converted, that no man might presume. I grant you it is written, Jesus is "able to save them to the uttermost that come to God by Him" (Heb. 7:25). But I warn you, it is also written by the same Spirit, "Because I have called, and ye refused, I also will laugh at your calamity; I will mock when your fear cometh" (Prov. 1:24-26).

Believe me, you will find it no easy matter to turn to God just when you please. It is a true saying of good Archbishop Leighton: "The way of sin is down hill; a man cannot stop when he would." Holy desires and serious convictions are not like the servants of the Centurion, ready to come and go at your desire; rather are they like the unicorn in Job, they will not obey your voice, nor attend at your bidding. It was said of a famous general[26] of old, when he could have taken the city[27] he warred against, he would not, and by and

---

[26] Hannibal.
[27] Rome.

by when he would, he could not. Beware, lest the same kind of event befall you in the matter of eternal life.

Why do I say all this? I say it because of the force of habit. I say it because experience tells me that people's hearts are seldom changed if they are not changed when young. Seldom indeed are men converted when they are old. Habits have long roots. Sin once allowed to nestle in your bosom, will not be turned out at your bidding. Custom becomes second nature, and its chains are threefold cords not easily broken. Well says the prophet, "Can the Ethiopian change his skin, or the leopard his spots? then may ye also do good, that are accustomed to do evil" (Jer. 13:23). Habits are like stones rolling down hill, the further they roll, the faster and more ungovernable is their course. Habits, like trees, are strengthened by age. A boy may bend an oak, when it is a sapling, a hundred men cannot root it up, when it is a full-grown tree. A child can wade over the Thames at its fountain-head, the largest ship in the world can float in it when it gets near the sea. So it is with habits: the older the stronger, the longer they have held possession, the harder they will be to cast out. They grow with our growth, and strengthen with our strength. Custom is the nurse of sin. Every fresh act of sin lessens fear and remorse, hardens our hearts, blunts the edge of our conscience, and increases our evil inclination.

Young men, you may fancy I am laying too much stress on this point. If you had seen old men, as I have done, on the brink of the grave, feelingless, seared, callous, dead, cold, hard as the nether mill-stone, you would not think so. Believe me, you cannot stand still in the affairs of your souls. Habits of good or evil are daily strengthening in your hearts. Every day you are either getting nearer to God, or further off. Every year that you continue impenitent, the wall of division between you and heaven becomes higher and thicker, and the gulf to be crossed deeper and broader. Oh, dread the hardening effect of constant lingering in sin! Now is the accepted time. See that your flight be not in the winter of your days. If you seek not the Lord when young, the strength of habit is such that you will probably never seek Him at all.

I fear this, and therefore I exhort you.

(4) For another thing, the devil uses special diligence to destroy the souls of young men, and they seem not to know it.

Satan knows well that you will make up the next generation, and therefore he employs every art betimes to make you his own. I would not have you ignorant of his devices.

You are those on whom he plays off all his choicest temptations. He spreads his net with the most watchful carefulness, to entangle your hearts. He baits his traps with the sweetest morsels, to get you into his power. He displays his wares before your eyes with his utmost ingenuity, in order to make you buy his sugared poisons, and eat his accursed dainties. You are the grand object of his attack. May the Lord rebuke him, and deliver you out of his hands.

Young men, beware of being taken by his snares. He will try to throw dust in your eyes, and prevent you seeing anything in its true colours. He would fain make you think evil good, and good evil. He will paint, and gild, and dress up sin, in order to make you fall in love with it. He will deform, and misrepresent, and caricature true religion, in order to make you take a dislike to it. He will exalt the pleasures of wickedness,—but he will hide from you the sting. He will lift up before your eyes the cross and its painfulness,— but He will keep out of sight the eternal crown. He will promise you everything, as he did to Christ, if you will only serve him. He will even help you to wear a form of religion, if you will only neglect the power. He will tell you at the beginning of your lives, it is too soon to serve God,—he will tell you at the end, it is too late. Oh, be not deceived!

You little know the danger you are in from this enemy; and it is this very ignorance which makes me afraid. You are like blind men, walking amidst holes and pitfalls; you do not see the perils which are around you on every side.

Your enemy is mighty. He is called "The Prince of this world" (John 14:30). He opposed our Lord Jesus Christ all through His ministry. He tempted Adam and Eve to eat the forbidden fruit, and so brought sin and death into the world. He tempted even David, the man after God's own heart, and caused his latter days to be full of sorrow. He tempted even Peter, the chosen Apostle, and made him deny his Lord. Surely his enmity is not to be despised?

Your enemy is restless. He never sleeps. He is always going about as a roaring lion, seeking whom he may devour. He is ever going to and fro in the earth, and walking up and down in it. You may be careless about your souls: he is not. He wants them to make them miserable, like himself, and will have them if he can. Surely his enmity is not to be despised?

And your enemy is cunning. For near six thousand years he has been reading one book, and that book is the heart of man. He ought to know it well, and he does know it; all its weakness, all its deceitfulness, all its folly. And he has a store of temptations, such as are most likely to do it harm. Never will you go to the place where he will not find you. Go into towns,—he will be there. Go into a wilderness, he will be there also. Sit among drunkards and revilers,—and he will be there to help you. Listen to preaching,—and he will be there to distract you. Surely such enmity is not to be despised?

Young men, this enemy is working hard for your destruction, however little you may think it. You are the prize for which he is specially contending. He foresees you must either be the blessings or the curses of your day, and he is trying hard to effect a lodgment in your hearts thus early, in order that you may help forward his kingdom by and by. Well does he understand that to spoil the bud is the surest way to mar the flower.

Oh that your eyes were opened, like those of Elisha's servant in Dothan! Oh that you did but see what Satan is scheming against your peace! I must warn you,—I must exhort you. Whether you will hear or not, I cannot, dare not, leave you alone.

(5) For another thing, young men need exhorting, because of the sorrow it will save them, to begin serving God now.

Sin is the mother of all sorrow, and no sort of sin appears to give a man so much misery and pain as the sins of his youth. The foolish acts he did, the time he wasted,—the mistakes he made, the bad company he kept,—the harm he did himself, both body and soul, the chances of happiness he threw away, the openings of usefulness he neglected; all these are things that often embitter the conscience of an old man, throw a gloom on the evening of his days, and fill the later hours of his life with self-reproach and shame.

Some men could tell you of the untimely loss of health, brought on by youthful sins. Disease racks their limbs with pain, and life is almost a weariness. Their muscular strength is so wasted, that a grasshopper seems a burden. Their eye has become prematurely dim, and their natural force abated. The sun of their health has gone down while it is yet day, and they mourn to see their flesh and body consumed. Believe me, this is a bitter cup to drink.

Others could give you sad accounts of the consequences of idleness. They threw away the golden opportunity for learning. They would not get wisdom at the time when their minds were most able to receive it, and their memories most ready to retain it. And now it is too late. They have not leisure to sit down and learn. They have no longer the same power, even if they had the leisure. Lost time can never be redeemed. This too is a bitter cup to drink.

Others could tell you of grievous mistakes in judgment, from which they suffer all their lives long. They would have their own way. They would not take advice. They formed some connection which has been altogether ruinous to their happiness. They chose a profession for which they were entirely unsuited. And they see it all now. But their eyes are only open when the mistake cannot be retrieved. Oh, this is also a bitter cup to drink!

Young men, young men, I wish you did but know the comfort of a conscience not burdened with a long list of youthful sins. These are the wounds that pierce the deepest. These are the arrows that drink up a man's spirit. This is the iron that enters into the soul. Be merciful to yourselves. Seek the Lord early, and so you will be spared many a bitter tear.

This is the truth that Job seems to have felt. He says, "Thou writest bitter things against me, and makest me to possess the iniquities of my youth" (Job 13:26). So also his friend Zophar, speaking of the wicked, says, "His bones are full of the sins of his youth, which shall lie down with him in the dust" (Job 20:11).

David also seems to have felt it. He says to the Lord, "Remember not the sins of my youth, nor my transgressions" (Ps. 25:7).

Beza, the great Swiss Reformer, felt it so strongly, that he named it in his will as a special mercy that he had been called out from the world, by the grace of God, at the age of sixteen.

Go and ask believers now, and I think many of them will tell you much the same. "Oh that I could live my young days over again!" he will most probably say. "Oh that I had spent the beginning of my life in a better fashion! Oh that I had not laid the foundation of evil habits so strongly in the spring-time of my course!"

Young men, I want to save you all this sorrow, if I can. Hell itself is truth known too late. Be wise in time. What youth sows, old age must reap. Give not the most precious season of your life to that which will not comfort you in your latter end. Sow to yourselves rather in righteousness: break up your fallow ground, sow not among thorns.

Sin may go lightly from your hand, or run smoothly off your tongue now, but depend on it, sin and you will meet again by and by, however little you may like it. Old wounds will often ache and give pain long after they are healed, and only a scar remains:—so may you find it with your sins. The footprints of animals have been found on the surface of rocks that were once wet sand, thousands of years after the animal that made them has perished and passed away;[28] so also it may be with your sins.

"Experience," says the proverb, "keeps a dear school, but fools will learn in no other." I want you all to escape the misery of learning in that school. I want you to avoid the wretchedness that youthful sins are sure to entail. This is the last reason why I exhort you.

II. Dangers of Young Men.

In the second place, there are some special dangers against which young men need to be warned.

(1) One danger to young men is pride.

---

[28] See Buckland's Bridgewater Treatise, vol. ii. plate 26.

I know well that all souls are in fearful peril. Old or young, it matters not; all have a race to run, a battle to fight, a heart to mortify, a world to overcome, a body to keep under control, a devil to resist; and we may well say, Who is sufficient for these things? But still every age and condition has its own peculiar snares and temptations, and it is well to know them. He that is forewarned is forearmed. If I can only persuade you to be on your guard against the dangers I am going to name, I am sure I shall do your souls an essential service.

Pride is the oldest sin in the world. Indeed, it was before the world. Satan and his angels fell by pride. They were not satisfied with their first estate. Thus pride stocked hell with its first inhabitants.

Pride cast Adam out of paradise. He was not content with the place God assigned him. He tried to raise himself, and fell. Thus sin, sorrow, and death entered in by pride.

Pride sits in all our hearts by nature. We are born proud. Pride makes us rest satisfied with ourselves,—think we are good enough as we are,—stop our ears against advice,—refuse the gospel of Christ,—turn every one to his own way. But pride never reigns anywhere so powerfully as in the heart of a young man.

How common is it to see young men heady, highminded, and impatient of counsel! How often they are rude and uncourteous to all about them, thinking they are not valued and honoured as they deserve! How often they will not stop to listen to a hint from an older person! They think they know everything. They are full of conceit of their own wisdom. They reckon elderly people, and especially their relations, stupid, and dull, and slow. They fancy they want no teaching or instruction themselves: they understand all things. It makes them almost angry to be spoken to. Like young horses, they cannot bear the least control. They must be independent, and have their own way. They seem to think, like those whom Job mentioned, "We are the people, and wisdom shall die with us" (Job 12:2). And this is all pride.

Such an one was Rehoboam, who despised the counsel of the old experienced men who stood before his father, and hearkened to the advice of the young men of his own generation. He lived to reap the consequences of his folly. There are many like him.

Such an one was the prodigal son in the parable, who had to have the portion of goods which fell to him, and set up life for himself. He could not submit to live quietly under his father's roof, but would go into a far country, and be his own master. Like the little child that will leave its mother's hand and walk alone, he soon smarted for his folly. He became wiser when he had to eat husks with the swine. But there are many like him.

Young men, I beseech you earnestly, beware of pride. Two things are said to be very rare sights in the world, one is a young man humble, and the other is an old man content. I fear this saying is only too true.

Be not proud of your own abilities, your own strength,—your own knowledge,—your own appearance, your own cleverness. Be not proud of yourself, and your endowments of any kind. It all comes from not knowing yourself and the world. The older you grow, and the more you see, the less reason you will find for being proud. Ignorance and inexperience are the pedestal of pride; once let the pedestal be removed, and pride will soon come down.

Remember how often Scripture sets before us the excellence of a humble spirit. How strongly we are warned "not to think of ourselves more highly than we ought to think"! (Rom. 12:3). How plainly we are told, "If any man think that he knoweth anything, he knoweth nothing yet as he ought to know"! (1 Cor. 8:2). How strict is the command, "Put on humbleness of mind"! (Col. 3:12). And again, "Be clothed with humility" (1 Pet. 5:5). Alas, this is a garment of which many seem not to have so much as a rag.

Think of the great example our Lord Jesus Christ leaves us in this respect. He washed the feet of His disciples, saying, "Ye should do as I have done to you" (John 13:15). It is written, "Though He was rich, yet for your sakes He became poor" (2 Cor. 8:9). And again, "He made Himself of no reputation, and took upon Him the form of a servant, and was made in the likeness of men; and being found in fashion as a man, He humbled Himself" (Phil. 2:7-8). Surely to be proud is to be more like the devil and fallen Adam, than like Christ. Surely it can never be mean and low-spirited to be like Him.

Think of the wisest man that ever lived—I mean Solomon. See how he speaks of himself as a "little child,"—as one who "knew not how to go out or come in," or manage for himself (1 Kings 3:7-8). That was a very different spirit from his brother Absalom's, who thought himself equal to anything: "Oh that I were made judge in the land, that every man which hath any suit or cause might come unto me, and I would do him justice" (2 Sam. 15:4). That was a very different spirit from his brother Adonijah's, who "exalted himself, saying, I will be king" (1 Kings 1:5). Humility was the beginning of Solomon's wisdom. He writes it down as his own experience, "Seest thou a man wise in his own conceit? there is more hope of a fool than of him" (Prov. 26:12).

Young men, lay to heart the Scriptures here quoted. Do not be too confident in your own judgment. Cease to be sure that you are always right, and others wrong. Be distrustful of your own opinion, when you find it contrary to that of older men than yourselves, and specially to that of your own parents. Age gives experience, and therefore deserves respect. It is a mark of Elihu's wisdom, in the book of Job, that "he waited till Job had spoken, because they were older than himself" (Job 32:4). And afterwards he said, "I am young, and you are very old; wherefore I was afraid, and durst not show you mine opinion. I said, Days should speak, and multitude of years should teach wisdom" (Job 32:6-7). Modesty and silence are beautiful graces in young people. Never be ashamed of being a learner: Jesus was one at twelve years; when He was found in the temple, He was "sitting in the midst of the doctors, both hearing them, and asking them questions" (Luke 2:46). The wisest men would tell you they are always learners, and are humbled to find after all how little they know. The great Sir Isaac Newton used to say that he felt himself no better than a little child, who had picked up a few precious stones on the shore of the sea of knowledge.

Young men, if you would be wise, if you would be happy, remember the warning I give you,—Beware of pride.

(2) Another danger to young men is the love of pleasure.

Youth is the time when our passions are strongest,—and like unruly children, cry most loudly for indulgence. Youth is the time when we have generally most health and strength: death seems far away, and to enjoy ourselves in this life seems everything. Youth is the time when most people have few earthly cares or anxieties to take up their attention. And all these things help to make young men think of nothing so much as pleasure. "I serve lusts and pleasures;" that is the true answer many a young man should give, if asked, "Whose servant are you?"

Young men, time would fail me if I were to tell you all the fruits this love of pleasure produces, and all the ways in which it may do you harm. Why should I speak of revelling, feasting, drinking, gambling, theatre-going, dancing, and the like? Few are to be found who do not know something of these things by bitter experience. And these are only instances. All things that give a feeling of excitement for the time,—all things that drown thought, and keep the mind in a constant whirl,—all things that please the senses and gratify the flesh;—these are the sort of things that have mighty power at your time of life, and they owe their power to the love of pleasure. Be on your guard. Be not like those of whom Paul speaks, "Lovers of pleasure more than lovers of God" (2 Tim. 3:4).

Remember what I say: if you would cling to earthly pleasures, these are the things which murder souls. There is no surer way to get a seared conscience and a hard impenitent heart, than to give way to the desires of the flesh and mind. It seems nothing at first, but it tells in the long run.

Consider what Peter says: "Abstain from fleshly lusts, which war against the soul" (1 Pet. 2:11). They destroy the soul's peace, break down its strength, lead it into hard captivity, make it a slave.

Consider what Paul says: "Mortify your members which are upon the earth" (Col. 3:5). "They that are Christ's have crucified the flesh, with its affections and lusts" (Gal. 5:24). "I keep under my body, and bring it into subjection" (1 Cor. 9:27). Once the body was a perfect mansion of the soul; now it is all corrupt and disordered, and needs constant watching. It is a burden to the soul,—not a helpmeet; a hindrance,—not an assistance. It may become a useful servant, but it is always a bad master.

Consider, again, the words of Paul: "Put ye on the Lord Jesus Christ, and make not provision for the flesh, to fulfil the lusts thereof" (Rom. 13:14). "These," says Leighton, "are the words, the very reading of which so wrought with Augustine, that from a licentious young man he turned a faithful servant of Jesus Christ." Young men, I wish this might be the case with all of you.

Remember, again, if you will cling to earthly pleasures, they are all unsatisfying, empty, and vain. Like the locusts of the vision in Revelation, they seem to have crowns on their heads: but like the same locusts, you will find they have stings,—real stings,—in their tails. All is not gold that glitters. All is not good that tastes sweet. All is not real pleasure that pleases for a time.

Go and take your fill of earthly pleasures if you will, you will never find your heart satisfied with them. There will always be a voice within, crying, like the leech in the Proverbs 30:15, "Give and give!" There is an empty place there, which nothing but God can fill. You will find, as Solomon did by experience, that earthly pleasures are but a vain show,—vanity and vexation of spirit,—whited sepulchres, fair to look at without, full of ashes and corruption within. Better be wise in time. Better write "poison" on all earthly pleasures. The most lawful of them must be used with moderation. All of them are soul-destroying if you give them your heart.[29]

And here I will not shrink from warning all young men to remember the seventh commandment; to beware of adultery and fornication, of all impurity of every kind. I fear there is often a want of plain speaking on this part of God's law. But when I see how prophets and Apostles have dealt with this subject,—when I observe the open way in which the Reformers of our own Church denounce it,—when I see the number of young men who walk in the footsteps of Reuben, and Hophni, and Phinehas, and Amnon,—I for one cannot, with a good conscience, hold my peace. I doubt whether the world is any better for the excessive silence which prevails upon this commandment. For my own part,

---

[29] "Pleasure," says Adams on Second Peter, "must first have the warrant, that it be without sin;—then the measure, that it be without excess."

I feel it would be false and unscriptural delicacy, in addressing young men, not to speak of that which is pre-eminently "the young man's sin."

The breach of the seventh commandment is the sin above all others, that, as Hosea says, "takes away the heart" (Hos. 4:11). It is the sin that leaves deeper scars upon the soul than any sin that a man can commit. It is a sin that slays its thousands in every age, and has overthrown not a few of the saints of God in time past. Lot, and Samson, and David are fearful proofs. It is the sin that man dares to smile at, and smoothes over under the names of gaiety, unsteadiness, wildness, and irregularity. But it is the sin that the devil particularly rejoices over, for he is the "unclean spirit;" and it is the sin that God particularly abhors, and declares He "will judge" (Heb. 13:4).

Young men, "flee fornication" (1 Cor. 6:18) if you love life. "Let no man deceive you with vain words: for because of these things cometh the wrath of God upon the children of disobedience" (Eph. 5:6). Flee the occasions of it,—the company of those who might draw you into it, the places where you might be tempted to it. Read what our Lord says about it in Matt. 5:28. Be like holy Job: "Make a covenant with your eyes" (Job 31:1). Flee talking of it. It is one of the things that ought not so much as to be named. You cannot handle pitch and not be defiled. Flee the thoughts of it; resist them, mortify them, pray against them,—make any sacrifice rather than give way. Imagination is the hotbed where this sin is too often hatched. Guard your thoughts, and there is little fear about your deeds.

Consider the caution I have been giving. If you forget all else, do not let this be forgotten.

(3) Another danger to young men is thoughtlessness and inconsideration.

Want of thought is one simple reason why thousands of souls are cast away for ever. Men will not consider, will not look forward, will not look around them,—will not reflect on the end of their present course, and the sure consequences of their present ways,—and awake at last to find they are damned for want of thinking.

Young men, none are in more danger of this than yourselves. You know little of the perils around you, and so you are heedless how you walk. You hate the trouble of sober, quiet thinking, and so you form wrong decisions and run your heads into sorrow. Young Esau had to have his brother's pottage and sell his birthright: he never thought how much he should one day want it. Young Simeon and Levi had to avenge their sister Dinah, and slay the Shechemites: they never considered how much trouble and anxiety they might bring on their father Jacob and his house. Job seems to have been specially afraid of this thoughtlessness among his children: it is written, that when they had a feast, and "the days of their feasting were gone about, Job sent and sanctified them, and rose up early in the morning and offered burnt-offerings, according to the number of them all: for Job said, It may be that my sons have sinned, and cursed God in their hearts. Thus did Job continually" (Job 1:5).

Believe me, this world is not a world in which we can do well without thinking, and least of all do well in the matter of our souls. "Don't think," whispers Satan: he knows that an unconverted heart is like a dishonest tradesman's books, it will not bear close inspection. "Consider your ways," says the Word of God, stop and think,—consider and be wise. Well says the Spanish proverb, "Hurry comes from the devil." Just as men marry in haste and then repent at leisure, so they make mistakes about their souls in a minute, and then suffer for it for years. Just as a bad servant does wrong, and then says, "I never gave it a thought," so young men run into sin, and then say, "I did not think about it,—it did not look like sin." Not look like sin! What would you have? Sin will not come to you, saying, "I am sin;" it would do little harm if it did. Sin always seems "good, and pleasant, and desirable," at the time of commission. Oh, get wisdom, get discretion! Remember the words of Solomon: "Ponder the paths of thy feet, and let thy ways be established" (Prov. 4:26). It is a wise saying of Lord Bacon, "Do nothing rashly. Stay a little, that you make an end the sooner."

Some, I dare say, will object that I am asking what is unreasonable; that youth is not the time of life when people ought to be grave and thoughtful. I answer, there is little danger of their being too much so in the present day. Foolish talking, and jesting, and joking, and excessive merriment, are only too common. Doubtless there is a time for all things; but to be always light and trifling is anything but wise. What says the wisest of men? "It is better to go to the house of mourning than to go to the house of feasting: for that is the end of all men; and the living will lay it to heart. Sorrow is better than laughter: for by the sadness of the countenance the heart is made better. The heart of the wise is in the house of mourning; but the heart of fools is in the house of mirth" (Eccles. 7:2-4). Matthew Henry tells a story of a great statesman[30] in Queen Elizabeth's time, who retired from public life in his latter days, and gave himself up to serious thought. His former gay companions came to visit him, and told him he was becoming melancholy: "No," he replied, "I am serious; for all are serious round about me. God is serious in observing us,—Christ is serious in interceding for us, the Spirit is serious in striving with us,—the truths of God are serious,—our spiritual enemies are serious in their endeavours to ruin us,—poor lost sinners are serious in hell;—and why then should not you and I be serious too?"

Oh, young men, learn to be thoughtful! Learn to consider what you are doing, and whither you are going. Make time for calm reflection. Commune with your own heart, and be still. Remember my caution:—Do not be lost merely for the want of thought.

(4) Another danger to young men is contempt of religion.

This also is one of your special dangers. I always observe that none pay so little outward respect to religion as young men. None attend so badly on means of grace, none take so little part in our services, when they are present at them,—use Bibles and Prayer Books so little,—sing so little,—listen to preaching so little. None are so generally absent at prayer-meetings, and lectures, and all such week-day helps to the soul. Young men seem to think they do not need these things,—they may be good for women and old men, but not for them. They appear ashamed of seeming to care about their souls: one would almost fancy they reckoned it a disgrace to go to heaven at all. And this is contempt of religion;—it is the same spirit which made the young people of Bethel mock Elisha;—and of this spirit I say to all young men, Beware! If it be worth while to have a religion, it is worth while to be in earnest about it.

Contempt of holy things is the high road to infidelity. Once let a man begin to make a jest and joke of any part of Christianity, and I am never surprised to hear that he has turned out a downright unbeliever.

Young men, have you really made up your minds to this? Have you fairly looked into the gulf which is before you, if you persist in despising religion? Call to mind the words of David: "The fool hath said in his heart, There is no God" (Ps. 14:1). The fool, and none but the fool!—He has said it: but he has never proved it! Remember, if ever there was a book which has been proved true from beginning to end, by every kind of evidence, that book is the Bible. It has defied the attacks of all enemies and fault-finders. "The Word of

---

[30]Secretary Walsingham.

the Lord is indeed tried" (Ps. 18:30). It has been tried in every way, and the more it has been tried, the more evidently has it been shown to be the very handiwork of God Himself. What will you believe, if you do not believe the Bible? There is no choice but to believe something ridiculous and absurd.[31] Depend on it, no man is so grossly credulous as the man who denies the Bible to be the Word of God;—and if it be the Word of God, take heed that you despise it not.

Men may tell you there are difficulties in the Bible;—things hard to be understood. It would not be God's book if there were not. And what if there are? You do not despise medicines because you cannot explain all that your doctor does by them. But whatever men may say, the things needful to salvation are as clear as daylight. Be very sure of this,—people never reject the Bible because they cannot understand it. They understand it only too well; they understand that it condemns their own behaviour; they understand that it witnesses against their own sins, and summons them to judgment. They try to believe it is false and useless, because they do not like to allow it is true. "A bad life," said the celebrated Lord Rochester,[32] laying his hand on the Bible, "a bad life is the only grand objection to this book." "Men question the truth of Christianity," says South,[33] "because they hate the practice of it."

Young men, when did God ever fail to keep His word? Never. What He has said, He has always done; and what He has spoken, He has always made good. Did He fail to keep His word at the flood?—No. Did He fail with Sodom and Gomorrah?—No. Did He fail with unbelieving Jerusalem?—No. Has He failed with the Jews up to this very hour?—No. He has never failed to fulfil His word. Take care, lest you be found amongst those by whom God's Word is despised.

Never laugh at religion. Never make a jest of sacred things. Never mock those who are serious and in earnest about their souls. The time may come when you will count those happy whom you laughed at,—a time when your laughter will be turned into sorrow, and your mockery into heaviness.

(5) Another danger to young men is the fear of man's opinion.

"The fear of man" does indeed "bring a snare" (Prov. 29:25). It is terrible to observe the power which it has over most minds, and especially over the minds of the young. Few seem to have any opinions of their own, or to think for themselves. Like dead fish, they go with the stream and tide: what others think right, they think right; and what others call wrong, they call wrong too. There are not many original thinkers in the world. Most men are like sheep, they follow a leader. If it was the fashion of the day to be Romanists, they would be Romanists,—if to be Mahometans, they would be Mahometans. They dread the idea of going against the current of the times. In a word, the opinion of the day becomes their religion, their creed, their Bible, and their God.

The thought, "What will my friends say or think of me?" nips many a good inclination in the bud. The fear of being observed upon, laughed at, ridiculed, prevents many a good habit being taken up. There are Bibles that would be read this very day, if the owners dared. They know they ought to read them, but they are afraid:—"What will people say?" There are knees that would be bent in prayer this very night, but the fear of man forbids it:—"What would my wife, my brother, my friend, my companion say, if they saw me

---

[31] See Faber's Difficulties of Infidelity on this subject.
[32] John Rochester (1647-1680).
[33] Robert South (1634-1716).

praying?" Alas, what wretched slavery this is, and yet how common! "I feared the people," said Saul to Samuel: and so he transgressed the commandment of the Lord (1 Sam. 15:24). "I am afraid of the Jews," said Zedekiah, the graceless king of Judah: and so he disobeyed the advice which Jeremiah gave him (Jer. 38:19). Herod was afraid of what his guests would think of him: so he did that which made him "exceeding sorry,"—he beheaded John the Baptist. Pilate feared offending the Jews: so he did that which he knew in his conscience was unjust, he delivered up Jesus to be crucified. If this be not slavery, what is?

Young men, I want you all to be free from this bondage. I want you each to care nothing for man's opinion, when the path of duty is clear. Believe me, it is a great thing to be able to say "No!" Here was good King Jehoshaphat's weak point,—he was too easy and yielding in his dealings with Ahab, and hence many of his troubles (1 Kings 22:4). Learn to say "No!" Let not the fear of not seeming good-natured make you unable to do it. When sinners entice you, be able to say decidedly, "I will not consent" (Prov. 1:10).

Consider only how unreasonable this fear of man is. How short-lived is man's enmity, and how little harm he can do you! "Who art thou, that thou shouldest be afraid of a man that shall die, and of the son of man, which shall be as grass: and forgettest the Lord thy Maker, that hath stretched forth the heavens, and laid the foundations of the earth?" (Isa. 51:12-13). And how thankless is this fear! None will really think better of you for it. The world always respects those most who act boldly for God. Oh, break these bonds, and cast these chains from you! Never be ashamed of letting men see you want to go to heaven. Think it no disgrace to show yourself a servant of God. Never be afraid of doing what is right.

Remember the words of the Lord Jesus: "Fear not them which kill the body, but are not able to kill the soul: but rather fear Him which is able to destroy both soul and body in hell" (Matt. 10:28). Only try to please God, and He can soon make others pleased with you. "When a man's ways please the Lord, he maketh even his enemies to be at peace with him" (Prov. 16:7).

Young men, be of good courage.—Care not for what the world says or thinks: you will not be with the world always. Can man save your soul? No. Will man be your judge in the great and dreadful day of account?—No. Can man give you a good conscience in life, a good hope in death, a good answer in the morning of resurrection? No! no! no! Man can do nothing of the sort. Then "fear not the reproach of men, neither be afraid of their revilings: for the moth shall eat them up like a garment, and the worm shall eat them like wool" (Isa. 51:7-8). Call to mind the saying of good Colonel Gardiner: "I fear God, and therefore I have none else to fear." Go and be like him.

Such are the warning I give you. Lay them to heart. They are worth thinking over. I am much mistaken if they are not greatly needed. The Lord grant they may not have been given you in vain.

III. General Counsels to Young Men.

In the third place, I wish to give some general counsels to young men.

(1) For one thing, try to get a clear view of the evil of sin.

Young men, if you did but know what sin is, and what sin has done, you would not think it strange that I exhort you as I do. You do not see it in its true colours. Your eyes are naturally blind to its guilt and danger, and hence you cannot understand what makes me so anxious about you. Oh, let not the devil succeed in persuading you that sin is a small matter!

Think for a moment what the Bible says about sin;-how it dwells naturally in the heart of every man and woman alive (Eccles. 7:20; Rom. 3:23),—how it defiles our thoughts, words, and actions, and that continually (Gen. 6:5; Matt. 15:19),—how it renders us all guilty and abominable in the sight of a holy God (Isa. 64:6; Hab. 1:13),—how it leaves us utterly without hope of salvation, if we look to ourselves (Ps. 143:2; Rom. 3:20),—how its fruit in this world is shame, and its wages in the world to come, death (Rom. 6:21-23). Think calmly of all this. I tell you this day, it is not more sad to be dying of consumption, and not to know it, than it is to be a living man, and not know it.

Think what an awful change sin has worked on all our natures. Man is no longer what he was when God formed him out of the dust of the ground. He came out of God's hand upright and sinless (Eccles. 7:29). In the day of his creation he was, like everything else, "very good" (Gen. 1:31). And what is man now?—A fallen creature, a ruin, a being that shows the marks of corruption all over, his heart like Nebuchadnezzar, degraded and earthly, looking down and not up,—his affections like a household in disorder, calling no man master, all extravagance and confusion,—his understanding like a lamp flickering in the socket, impotent to guide him, not knowing good from evil,—his will like a rudderless ship, tossed to and fro by every desire, and constant only in choosing any way rather than God's. Alas, what a wreck is man, compared to what he might have been! Well may we understand such figures being used as blindness, deafness, disease, sleep, death, when the Spirit has to give us a picture of man as he is. And mail as he is, remember, was so made by sin.

Think, too, what it has cost to make atonement for sin, and to provide a pardon and forgiveness for sinners. God's own Son must come into the world, and take upon Him our nature, in order to pay the price of our redemption, and deliver us from the curse of a broken law. He who was in the beginning with the Father, and by whom all things were made, must suffer for sin the just for the unjust,—must die the death of a malefactor, before the way to heaven can be laid open to any soul. See the Lord Jesus Christ despised and rejected of men, scourged, mocked, and insulted;—behold Him bleeding on the cross of Calvary;—hear Him crying in agony, "My God, My God, why hast Thou forsaken Me?" mark how the sun was darkened, and the rocks rent at the sight;-and then consider, young men, what must be the evil and guilt of sin.

Think, also, what sin has done already upon the earth. Think how it cast Adam and Eve out of Eden,—brought the flood upon the old world, caused fire to come down on Sodom and Gomorrah, drowned Pharaoh and his host in the Red Sea, destroyed the seven wicked nations of Canaan, scattered the twelve tribes of Israel over the face of the globe. Sin alone did all this.

Think, moreover, of all the misery and sorrow that sin has caused, and is causing at this very day. Pain, disease, and death, strifes, quarrels, and divisions, envy, jealousy, and malice, deceit, fraud, and cheating, violence, oppression, and robbery, selfishness, unkindness, and ingratitude; all these are the fruits of sin. Sin is the parent of them all. Sin it is that has so marred and spoiled the face of God's creation.

Young men, consider these things, and you will not wonder that we preach as we do. Surely, if you did but think of them, you would break with sin for ever. Will you play with poison? Will you sport with hell? Will you take fire in your hand? Will you harbour your deadliest enemy in your bosom? Will you go on living as if it mattered nothing whether your own sins were forgiven or not, whether sin had dominion over you, or you over sin?

Oh, awake to a sense of sin's sinfulness and danger! Remember the words of Solomon: "Fools," none but fools, "make a mock at sin" (Prov. 14:9).

Hear, then, the request that I make of you this day,—pray that God would teach you the real evil of sin. As you would have your soul saved, arise and pray.

(2) For another thing, seek to become acquainted with our Lord Jesus Christ.

This is, indeed, the principal thing in religion. This is the corner-stone of Christianity. Till you know this, my warnings and advice will be useless, and your endeavours, whatever they may be, will be in vain. A watch without a mainspring is not more unserviceable than is religion without Christ.

But let me not be misunderstood. It is not the mere knowing Christ's name that I mean,—it is the knowing His mercy, grace, and power, the knowing Him not by the hearing of the ear, but by the experience of your hearts. I want you to know Him by faith,—I want you, as Paul says, to know "the power of His resurrection; being made conformable unto His death" (Phil. 3:10). I want you to be able to say of Him, He is my peace and my strength, my life and my consolation, my Physician and my Shepherd, my Saviour and my God.

Why do I make such a point of this? I do it because in Christ alone "all fulness dwells" (Col. 1:19),—because in Him alone there is full supply of all that we require for the necessities of our souls. Of ourselves we are all poor, empty creatures,—empty of righteousness and peace,—empty of strength and comfort,—empty of courage and patience,—empty of power to stand, or go on, or make progress in this evil world. It is in Christ alone that all these things are to be found,—grace, peace, wisdom, righteousness, sanctification, and redemption. It is just in proportion as we bye upon Him, that we are strong Christians. It is only when self is nothing and Christ is all our confidence, it is then only that we shall do great exploits. Then only are we armed for the battle of life, and shall overcome. Then only are we prepared for the journey of life, and shall get forward. To live on Christ into draw all from Christ,—to do all in the strength of Christ,—to be ever looking unto Christ;—this is the true secret of spiritual prosperity. "I can do all things," says Paul, "through Christ which strengtheneth me" (Phil. 4:13).

Young men, I set before you Jesus Christ this day, as the treasury of your souls; and I invite you to begin by going to Him, if you would so run as to obtain. Let this be your first step,—go to Christ. Do you want to consult friends?—He is the best friend: "a friend that sticketh closer than a brother" (Prov. 18:24). Do you feel unworthy because of your sins? Fear not: His blood cleanseth from all sin. He says, "Though your sins be as scarlet, they shall be as white as snow: though they be red like crimson, they shall be as wool" (Isa. 1:18). Do you feel weak, and unable to follow Him?—Fear not: He will Eve you power to become sons of God. He will give you the Holy Ghost to dwell in you, and seal you for His own; a new heart will He give you, and a new spirit will He put within you. Are you troubled or beset with peculiar infirmities?—Fear not: there is no evil spirit that Jesus cannot cast out,—there is no disease of soul that He cannot heal. Do you feel doubts and fears?—Cast them aside: "Come unto Me," He says; "him that cometh I will in no wise cast out." He knows well the heart of a young man. He knows your trials and your temptations, your difficulties and your foes. In the days of His flesh He was like yourselves,—a young man at Nazareth. He knows by experience a young man's mind. He can be touched with the feeling of your infirmities,—for He suffered Himself, being tempted. Surely you will be without excuse if you turn away from such a Saviour and Friend as this.

Hear the request I make of you this day,—if you love life, seek to become acquainted with Jesus Christ.

(3) For another thing, never forget that nothing is so important as your soul.

Your soul is eternal. It will live for ever. The world and all that it contains shall pass away,—firm, solid, beautiful, well-ordered as it is, the world shall come to an end. "The earth and the works that are therein shall be burned up" (2 Pet. 3:10). The works of statesmen, writers, painters, architects, are all short-lived: your soul will outlive them all. The angel's voice shall proclaim one day, that "Time shall be no longer" (Rev. 10:6).—But that shall never be said of your souls.

Try, I beseech you, to realize the fact, that your soul is the one thing worth living for. It is the part of you which ought always to be first considered. No place, no employment is good for you, which injures your soul. No friend, no companion deserves your confidence, who makes light of your soul's concerns. The man who hurts your person, your property, your character, does you but temporary harm. He is the true enemy who contrives to damage your soul.

Think for a moment what you were sent into the world for. Not merely to eat and drink, and indulge the desires of the flesh,—not merely to dress out your body, and follow its lusts whithersoever they may lead you,—not merely to work, and sleep, and laugh, and talk, and enjoy yourselves, and think of nothing but time. No! you were meant for something higher and better than this. You were placed here to train for eternity. Your body was only intended to be a house for your immortal spirit. It is flying in the face of God's purposes to do as many do,—to make the soul a servant to the body, and not the body a servant to the soul.[34]

Young men, God is no respecter of persons. He regards no man's coat, or purse, or rank, or position. He sees not with man's eyes. The poorest saint that ever died in a workhouse is nobler in His sight than the richest sinner that ever died in a palace. God does not look at riches, titles, learning, beauty, or anything of the kind. One thing only God does look at, and that is the immortal soul. He measures all men by one standard, one measure, one test, one criterion, and that is the state of their souls.

Do not forget this. Keep in view, morning, noon, and night, the interests of your soul. Rise up each day desiring that it may prosper,—lie down each evening inquiring of yourself whether it has really got on. Remember Zeuxis, the great painter of old. When men asked him why he laboured so intensely, and took such extreme pains with every picture, his simple answer was, "I paint for eternity." Do not be ashamed to be like him. Set your immortal soul before your mind's eye, and when men ask you why you live as you do, answer them in his spirit, "I live for my soul." Believe me, the day is fast coming when the soul will be the one thing men will think of, and the only question of importance will be this, "Is my soul lost or saved?"

(4) For another thing, remember it is possible to be a young man and yet to serve God.

I fear the snares that Satan lays for you on this point. I fear lest he succeed in filling your minds with the vain notion, that to be a true Christian in youth is impossible. I have seen many carried away by this delusion. I have heard it said, "You are requiring impossibilities in expecting so much religion from young people. Youth is no time for seriousness. Our desires are strong, and it was never intended that we should keep them

---

[34] The Assembly's Larger Catechism begins with this admirable question and answer. "What is the chief and highest end of man?" "To glorify God, and fully to enjoy Him for ever."

under, as you wish us to do. God meant us to enjoy ourselves. There will be time enough for religion by and by." And this kind of talk is only too much encouraged by the world. The world is only too ready to wink at youthful sins. The world appears to think it a matter of course that young men must "sow their wild oats." The world seems to take it for granted young people must be irreligious, and that it is not possible for them to follow Christ.

Young men, I will ask you this simple question,—Where will you find anything of all this in the Word of God? Where is the chapter or verse in the Bible which will support this talking and reasoning of the world? Does not the Bible speak to old and young alike, without distinction? Is not sin, sin, whether committed at the age of twenty or fifty? Will it form the slightest excuse, in the day of judgment, to say, "I know I sinned, but then I was young"? Show your common sense, I beg of you, by giving up such vain excuses. You are responsible and accountable to God from the very moment that you know right and wrong.

I know well there are many difficulties in a young man's way, I allow it fully. But there are always difficulties in the way of doing right. The path to heaven is always narrow, whether we be young or old.

There are difficulties,—but God will give you grace to overcome them. God is no hard master. He will not, like Pharaoh, require you to make bricks without straw. He will take care the path of plain duty is never impossible. He never laid commands on man which He would not give man power to perform.

There are difficulties, but many a young man has overcome them hitherto, and so may you. Moses was a young man of like passions with yourselves;—but see what is said of him in Scripture: "By faith Moses, when he was come to age, refused to be called the son of Pharaoh's daughter; choosing rather to suffer affliction with the people of God, than to enjoy the pleasures of sin for a season; esteeming the reproach of Christ greater riches than the treasures of Egypt: for he had respect unto the recompense of the reward" (Heb. 11:24-26). Daniel was a young man when he began to serve God in Babylon. He was surrounded by temptations of every kind. He had few with him, and many against him. Yet Daniel's life was so blameless and consistent, that even his enemies could find no fault in him, except "concerning the law of his God" (Dan. 6:5). And these are not solitary cases. There is a cloud of witnesses whom I could name. Time would fail me, if I were to tell you of young Isaac, young Joseph, young Joshua, young Samuel, young David, young Solomon, young Abijah, young Obadiah, young Josiah, young Timothy. These were not angels, but men, with hearts naturally like your own. They too had obstacles to contend with, lusts to mortify, trials to endure, hard places to fill, like any of yourselves. But young as they were, they all found it possible to serve God. Will they not all rise in judgment and condemn you, if you persist in saying it cannot be done?

Young men, try to serve God. Resist the devil when he whispers it is impossible. Try,—and the Lord God of the promises will give you strength in the trying. He loves to meet those who struggle to come to Him, and He will meet you and give you the power that you feel you need. Be like the man whom Bunyan's Pilgrim saw in the Interpreter's house,—go forward boldly, saying, "Set down my name." Those words of our Lord are true, though I often hear them repeated by heartless and unfeeling tongues: "Seek, and ye shall find; knock, and it shall be opened unto you" (Matt. 7:7). Difficulties which seemed like mountains shall melt away like snow in spring. Obstacles which seemed like giants in the mist of distance, shall dwindle into nothing when you fairly face them. The lion in the way which you fear, shall prove to be chained. If men believed the promises more, they would never be afraid of duties. But remember that little word I press upon you, and when Satan says, "You cannot be a Christian while you are young:" answer him, "Get thee behind me, Satan: by God's help I will try."

(5) For another thing, determine as long as you live to make the Bible your guide and adviser.

The Bible is God's merciful provision for sinful man's soul,—the map by which he must steer his course, if he would attain eternal life. All that we need to know, in order to make us peaceful, holy, or happy, is there richly contained. If a young man would know how to begin life well, let him hear what David says: "Wherewithal shall a young man cleanse his way? by taking heed thereto according to Thy word" (Ps. 119:9).

Young men, I charge you to make a habit of reading the Bible, and not to let the habit be broken. Let not the laughter of companions,—let not the bad customs of the family you may live in,—let none of these things prevent your doing it. Determine that you will not only have a Bible, but also make time to read it too. Suffer no man to persuade you that it is only a book for Sunday-school children and old women. It is the book from which King David got wisdom and understanding. It is the book which young Timothy knew from his childhood. Never be ashamed of reading it. Do not "despise the Word" (Prov. 13:13).

Read it with prayer for the Spirit's grace to make you understand it Bishop Beveridge says well, "A man may as soon read the letter of Scripture without eyes, as understand the spirit of it without grace."

Read it reverently, as the Word of God, not of man,—believing implicitly that what it approves is right, and what it condemns is wrong. Be very sure that every doctrine which will not stand the test of Scripture is false. This will keep you from being tossed to and fro, and carried about by the dangerous opinions of these latter days. Be very sure that every practice in your life which is contrary to Scripture, is sinful and must be given up. This will settle many a question of conscience, and cut the knot of many a doubt. Remember how differently two kings of Judah read the Word of God: Jehoiakim read it, and at once cut the writing to pieces, and burned it on the fire (Jer. 36:23). And why?—Because his heart rebelled against it, and he was resolved not to obey. Josiah read it, and at once rent his clothes, and cried mightily to the Lord (2 Chron. 34:19). And why?—Because his heart was tender and obedient. He was ready to do anything which Scripture showed him was his duty. Oh that you may follow the last of these two, and not the first!

And read it regularly. This is the only way to become "mighty in the Scriptures." A hasty glance at the Bible now and then does little good. At that rate you will never become familiar with its treasures, or feel the sword of the Spirit fitted to your hand in the hour of conflict. But get your mind stored with Scripture, by diligent reading, and you will soon discover its value and power. Texts will rise up in your hearts in the moment of temptation. Commands will suggest themselves in seasons of doubt. Promises will come across your thoughts in the time of discouragement.—And thus you will experience the truth of David's words, "Thy word have I hid in mine heart, that I might not sin against Thee" (Ps. 119:11); and of Solomon's words, "When thou goest, it shall lead thee; when thou sleepest, it shall keep thee; and when thou awakest, it shall talk with thee" (Prov. 6:22).

I dwell on these things more because this is an age of reading. Of making many books there seems no end, though few of them are really profitable. There seems a rage for cheap printing and publishing. Newspapers of every sort abound, and the tone of some, which have the widest circulation, tells badly for the taste of the age. Amidst the flood of dangerous reading, I plead for my Master's book,—I call upon you not to forget the book of the soul. Let not newspapers, novels, and romances be read, while the prophets and Apostles are despised. Let not the exciting and licentious swallow up your attention, while the edifying and the sanctifying can find no place in your mind.

Young men, give the Bible the honour due to it every day you live. Whatever you read, read that first. And beware of bad books: there are plenty in this day. Take heed what you read. I suspect there is more harm done to souls in this way than most people have an idea is possible. Value all books in proportion as they are agreeable to Scripture. Those that are nearest to it are the best, and those that are farthest from it, and most contrary to it, the worst.

(6) For another thing, never make an intimate friend of any one who is not a friend of God.

Understand me,—I do not speak of acquaintances. I do not mean that you ought to have nothing to do with any but true Christians. To take such a line is neither possible nor desirable in this world. Christianity requires no man to be uncourteous.

But I do advise you to be very careful in your choice of friends. Do not open all your heart to a man merely because he is clever, agreeable, good-natured, high-spirited, and kind. These things are all very well in their way, but they are not everything. Never be satisfied with the friendship of any one who will not be useful to your soul.

Believe me, the importance of this advice cannot be overrated. There is no telling the harm that is done by associating with godless companions and friends. The devil has few better helps in ruining a man's soul. Grant him this help, and he cares little for all the armour with which you may be armed against him. Good education, early habits of morality, sermons, books, regular homes, letters of parents, all, he knows well, will avail you little, if you will only cling to ungodly friends. You may resist many open temptations, refuse many plain snares; but once take up a bad companion, and he is content. That awful chapter which describes Amnon's wicked conduct about Tamar, almost begins with these words, "But Amnon had a friend, a very subtle man" (2 Sam. 13:3).

You must recollect, we are all creatures of imitation: precept may teach us, but it is example that draws us. There is that in us all, that we are always disposed to catch the ways of those with whom we live; and the more we like them, the stronger does the disposition grow. Without our being aware of it, they influence our tastes and opinions;— we gradually give up what they dislike, and take up what they like, in order to become more close friends with them. And, worst of all, we catch their ways in things that are wrong, far quicker than in things that are right. Health, unhappily, is not contagious, but disease is. It is far more easy to catch a chill than to impart a glow; and to make each other's religion dwindle away, than grow and prosper.

Young men, I ask you to lay these things to heart. Before you let any one become your constant companion, before you get into the habit of telling him everything, and going to him in all your troubles and all your pleasures,—before you do this, just think of what I have been saying; ask yourself, "Will this be a useful friendship to me or not?"

"Evil communications" do indeed "corrupt good manners" (1 Cor. 15:33). I wish that text were written in hearts as often as it is in copy-books. Good friends are among our greatest blessings;—they may keep us back from much evil, quicken us in our course, speak a word in season, draw us upward, and draw us on. But a bad friend is a positive misfortune, a weight continually dragging us down, and chaining us to earth. Keep company with an irreligious man, and it is more than probable you will in the end become like him. That is the general consequence of all such friendships. The good go down to the bad, and the bad do not come up to the good. Even a stone will give way before a continual dropping. The world's proverb is only too correct: "Clothes and company tell true tales about character." "Show me who a man lives with," says the Spaniards, "and I will show you what he is."

I dwell the more upon this point, because it has more to do with your prospects in life than at first sight appears. If ever you marry, it is more than probable you will choose a wife among the connections of your friends. If Jehoshaphat's son Jehoram had not formed a friendship with Ahab's family, he would most likely not have married Ahab's daughter. And who can estimate the importance of a right choice in marriage? It is a step which, according to the old saying, "either makes a man or mars him." Your happiness in both lives may depend on it. Your wife must either help your soul or harm it: there is no medium. She will either fan the flame of religion in your heart, or throw cold water upon it, and make it burn low. She will either be wings or fetters, a rein or a spur to your Christianity, according to her character. He that findeth a good wife doth indeed "find a good thing;" but if you have the least wish to find one, be very careful how you choose your friends.

Do you ask me what kind of friends you shall choose? Choose friends who will benefit your soul,—friends whom you can really respect,—friends whom you would like to have near you on your death-bed,—friends who love the Bible, and are not afraid to speak to you about it,—friends such as you will not be ashamed of owning at the coming of Christ, and the day of judgment. Follow the example that David sets you: he says, "I am a companion of all them that fear Thee, and of them that keep Thy precepts" (Ps. 119:63). Remember the words of Solomon: "He that walketh with wise men shall be wise; but a companion of fools shall be destroyed" (Prov. 13:20). But depend on it, bad company in the life that now is, is the sure way to procure worse company in the life to come.

IV. Special Rules for Young Men.

In the last place, I will set down some particular rules of conduct which I strongly advise all young men to follow.

(1) For one thing, resolve at once, by God's help, to break off every known sin, however small.

Look within, each one of you. Examine your own hearts. Do you see there any habit or custom which you know to be wrong in the sight of God? If you do, delay not a moment in attacking it. Resolve at once to lay it aside.

Nothing darkens the eyes of the mind so much, and deadens the conscience so surely, as an allowed sin. It may be a little one, but it is not the less dangerous for all that. A small leak will sink a great ship, and a small spark will kindle a great fire, and a little allowed sin in like manner will ruin an immortal soul. Take my advice, and never spare a little sin. Israel was commanded to slay every Canaanite, both great and small. Act on the same principle, and show no mercy to little sins. Well says the book of Canticles, "Take us the foxes, the little foxes, that spoil the vines" (Cant. 2:15).[35]

Be sure no wicked man ever meant to be so wicked at his first beginnings. But he began with allowing himself some little transgression, and that led on to something greater, and that in time produced something greater still, and thus he became the miserable being that he now is. When Hazael heard from Elisha of the horrible acts that

---

[35] Song of Solomon.

he would one day do, he said with astonishment, "Is thy servant a dog, that he should do this great thing?" (2 Kings 8:13). But he allowed sin to take root in his heart, and in the end he did them all.

Young men, resist sin in its beginnings. They may look small and insignificant, but mind what I say, resist them,—make no compromise, let no sin lodge quietly and undisturbed in your heart. "The mother of mischief," says an old proverb, "is no bigger than a midge's wing." There is nothing finer than the point of a needle, but when it has made a hole, it draws all the thread after it. Remember the Apostle's words, "A little leaven leaveneth the whole lump" (1 Cor. 5:6).

Many a young man could tell you with sorrow and shame, that he traces up the ruin of all his worldly prospects to the point I speak of,—to giving way to sin in its beginnings. He began habits of falsehood and dishonesty in little things, and they grew upon him. Step by step, he has gone on from bad to worse, till he has done things that at one time he would have thought impossible; till at last he has lost his place, lost his character, lost his comfort, and well-nigh lost his soul. He allowed a gap in the wall of his conscience, because it seemed a little one,—and once allowed, that gap grew larger every day, till at length the whole wall seemed to come down.

Remember this especially in matters of truth and honesty. Make conscience of pins and syllables. "He that is faithful in that which is least, is faithful also in much" (Luke 16:10). Whatever the world may please to say, there are no little sins. All great buildings are made up of little parts;—the first stone is as important as any other. All habits are formed by a succession of little acts, and the first little act is of mighty consequence. The axe in the fable only begged the trees to let him have one little piece of wood to make a handle, and he would never trouble them any more. He got it, and then he soon cut them all down. The devil only wants to get the wedge of a little allowed sin into your heart, and you will soon be all his own. It is a wise saying of old William Bridge, "There is nothing small betwixt us and God, for God is an infinite God."

There are two ways of coming down from the top of a church steeple; one is to jump down,—and the other is to come down by the steps: but both will lead you to the bottom. So also there are two ways of going to hell; one is to walk into it with your eyes open,—few people do that; the other is to go down by the steps of little sins,—and that way, I fear, is only too common. Put up with a few little sins, and you will soon want a few more. Even a heathen could say, "Who ever was content with only one sin?" And then your course will be regularly worse and worse every year. Well did Jeremy Taylor describe the progress of sin in a man: "First it startles him, then it becomes pleasing, then easy, then delightful, then frequent, then habitual, then confirmed, then the man is impenitent, then obstinate, then resolves never to repent, and then he is damned."

Young men, if you would not come to this, recollect the rule I give you this day,—resolve at once to break off every known sin.

(2) For another thing, resolve, by God's help, to shun everything which may prove an occasion of sin.

It is an excellent saying of good Bishop Hall, "He that would be safe from the acts of evil, must widely avoid the occasions."[36] It is not enough that we determine to commit no sin, we must carefully keep at a distance from all approaches to it. By this test we ought

---

[36]There is an old fable, that the butterfly once asked the owl how she should deal with the fire, which had singed her wings; and the owl counselled her, in reply, not to behold so much as its smoke.

to try our ways of spending our time,—the books that we read, the families that we visit, the society into which we go. We must not content ourselves with saying, "There is nothing positively wrong here;" we must go further, and say, "Is there anything here which may prove to me the occasion of sin?"

This, be it remembered, is one great reason why idleness is so much to be avoided. It is not that doing nothing is of itself so positively wicked; it is the opportunity it affords to evil thoughts, and vain imaginations; it is the wide door it opens for Satan to throw in the seeds of bad things; it is this which is mainly to be feared. If David had not given occasion to the devil, by idling on his house-top at Jerusalem, he would probably never have seen Bathsheba, nor murdered Uriah.

This, too, is one great reason why worldly amusements are so objectionable. It may be difficult, in some instances, to show that they are, in themselves, positively unscriptural and wrong. But there is little difficulty in showing that the tendency of almost all of them is most injurious to the soul. They sow the seeds of an earthly and sensual frame of mind. They war against the life of faith. They promote an unhealthy and unnatural craving after excitement. They minister to the lust of the flesh, and the lust of the eye, and the pride of life. They dim the view of heaven and eternity, and give a false colour to the things of time. They indispose the heart for private prayer, and Scripture-reading, and calm communion with God. The man who mingles in them is like one who gives Satan vantage-ground. He has a battle to fight, and he gives his enemy the help of sun, and wind, and hill. It would be strange indeed if he did not find himself continually overcome.

Young men, endeavour, as much as in you lies, to keep clear of everything which may prove injurious to your soul. Never hold a candle to the devil. People may say you are over scrupulous, too particular, where is the mighty harm of such and such things? But heed them not. It is dangerous to play tricks with edged tools: it is far more dangerous to take liberties with your immortal soul. He that would be safe must not come near the brink of danger. He must look on his heart as a magazine of gunpowder, and be cautious not to handle one spark of temptation more than he can help.

Where is the use of your praying, "Lead us not into temptation," unless you are yourselves careful not to run into it; and "deliver us from evil," unless you show a desire to keep out of its way? Take example from Joseph,—Not merely did he refuse his mistress's solicitation to sin, but he showed his prudence in refusing to be "with her" at all (Gen. 39:10). Lay to heart the advice of Solomon, not merely to "go not in the path of wickedness," but to "avoid it, pass not by it, turn from it, and pass away" (Prov. 4:15); not merely not to be drunken, but not even to "look upon the wine when it is red" (Prov. 23:31). The man who took the vow of a Nazarite in Israel, not only took no wine, but he even abstained from grapes in any shape whatever. "Abhor that which is evil," says Paul to the Romans (Rom. 12:9); not merely do not do it;—"Flee youthful lusts," he writes to Timothy; get away from them as far as possible (2 Tim. 2:22). Alas, how needful are such cautions! Dinah had to go out among the wicked Shechemites, to see their ways, and she lost her character. Lot had to pitch his tent near sinful Sodom, and he lost everything but his life.

Young men, be wise in time. Do not be always trying how near you can allow the enemy of souls to come, and yet escape him. Hold him at arm's length. Try to keep clear of temptation as far as possible, and this will be one great help to keep clear of sin.

(3) For another thing, resolve never to forget the eye of God.

The eye of God! Think of that. Everywhere, in every house, in every field, in every room, in every company, alone or in a crowd, the eye of God is always upon you. "The eyes of the Lord are in every place, beholding the evil and the good" (Prov. 15:3), and they are eyes that read hearts as well as actions.

Endeavour, I beseech you all, to realize this fact. Recollect that you have to do with an all-seeing God,—a God who never slumbereth nor sleepeth,—a God who understands your thoughts afar off, and with whom the night shines as the day. You may leave your father's roof, and go away, like the prodigal, into a far country, and think that there is nobody to watch your conduct; but the eye and ear of God are there before you. You may deceive your parents or employers, you may tell them falsehoods, and be one thing before their faces, and another behind their backs, but you cannot deceive God. He knows you through and through. He heard what you said as you came here today. He knows what you are thinking of at this minute. He has set your most secret sins in the light of His countenance, and they will one day come out before the world to your shame, except you take heed.

How little is this really felt! How many things are done continually, which men would never do if they thought they were seen! How many matters are transacted in the chambers of imagination, which would never bear the light of day! Yes; men entertain thoughts in private, and say words in private, and do acts in private, which they would be ashamed and blush to have exposed before the world. The sound of a footstep coming has stopped many a deed of wickedness. A knock at the door has caused many an evil work to be hastily suspended, and hurriedly laid aside. But oh, what miserable driveling folly is all this! There is an all-seeing Witness with us wherever we go. Lock the door, draw down the blind, shut the shutters, put out the candle; it matters not, it makes no difference; God is everywhere, you cannot shut Him out, or prevent HIS seeing. "All things are naked and open unto the eyes of Him with whom we have to do" (Heb. 4:13). Well did young Joseph understand this when his mistress tempted him. There was no one in the house to see them,—no human eye to witness against him;—but Joseph was one who lived as seeing Him that is invisible: "How can I do this great wickedness," said he, "and sin against God?" (Gen. 39:9).

Young men, I ask you all to read Ps. 139. I advise you all to learn it by heart. Make it the test of all your dealings in this world's business: say to yourself often, "Do I remember that God sees me?"

Live as in the sight of God. This is what Abraham did,—he walked before Him. This is what Enoch did,—he walked with Him. This is what heaven itself will be,—the eternal presence of God. Do nothing you would not like God to see. Say nothing you would not like God to hear. Write nothing you would not like God to read. Go to no place where you would not like God to find you. Read no book of which you would not like God to say, "Show it Me." Never spend your time in such a way that you would not like to have God say, "What art thou doing?"

(4) For another thing, be diligent in the use of all public means of grace.

Be regular in going to the house of God, whenever it is open for prayer and preaching, and it is in your power to attend. Be regular in keeping the Lord's day holy, and determine that God's day out of the seven shall henceforth always be given to its rightful owner.

I would not leave any false impression on your minds. Do not go away and say I told you that keeping your church made up the whole of religion. I tell you no such thing. I have no wish to see you grow up formalists and Pharisees. If you think the mere carrying your body to a certain house, at certain times, on a certain day in the week, will make you a Christian, and prepare you to meet God, I tell you flatly you are miserably deceived. All services without heart-service are unprofitable and vain. They only are true worshippers who "worship God in spirit and in truth: the Father seeketh such to worship Him" (John 4:23).

But means of grace are not to be despised because they are not saviours. Gold is not food,—you cannot eat it, but you would not therefore say it is useless, and throw it away. Your soul's eternal well-doing most certainly does not depend on means of grace, but it is no less certain that without them, as a general rule, your soul will not do well. God might take all who are saved to heaven in a chariot of fire, as He did Elijah, but He does not do so. He might teach them all by visions, and dreams, and miraculous interpositions, without requiring them to read or think for themselves, but He does not do so. And why not? Because He is a God that works by means, and it is His law and will that in all man's dealings with him means shall be used. None but a fool or enthusiast would think of building a house without ladders and scaffolding, and just so no wise man will despise means.

I dwell the more on this point, because Satan will try hard to fill your minds with arguments against means.

He will draw your attention to the numbers of persons who use them and are no better for the using. "See there," he will whisper, "do you not observe those who go to church are no better than those who stay away?" But do not let this move you. It is never fair to argue against a thing because it is improperly used. It does not follow that means of grace can do no good because many attend on them and get no good from them. Medicine is not to be despised because many take it and do not recover their health. No man would think of giving up eating and drinking because others choose to eat and drink improperly, and so make themselves ill. The value of means of grace, like other things, depends, in a great measure, on the manner and spirit in which we use them.

I dwell on this point too, because of the strong anxiety I feel that every young man should regularly hear the preaching of Christ's gospel. I cannot tell you how important I think this is. By God's blessing, the ministry of the gospel might be the means of converting your soul;—of leading you to a saving knowledge of Christ, of making you a child of God in deed and in truth. This would be cause for eternal thankfulness indeed. This would be an event over which angels would rejoice. But even if this were not the case, there is a restraining power and influence in the ministry of the gospel, under which I earnestly desire every young man to be brought. There are thousands whom it keeps back from evil, though it has not yet turned them unto God;—it has made them far better members of society, though it has not yet made them true Christians. There is a certain kind of mysterious power in the faithful preaching of the gospel, which tells insensibly on multitudes who listen to it without receiving it into their hearts. To hear sin cried down, and holiness cried up, to hear Christ exalted, and the works of the devil denounced;—to hear the kingdom of heaven and its blessedness described, and the world and its emptiness exposed; to hear this week after week, Sunday after Sunday, is seldom without good effect to the soul. It makes it far harder afterwards to run into any excess of riot and profligacy. It acts as a wholesome check upon a man's heart. This, I believe, is one way in which that promise of God is made good, "My word shall not return unto Me void" (Isa. 55:11). There is much truth in that strong saying of Whitefield, "The gospel keeps many a one from the gaol and gallows, if it does not keep him from hell."

Let me here name another point which is closely connected with this subject. Let nothing ever tempt you to become a Sabbath-breaker. I press this on your attention. Make conscience of giving all your Sabbath to God. A spirit of disregard for this holy day is growing up amongst us with fearful rapidity, and not least among young men. Sunday travelling by railways and steamboats, Sunday visiting, Sunday excursions, are becoming every year more common than they were, and are doing infinite harm to souls.

Young men, be jealous on this point. Whether you live in town or country, take up a decided line; resolve not to profane your Sabbath. Let not the plausible argument of "needful relaxation for your body,"—let not the example of all around you,—let not the invitation of companions with whom you may be thrown;—let none of these things move you to depart from this settled rule, that God's day shall be given to God.

Once give over caring for the Sabbath, and in the end you will give over caring for your soul. The steps which lead to this conclusion are easy and regular. Begin with not honouring God's day, and you will soon not honour God's house;—cease to honour God's house, and you will soon cease to honour God's book; cease to honour God's book, and by and by you will give God no honour at all. Let a man lay the foundation of having no Sabbath, and I am never surprised if he finishes with the top-stone of no God. It is a remarkable saying of Judge Hale, "Of all the persons who were convicted of capital crimes while he was upon the bench, he found only a few who would not confess, on inquiry, that they began their career of wickedness by a neglect of the Sabbath."

Young men, you may be thrown among companions who forget the honour of the Lord's day; but resolve, by God's help, that you will always remember to keep it holy. Honour it by a regular attendance at some place where the gospel is preached. Settle down under a faithful ministry, and once settled, let your place in church never be empty. Believe me, you will find a special blessing following you: "If you call the Sabbath a delight, the holy of the Lord, honourable; and shalt honour Him, not doing thine own ways, nor finding thine own pleasure, nor speaking thine own words: then shalt thou delight thyself in the Lord; and I will cause thee to ride upon the high places of the earth" (Isa. 58:13-14). And one thing is very certain,—your feelings about the Sabbath will always be a test and criterion of your fitness for heaven. Sabbaths are a foretaste and fragment of heaven. The man who finds them a burden and not a privilege, may be sure that his heart stands in need of a mighty change.

(5) For another thing, resolve that wherever you are, you will pray.

Prayer is the life-breath of a man's soul. Without it, we may have a name to live, and be counted Christians; but we are dead in the sight of God. The feeling that we must cry to God for mercy and peace is a mark of grace; and the habit of spreading before Him our soul's wants is an evidence that we have the spirit of adoption. And prayer is the appointed way to obtain the relief of our spiritual necessities.—It opens the treasury, and sets the fountain flowing. If we have not, it is because we ask not.

Prayer is the way to procure the outpouring of the Spirit upon our hearts. Jesus has promised the Holy Ghost, the Comforter. He is ready to come down with all His precious gifts, renewing, sanctifying, purifying, strengthening, cheering, encouraging, enlightening, teaching, directing, guiding into all truth. But then He waits to be entreated.

And here it is, I say it with sorrow, here it is that men fall short so miserably. Few indeed are to be found who pray: many who go down on their knees, and say a form perhaps, but few who pray; few who cry unto God, few who call upon the Lord, few who seek as if they wanted to find, few who knock as if they hungered and thirsted, few who wrestle, few who strive with God earnestly for an answer, few who give Him no rest, few who continue in prayer, few who watch unto prayer, few who pray always without ceasing, and faint not. Yes: few pray! It is just one of the things assumed as a matter of course, but seldom practised; a thing which is everybody's business, but in fact hardly anybody performs.

Young men, believe me, if your soul is to be saved, you must pray. God has no dumb children. If you are to resist the world, the flesh, and the devil, you must pray: it is in vain to look for strength in the hour of trial, if it has not been sought for. You may be thrown with those who never do it, you may have to sleep in the same room with some one who never asks anything of God,—still, mark my words, you must pray.

I can quite believe you find great difficulties about it, difficulties about opportunities, and seasons, and places. I dare not lay down too positive rules on such points as these. I leave them to your own conscience. You must be guided by circumstances. Our Lord Jesus Christ prayed on a mountain; Isaac prayed in the fields; Hezekiah turned his face to the wall as he lay upon his bed; Daniel prayed by the river-side; Peter, the Apostle, on the house-top. I have heard of young men praying in stables and hay-lofts. All that I contend for is this, you must know what it is to "enter into your closet" (Matt. 6:6). There must be stated times when you must speak to God face to face,—you must every day have your seasons for prayer. You must pray.

Without this, all advice and counsel is useless. This is that piece of spiritual armour which Paul names last in his catalogue, in Eph. 6, but it is in truth first in value and importance. This is that meat which you must daily eat, if you would travel safely through the wilderness of this life. It is only in the strength of this that you will get onward towards the mount of God. I have heard it said that the needle-grinders of Sheffield sometimes wear a magnetic mouthpiece at their work, which catches all the fine dust that flies around them, prevents it entering their lungs, and so saves their lives. Prayer is the mouthpiece that you must wear continually, or else you will never work on uninjured by the unhealthy atmosphere of this sinful world. You must pray.

Young men, be sure no time is so well spent as that which a man spends upon his knees. Make time for this, whatever your employment may be. Think of David, king of Israel: what does he say? "Evening, and morning, and at noon will I pray and cry aloud, and He shall hear my voice" (Ps. 55:17). Think of Daniel. He had all the business of a kingdom on his hands; yet he prayed three times a day. See there the secret of his safety in wicked Babylon. Think of Solomon. He begins his reign with prayer for help and assistance, and hence his wonderful prosperity. Think of Nehemiah. He could find time to pray to the God of heaven, even when standing in the presence of his master, Artaxerxes. Think of the example these godly men have left you, and go and do likewise.

Oh that the Lord may give you all the spirit of grace and supplication! "Wilt thou not from this time cry unto God, My Father, Thou art the guide of my youth?" (Jer. 3:4). Gladly would I consent that all this address should be forgotten, if only this doctrine of the importance of prayer might be impressed on your hearts.

V. Conclusion.

And now I hasten towards a conclusion. I have said things that many perhaps will not like, and not receive; but I appeal to your consciences, Are they not true?

Young men, you have all consciences. Corrupt and ruined by the fall as we are, each of us has a conscience. In a corner of each heart there sits a witness for God,—a witness who condemns when we do wrong, and approves when we do right. To that witness I make my appeal this day, Are not the things that I have been saying true?

Go then, young men, and resolve this day to remember your Creator in the days of your youth. Before the day of grace is past,—before your conscience has become hardened by age, and deadened by repeated trampling under foot,—while you have strength, and time, and opportunities, go and join yourself to the Lord in an everlasting covenant not to be forgotten. The Spirit will not always strive. The voice of conscience will become feebler and fainter every year you continue to resist it. The Athenians said to Paul, "We will hear thee again of this matter," but they had heard him for the last time (Acts 17:32). Make haste, and delay not. Linger and hesitate no more.

Think of the unspeakable comfort you will give to parents, relations, and friends, if you take my counsel. They have expended time, money, and health to rear you, and make you what you are. Surely they deserve some consideration at your hands. Who can reckon up the joy and gladness which young people have it in their power to occasion? Who can tell the anxiety and sorrow that sons like Esau, and Hophni, and Phinehas, and Absalom may cause? Truly indeed does Solomon say, "A wise son maketh a glad father, but a foolish son is the heaviness of his mother" (Prov. 10:1). Oh, consider these things, and give God your heart! Let it not be said of you at last, as it is of many, that your "youth was a blunder, your manhood a struggle, and your old age a regret."

Think of the good you may be the instruments of doing to the world. Almost all the most eminent saints of God sought the Lord early. Moses, Samuel, David, Daniel, all served God from their youth. God seems to delight in putting special honour upon young servants;—remember the honour He placed upon our own young king, Edward the Sixth. And what might we not confidently expect, if young men in our own day would consecrate the spring-time of their lives to God? Agents are wanted now in almost every great and good cause, and cannot be found. Machinery of every kind for spreading truth exists, but there are not hands to work it.

Money is more easily got for doing good than men. Ministers are wanted for new churches, missionaries are wanted for new stations, visitors are wanted for neglected districts, teachers are wanted for new schools;—many a good cause is standing still merely for want of agents. The supply of godly, faithful, trustworthy men, for posts like those I have named, is far below the demand.

Young men of the present day, you are wanted for God. This is particularly an age of activity. We are shaking off some of our past selfishness. Men no longer sleep the sleep of apathy and indifference about others, as their forefathers did. They are beginning to be ashamed of thinking, like Cain,—"Am I my brother's keeper?" A wide field of usefulness is open before you, if you are only willing to enter upon it. The harvest is great, and the labourers are few. Be zealous of good works. Come, come to the help of the Lord against the mighty.[37]

This is, in some sort, to be like God, not only "good, but doing good" (Ps. 119:68). This is the way to follow the steps of your Lord and Saviour: "He went about doing good" (Acts 10:38).

This is to live as David did; he "served his own generation" (Acts 13:36).

---

[37]The Church of England Young Men's Society for Aiding Missions at Home and Abroad; and the Young Men's Christian Association, in London, deserve the support of all true Christians. It is one of the few cheering signs in an evil day, that such institutions have been formed. I rejoice to see that kindred societies have been established at other places.— I trust that God will abundantly bless them.

And who can doubt that this is the path which most becomes an immortal soul? Who would not rather leave this world like Josiah, lamented by all, than depart like Jehoram, "without being desired"? (2 Chron. 21:20). Whether is it better to be an idle, frivolous, useless cumberer of the ground, to live for your body, your selfishness, your lusts, and your pride,—or to spend and be spent in the glorious cause of usefulness to your fellow-men;—to be like Wilberforce or Lord Shaftesbury, a blessing to your country and the world,—to be like Howard, the friend of the prisoner and the captive,—to be like Schwartz, the spiritual father of hundreds of immortal souls in heathen lands,—to be like that man of God, Robert M'Cheyne, a burning and a shining light, an epistle of Christ, known and read of all men, the quickener of every Christian heart that comes across your path? Oh, who can doubt? Who can for one moment doubt?

Young men, consider your responsibilities. Think of the privilege and luxury of doing good. Resolve this day to be useful. At once give your hearts to Christ.

Think, lastly, of the happiness that will come to your own soul, if you serve God,—happiness by the way, as you travel through life,—and happiness in the end, when the journey is over. Believe me, whatever vain notions you may have heard, believe me, there is a reward for the righteous even in this world. Godliness has indeed the promise of this life, as well as of that which is to come. There is a solid peace in feeling that God is your friend. There is a real satisfaction in knowing that however great your unworthiness, you are complete in Christ,—that you have an enduring portion,—that you have chosen that good part which shall not be taken from you.

The backslider in heart may well be filled with his own ways, but "a good man shall be satisfied from himself" (Prov. 14:14). The path of the worldly man grows darker and darker every year that he lives;—the path of the Christian is as a shining light, brighter and brighter to the very end. His sun is just rising when the sun of the worldly is setting for ever;—his best things are all beginning to blossom and bloom for ever, when those of the worldly are all slipping out of his hands, and passing away.

Young men, these things are true. Suffer the word of exhortation. Be persuaded. Take up the cross. Follow Christ. Yield yourselves unto God.

CHAPTER XX

Questions About The Lord's Supper.

THE paper which begins at this page requires a few words of prefatory explanation. It consists of fifty-one questions about the Lord's Supper, with special reference to points which are the subject of much dispute and controversy in the present day. It supplies fifty-one answers to these questions, chiefly drawn from the New Testament, and the Articles, Communion Service, and Catechism of the Church of England. It contains, in addition, some valuable extracts from the writings of standard English divines.

It is a painful fact, and one which it is impossible to deny, that the principal cause of differences among Churchmen at this moment is the Sacrament of the Lord's Supper. Whether that blessed ordinance is to be regarded as a sacrifice or not, whether the Lord's Table is an altar or not, whether the officiating clergyman is a sacrificing priest or not,—whether there is a corporal, material presence of Christ's body and blood in the consecrated elements of bread and wine or not,—whether these elements and the Lord's Table ought to be regarded with as much lowly reverence and honour as if Christ was bodily present or not,—all these are questions which are continually coming to the front. To speak plainly, they seem likely to divide the English clergy into two distinct parties, and to rain the Church of England!

Nor is this all. It is another painful and dangerous fact that the great majority of English lay Churchmen seem utterly unable to understand the very serious nature of the question which is dividing the clergy, and the doctrinal consequences which are bound up with it. Most lay Churchmen can only see that the service in some churches is more ornamental and musical than in others, and that in some there is more importance attached to the Lord's Table, and to flowers, decorations, gestures, dress, and postures, than in others. But they can see no further. They cannot, or will not, perceive that the ceremonial actions in administering the Lord's Supper, about which the clergy disagree, are not mere ornamental trifles, as some suppose. So far from being "trifles," they are the outward and visible expressions of a most mischievous doctrine, which strikes at one of the first principles of the Reformed Church of England. They think all earnest, eloquent, zealous, hard-working clergymen cannot be far wrong. And when you tell them that there is an avowed determination among many clergymen to unprotestantize the Established Church, to get behind the Reformation, and to bring back the Romish Mass and the Confessional, you are too often smiled at as an alarmist, and are not believed. It is my deliberate conviction that unless English lay Churchmen can be awakened to see the real nature of the existing differences about the Lord's Supper, there will come in a few years the disestablishment, the disendowment, and the disruption of the Church of England. Half the lay Churchmen seem so absorbed in politics, or fine arts, or cotton, or iron, or coal, or corn, or shipping, or railways, that you cannot get them to look at religious questions. Of the other half, too many are crying "Peace, peace." when there is no peace, and insisting that every "earnest" clergyman should be allowed to" do what is right in his own eyes, to break the law, and to be let alone. In short, unless a change comes soon, our candlestick will be taken away, and our Church will be ruined.

The paper now in the reader's hands is a humble contribution to the cause of truth about the Lord's Supper. It is truth as I find it in the New Testament, truth as I find it in the authorized formularies of our Church, truth as I find it in the writings of our greatest English divines;—it is this truth which I advocate in these pages.

1. Is the Lord's Supper a subject of primary importance in the Christian religion? Do not thousands of Churchmen live and die without receiving it? Do not the majority of church-goers turn their backs on it, and always go away when it is administered? How is this?

Nothing can possibly be of small importance which the Lord Jesus Christ ordained and appointed. Our Lord most distinctly commanded His disciples to "eat bread" and "drink wine" in remembrance of Him. What right has any Christian to disobey this commandment? No doubt a man may be saved, like the penitent thief, without having received the Lord's Supper. It is not a matter of absolute and indispensable necessity, like repentance, faith, and conversion. But it is impossible to say that any professing Christian is in a safe, healthy, or satisfactory condition of soul, who habitually refuses to obey Christ and attend the Lord's Table. If he is not fit to be a communicant, as many say, he is confessing that he does not live as he ought to do, and is not fit to die and meet God. It is very difficult to see what habitual non-communicants will be able to say for themselves in the judgment-day. There is a judgment to come, a judgment of things left undone which we ought to have done, as well as of things done which we ought not to have done.

2. Is it of much importance to have right and true views of the Lord's Supper?

It is of the utmost possible importance. On no subject in Christianity has there been such an immense amount of superstitious error taught and held for nearly eighteen centuries. No error probably has done more harm to the souls of men. Those who think it does not signify what opinions we hold about the Lord's Supper, so long as we receive it, are under a strong delusion. No ordinance appointed by Christ does good to our souls "ex opere operato," or by the mere outward bodily use of it. The value of the Lord's Supper depends entirely on its being rightly understood, and rightly used.

3. Where shall we find right and true views of the Lord's Supper?

We shall find them in the four accounts of the institution of the ordinance given by St. Matthew, St. Mark, and St. Luke in their Gospels, and by St. Paul in the First Epistle to the Corinthians (see Matt. 26:26-28; Mark 14:22-24; Luke 22:19-20; 1 Cor. 11:23-29). These are our only full sources of information in God's Word. In the three Pastoral Epistles to Timothy and Titus, written especially for the instruction of ministers, the Lord's Supper is not once named. The views and principles of the Church of England are to be found in her Articles, Communion Service, Catechism, and Twenty-seventh Homily. Any views which cannot be reconciled with these formularies are not "Church views."

4. What is the Lord's Supper?

It is an ordinance or sacrament appointed by Jesus Christ the night before He was crucified, for the perpetual benefit and edification of His Church, until He comes again at the end of the world. The only other sacrament is baptism. The Church of Rome holds that Confirmation, Penance (or Confession and Absolution), Ordination.

Matrimony, and Extreme Unction, are sacraments of the gospel. The Church of England in her Twenty-fifth Article says distinctly that they are not.

5. How many Tarts are there in the Lord's Supper?

The Catechism of the Church of England rightly tells us that there are two parts. One is the outward and visible part, which is received by all communicants, both good and bad, without exception. The other is the inward and invisible part which is the thing signified by the outward part, and is only received by believers, and received by them, as the Twenty-eighth Article says, "after a heavenly and spiritual manner."

6. What is the outward and visible Tart or sign in the Lord's Supper?

The outward and visible part of the sacrament consists of bread and wine, which are placed on the Lord's Table, consecrated and set apart by the minister, seen, touched, received, eaten, and drunk by the communicants.

7. What is the inward part or thing signified in the Lord's Supper?

The inward or invisible part is that body and blood of Christ which were offered for our sins on the cross. It is neither seen, nor touched, nor tasted, nor received into the mouth by communicants. It is not a tangible and material thing, and can only be eaten and drunk, spiritually, with the heart, and by faith.

8. What did our Lord mean, when He said of the bread, "This is My body," and of the wine, "This is My blood," at the first institution of the Lord's Supper?

He certainly did not mean, "This bread is literally and materially My body, and this wine is literally My blood." It is quite plain that the Apostles did not so understand His words. As devout and well-taught Jews, they would have been shocked and horrified at the idea of drinking literal blood. Our Lord simply meant, "This bread and this wine represent, and are emblems of, My body and My blood." It is just the form of speech He had used when He said, "The field is the world; the good seed are the children of the kingdom" (Matt. 13:38).

9. Why was the sacrament of the Lord's Supper ordained?

The answer of the Church Catechism is the best that can be given. It was ordained "for the continual remembrance of the sacrifice of the death of Christ, and of the benefits which we receive thereby." The bread broken, given, and eaten, was intended to remind Christians of Christ's body given for our sins on the cross. The wine poured out and drunk was intended to remind Christians of Christ's blood shed for our sins. The whole ordinance was intended to keep the Church in perpetual recollection of Christ's death and substitution for us, and His atonement for our sins. Five times over in the Communion Office of the Prayer Book, the words "memory" and "remembrance" are expressly used, to describe the principal object of the Lord's Supper.

10. Who ought to come to the Lord's Supper?

Only those who have the marks and qualifications which are described in the last answer in the Church Catechism. People who "repent truly of their former sins, and stedfastly purpose to lead a new life,"—people who "have a lively faith in God's mercy through Christ, and a thankful remembrance of His death,"—people who are "in charity with all men,"—these, and only these, are fit to be communicants.

11. What good do fit communicants receive from the Lord's Supper?

Their souls, as the Catechism says, are "strengthened and refreshed" by inward spiritual communion with the body and blood of Christ, after the same manner that a material body is strengthened by bread and wine. Their repentance is deepened, their faith increased, their hope brightened, their knowledge enlarged, their habits of holy living strengthened.

12. Who ought not to come to the Lord's Supper?

Those who are living in open sin, those who are manifestly ignorant of true religion, thoughtless, careless, unconverted, and without the Spirit of Christ. To tell such persons that it will do them good to come to the Lord's Table is to do them positive harm. Justification is not by the sacraments. To eat the bread and drink the wine is not the way to obtain forgiveness of sins or converting grace. On the contrary, St. Paul says that a man may eat and drink to his own condemnation (1 Cor. 11:29). The Twenty-ninth Article says that" the wicked, and such as be void of a lively faith, although they do carnally and visibly press with their teeth the sacrament of the body and blood of Christ, yet in no wise are they partakers of Christ: but rather to their own condemnation do eat and drink the sign or sacrament of so great a thing."

13. But ought not all persons without exception to be pressed to come to the Lord's Table, in order that their souls may be saved? Is not reception of the Lord's Supper the truest, shortest, and best way to obtain forgiveness of sins and have eternal life? Does not our Lord Jesus Christ say in the 6th chapter of St. John's Gospel, "Except ye eat the flesh of the Son of man and drink His blood, ye have no life in you;" and again, "Whoso eateth My flesh and drinketh My blood hath eternal life"? (John 6:53-54). Do not these texts refer to the Lord's Supper?

Those two texts have nothing to do with the Lord's Supper. This is the opinion of all the best Protestant commentators, and also of some Romish ones. The "eating and drinking" here spoken of mean the spiritual eating and drinking of the heart by faith, and the "flesh and blood" mean Christ's vicarious sacrifice of His body upon the cross.—The penitent thief most certainly did not receive the bread and wine of the Lord's Supper, yet it is certain that he "had eternal life," and went to paradise when he died. Judas Iscariot did eat the bread and wine, but he did not "have eternal life," and died in his sins. The Prayer-book Service for the Communion of the Sick contains the following statement in one of its concluding rubrics: "If the sick man do truly repent him of his sins, and stedfastly believe that Jesus Christ hath suffered death on the cross for him, and shed His blood for his redemption, earnestly remembering the benefits he hath thereby, and giving Him thanks therefore, he doth eat and drink the body and blood of Christ profitably to his soul's health, although he do not receive the sacrament with his mouth." In fact, to maintain that no one "has eternal life" who does not receive the Lord's Supper, is a most narrow, cruel, and illiberal doctrine. It condemns to eternal death myriads of our fellow-Christians who, from one cause or another, have never become communicants. It condemns the whole body of the Quakers, who allow no sacraments. He that can hold such doctrine must be in a strange state of mind.

14. Does not St. Paul tell the Corinthians, that "the cup of blessing is a communion of the blood of Christ, and the bread a communion of the body of Christ"? (1 Cor. 10:16). Is not this a proof that there is a real corporal presence of Christ's natural body and blood in the Lord's Supper?

It is no proof at all. St. Paul does not say that the bread and wine are the body and blood of Christ, but only a COMMMUNION of them. By that he means that every communicant who rightly, worthily, and with faith receives the bread and wine, does in so receiving have spiritual and heart communion with the sacrifice of Christ's body and blood which was offered for his sins on the cross. For this is precisely one of the objects for which the Lord's Supper was appointed. It was intended to deepen and strengthen the heart union of believers with their crucified Saviour. More than this cannot be fairly got out of the text.

15. Does not the Church Catechism say that the "body and blood of Christ are verily and indeed taken and received by the faithful in the Lord's Supper"? Do not the words "verily and indeed" mean that, in the judgment of those who drew up the Catechism, there is a real corporal presence of Christ's natural body and blood in the consecrated bread and wine?

The simplest answer to this question is to be found in the Twenty-eighth Article: "The body of Christ is given, taken, and eaten in the Supper only after an heavenly and spiritual manner. And the mean whereby the body of Christ is received and eaten in the Supper is faith." The following quotation from the work of a very learned divine, Archdeacon Waterland, deserves close attention:—"The words of the Church Catechism, Verily and indeed taken and received by the faithful, are rightly interpreted of a real participation in the benefits purchased by Christ's death. The body and blood of Christ are taken and received by the faithful, not corporally, not internally, but verily and indeed, that is, effectually."—Waterland's Works, vol. iv. p. 42.

16. Does any change take place in the bread and wine when the minister consecrates them in the Lord's Supper?

Most certainly not. The bread continues bread just as it was before, and the wine continues wine, the same in colour, taste, and composition. The Twenty-eighth Article of the Church of England declares, "Transubstantiation, or the change of the substance of bread and wine in the Supper of the Lord, cannot be proved by holy writ; but it is repugnant to the plain words of Scripture, over-throweth the nature of a sacrament, and hath given occasion to many superstitions."

17. Is there any real presence of Christ's natural body and blood in the bread and wine after consecration?

Most certainly not, if by "real" is meant a corporal and material presence. The rubric at the end of the Prayer-book Communion Service distinctly says, "The natural body and blood of our Saviour Christ are in heaven and not here, it being against the truth of Christ's natural body to be at one time in more places than one." If the body of Him who was born of the Virgin Mary can be present in the bread and wine on the Lord's Table, it cannot be a true human body, and the comfortable truth that our Saviour is perfect man would be overthrown. Those who tell us that as soon as the words of consecration are pronounced, at once the body and blood of Christ come down into the bread and wine, are in great error, and assert what they cannot prove.

18. Ought the consecrated bread and wine in the Lord's Sapper to be elevated, adored, and worshipped?

Most certainly not. The bread is still really and truly bread, and the wine really and truly wine. They ought to be reverently and carefully handled, as signs and emblems of very holy things after consecration. But the change is in the use of them, not in the substance; and to adore them is to break the second commandment. The Prayer-book rubric expressly says, "The sacramental bread and wine remain still in their very natural substance, and may not be adored; for that were idolatry to be abhorred of all faithful Christians." The Twenty-eighth Article says, "The sacrament of the Lord's Supper was not by Christ's ordinance reserved, carried about, lifted up, or worshipped."

19. Is there any sacrifice of Christ's body and blood in the Lord's Supper?

Most certainly not. The ordinance is never once caned a sacrifice in the New Testament. There is not the slightest trace of any sacrifice in the four accounts of its first institution. There is not a word to show that the Apostles thought they saw any sacrifice offered up. Moreover, we are repeatedly taught in the New Testament, that as soon as Christ was sacrificed for our sins on the cross, there was no more sacrifice needed, and that after His one offering of Himself there was no need of other offering for sin (Heb. 10:14-18). To attempt to offer up Christ again is an act of ignorance akin to blasphemy. The Prayer Book never once calls the Lord's Supper a sacrifice. The "oblations" it speaks of in one place are the offering of money in the offertory. The only "sacrifice" it mentions is that of "praise and thanksgiving;" and the only offering it mentions is that of "ourselves, souls and bodies," to be a "reasonable, holy, and lively sacrifice" unto God. Those who call the sacrament a sacrifice cannot possibly prove what they say.

20. Is the minister who consecrates the bread and wine in the Lord's Supper a priest?

He is a priest no doubt, if by the word "priest" we only mean a presbyter, or one in the second order of the ministry; and in this sense only he is called a priest in the Prayer Book. But he is certainly not a priest, if we mean by that word one who offers up a sacrifice. He cannot be, because he has no sacrifice to offer, and a priest without a sacrifice is an unmeaning title. He cannot be, because Christian ministers are never once called "priests" in the New Testament. The Jewish priests in the Old Testament had to offer sacrifices daily, and were types and figures of the great High Priest who was to come. But when Christ offered up Himself on the cross, a sacerdotal ministry was at once done away for ever. All believers are now "kings and priests," because they "present their bodies a living sacrifice to God" (Rom. 12:1). But Christian ministers are not sacrificing priests, and cannot be. They are Christ's ambassadors, messengers, witnesses, watchmen, shepherds, and stewards of the mysteries of God, but nothing more, whatever dress they may wear, and whatever title they may assume. Christians have only one Priest, even Him who is "passed into the heavens, Jesus, the Son of God" (Heb. 4:14).

21. Is the table in the Lord's Supper rightly called an altar?

Most certainly not. It is never once called an altar in the New Testament. The text in (Hebrews 13:10), "We have an altar," has nothing whatever to do with the Lord's Supper. That learned divine, Dr. Waterland, says, "That altar is Christ our Lord, who is Altar, Priest, and Sacrifice all in one" (Waterland's Works, vol. v. p. 268, Oxford ed.). Not once is the Lord's Table called an "altar" in the English Prayer Book. The Reformers of our Church ordered altars everywhere to be pulled down and removed, and wooden tables to be set up. Those Churchmen who carelessly call the Lord's Table an "altar," and talk of "altar services," and brides being "led to the altar" at weddings, are doing immense harm, ignorantly borrowing the language of the corrupt Church of Rome, and countenancing a mischievous error. If St. Paul rose from the grave, and was shown an "altar" in a Christian Church, he would not understand what it meant.

22. Is there anything sinful or wrong "in having the Lord's Supper in the evening?

Most certainly not. It cannot possibly be sinful to follow the example of Christ and His Apostles. Every reader of the New Testament must know that the institution of the Lord's Supper took place in the evening. It is certain that no special hour is recommended to us in the Acts or Epistles. It is equally certain that the Prayer Book leaves the matter to the discretion of every clergyman, and allows him to do what is best for his congregation, and wisely lays down no hard and fast rule about the time. To forbid evening communions would completely shut out many persons in large town parishes from the Lord's Table. The mothers of many families among the working classes cannot possibly leave home in the morning. The very name "Supper" seems to point to the evening of a day rather than the morning. In the face of these facts, to denounce evening communion as irreverent and profane is neither reasonable nor wise.

23. Is it needful, advantageous, and desirable to receive the Lord's Supper fasting?

It is certainly not necessary, because the practice is neither commanded nor recommended in Scripture. Moreover, it is perfectly clear that at the first institution of the sacrament, the Apostles could not have received the elements fasting, because they had just eaten the passover. There cannot, therefore, be anything very important in this point, and every believer may use his liberty, and do what he finds edifying to himself without condemning others. But it may be feared that there lies in the minds of many who attach immense value to fasting communion, a vague belief that the consecrated bread and wine which we receive are in some mysterious way not real bread and wine, and ought not therefore to be mixed with other food in our bodies! Such a belief cannot be praised. Those who teach that fasting communion is a rule obligatory on all take up a position which is not only unscriptural, but cruel. To go fasting to an early morning communion is likely to cause the death of delicate persons.

24. Is it necessary, or desirable, or useful for communicants to confess their sins privately to a minister, and to receive absolution, before they come to the Lord's Supper?

Necessary it cannot be. There is not a single verse in the New Testament to show that the Apostles recommended such confession, or that the first Christians practised it. Desirable or useful it certainly is not. The habit of private or auricular confession to a minister, under any circumstances, is one of the most mischievous and dangerous inventions of the corrupt Church of Rome, and has been the cause of enormous immorality and wickedness. Moreover, it is so expressly condemned in the "Homily of Repentance," that no minister of the Church of England has any right to recommend, encourage, or permit it, if he is honest, and faithful to his ordination VOWS.

25. But is not private confession before communion sanctioned by that passage in the Communion Service of our Prayer Book, in which the minister says, "If any of you cannot quiet his own conscience, but requireth further comfort or counsel, let him come to me or some other discreet and learned minister of God's Holy Word, and open his grief, that by the ministry of God's Word he may receive the benefit of absolution"?

It is impossible, with any fairness, to extract auricular confession and sacramental absolution out of this passage. The simple meaning is, that people who are troubled in mind with some special difficulties of conscience, are advised to go to some minister and talk privately with him about them, and to get them cleared up and resolved by texts of Scripture, that is, "by the ministry of God's Word." This is exactly what every wise minister in the present day does with those who seek private interviews with him, or wait for an after-meeting at the end of a sermon. But it is as utterly unlike the mischievous practice of habitual confession before communion, as wholesome medicine is unlike opium-eating, and water is unlike poison.

26. Does a minister do anything wicked or wrong if he pronounces the words of administration, once in giving the bread and wine to a number of communicants altogether, and not to each one separately he certainly does nothing wrong according to Scripture? He does exactly what our Lord Jesus Christ did when He first instituted the Lord's Supper. In each of the four accounts given in the New Testament, He used the plural number and not the singular. In each He pronounced the words once, and only once, and then gave the bread and wine to the whole company of the Apostles. In the face of our Lord's own example, to blame and condemn ministers who find it necessary to do the same, is surely not wise.

27. Does not the rubric of the Prayer Book order that the minister shall say the words of administration to each communicant separately?

Most certainly it does. Yet reason and common sense point out that the compilers of the Prayer Book could not have meant this rubric to be interpreted and obeyed literally and exactly, when such obedience is seriously inconvenient, if not impossible. When a clergyman with only one curate has to give the elements of bread and wine to 300 or 400 persons, the service must necessarily be so long, that aged and delicate people are wearied, and any following service is interfered with, or prevented altogether. No doubt, when the rubric was drawn up, parishes were small, communicants were few, there were no Sunday Schools, and few clergymen had more than one full service a day. Rules drawn up at that date, under such circumstances, are not to be rigorously applied to this day, especially when the application injures the Sunday services, and does more harm than good.

28. Does any clergyman literally obey all the rubrics of the Communion Service in the Prayer Book?

It is probable that there is not one who obeys then: all, and certainly no one obeys the four which immediately precede the Communion Service. The order to place the table "in the body of the church" is never attended to by any one! Custom in this matter has completely overridden the rubric. But this being the case, there must evidently be some discretion allowed in interpreting the communion rubrics.

29. Are communicants more likely to be edified if the words of administration are said to each one separately, than they are if they are said to the whole rail collectively?

It is impossible to answer this question. It is a matter of feeling and opinion. It is certain that many communicants feel pained and offended if they do not each hear the words addressed to themselves. It is equally certain that many others strongly dislike the incessant repetition of the words of administration, and especially where seven or eight ministers are employed, some giving the bread and some the wine, at the same time. Many complain that it confuses and distracts their minds. On such a point we must think and let think, and not judge one another. Let every man be fully persuaded in his own mind. The argument that some clergymen will not repeat the words to each communicant separately, because they hold the doctrine of "particular redemption," is an absurd, baseless, and ignorant suggestion, destitute of truth.

30. In receiving the bread and wine, are any bodily actions, attitudes, or gestures specially obligatory on communicants?

None are prescribed in Scripture. The Apostles at the first institution of the Lord's Supper were evidently reclining after the manner of the times. Kneeling is wisely ordered in the Prayer Book, to use the words of the rubric: "For a signification of our humble and grateful acknowledgment of the benefits of Christ given in the sacrament to all worthy receivers, and for the avoiding of profanation and disorder." Whether we should receive the bread with our fingers or upon the open palm of our hands, seems an open question, which each must decide for himself. Let it only be remembered, that to refrain to touch the bread with our hands, and to require it to be put into our mouths, has a strong appearance of superstition. As to bowing down till we almost grovel on the ground like serfs, it is a posture unworthy of Christ's freemen, and is a painfully suspicious symptom of ignorance of the real nature of the consecrated elements.

31. Does it add to the value and usefulness of the Lord's Supper, or promote the edification of the communicants, to have the sacrament administrated with the following accompaniments, viz.

1. Lights on the Communion Table in broad day;
2. Mixing water with the wine;
3. Clothing the minister in a peculiar dress called a chasuble;
4. Burning incense?

These things cannot be shown to be of any real value. Not one of them is recommended, or even named, in the New Testament. Not one of them is prescribed or ordered in the Prayer Book, and the best English lawyers pronounce them illegal. They are borrowed from the corrupt Church of Rome, and not a few clergymen, after beginning by using them, have ended by believing the sacrifice of the Mass, and joining the Romish communion. Such things no doubt have "a show of wisdom," and "satisfy the flesh" (Col. 2:23). They suit the many ignorant people who like a mere outward religion. But it is vain to suppose that they please God. In the nature of things, they tend to distract and divert the minds of communicants from the true, scriptural, and simple view of the Lord's Supper. No one in his senses can dare to say that they are essential to the validity of the sacrament, or that our Lord or His Apostles ever used them. They are neither more nor less than "will-worship," and the invention of man (Col. 2:23). The clergyman who persists in using these illegal ceremonial acts, in defiance of his bishop's monitions, causes divisions, offences, strife, and controversy in the Church about things not essential, and is justly deserving of censure.

32. Did the reformers of the Church of England, to whom we owe our Articles and Prayer Book, attach much weight to right and true views of the lord's Supper, and especially of the real meaning of the presence of Christ in that sacrament?

Yes! most certainly. It was precisely on this point that our Protestant Reformers differed most widely from the Church of Rome. It was precisely because they would not admit that the natural body and blood of Christ were corporally present under the forms of bread and wine after the words of consecration were pronounced, that many of them were condemned to death and burned at the stake in Queen Mary's reign. Fuller, the famous Church historian, says:—"The sacrament of the altar was the main touchstone to discover the poor Protestants. This point of the real corporal presence of Christ in the sacrament., the same body that was crucified, was the compendious way to discover those of the opposite opinion."—Fuller's Church History, vol. iii. p. 399, Tegg's edition.

33. Why was John Rogers, the protomartyr, Vicar of St. Sepulchre's and Prebendary of St. Paul's, burned in Smithfield, on February 4, 1555?

Let us hear his own account:—

"I was asked whether I believed in the sacrament to be the very body and blood of our Saviour Christ that was born of the Virgin Mary, and hanged on the cross, really and substantially? I answered, 'I think it to be false. I cannot understand really and substantially to signify otherwise than corporally. But corporally Christ is only in heaven, and so Christ cannot be corporally in your sacrament.'" Foxe in loco, vol. iii. p. 101, edit. 1684.

And so he was burned.

34. Why was Hugh Latimer, sometime Bishop of Worcester, burned at Oxford, on October 16, 1555?

Let us hear what Foxe says were the articles exhibited against him:—

"That thou hast openly affirmed, defended, and maintained that the true and natural body of Christ after the consecration of the priest, is not really present in the sacrament of the altar, and that in the sacrament of the altar remaineth still the substance of bread and wine."

And to this article the good old man replied:—

"After a corporal being, which the Romish Church furnisheth, Christ's body and blood is not in the sacrament under the forms of bread and wine." Foxe in loco, vol. iii. p. 426.

And so he was burned.

35. Why was Nicholas Ridley, Bishop of London, burned at Oxford, on October 16, 1555?

Once more let us hear what Foxe says were the words of his sentence of condemnation:—

"The said Nicholas Ridley affirms, maintains, and stubbornly defends certain opinions, assertions, and heresies, contrary to the Word of God and the received faith of the Church, as in denying the true and natural body and blood of Christ to be in the sacrament of the altar, and secondarily, in affirming the substance of bread and wine to remain after the words of consecration." Foxe in loco, vol. iii. p. 426.

And so he was burned.

36. Why was John Bradford, Prebendary of St. Paul's, chaplain to Bishop Ridley, and one of Edward the Sixth's chaplains, burned at Smithfield, on July 1, 1555?

Let us hear what Foxe says he wrote to the men of Lancashire and Cheshire while he was in prison:—

"The chief thing which I am condemned for as an heretic is because I deny the sacrament of the altar (which is not Christ's Supper, but a plain perversion as the Papists now use it) to be a real, natural, and corporal presence of Christ's body and blood under the forms and accidents of bread and wine, that is, because I deny transubstantiation, which is the darling of the devil, and daughter and heir to Antichrist's religion."—Foxe in loco, vol. iii. p. 260.

And so he was burned.

37. But may not these four men who were burned have been isolated cases, and not true representatives of the Church of England? May they not have been violent fanatics, and unlearned and ignorant men?

Nothing can be further from the truth than these suggestions. The doctrines for which these four men laid down their lives were the doctrines professed by the whole Church of England in the reign of Edward the Sixth. So far from standing alone, their opinions were shared by 280 other persons, who were burned in Queen Mary's reign. As to ignorance and want of learning, Ridley and Rogers were among the most learned men of their day, and to Ridley in particular we are indebted for the foundations of our English Prayer Book.

38. But is it not said that the English Reformers, having just come out of Rome, adopted very extreme and rather defective views of the Lord's Supper? Have not English divines since the Reformation taken up much more moderate and temperate opinions about the doctrine of the Real Presence?

Whosoever says this says what he cannot possibly prove. With very few exceptions, all the greatest, ablest, and most learned English theologians of every school of thought, for three hundred years, have agreed in maintaining that there is no real corporal presence of Christ's natural body and blood in the consecrated bread and wine in the Lord's Supper.

39. What does Bishop Jewell, in his work on the Sacraments, say?

"Let us examine what difference there is between the body of Christ and the Sacrament of His body.

"The difference is this: a sacrament is a figure or token; the body of Christ is figured or tokened. The sacramental bread is bread, it is not the body of Christ; the body of Christ is flesh; it is no bread. The bread is beneath; the body is above. The bread is on the table; the body is in heaven. The bread is in the mouth; the body is in the heart. The bread feedeth the body; the body feedeth the soul. The bread shall come to nothing; the body is immortal and shall not perish. The bread is vile; the body of Christ is glorious. Such a difference is there between the bread which is a sacrament of the body, and the body of Christ itself. The sacrament is eaten as well of the wicked as of the faithful; the body is only eaten of the faithful. The sacrament may be eaten unto judgment; the body cannot be eaten but unto salvation. Without the sacrament we may be saved; but without the body of Christ we have no salvation: we cannot be saved."—Jewell's Works, vol. ii., Treatise on Sacraments, Parker Society edition, p. 1121.

40. What does Richard Hooker, in his "Ecclesiastical Polity," say?

"The real presence of Christ's most blessed body and blood is not to be sought for in the sacrament, but in the worthy receiver of the sacrament.

"And with this the very order of our Saviour's words agreeth. First, 'Take and eat;' then,' This is My body which is broken for you.' First, 'Drink ye all of this;' then followeth, 'This is My blood of the New Testament, which is shed for many for the remission of sins.' I see not which way it should be gathered by the words of Christ,—when and where the bread is His body or the wine His blood, but only in the very heart and soul of him which receiveth them. As for the sacraments, they really exhibit, but for aught we can gather out of that which is written of them, they are not really nor do really contain in themselves that grace which with them or by them it pleaseth God to bestow." Hooker, Eccl. Pol., book v. p. 67.

41. What does Jeremy Taylor, in his book on the Real Presence (edit. 1654, pp. 13-15), say?

"We say that Christ's body is in the sacrament really, but spiritually. The Roman Catholics say that it is there really, but spiritually. For so Bellarmine is bold to say that the word may be allowed in this question. Where now is the difference? Here by spiritually, they mean spiritual after the manner of a spirit. We by spiritually, mean present to our spirit only. They say that Christ's body is truly present there as it was upon the cross, but not after the manner of all or anybody, but after that manner of being as an angel is in a place. That's their spiritually.—But we by the real spiritual presence of Christ do understand Christ to be present, as the Spirit of God is present, in the hearts of the faithful by blessing and grace; and this is all which we mean beside topical and figurative presence."

42. What did Archbishop Usher, in his sermon before the House of Commons, say?

"In the sacrament of the Lord's Supper, the bread and wine are not changed in substance from being the same with that which is served at ordinary tables. But in respect of the sacred use whereunto they are consecrated, such a change is made that now they differ as much from common bread and wine as heaven from earth. Neither are they to be accounted barely significative, but truly exhibitive also of those heavenly things whereunto they have relation; as being appointed by God to be a means of conveying the same to us, and putting us in actual possession thereof. So that in the use of this holy ordinance, as verily as a man with his bodily hand and mouth receiveth the earthly creatures of bread and wine, so verily with his spiritual hand and mouth, if he have any, doth he receive the body and blood of Christ. And this is that real and substantial presence which we affirm to be in the inward part of this sacred action."

43. What does Waterland say?

"The Fathers well understood that to make Christ's natural body the real sacrifice of the Eucharist, would not only be absurd in reason, but highly presumptuous and profane; and that to make the outward symbols a proper sacrifice, a material sacrifice, would be entirely contrary to gospel principles, degrading the Christian sacrifice into a Jewish one, yea, and making it much lower and meaner than the Jewish one, both in value and dignity. The right way, therefore, was to make the sacrifice spiritual, and it could be no other upon gospel principles."—Works, vol. iv. p. 762.

"No one has any authority or right to offer Christ as a sacrifice, whether really or symbolically, but Christ Himself; such a sacrifice is His sacrifice, not ours—offered for us, not by us, to God the Father." Works, vol. iv. p. 753.

44. What does Bishop Burnet, in his work on the Articles, say?

"We assert a real presence of the body and blood of Christ; but not of His body as it is now glorified in heaven, but of His body as it was broken on the cross, when His blood was shed and separated from it; that is, His death, with the merits and effects of it, are in a visible and federal act offered in the sacrament to all worthy believers.—By real we understand true, in opposition both to fiction and imagination, and to those shadows that were in the Mosaical dispensation, in which the manna, the rock, the brazen serpent, but eminently the cloud of glory, were types and shadows of Messiah that was to come, with whom came grace and truth, that is, a most wonderful manifestation of the mercy and grace of God, and a verifying of promises made under the law.—In this sense we acknowledge a real presence of Christ in the sacrament. Though we are convinced that our first Reformers judged right concerning the use of the phrase, Real Presence, that it was better to be let fall than to be continued, since the use of it, and that idea which does naturally arise from the common acceptation of it, may stick deeper, and feed superstition more than all those larger explanations that are given to it can be able to cure."—Burnet on Twenty-eighth Article.

45. What does Henry Philpotts, Bishop of Exeter; in his letter to Charles Butler, say? "The Church of Rome holds that the body and blood of Christ are present under the accidents of bread and wine; the Church of England holds that their real presence is in the soul of the communicant at the sacrament of the Lord's Supper.

"She holds that after the consecration of the bread and wine they are changed, not in their nature, but in their use, that instead of nourishing our bodies only, they now are instruments by which, when worthily received, God gives to our souls the body and blood of Christ to nourish and sustain them, that this is not a fictitious or imaginary exhibition of our crucified Redeemer to us, but a real though spiritual one, more real, indeed, because more effectual, than the carnal exhibition and manducation of Him could be, for the flesh profiteth nothing."

"In the same manner, then, as oar Lord Himself said, 'I am the true bread that came down from heaven' (not meaning thereby that he was a lump of baked dough or manna, but the true means of sustaining the true life of man, which is spiritual, not corporeal), so in the sacrament to the worthy receiver of the consecrated elements, though in their nature mere bread and wine, are yet given truly, really, and effectively, the crucified body and blood of Christ; that body and blood which are the instruments of man's redemption, and upon which our spiritual life and strength solely depend. It is in this sense that the crucified Jesus is present in the sacrament of His Supper, not in, nor with, the bread and wine, nor under their accidents, but in the souls of communicants; not carnally, but effectually and faithfully, and therefore most really."—Philpotts' Letter to Butler, 8vo edit. 1825, pp. 235, 236.

46. What did Archbishop Longley say in his last Charge, printed and published after his death in 1868?

"The doctrine of the real presence is, in one sense, the doctrine of the Church of England. She asserts that the body and blood of Christ are 'verily and indeed taken and received by the faithful in the Lord's Supper.' And she asserts equally that such presence, is not material or corporal, but that Christ's body 'is given, taken, and eaten in the Supper, only after a heavenly and spiritual manner' (Art. 28.). Christ's presence is effectual for all those intents and purposes for which His body was broken and His blood shed. As to a presence elsewhere than in the heart of a believer, the Church of England is silent, and the words of Hooker therefore represent her views: 'The real presence of Christ's most blessed body and blood is not to be sought in the sacrament, but in the worthy receiver of the sacrament.'"

47. What did the Judicial Committee of Privy Council declare in the famous case of Shepherd V. Bennet.

"It is not lawful for a clergyman to teach that the sacrifice and offering of Christ upon the cross, or the redemption, propitiation, or satisfaction wrought by it, is or can be repeated in the ordinance of the Lord's Supper; nor that in that ordinance there is or can be any sacrifice or offering of Christ which is efficacious in the sense in which Christ's death is efficacious, to procure the remission of guilt or punishment of sins."

"Any presence of Christ in the Holy Communion, which is not a presence to the soul of the faithful receiver, the Church of England does not by her Articles and formularies affirm, or require her ministers to accept. This cannot be stated too plainly."

48. What is the declaration which, under the "Act of Settlement," and by the law of England, every Sovereign of this country, at his or her Coronation, must "make, subscribe, and audibly repeat"!

It is the declaration, be it remembered, which was made, subscribed, and repeated by Her Gracious Majesty Queen Victoria.

"I, Victoria, do solemnly and sincerely, in the presence of God, profess, testify, and declare that I do believe that in the sacrament of the Lord's Supper there is not any transubstantiation of the elements of bread and wine into the body and blood of Christ, at or after the consecration thereof, by any person whatsoever; and that the invocation or adoration of the Virgin Mary or any other saint, and the sacrifice of the mass, as they are now used in the Church of Rome, are superstitious and idolatrous. And I do solemnly, in the presence of God, profess, testify, and declare, that I do make this declaration, and every part thereof, in the plain and ordinary sense of the words read unto me, as they are commonly understood by English Protestants, without any evasion, equivocation, or mental reservation, and without any dispensation already granted me for this purpose by the Pope or any other authority or person whatsoever, or without any hope of any such dispensation from any person or authority whatsoever, or without thinking that I am or can be acquitted before God or man, or absolved of this declaration or any part thereof, although the Pope or any other person or persons or power whatsoever shall dispense with or annul the same, or declare that it was null and void from the beginning."

49. After all, are these nice and deep questions about a real corporal presence and a sacrifice in the Lord's Supper of any vital importance? Do they really interfere with any leading truths of the gospel? Are they not all strifes about words which are of no consequence? Are they not all mere aesthetic squabbling about ornaments, on which tastes may be allowed to differ?

The man who can say such things as this, exhibits most woeful ignorance of Christian theology, as laid down in the New Testament, and has very much to learn. The harmless theory, as some people call it, of a real corporal presence of Christ's natural body and blood in the bread and wine, if pursued to its legitimate consequences, obscures every leading doctrine of the gospel, and damages and interferes with the whole system of Christ's truth. Grant for a moment that the Lord's Supper is a sacrifice, and not a sacrament—grant that every time the words of consecration are used, the natural body and blood of Christ are present on the communion table under the forms of bread and wine—grant that every one who eats that consecrated bread and drinks that consecrated wine, does really eat and drink the body and blood of Christ—grant for a moment these things, and the most momentous consequences result from these premises. You spoil the blessed doctrine of Christ's finished work when He died on the cross. A sacrifice that needs to be repeated is not a perfect and complete thing. You spoil the priestly office of Christ. If there are priests that can offer an acceptable sacrifice to God besides Him, the great High Priest is robbed of His glory.—You spoil the scriptural doctrine of the Christian ministry. You exalt sinful men into the position of mediators between God and man. You give to the sacramental elements of bread and wine an honour and veneration they were never meant to receive, and produce an idolatry to be abhorred of faithful Christians.—Last, but not least, you overthrow the true doctrine of Christ's human nature. If the body born of the Virgin Mary can be in more places than one at the same time, it is not a body like our own, and Jesus was not the second Adam in the truth of our nature. Our martyred Reformers saw and felt these things even more clearly than we do, and, seeing and feeling them, chose to die rather than admit the doctrine of the Real Presence.

50. But may not these unhappy divisions about the, Lord's Supper be healed and laid to rest by sanctioning a policy of general compromise and toleration? Why should not Churchmen agree to allow every clergyman to believe and teach just what he likes about the Lord's Supper? Why not proclaim by authority, that for peace' sake one clergyman may call this ordinance a sacrament, and another clergyman in the next parish may call it a sacrifice,—one man may tell his people that there is a real corporal presence of Christ on the Lord's Table, and another tell his people that there is no such presence at all? Why not permit all this for the sake of peace? Why not sacrifice all distinct doctrine in order to avoid controversy?

The answer is plain and obvious. This "policy of compromise and toleration" would bring no peace at all, but would rather increase, emphasize, crystallize, and solidify our unhappy divisions. It would be regarded by the laity of the middle and lower classes as a deliberate attempt to bring back the Romish Mass, and get behind the Protestant Reformation. It would: split the clergy of every diocese into two distinct bodies, neither of which would hold any communion with the other. It would increase the difficulties of bishops tenfold, and make it impossible to examine any candidate for orders about the Lord's Supper. Above all, this policy of universal toleration would sooner or later bring down the displeasure of God, and ruin the Church of England. Peace, cessation of controversy, free thought, and liberty in administering sacraments, are excellent things to talk about, and they look beautiful at a distance. But they must have some bounds. The Church which, in zeal for peace, throws creeds and rubrics overboard, and regards Deism, Socinianism, Romanism, and Protestantism with equal favour or equal indifference, is a mere Babel, a city of confusion, and not a city of God. This is what the Church of England will come to, if she ever gives up the principles of her martyred Reformers about the Lord's Supper.

51. What is the Real Presence that the Church of England specially needs in these latter days?

It is the presence of God the Holy Spirit. This is of far more importance than any corporal presence of Christ. Our question in every place of worship should be, not, "Is Christ's body here?" but, "Is the Spirit, the Comforter, here?" Excessive craving after Christ's material bodily presence before the Second Advent is in reality dishonouring the Holy Spirit. Where He is, there will be God's blessing. Where He is, there will be true honour given to the body and blood of Christ. What the Church of Christ needs everywhere is the real presence of the Holy Ghost. If the Holy Spirit is not present, the highest show of reverence for the consecrated bread and wine in the Lord's Supper is useless formality, and completely worthless in God's sight.

CHAPTER XXI

1 Thess. 2:1-2
"For Kings."

"I exhort, therefore, that, first of all, supplications, prayers, intercessions, and giving of thanks, be made for all men; For kings, and for all that are in authority." —1 Thess. 2:1-2.

THE words which head this page are taken from a passage of Scripture which is eminently suitable to the solemn occasion which gathers us together, the Jubilee of our gracious Sovereign Queen Victoria's reign. A royal Jubilee is a very rare event in history, and in all human probability this is the only one in England which any of us will ever live to see. Let us lay this seriously to heart in today's service of prayer and praise!

The words of the text occur in the first direction which St. Paul gave, by inspiration of the Holy Ghost, to his young friend Timothy about the conduct of public worship. "First of all," he says emphatically—"first of all, I exhort that supplications, prayers, intercessions, and giving of thanks, be made for all men; for kings, and for all that are in authority; that we may lead a quiet and peaceable life."

I might say something about the striking contrast between the elaborate and minute ritual of the Old.

The paper now in the reader's hands contains file substance of a sermon preached in Liverpool Cathedral, on June 20th, 1887, on the occasion of the Jubilee of Queen Victoria, before the Mayor and leading inhabitants of Liverpool.

Testament Church under the ceremonial law, and the remarkable simplicity and brevity of the ritual provided for the Church of the new dispensation. It is a contrast easily explained. The worship of the Old Testament was designed for the Jews alone,—for one single nation practically cut off from the rest of mankind,—and was full of types and emblems of good things to come. The worship of the New Testament was intended for all the world, and as the Thirty-fourth Article of our Church has wisely said—"Ceremonies may be changed according to the diversities of countries, times, and men's manners."

One thing, however, is very certain. The rule, or rubric, laid down by St. Paul for the guidance of Timothy at Ephesus, is meant to be a rule of perpetual obligation as long as the world stands, and until the Lord comes. Whenever Christians meet together for public worship, there ought to be "prayers and intercessions for all men," and specially "for kings," as well as "thanksgiving for mercies received." This primary rule you are invited to observe this day.

I. Concerning the general duty of praying for others, I think it useful to say something. But my words shall be few.

I suspect the thought crosses some minds—"What is the use of my intercession? What am I but a debtor to Christ's mercy and grace? How can the prayer of such a poor sinner be of any use to others? Praying for myself I can understand, but not praying for another."

The answer to all such thoughts is short and simple. It is the command of God, and it is a plain duty to obey it. In this, as in many other matters, it becomes a mortal man to believe that the light of the last day shall make all clear. In the meantime, the "how" and the "why" and the "wherefore" had better be left alone. What we know not now we shall know hereafter. The practice of almost every saint in the Bible, of whom much is recorded, ought to silence all objections. Patriarchs, prophets, kings, and apostles have left us examples of intercession. Do we know more than they did? Do we think they wasted their time when they named others before God? Are we wiser than they?

I have a firm conviction that in this matter God tests our faith and our love. Do we believe that the eternal God is too wise to make any mistake? Then, when He says "Pray for others," let us not stand still, reasoning and arguing, but do as He tells us. When our Lord Jesus Christ says the best proof of a high standard of love is to "Pray for them which despitefully use you and persecute you" (Matt. 5:44), let us believe and obey. I always thank God that our time-honoured Prayer Book contains such a grand specimen of intercession as the Litany. I believe the last day alone will show how the prayers of God's elect have affected the history of this world, and influenced the rise and fall of nations. There was deep truth in the saying of unhappy Mary Queen of Scots—"I fear the prayers of John Knox more than an army of 20,000 men." So, when we kneel to pray for ourselves, let us never forget to pray for others.

II. Concerning the special duty of praying for kings and all that are in authority, I must not omit to say something. But once again my words shall be few.

A moment's reflection will tell us that St. Paul's injunction to "pray for kings" is a very singular and remarkable one. For consider in whose hands the government of the world lay at the time when the Epistle to Timothy was written. Think what a monster of iniquity wore the imperial purple at Rome—Nero—whose very name is a proverb. Think of such rulers of provinces as Felix and Festus, Herod, Agrippa and Gallio. Think of the ecclesiastical heads of the Jewish Church Annas and Caiaphas. Yet these were the men for whom St. Paul says Christians were to pray! Their personal characters might be bad. But they were persons ordained by God to keep some outward order in this sin-burdened world. As such, for their office' sake, they were to be prayed for.

After all, we must never forget that none are so truly to be pitied—none in such spiritual danger—none so likely to make shipwreck to all eternity—and none stand in such need of our prayers, as the kings of this world. Few out of the many who criticise their conduct seriously consider the enormous difficulties of their position.

Think of the temptations which surround them. Seldom advised, seldom contradicted, seldom warned, they dwell in bodies like our own, and have like passions with ourselves, and are liable to be overcome by the world, the flesh, and the devil, just like other men. I do not wonder to read that when Buchanan, once tutor to James the First, was lying on his deathbed, he sent a last message to his royal pupil, "that he was going to a place to which few kings and princes ever came." If it be true, as of course it must be, because our Lord said it. How hardly shall a rich man enter the kingdom of God," how much more hard shall entrance be for a king!

Think of the countless knots which a king has to untie, and the awkward questions which he often has to decide. How to arrange differences with other countries,—how to promote the prosperity of all classes of the community,—how to decide when to tighten the reins of government, and when to loosen them,—how to select the right men to fill vacant posts,—how to deal fairly and justly with all ranks, sorts, and conditions of men, attending impartially to all and neglecting none—all these are difficulties which the poor fallible occupant of a throne has to face every week of his life. Can we wonder if he makes mistakes? Well might a poet of our own say—"Uneasy sleeps the head that wears a crown."

Think of the immense responsibility of a king's office, and the tremendous issues which depend on his decisions. A single error in judgment in managing a negotiation, a want of temper in dealing with an ambassador, a hasty reliance on erroneous information—any one of these things may involve his subjects in a war attended by fearful bloodshed, losses abroad, discontent at home, heavy taxation, and, finally perhaps, revolution and deposition from his throne. And all may come from one man's mistake.'

Yes! we may well be exhorted to "pray for kings." If we could only believe it, of all the children of Adam they most deserve our daily intercessions. Raised above their fellows by their position, they find themselves, like the Alpine traveller who scales the Matterhorn, fearfully alone. In the nature of things, they can have no equals with whom to exchange hearts and sympathies. They are surrounded by those who are tempted to be flatterers and sycophants, and to make things pleasant to royal ears. They seldom hear the whole truth. They are only human beings like ourselves, needing the same Christ—the same Holy Spirit. Yet they are expected never to err, and are blamed if they do.

Yes! we may well "pray for kings." It is easy to criticise and find fault with their conduct, and write furious articles against them in newspapers, or make violent speeches about them on platforms. Any fool can rip and rend a costly garment, but not every man can cut out and make one. To expect perfection in kings, prime ministers, or rulers of any kind, is senseless and unreasonable. We should exhibit more wisdom if we prayed for them more, and criticised less.

III. Let me now invite your attention to the special subject which calls us together this day, viz. the celebration of the Royal English Jubilee. This very day our gracious Queen Victoria completes the fiftieth year of her reign. I ask you to come with me and look back on the half century which is just concluded. My aim is to show you as briefly as possible some of the great reasons why we ought to be a very thankful people this day. In a fallen world like ours there always will be many unredressed evils, and murmurers and complainers will be found in every quarter. For myself, I can only say that, on a calm retrospect of the last fifty years, I see so many causes for national thankfulness, that I find it hard to know what I should select, and where to begin. Let me, however, try to name a few.

(a) First and foremost among the reasons for thankfulness, let me mention the stainless and blameless personal character which our gracious Sovereign has borne during the long fifty years of her reign. In all the relations of life as a mother and a wife—in the high moral standard which she has maintained in her Court and household—in her scrupulous and diligent discharge of the countless daily duties which her high office entails upon her in her boundless sympathy with the sorrows of her humblest subjects—where, in the long roll of English sovereigns, will you find one who can be compared with our good Queen Victoria?

I believe we do not realize sufficiently the immense importance of a Sovereign's personal character in the present day. The character of a ruler, like the insensible pressure of the atmosphere on every square inch of our bodies, will always have a silent, quiet influence on the conduct of subjects. The lives of sovereigns are an open book which all can read, and the example of a crowned head often does more than legal enactments. There can be no doubt that the enormous immorality of the French Court in the eighteenth century was the true cause of the first French Revolution, and the Reign of Terror. During the last half century the foundations of not a few governments in the world have been rudely shaken, and some have been completely overturned. Nothing, I suspect, had contributed so largely to the stability of the British throne as the high character of the Royal Lady who has occupied it. A revolutionary spirit, we all know, has been frequently in the air during the last fifty years, and a disposition to pull down all established institutions, and substitute new-fangled schemes of government, has repeatedly shown itself. The rise and progress of Chartism and Socialism have often made many afraid. Nothing, I firmly believe, has kept the ship of the British State on an even keel so much as the inner life of our beloved Queen. If that inner life had been such as the lives of some of the Plantagenets, Tudors, and Stuarts, I doubt extremely whether the royal standard would have been flying at Windsor Castle this week.

(b) In the next place, let us be thankful for the singularly long period of time during which God has permitted our gracious Sovereign to sit on the throne of her ancestors. Of all the kings of Judah who reigned in Jerusalem, Uzziah and Manasseh were the only two who held the sceptre for more than fifty years, and even David and Solomon's reigns were only forty years long. Our own kings, Henry the Third, Edward the Third, and George the Third, each reigned more than fifty years. But, since the world began, we know of no female sovereign in historic times, on the face of the globe, who has worn a crown so long as our good Queen Victoria. I am sure we are not sufficiently grateful for this. Even under a constitutional monarchy like ours—in which everything does not depend on the whim of an imperial autocrat—frequent changes on the throne are calculated to have a disturbing influence, and a new sovereign's views of his power and duties may not always coincide with those of his predecessor. There is a deep meaning in Solomon's words—"For the transgression of a land many are the princes thereof" (Prov. 28:2). In early English history, the bloody wars of the Roses swept away the flower of our nobility, and struggles between the rival houses of York and Lancaster frequently shook the throne, and desolated the realm. At a later date, the unhappy Commonwealth struggle overturned for a time our long-established institutions. Happy is the land in which there are few changes on the throne. "Grant our Sovereign a long life," and "God save the Queen," should be the daily prayer of every British patriot.

(c) In the next place, let us thank God for the enormous growth in national wealth and prosperity by which the half century of Queen Victoria's reign has been distinguished. It is a simple matter of fact, that in no preceding fifty years of English history has there been anything like it. To use a well-known phrase, the capital or income of the country has moved on "by leaps and bounds." In spite of occasional cycles of bad times and commercial depression,—in spite of bloody and expensive wars, such as the Crimean War and the Indian Mutiny,—in spite of providential visitation, such as cholera and the Irish potato famine,—the progress of the nation and the increase of wealth have been something astounding. The waves on the shore have seemed to come and go, to advance and retire, but on the whole the tide has been steadily rising every year. In 1837, the sums of money deposited in Savings Banks were only 14 millions. They are now 90 millions.—In 1843, when the income tax was first imposed, each penny in the pound brought into the National Exchequer £772,000. In 1885, each penny produced £1,992,000.—In 1843, the assessable value of lands and tenements was only 95 millions. In 1885, it was 180 millions. The assessable value of trades and professions in 1843 was only 71 millions. In 1885, it was 282 millions.—The population of the United Kingdom was 25 millions in 1837. It is now, in spite of the Irish famine and a ceaseless emigration, 37 millions. In our own city of Liverpool, the population in 1837 was only 246,000. It is now, including suburbs, 700,000.—The tonnage of shipping at our port in 1837 was only 1,953,894. It is now 7,546,623.—The number of ships entering was 15,038. It is now 21,529.—In 1837, Liverpool had 9 docks, with a frontage of two miles and a half to the river. There are now fifty docks and basins with a frontage of six miles.—In 1837, Liverpool dock dues were £173,853. They are now £694,316.—Surely we ought to be thankful.—This is the finger of God. It is "the blessing of the Lord that maketh rich."—"Both riches and honour come from Him" (Prov. 10:22; 1 Chron. 29:12).[38]

(d) In the next place, we ought to be thankful for the extraordinary advances which science has made during the half century of our gracious Sovereign's reign. We have bridged the Atlantic with our steamers, and brought our English-speaking cousins within a week of our shores—a thing which I well remember Dr. Lardner declared to be impossible. We have covered the land with a network of railways, making journeys possible in a few hours, which formerly occupied days. We have opened communication with every part of the world by electric telegraph, and can send messages in a few hours, which formerly would not have been conveyed in as many months.

All these things, and many others, have budded, blossomed, and bloomed since Queen Victoria ascended her throne. They have added immensely to the comfort and convenience of modern life. They have practically annihilated time and space, and lengthened life, and enabled us to do an amount of work in twenty-four hours, which our grandfathers would have thought Quixotical, romantic, absurd, and impossible. But they are simple facts. Surely we ought to be thankful.

(e) Finally, and above all, we ought to be most thankful for the immense advance which the cause of religion, education, and morality has made throughout the realm since Queen Victoria came to the throne. Human nature, no doubt, is not changed. The millennium has not begun, and much evil abounds. But still, that man must be blind or obstinately prejudiced, who does not see an immense change for the better, both as regards duty to God and duty to our neighbours throughout the country, in the last half century. Church building, no doubt, is not everything, and bricks and mortar do not constitute religion. Yet the mere fact that 2000 new churches, besides Nonconformist chapels, have been built in England and Wales during the last fifty years, by voluntary efforts, and nearly thirty millions of money have been spent in restoring old places of worship and building new ones, speaks volumes. Even here in Liverpool and its suburbs, there were only 36 churches and about 70 clergymen in 1837. At this moment there are 90 churches and 185 clergy in 1837, the income of the Church Missionary Society was £71,000. It is now £232,000. The Pastoral Aid Society only received £7363. It now receives £50,122.—In 1837, there were only 58,000 children receiving education in all the schools of the National and British and Foreign School Societies throughout England and Wales. In 1885, there were nearly 4,000,000 under instruction and inspection. It is a striking fact that during the half century of Queen Victoria's reign, her Governments have spent fifty millions on education.

As to works of philanthropy and efforts to promote morality, time would fail me if I tried to recount them. The labours of men like Lord Shaftesbury and others have raised the condition of the working classes one-hundred per cent. The Ten Hours Factory Act, the legislation about women and children working in mines, the creation of ragged schools and reformatories, the rise and progress of the temperance movement, the many efforts to ameliorate the condition of the working classes by education, sanitation, public parks, and recreation grounds, hall these things have been the creation of the last fifty years. I call

---

[38] For the figures in this paragraph I am chiefly indebted to my friend Sir James Picton, of Liverpool, a well-known master of statistics.

them healthy symptoms of our condition as a nation. I humbly confess that we are still very imperfect. There is still a vast amount of improvidence, willful poverty, drunkenness, impurity, and Sabbath-breaking in the land which is greatly to be regretted. But these evils are less than they were in proportion to the population. And, at any rate, we see them, know them, and are honestly using means to prevent them. Surely our hearts, when we compare 1837 and 1887, ought to be deeply thankful.

It is very meet, right, and our bounden duty to praise God.[39] Let me earnestly entreat all whom I address today to turn from the black clouds in his horizon, to look at the blue sky, and to be thankful. Where is the nation on the face of the globe which has had such reason to thank God for the last half century as Great Britain? And who can deny that, in reckoning up the many blessings of that period, we have reason to thank God for the wise and beneficent reign of our Queen? There are names in the long roll of English kings which no Englishman can think of without shame. The memory of a Royal William, or Henry, or Edward, or James, or Charles, or George, is by no means always fragrant. But I doubt if the future historian will ever record the name of a monarch whose subjects will have had such cause to be thankful as we have for Queen Victoria.

And now to these praises and thanksgivings let us add an earnest prayer that the life of our beloved Sovereign may yet be spared to us for many years, and that these years may be years of increasing happiness and usefulness to the end. We all know that she has had many sorrowful times to pass through. The deaths of the Prince Consort, the Princess Alice, and the Duke of Albany, were crushing trials which will never be forgotten. Let us pray that she may be spared further trials of this kind, that she may long continue to live in the affections of a prosperous, united, and contented people, and that when she is removed from this world of sorrow, she may enter with an abundant entrance into that kingdom where tears are wiped from all eyes, and receive that crown of glory which alone never fades away.

Bonus Sermon: A Call to Prayer

"Men ought always to pray." Luke 18:1

"I will that men pray everywhere." I Tim 2:1

I have a question to offer you. It is contained in three words, Do you pray?

The question is one that none but you can answer. Whether you attend public worship or not, your minister knows. Whether you have family prayers in your house or not, your relations know. But whether you pray in private or not, is a matter between yourself and God.

I beseech you in all affection to attend to the subject I bring before you. Do not say that my question is too close. If your heart is right in the sight of God, there is nothing in it to make you afraid. Do not turn off my question by replying that you say your prayers. It is one thing to say your prayers and another to pray. Do not tell me that my question is unnecessary. Listen to me for a few minutes, and I will show you good reasons for asking it.

---

[39]It is very meet, right, and our bounden duty, that we should at all times, and in all places, give thanks unto thee, O Lord, holy Father, almighty, everlasting God. —From the Book of Common Prayer.

I. I ask whether you pray, because prayer is absolutely needful to a man's salvation.

I say, absolutely needful, and I say so advisedly. I am not speaking now of infants or idiots. I am not settling the state of the heathen. I know that where little is given, there little will be required. I speak especially of those who call themselves Christians, in a land like our own. And of such I say, no man or woman can expect to be saved who does not pray.

I hold salvation by grace as strongly as any one. I would gladly offer a free and full pardon to the greatest sinner that ever lived. I would not hesitate to stand by his dying bed, and say, "Believe on the Lord Jesus Christ even now, and you shall be saved." But that a man can have salvation without *asking* for it, I cannot see in the Bible. That a man will receive pardon of his sins, who will not so much as lift up his heart inwardly, and say, "Lord Jesus, give it to me," this I cannot find. I can find that nobody will be saved by his prayers, but I cannot find that without prayer anybody will be saved.

It is not absolutely needful to salvation that a man should *read* the Bible. A man may have no learning, or be blind, and yet have Christ in his heart. It is not absolutely needful that a man should hear public preaching of the gospel. He may live where the gospel is not preached, or he may be bedridden, or deaf. But the same thing cannot be said about prayer. It is absolutely needful to salvation that a man should *pray*.

There is no royal road either to health or learning. Princes and kings, poor men and peasants, all alike must attend to the wants of their own bodies and their own minds. No man can eat, drink, or sleep by proxy. No man can get the alphabet learned for him by another. All these are things which everybody must do for himself, or they will not be done at all.

Just as it is with the mind and body, so it is with the soul. There are certain things absolutely needful to the soul's health and well-being. Each must attend to these things for himself. Each must repent for himself. Each must apply to Christ for himself. And for himself each must speak to God and pray. You must do it for yourself, for by nobody else can it be done.

To be prayerless is to be without God, without Christ, without grace, without hope, and without heaven. It is to be on the road to hell. Now can you wonder that I ask the question, Do you pray?

II. I ask again whether you pray, because a habit of prayer is one of the surest marks of a true Christian.

All the children of God on earth are alike in this respect. From the moment there is any life and reality about their religion, they pray. Just as the first sign of life in an infant when born into the world is the act of breathing, so the first act of men and women when they are born again is *praying*.

This is one of the common marks of all the elect of God, "They cry unto him day and night" (Luke 18:1). The Holy Spirit, who makes them new creatures, works in them the feeling of adoption, and makes them cry, "Abba, Father" (Rom. 8:15). The Lord Jesus, when he quickens them, gives them a voice and a tongue, and says to them, "Be dumb no more." God has no dumb children. It is as much a part of their new nature to pray, as it is of a child to cry. They see their need of mercy and grace. They feel their emptiness and weakness. They can not do otherwise than they do. They *must* pray.

I have looked carefully over the lives of God's saints in the Bible. I cannot find one of whose history much is told us, from Genesis to Revelation, who was not a man of prayer. I find it mentioned as a characteristic of the godly, that "they call on the Father" (1 Peter 1:17), that "they call on the name of the Lord Jesus Christ" (1 Cor. 1:2). Recorded as a characteristic of the wicked is the fact that "they call not upon the Lord" (Ps. 14:4).

I have read the lives of many eminent Christians who have been on earth since the Bible days. Some of them, I see, were rich, and some poor. Some were learned, and some unlearned. Some of them were Episcopalians, and some Christians of other names. Some were Calvinists, and some were Arminians. Some have loved to use a liturgy, and some to use none. But one thing, I see, they all had in common. They have all been *men of prayer*.

I study the reports of missionary societies in our own times. I see with joy that heathen men and women are receiving the gospel in various parts of the globe. There are conversions in Africa, in New Zealand, in Hindustan, in China. The people converted are naturally unlike one another in every respect. But one striking thing I observe at all the missionary stations: the converted people *always pray*.

I do not deny that a man may pray without heart and without sincerity. I do not for a moment pretend to say that the mere fact of a person's praying proves is everything about his soul. As in every other part of religion, so also in this, there may be deception and hypocrisy.

But this I do say, that not praying is a clear proof that a man is not yet a true Christian. He cannot really feel his sins. He cannot love God. He cannot feel himself a debtor to Christ. He cannot long after holiness. He cannot desire heaven. He has yet to be born again. He has yet to be made a new creature. He may boast confidently of election, grace, faith, hope, and knowledge, and deceive ignorant people. But you may rest assured it is all vain talk *if he does not pray.*

And I say, furthermore, that of all the evidences of the real work of the Spirit, a habit of hearty private prayer is one of the most satisfactory that can be named. A man may preach from false motives. A man may write books and make fine speeches and seem diligent in good works, and yet be a Judas Iscariot. But a man seldom goes into his closet, and pours out his soul before God in secret, unless he is in earnest. The Lord himself has set his stamp on prayer as the best proof of a true conversion. When he sent Ananias to Saul in Damascus, he gave him no other evidence of his change of heart than this, "*Behold, he prayeth*" (Acts 9: 11).

I know that much may go on in a man's mind before he is brought to pray. He may have many convictions, desires, wishes, feelings, intentions, resolutions, hopes, and fears. But all these things are very uncertain evidences. They are to be found in ungodly people, and often come to nothing. In many a case they are not more lasting than the morning cloud, and the dew that passeth away. A real, hearty prayer, coming from a broken and contrite spirit, is worth all these things put together.

I know that the Holy Spirit, who calls sinners from their evil ways, does in many instances lead them by very slow degrees to acquaintance with Christ. But the eye of man can only judge by what it sees. I cannot call any one justified until he believes. I dare not say that any one believes until he prays. I cannot understand a dumb faith. The first act of faith will be to speak to God. Faith is to the soul what life is to the body. Prayer is to faith what breath is to life. How a man can live and not breathe is past my comprehension, and how a man can believe and not pray is past my comprehension too.

Never be surprised if you hear ministers of the gospel dwelling much on the importance of prayer. This is the point we want to bring you to; we want to know that you pray. Your views of doctrine may be correct. Your love of Protestantism may be warm and unmistakable. But still this may be nothing more than head knowledge and party spirit. We want to know whether you are actually acquainted with the throne of grace, and whether you can speak *to* God as well as speak *about* God.

Do you wish to find out whether you are a true Christian? Then rest assured that my question is of the very first importance—Do you pray?

> *III. I ask whether you pray, because*
> *there is no duty in religion so neglected as private prayer.*

We live in days of abounding religious profession. There are more places of public worship now than there ever were before. There are more persons attending them than there ever were before. And yet in spite of all this public religion, I believe there is a vast neglect of private prayer. It is one of those private transactions between God and our souls which no eye sees, and therefore one which men are tempted to pass over and leave undone.

I believe that thousands *never utter a word of prayer at all*. They eat. They drink. They sleep. They rise. They go forth to their labor. They return to their homes. They breathe God's air. They see God's sun. They walk on God's earth. They enjoy God's mercies. They have dying bodies. They have judgment and eternity before them. But they *never speak to God*. They live like the beasts that perish. They behave like creatures without souls. They have not one word to say to Him in whose hand are their life and breath, and all things, and from whose mouth they must one day receive their everlasting sentence. How dreadful this seems; but if the secrets of men were only known, how common.

I believe there are tens of thousands *whose prayers are nothing but a mere form*, a set of words repeated by rote, without a thought about their meaning.

Some say over a few hasty sentences picked up in the nursery when they were children. Some content themselves with repeating the Creed, forgetting that there is not a request in it. Some add the Lord's Prayer, but without the slightest desire that its solemn petitions may be granted.

Many, even of those who use good forms, mutter their prayers after they have gotten into bed, or while they wash or dress in the morning. Men may think what they please, but they may depend upon it that in the sight of God *this is not praying*. Words said without heart are as utterly useless to our souls as the drum beating of the poor heathen before their idols. Where there is no heart, there may be lip work and tongue work, but there is nothing that God listens to; there is no prayer. Saul, I have no doubt, said many a long prayer before the Lord met him on the way to Damascus. But it was not till his heart was broken that the Lord said, "He prayeth."

Does this surprise you? Listen to me, and I will show you that I am not speaking as I do without reason. Do you think that my assertions are extravagant and unwarrantable? Give me your attention, and I will soon show you that I am only telling you the truth.

Have you forgotten that it is *not natural* to any one to pray? "The carnal mind is enmity against God." The desire of man's heart is to get far away from God, and have nothing to do with him. His feeling towards him is not love, but fear. Why then should a man pray when he has no real sense of sin, no real feeling of spiritual wants, no thorough belief in unseen things, no desire after holiness and heaven? Of all these things the vast majority of men know and feel nothing. The multitude walk in the broad way. I cannot forget this. Therefore I say boldly, I believe that few pray.

Have you forgotten that it is *not fashionable* to pray? It is one of the things that many would be rather ashamed to own. There are hundreds who would sooner storm a breach, or lead a forlorn hope, than confess publicly that they make a habit of prayer. There are thousands who, if obliged to sleep in the same room with a stranger, would lie down in bed without a prayer. To dress well, to go to theaters, to be thought clever and agreeable, all this is fashionable, but not to pray. I cannot forget this. I cannot think a habit is common which so many seem ashamed to own. I believe that few pray.

Have you forgotten *the lives that many live*? Can we really believe that people are praying against sin night and day, when we see them plunging into it? Can we suppose they pray against the world, when they are entirely absorbed and taken up with its pursuits? Can we think they really ask God for grace to serve him, when they do not show the slightest desire to serve him at all? Oh, no, it is plain as daylight that the great majority of men either ask nothing of God or *do not mean what they say* when they do ask, which is just the same thing. Praying and sinning will never live together in the same heart. Prayer will consume sin, or sin will choke prayer. I cannot forget this. I look at men's lives. I believe that few pray.

Have you forgotten *the deaths that many die*? How many, when they draw near death, seem entirely strangers to God. Not only are they sadly ignorant of his gospel, but sadly wanting in the power of speaking to him. There is a terrible awkwardness and shyness in their endeavors to approach him. They seem to be taking up a fresh thing. They appear as if they wanted an introduction to God, and as if they had never talked with him before. I remember having heard of a lady who was anxious to have a minister to visit her in her last illness. She desired that he would pray with her. He asked her what he should pray for. She did not know, and could not tell. She was utterly unable to name any one thing which she wished him to ask God for her soul. All she seemed to want was the form of a minister's prayers. I can quite understand this. Death beds are great revealers of secrets. I cannot forget what I have seen of sick and dying people. This also leads me to believe that few pray.

I cannot see your heart. I do not know your private history in spiritual things. But from what I see in the Bible and in the world I am certain I cannot ask you a more necessary question than that before you—Do you pray?

> *IV. I ask whether you pray, because*
> *prayer is an act in religion to which there is great encouragement.*

There is everything on God's part to make prayer easy, if men will only attempt it. All things are ready on his side. Every objection is anticipated. Every difficulty is provided for. The crooked places are made straight and the rough places are made smooth. There is no excuse left for the prayerless man.

There is *a way* by which any man, however sinful and unworthy, may draw near to God the Father. Jesus Christ has opened that way by the sacrifice he made for us upon the cross. The holiness and justice of God need not frighten sinners and keep them back. Only let them cry to God in the name of Jesus, only let them plead the atoning blood of Jesus, and they shall find God upon a throne of grace, willing and ready to hear. The name of Jesus is a never-failing passport for our prayers. In that name a man may draw near to God with boldness, and ask with confidence. God has engaged to hear him. Think of this. Is not this encouragement?

There is an *Advocate* and Intercessor always waiting to present the prayers of those who come to God through him. That advocate is Jesus Christ. He mingles our prayers with the incense of his own almighty intercession. So mingled, they go up as a sweet savor before the throne of God. Poor as they are in themselves, they are mighty and powerful in the hand of our High Priest and Elder Brother. The bank note without a signature at the bottom is nothing but a worthless piece of paper. The stroke of a pen confers on it all its value. The prayer of a poor child of Adam is a feeble thing in itself, but once endorsed by the hand of the Lord Jesus it availeth much. There was an officer in the city of Rome who was appointed to have his doors always open, in order to receive any Roman citizen who applied to him for help. Just so the ear of the Lord Jesus is ever open to the cry of all who want mercy and grace. It is his office to help them. Their prayer is his delight. Think of this. Is not this encouragement?

There is *the Holy Spirit* ever ready to help our infirmities in prayer. It is one part of his special office to assist us in our endeavors to speak with God. We need not be cast down and distressed by the fear of not knowing what to say. The Spirit will give us words if we seek his aid. The prayers of the Lord's people are the inspiration of the Lord's Spirit, the work of the Holy Ghost who dwells within them as the Spirit of grace and supplication. Surely the Lord's people may well hope to be heard. It is not they merely that pray, but the Holy Ghost pleading in them. Reader, think of this. Is not this encouragement?

There are exceeding great and precious *promises* to those who pray. What did the Lord Jesus mean when he spoke such words as these: "Ask, and it shall be given you; seek, and ye shall find; knock, and it shall be opened unto you: for every one that asketh, receiveth; and he that seeketh, findeth; and to him that knocketh, it shall be opened" (Matt. 7:7, 8). "All things whatsoever ye shall ask in prayer believing, ye shall receive" (Matt. 21:22). "Whatsoever ye shall ask in my name, that will 1 do, that the Father may be glorified in the Son. If ye shall ask anything in my name, I will do it" (John 14:13, 14). What did the Lord mean when he spoke the parables of the friend at midnight and the importunate widow (Luke 11:5; 18:1)? Think over these passages. If this is not encouragement to pray, words have no meaning.

There are wonderful *examples* in Scripture of the power of prayer. Nothing seems to be too great, too hard, or too difficult for prayer to do. It has obtained things that seemed impossible and out of reach. It has won victories over fire, air, earth, and water. Prayer opened the Red Sea. Prayer brought water from the rock and bread from heaven. Prayer made the sun stand still. Prayer brought fire from the sky on Elijah's sacrifice. Prayer turned the counsel of Ahithophel into foolishness. Prayer overthrew the army of Sennacherib. Well might Mary Queen of Scots say, "I fear John Knox's prayers more than an army of ten thousand men." Prayer has healed the sick. Prayer has raised the dead. Prayer has procured the conversion of souls. "The child of many prayers," said an old Christian to Augustine's mother, "shall never perish." Prayer, pains, and faith can do anything. Nothing seems impossible when a man has the spirit of adoption. "Let me alone," is the remarkable saying of God to Moses when Moses was about to intercede for the children of Israel—the Chaldee version has, "Leave off praying"—(Exod. 32:10). So long as Abraham asked mercy for Sodom, the Lord went on giving. He never ceased to give till Abraham ceased to pray. Think of this. Is not this encouragement?

What more can a man want to lead him to take any step in religion, than the things I have just told him about prayer? What more could be done to make the path to the mercy seat easy, and to remove all occasions of stumbling from the sinner's way? Surely if the devils in hell had such a door set open before them, they would leap for gladness, and make the very pit ring with joy.

But where will the man hide his head at last who neglects such glorious encouragements? What can possibly be said for the man who, after all, dies without prayer? Surely I may feel anxious that you should not be that man. Surely I may well ask—Do you pray?

> *V. I ask whether you pray, because*
> *diligence in prayer is the secret of eminent holiness.*

Without controversy there is a vast difference among true Christians. There is an immense interval between the foremost and the hindermost in the army of God.

They are all fighting the same good fight but how much more valiantly some fight than others. They are all doing the Lord's work but how much more some do than others. They are all light in the Lord; but how much more brightly some shine than others. They are all running the same race; but how much faster some get on than others. They all love the same Lord and Saviour; but how much more some love him than others. I ask any true Christian whether this is not the case. Are not these things so?

There are some of the Lord's people who seem *never able to get on* from the time of their conversion. They are born again, but they remain babes all their lives. You hear from them the same old experience. You remark in them the same want of spiritual appetite, the same want of interest in any thing beyond their own little circle, which you remarked ten years ago. They are pilgrims, indeed, but pilgrims like the Gibeonites of old; their bread is always dry and moldy, their shoes always old, and their garments always rent and torn. I say this with sorrow and grief; but I ask any real Christian, Is it not true?

There are others of the Lord's people who seem to be *always advancing*. They grow like the grass after rain; they increase like Israel in Egypt; they press on like Gideon, though sometimes faint, yet always pursuing. They are ever adding grace to grace, and faith to faith, and strength to strength. Every time you meet them their hearts seem larger, and their spiritual stature taller and stronger. Every year they appear to see more, and know more, and believe more, and feel more in their religion. They not only have good works to prove the reality of their faith, but they are *zealous* of them. They not only do well, but they are *unwearied* in well-doing. They attempt great things, and they do great things. When they fail they try again, and when they fall they are soon up again. And all this time they think themselves poor, unprofitable servants, and fancy they do nothing at all. These are those who make religion lovely and beautiful in the eyes of all. They wrest praise even from the unconverted and win golden opinions even from the selfish men of the world. It does one good to see, to be with, and to hear them. When you meet them, you could believe that like Moses, they had just come out from the presence of God. When you part with them you feel warmed by their company, as if your soul had been near a fire. I know such people are rare. I only ask, Are there not many such?

Now how can we account for the difference which I have just described? What is the reason that some believers are so much brighter and holier than others? I believe the difference, in nineteen cases out of twenty, arises from different habits about private prayer. I believe that those who are not eminently holy pray *little*, and those who are eminently holy pray *much*.

I dare say this opinion will startle some readers. I have little doubt that many look on eminent holiness as a kind of special gift, which none but a few must pretend to aim at. They admire it at a distance in books. They think it beautiful when they see an example near themselves. But as to its being a thing within the reach of any but a very few, such a notion never seems to enter their minds. In short, they consider it a kind of monopoly granted to a few favored believers, but certainly not to all.

Now I believe that this is a most dangerous mistake. I believe that spiritual as well as natural greatness depends in a high degree on the faithful use of means within everybody's reach. Of course I do not say we have a right to expect a miraculous grant of intellectual gifts; but this I do say, that when a man is once converted to God, his progress in holiness will be much in accordance with his own diligence in the use of God's appointed means. And I assert confidently that the principal means by which most believers have become great in the church of Christ is the habit of *diligent private prayer*.

Look through the lives of the brightest and best of God's servants, whether in the Bible or not. See what is written of Moses and David and Daniel and Paul. Mark what is recorded of Luther and Bradford the Reformers. Observe what is related of the private devotions of Whitefield and Cecil and Venn and Bickersteth and M'Cheyne. Tell me of one of all the goodly fellowship of saints and martyrs, who has not had this mark most prominently—*he was a man of prayer*. Depend upon it, prayer is power.

Prayer obtains fresh and continued outpourings of the Spirit. He alone begins the work of grace in a man's heart. He alone can carry it forward and make it prosper. But the good Spirit loves to be entreated. And those who ask most will have most of his influence.

Prayer is the surest remedy. Against the devil and besetting sins. That sin will never stand firm which is heartily prayed against. That devil will never long keep dominion over us which we beseech the Lord to cast forth. But then we must spread out all our cage before our heavenly Physician, if he is to give us daily relief.

Do you wish to grow in grace and be a devoted Christian? Be very sure, if you wish it, you could not have a more important question than this—Do you pray?

> *VI. I ask whether you pray, because
> neglect of prayer is one great cause of backsliding.*

There is such a thing as going back in religion after making a good profession. Men may run well for a season, like the Galatians, and then turn aside after false teachers. Men may profess loudly while their feelings are warm, as Peter did, and then in the hour of trial deny their Lord. Men may lose their first love as the Ephesians did. Men may cool down in their zeal to do good, like Mark the companion of Paul. Men may follow an apostle for a season, and like Demas go back to the world. All these things men may do.

It is a miserable thing to be a backslider. Of all unhappy things that can befall a man, I suppose it is the worst. A stranded ship, a brokenwinged eagle, a garden overrun with weeds, a harp without strings, a church in ruins, all these are sad sights, but a backslider is a sadder sight still. A wounded conscience—a mind sick of itself—a memory full of self-reproach—a heart pierced through with the Lord's arrows—a spirit broken with a load of inward accusation—all this is *a taste of hell*. It is a hell on earth. Truly that saying of the wise man is solemn and weighty, "The backslider in heart shall be filled with his own ways" (Prov. 14:14).

Now what is the cause of most backslidings? I believe, as a general rule, one of the chief causes is neglect of private prayer. Of course the secret history of falls will not be known till the last day. I can only give my opinion as a minister of Christ and a student of the heart. That opinion is, I repeat distinctly, that backsliding generally first begins with *neglect of private prayer*.

Bibles read without prayer; sermons heard without prayer; marriages contracted without prayer; journeys undertaken without prayer; residences chosen without prayer; friendships formed without prayer; the daily act of private prayer itself hurried over, or gone through without heart: these are the kind of downward steps by which many a Christian descends to a condition of spiritual palsy, or reaches the point where God allows him to have a tremendous fall. This is the process which forms the lingering Lots, the unstable Samsons, the wife-idolizing Solomons, the inconsistent Asas, the pliable Jehoshaphats, the over-careful Marthas, of whom so many are to be found in the church of Christ. Often the simple history of such cases is this: they became *careless about private prayer*.

You may be very sure men fall in private long before they fall in public. They are backsliders on their knees long before they backslide openly in the eyes of the world. Like Peter, they first disregard the Lord's warning to watch and pray, and then like Peter, their strength is gone, and in the hour of temptation they deny their Lord.

The world takes notice of their fall, and scoffs loudly. But the world knows nothing of the real reason. The heathen succeeded in making a well-known Christian offer incense to an idol, by threatening him with a punishment worse than death. They then triumphed greatly at the sight of his cowardice and apostasy. But the heathen did not know the fact of which history informs us, that on that very morning he had left his bed chamber hastily, and without finishing his usual prayers.

If you are a Christian indeed, I trust you will never be a backslider. But if you do not wish to be a backsliding Christian, remember the question I ask you: Do you pray?

> *VII. I ask, lastly, whether you pray because*
> *prayer is one of the best means of happiness and contentment.*

We live in a world where sorrow abounds. This has always been its state since sin came in. There cannot be sin without sorrow. And until sin is driven out from the world, it is vain for any one to suppose he can escape sorrow.

Some without doubt have a larger cup of sorrow to drink than others. But few are to be found who live long without sorrows or cares of one sort or another. Our bodies, our property, our families, our children, our relations, our servants, our friends, our neighbors, our worldly callings, each and all of these are fountains of care. Sicknesses, deaths, losses, disappointments, partings, separations, ingratitude, slander, all these are common things. We cannot get through life without them. Some day or other they find us out. The greater are our affections the deeper are our afflictions, and the more we love the more we have to weep.

And what is the best means of cheerfulness in such a world as this? How shall we get through this valley of tears with least pain? I know no better means than the regular, habitual practice of *taking everything to God in prayer*.

This is the plain advice that the Bible gives, both in the Old Testament and the New. What says the psalmist? "Call upon me in the day of trouble, and I will deliver thee, and thou shalt glorify me" (Ps. 50:15). "Cast thy burden upon the Lord, and he shall sustain thee: he shall never suffer the righteous to be moved" (Ps. 55:22). What says the apostle Paul? "Be careful for nothing; but in everything, by prayer and supplication with thanksgiving, let your requests be made known unto God: and the peace of God, which passeth all understanding shall keep your hearts and minds through Christ Jesus" (Phil. 4:6, 7). What says the apostle James? "Is any afflicted among you? let him pray" (James 5:13).

This was the practice of all the saints whose history we have recorded in the Scriptures. This is what Jacob did when he feared his brother Esau. This is what Moses did when the people were ready to stone him in the wilderness. This is what Joshua did when Israel was defeated before the men of Ai. This is what David did when he was in danger at Keilah. This is what Hezekiah did when he received the letter from Sennacherib. This is what the church did when Peter was put in prison. This is what Paul did when he was cast into the dungeon at Philippi.

The only way to be really happy in such a world as this, is to be ever casting all our cares on God. It is trying to carry their own burdens which so often makes believers sad. If they will tell their troubles to God, he will enable them to bear them as easily as Samson did the gates of Gaza. If they are resolved to keep them to themselves, they will find one day that the very grasshopper is a burden.

There is a friend ever waiting to help us, if we will unbosom to him our sorrow—a friend who pitied the poor and sick and sorrowful, when he was upon earth—a friend who knows the heart of man, for he lived thirty-three years as a man among us—a friend who can weep with the weepers, for he was a man of sorrows and acquainted with grief—a friend who is able to help us, for there never was earthly pain he could not cure. That friend is Jesus Christ. The way to be happy is to be always opening our hearts to him. Oh that we were all like that poor Christian who only answered, when threatened and punished, "*I must tell the Lord.*"

Jesus can make those happy who trust him and call on him, whatever be their outward condition. He can give them peace of heart in a prison, contentment in the midst of poverty, comfort in the midst of bereavements, joy on the brink of the grave. There is a mighty fulness in him for all his believing members—a fulness that is ready to be poured out on every one that will ask in prayer. Oh that men would understand that happiness, does not depend on outward circumstances, but on the state of the heart.

Prayer can lighten crosses for us however heavy. It can bring down to our side One who will help us to bear them. Prayer can open a door for us when our way seems hedged up. It can bring down One who will say, "This is the way, walk in it." Prayer can let in a ray of hope when all our earthly prospects seem darkened. It can bring down One who will say, "I will never leave thee, nor forsake thee." Prayer can obtain relief for us when those we love most are taken away, and the world feels empty. It can bring down One who can fill the gap in our hearts with himself, and say to the waves within, "Peace; be still." Oh that men were not so like Hagar in the wilderness, blind to the well of living waters close beside them.

I want you to be happy. I know I cannot ask you a more useful question than this: Do you pray?

And now it is high time for me to bring this tract to an end. I trust I have brought before you things that will be seriously considered. I heartily pray God that this consideration may be blessed to your soul.

1. Let me speak a parting word TO THOSE WHO DO NOT PRAY. I dare not suppose that all who read these pages are praying people. If you are a prayerless person, suffer me to speak to you this day on God's behalf.

Prayerless reader, I can only warn you, but I do warn you most solemnly. I warn you that you are in a position of fearful danger. If you die in your present state, you are a lost soul. You will only rise again to be eternally miserable. I warn you that of all professing Christians you are most utterly without excuse. There is not a single good reason that you can show for living without prayer.

It is useless to say you *know not how to pray*. Prayer is the simplest act in all religion. It is simply speaking to God. It needs neither learning nor wisdom nor book knowledge to begin it. It needs nothing but heart and will. The weakest infant can cry when he is hungry. The poorest beggar can hold out his hand for alms, and does not wait to find fine words. The most ignorant man will find something to say to God, if he has only a mind.

It is useless to say you have *no convenient place* to pray in. Any man can find a place private enough, if he is disposed. Our Lord prayed on a mountain; Peter on the housetop; Isaac in the field; Nathanael under the fig tree; Jonah in the whale's belly. Any place may become a closet, an oratory, and a Bethel, and be to us the presence of God.

It is useless to say you *have no time*. There is plenty of time, if men will employ it. Time may be short, but time is always long enough for prayer. Daniel had the affairs of a kingdom on his hands, and yet he prayed three times a day. David was ruler over a mighty nation, and yet he says, "Evening and morning and at noon will I pray" (Ps. 55:17). When time is really wanted, time can always be found.

It is useless to say you *cannot pray till you have faith and a new heart*, and that you must sit still and wait for them. This is to add sin to sin. It is bad enough to be unconverted and going to hell. It is even worse to say, "I know it, but will not cry for mercy." This is a kind of argument for which there is no warrant in Scripture. "Call ye upon the Lord," saith Isaiah, "while he is near" (Isa. 55:6). "Take with you words, and turn unto the Lord," says Hosea (Hos. 14:1). "Repent and pray," says Peter to Simon Magus (Acts 8:22). If you want faith and a new heart, go and cry to the Lord for them. The very attempt to pray has often been the quickening of a dead soul.

Oh, prayerless reader, who and what are you that you will not ask anything of God? Have you made a covenant with death and hell? Are you at peace with the worm and the fire? Have you no sins to be pardoned? Have you no fear of eternal torment? Have you no desire after heaven? Oh that you would awake from your present folly. Oh that you would consider your latter end. Oh that you would arise and call upon God. Alas, there is a day coming when many shall pray loudly, "Lord, Lord, open to us," but all too late; when many shall cry to the rocks to fall on them and the hills to cover them, who would never cry to God. In all affection, I warn you, beware lest this be the end of your soul. Salvation is very near you. Do not lose heaven for want of asking.

2. Let me speak TO THOSE WHO HAVE REAL DESIRES FOR SALVATION, but know not what steps to take, or where to begin. I cannot but hope that some readers may be in this state of mind, and if there be but one such I must offer him affectionate counsel.

In every journey there must be a first step. There must be a change from sitting still to moving forward. The journeyings of Israel from Egypt to Canaan were long and wearisome. Forty years pass away before they crossed Jordan. Yet there was some one who moved first when they marched from Ramah to Succoth. When does a man really take his first step in coming out from sin and the world? He does it in the day when he first prays with his heart.

In every building the first stone must be laid, and the first blow must be struck. The ark was one hundred and twenty years in building. Yet there was a day when Noah laid his axe to the first tree he cut down to form it. The temple of Solomon was a glorious building. But there was a day when the first huge stone was laid deep in mount Moriah. When does the building of the Spirit really begin to appear in a man's heart? It begins, so far as we can judge, when he first pours out his heart to God in prayer.

If you desire salvation, and want to know what to do, I advise you to go this very day to the Lord Jesus Christ, in the first private place you can find, and earnestly and heartily entreat him in prayer to save your soul.

Tell him that you have heard that he receives sinners, and has said, "Him that cometh unto me I will in no wise cast out." Tell him that you are a poor vile sinner, and that you come to him on the faith of his own invitation. Tell him you put yourself wholly and entirely in his hands; that you feel vile and helpless, and hopeless in yourself: and that except he saves you, you have no hope of being saved at all. Beseech him to deliver you from the guilt, the power, and the consequences of sin. Beseech him to pardon you, and wash you in his own blood. Beseech him to give you a new heart, and plant the Holy Spirit in Your Soul. Beseech him to give you grace and faith and will and power to be his disciple and servant from this day forever. Oh, reader, go this very day, and tell these things to the Lord Jesus Christ, if you really are in earnest about your soul.

Tell him in your own way, and your own words. If a doctor came to see you when sick you could tell him where you felt pain. If your soul feels its disease indeed, you can surely find something to tell Christ.

Doubt not his willingness to save you, because you are a sinner. It is Christ's office to save sinners. He says himself, "I came not to call the righteous, but sinners to repentance" (Luke 5:32).

Wait not because you feel unworthy. Wait for nothing. Wait for nobody. Waiting comes from the devil. Just as you are, go to Christ. The worse you are, the more need you have to apply to him. You will never mend yourself by staying away.

Fear not because your prayer is stammering, your words feeble, and your language poor. Jesus can understand you. Just as a mother understands the first lispings of her infant, so does the blessed Saviour understand sinners. He can read a sigh, and see a meaning in a groan.

Despair not because you do not get an answer immediately. While you are speaking, Jesus is listening. If he delays an answer, it is only for wise reasons, and to try if you are in earnest. The answer will surely come. Though it tarry, wait for it. It will surely come.

Oh, reader, if you have any desire to, be saved, remember the advice I have given you this day. Act upon it honestly and heartily, and you shall be saved.

3. Let me speak, lastly, TO THOSE WHO DO PRAY. I trust that some who read this tract know well what prayer is, and have the Spirit of adoption. To all such, I offer a few words of brotherly counsel and exhortation. The incense offered in the tabernacle was ordered to be made in a particular way. Not every kind of incense would do. Let us remember this, and be careful about the matter and manner of our prayers.

Brethren who pray, if I know anything of a Christian's heart, you are often sick of your own prayers. You never enter into the apostle's words, "When I would do good, evil is present with me," so thoroughly as you sometimes do upon your knees. You can understand David's words, I hate vain thoughts." You can sympathize with that poor converted Hottentot who was overheard praying, "Lord, deliver me from all my enemies, and above all, from that bad man myself." There are few children of God who do not often find the season of prayer a season of conflict. The devil has special wrath against us when he sees us on our knees. Yet, I believe that prayers which cost us no trouble should be regarded with great suspicion. I believe we are very poor judges of the goodness of our prayers, and that the prayer which pleases us least, often pleases God most. Suffer me then, as a companion in the Christian warfare, to offer you a few words of exhortation. One thing, at least, we all feel: we must pray. We cannot give it up. We must go on.

I commend then to your attention, the importance of *reverence and humility* in prayer. Let us never forget what we are, and what a solemn thing it is to speak with God. Let us beware of rushing into his presence with carelessness and levity. Let us say to ourselves: "I am on holy ground. This is no other than the gate of heaven. If I do not mean what I say, I am trifling with God. If I regard iniquity in my heart, the Lord will not hear me." Let us keep in mind the words of Solomon, "Be not rash with thy mouth, and let not thy heart be hasty to utter anything before God; for God is in heaven, and thou on earth" (Eccl. 5:2). When Abraham spoke to God, he said, "I am dust and ashes." When Job spoke to God, he said, I am vile." Let us do likewise.

I commend to you the importance of praying *spiritually*. I mean by that, that we should labor always to have the direct help of the Spirit in our prayers, and beware above all things of formality. There is nothing so spiritual but that it may become a form, and this is specially true of private prayer. We may insensibly get into the habit of using the fittest possible words, and offering the most scriptural petitions, and yet do it all by rote without feeling it, and walk daily round an old beaten path. I desire to touch this point with caution and delicacy. I know that there are certain great things we daily want, and that there is nothing necessarily formal in asking for these things in the same words. The world, the devil, and our hearts, are daily the same. Of necessity we must daily go over old ground. But this I say, we must be very careful on this point. If the skeleton and outline of our prayers be by habit almost a form, let us strive that the clothing and filling up of our prayers be as far as possible of the Spirit. As to praying out of a book in our *private* devotions, it is a habit I cannot praise. If we can tell our doctors the state of our bodies without a book, we ought to be able to tell the state of our souls to God. I have no objection to a man using crutches when he is first recovering from a broken limb. It is better to use crutches, than not to walk at all. But if I saw him all his life on crutches, I should not think it matter for congratulation. I should like to see him strong enough to throw his crutches away.

I commend to you the importance of making prayer a *regular business of life*. I might say something of the value of regular times in the day for prayer. God is a God of order. The hours for morning and evening sacrifice in the Jewish temple were not fixed as they were without a meaning. Disorder is eminently one of the fruits of sin. But I would not bring any under bondage. This only I say, that it is essential to your soul's health to make praying a part of the business of every twenty four hours in your life. Just as you allot time to eating, sleeping, and business, so also allot time to prayer. Choose your own hours and seasons. At the very least, speak with God in the morning, before you speak with the world: and speak with God at night, after you have done with the world. But settle it in your minds, that prayer is one of the great things of every day. Do not drive it into a corner.

Do not give it the scraps and parings of your duty. Whatever else you make a business of, make a business of prayer.

I commend to you the importance of *perseverance* in prayer. Once having begun the habit, never give it up. Your heart will sometimes say, "You have had family prayers: what mighty harm if you leave private prayer undone?" Your body will sometimes say, "You are unwell, or sleepy, or weary; you need not pray." Your mind will sometimes say, "You have important business to attend to today; cut short your prayers." Look on all such suggestions as coming direct from Satan. They are all as good' as saying, "Neglect your soul." I do not maintain that prayers should always be of the same length; but I do say, let no excuse make you give up prayer. Paul said, "Continue in prayer, and, "Pray without ceasing." He did not mean that men should be always on their knees, but he did mean that our prayers should be, like the continual burnt offering, steadily persevered in every day; that it should be like seed time and harvest, and summer and winter, unceasingly coming round at regular seasons; that it should be like the fire on the altar, not always consuming sacrifices, but never completely going out. Never forget that you may tie together morning and evening devotions, by an endless chain of short ejaculatory prayers throughout the day. Even in company, or business, or in the very streets, you may be silently sending up little winged messengers to God, as Nehemiah did in the very presence of Artaxerxes. And never think that time is wasted which is given to God. A nation does not become poorer because it loses one year of working days in seven, by keeping the Sabbath. A Christian never finds he is a loser, in the long run, by persevering in prayer.

I commend to you the importance of *earnestness* in prayer. It is not necessary that a man should shout, or scream, or be very loud, in order to prove that he is in earnest. But it is desirable that we should be hearty and fervent and warm, and ask as if we were really interested in what we were doing. It is the "effectual fervent" prayer that "availeth much." This is the lesson that is taught us by the expressions used in Scripture about prayer. It is called, "crying, knocking, wrestling, laboring, striving." This is the lesson taught us by scripture examples. Jacob is one. He said to the angel at Penuel, "I will not let thee go, except thou bless me" (Gen. 32:26). Daniel is another. Hear how he pleaded with God: "O Lord, hear; O Lord, forgive; O Lord, hearken and do; defer not, for thine own sake, O my God" (Dan. 9:19). Our Lord Jesus Christ is another. It is written of him, "In the days of his flesh, he offered up prayers and supplications with strong crying and tears" (Heb. 5:7). Alas, how unlike is this to many of our supplications! How tame and lukewarm they seem by comparison. How truly might God say to many of us, "You do not really want what you pray for." Let us try to amend this fault. Let us knock loudly at the door of grace, like Mercy in Pilgrim's Progress, as if we must perish unless heard. Let us settle it in our minds, that cold prayers are a sacrifice without fire. Let us remember the story of Demosthenes the great orator, when one came to him, and wanted him to plead his cause. He heard him without attention, while he told his story without earnestness. The man saw this, and cried out with anxiety that it was all true. "Ah," said Demosthenes, "I believe you *now*."

I commend to you the importance of *praying with faith*. We should endeavor to believe that our prayers are heard, and that if we ask things according to God's will, we shall be answered. This is the plain command of our Lord Jesus Christ: "Whatsoever things ye desire, when ye pray, believe that ye receive them, and ye shall have them" (Mark 11:24). Faith is to prayer what the feather is to the arrow: without it prayer will not hit the mark. We should cultivate the habit of pleading promises in our prayers.

We should take with us some promise, and say, "Lord, here is thine own word pledged. Do for us as thou hast said." This was the habit of Jacob and Moses and David. The 119th Psalm is full of things asked, "according to thy word." Above all, we should cultivate the habit of expecting answers to our prayers. We should do like the merchant who sends his ships to sea. We should not be satisfied, unless we see some return. Alas, there are few points on which Christians come short so much as this. The church at Jerusalem made prayer without ceasing for Peter in prison; but when the prayer was answered, they would hardly believe it (Acts 12:15). It is a solemn saying of Traill, "There is no surer mark of trifling in prayer, than when men are careless what they get by prayer."

I commend to you the importance of *boldness* in prayer. There is an unseemly familiarity in some men's prayers which I cannot praise. But there is such a thing as a holy boldness, which is exceedingly to be desired. I mean such boldness as that of Moses, when he pleads with God not to destroy Israel "Wherefore," says he, "should the Egyptians speak and say, For mischief did he bring them out, to slay them in the mountains? Turn from thy fierce anger" (Exod. 32:12). I mean such boldness as that of Joshua, when the children of Israel were defeated before men of Ai: "What," says he, "wilt thou do unto thy great name?" (Josh. 7:9). This is the boldness for which Luther was remarkable. One who heard him praying said, "What a spirit, what a confidence was in his very expressions. With such a reverence he sued, as one begging of God, and yet with such hope and assurance, as if he spoke with a loving father or friend." This is the boldness which distinguished Bruce, a great Scotch divine of the seventeenth century. His prayers were said to be "like bolts shot up into heaven." Here also I fear we sadly come short. We do not sufficiently realize the believer's privileges. We do not plead as often as we might, "Lord, are we not thine own people? Is it not for thy glory that we should be sanctified? Is it not for thy honor that thy gospel should increase?"

I commend to you the importance of *fullness* in prayer. I do not forget that our Lord warns us against the example of the Pharisees, who, for pretense, made long prayers; and commands us when we pray not to use vain repetitions. But I cannot forget, on the other hand, that he has given his own sanction to large and long devotions by continuing all night in prayer to God. At all events, we are not likely in this day to err on the side of praying *too much*. Might it not rather be feared that many believers in this generation pray *too little*? Is not the actual amount of time that many Christians give to prayer, in the aggregate, very small? I am afraid these questions cannot be answered satisfactorily. I am afraid the private devotions of many are most painfully scanty and limited; just enough to prove they are alive and no more. They really seem to want little from God. They seem to have little to confess, little to ask for, and little to thank him for. Alas, this is altogether wrong. Nothing is more common than to hear believers complaining that they do not get on. They tell us that they do not grow in grace as they could desire. Is it not rather to be suspected that many have quite as much grace as they ask for? Is it not the true account of many, that they have little, because they ask little? The cause of their weakness is to be found in their own stunted, dwarfish, clipped, contracted, hurried, narrow, diminutive prayers. *They have not, because they ask not.* Oh, we are not straitened in Christ, but in ourselves. The Lord says, "Open thy mouth wide, and I will fill it." But we are like the King of Israel who smote on the ground thrice and stayed, when he ought to have smitten five or six times.

I commend to you the importance of *particularity* in prayer. We ought not to be content with great general petitions. We ought to specify our wants before the throne of grace. It should not be enough to confess we are sinners: we should name the sins of which our conscience tells us we are most guilty. It should not be enough to ask for holiness; we should name the graces in which we feel most deficient. It should not be enough to tell the Lord we are in trouble; we should describe our trouble and all its peculiarities. This is what Jacob did when he feared his brother Esau. He tells God exactly what it is that he fears (Gen. 32:11). This is what Eliezer did, when he sought a wife for his master's son. He spreads before God precisely what he wants (Gen. 24:12). This is what Paul did when he had a thorn in the flesh. He besought the Lord (2 Cor. 12:8). This is true faith and confidence. We should believe that nothing is too small to be named before God. What should we think of the patient who told his doctor he was ill, but never went into particulars? What should we think of the wife who told her husband she was unhappy, but did not specify the cause? What should we think of the child who told his father he was in trouble, but nothing more? Christ is the true bridegroom of the soul, the true physician of the heart, the real father of all his people. Let us show that we feel this by being unreserved in our communications with him. Let us hide no secrets from him. Let us tell him all our hearts.

I commend to you the importance of *intercession* in our prayers. We are all selfish by nature, and our selfishness is very apt to stick to us, even when we are converted. There is a tendency in us to think only of our own Souls, our own spiritual conflicts, our own progress in religion, and to forget others. Against this tendency we all have need to watch and strive, and not least in our prayers. We should study to be of a public spirit. We should stir ourselves up to name other names besides our own before the throne of grace. We should try to bear in our hearts the whole world, the heathen, the Jews, the Roman Catholics, the body of true believers, the professing Protestant churches, the country in which we live, the congregation to which we belong, the household in which we sojourn, the friends and relations we are connected with. For each and all of these we should plead. This is the highest charity. He loves me best who loves me in his prayers. This is for our soul's health. It enlarges our sympathies and expands our hearts. This is for the benefit of the church. The wheels of all machinery for extending the gospel are moved by prayer. They do as much for the Lord's cause who intercede like Moses on the mount, as they do who fight like Joshua in the thick of the battle. This is to be like Christ. He bears the names of his people, as their High Priest, before the Father. Oh, the privilege of being like Jesus! This is to be a true helper to ministers. If I must choose a congregation, give me a people that pray.

I commend to you the importance of *thankfulness* in prayer. I know well that asking God is one thing and praising God is another. But I see so close a connection between prayer and praise in the Bible, that I dare not call that true prayer in which thankfulness has no part. It is not for nothing that Paul says, "By prayer and supplication, with thanksgiving, let your requests be made known unto God" (Phil. 4:6). "Continue in prayer, and watch in the same with thanksgiving" (Col. 4:2). It is of mercy that we are not in hell. It is of mercy that we have the hope of heaven. It is of mercy that we live in a land of spiritual light. It is of mercy that we have been called by the Spirit, and not left to reap the fruit of our own ways. It is of mercy that we still live and have opportunities of glorifying God actively or passively. Surely these thoughts should crowd on our minds whenever we speak with God. Surely we should never open our lips in prayer without blessing God for that free grace by which we live, and for that loving kindness which endureth for ever. Never was there an eminent saint who was not full of thankfulness. St. Paul hardly ever writes an epistle without beginning with thankfulness. Men like Whitefield in the last century, and Bickersteth in our time, abounded in thankfulness. Oh, reader, if we would be bright and shining lights in our day, we must cherish a spirit of praise. Let our prayers be thankful prayers.

I commend to you the importance of *watchfulness over your prayers*. Prayer is that point in religion at which you must be most of all on your guard. Here it is that true religion begins; here it flourishes, and here it decays. Tell me what a man's prayers are, and I will soon tell you the state of his soul. Prayer is the spiritual pulse. By this the spiritual health may be tested. Prayer is the spiritual weatherglass. By this we may know whether it is fair or foul with our hearts. Oh, let us keep an eye continually upon our private devotions. Here is the pith and marrow of our practical Christianity. Sermons and books and tracts, and committee meetings and the company of good men, are all good in their way, but they will never make up for the neglect of private prayer. Mark well the places and society and companions that unhinge your hearts for communion with God and make your prayers drive heavily. *There be on your guard.* Observe narrowly what friends and what employments leave your soul in the most spiritual frame, and most ready to speak with God. *To these cleave and stick fast.* If you will take care of your prayers, nothing shall go very wrong with your soul.

I offer these points for your private consideration. I do it in all humility. I know no one who needs to be reminded of them more than I do myself. But I believe them to be God's own truth, and I desire myself and all I love to feel them more.

I want the times we live in to be praying times. I want the Christians of our day to be praying Christians. I want the church to be a praying church. My heart's desire and prayer in sending forth this tract is to promote a spirit of prayerfulness. I want those who never prayed yet, to arise and call upon God, and I want those who do pray, to see that they are not praying amiss.

Bonus Sermon: On Christmas[40]

"What think ye of Christ?" (Mt. 22:42)

Christmas is a season which almost all Christians observe in one way or another. Some keep it as a religious season. Some keep it as a holiday. But all over the world, wherever there are Christians, in one way or another Christmas is kept.

Perhaps there is no country in which Christmas is so much observed as it is in England. Christmas holidays, Christmas parties, Christmas family-gatherings, Christmas services in churches, Christmas hymns and carols, Christmas holly and mistletoe,—who has not heard of these things? They are as familiar to English people as anything in their lives. They are among the first things we remember when we were children. Our grandfathers and grandmothers were used to them long before we were born. They have been going on in England for many hundred years. They seem likely to go on as long as the world stands.

But, reader, how many of those who keep Christmas ever consider why *Christmas is kept?* How many, in their Christmas plans and arrangements, give a thought to Him, without whom there would have been no Christmas at all? How many ever remember that

---

[40]From the December 1863 Tract.

the Lord Jesus Christ is the cause of Christmas? How many ever reflect that the first intention of Christmas was to remind Christians of Christ's birth and coming into the world? Reader, how is it with you? What do you think of at Christmas?

Bear with me a few minutes, while I try to press upon you the question which heads this tract. I do not want to make your Christmas merriment less. I do not wish to spoil your Christmas cheer. I only wish to put things in their right places. I want Christ Himself to be remembered at Christmas! Give me your attention while I unfold the question—"What think ye of Christ?"

    I.   Let us consider, firstly, *why all men ought to think of Christ.*
    II.   Let us examine, secondly, *the common thoughts of many about Christ.*
    III. Let us count up, lastly, *the thoughts of true Christians about Christ.*

Reader, I dare say the demands upon your time this Christmas are many. Your holidays are short. You have friends to see. You have much to talk about. But still, in the midst of all your hurry and excitement, give a little time to your soul. There will be a Christmas some year, when your place will be empty. Before that time comes, suffer me as a friend to press home on your conscience the inquiry,—"What think ye of Christ?"

    I. First, then,
       let us consider why all men ought to think of Christ.

This is a question which needs to be answered, at the very outset of this tract. I know the minds of some people when they are asked about such things as I am handling today. I know that many are ready to say, "Why should we think about Christ at all? We want meat, and drink, and money, and clothes, and amusements. We have no time to think about these high subjects. We do not understand them. Let parsons, and old women, and Sunday-school children mind such things if they like. We have no time in a world like this to be thinking of Christ."

Such is the talk of thousands in this country. They never go either to church or chapel. They never read their Bibles. The world is their god. They think themselves very wise and clever. They despise those whom they call "religious people." But whether they like it or not, they will all have to die one day. They have all souls to be lost or saved in a world to come. They will all have to rise again from their graves, and to have a reckoning with God. And shall their scoffing and contempt stop our mouths, and make us ashamed? No, indeed! not for a moment! Listen to me and I will tell you why.

All men ought to think of Christ, because of *the office Christ fills between God and man.* He is the eternal Son of God, through whom alone the Father can be known, approached, and served. He is the appointed Mediator between God and man, through whom alone we can be reconciled with God, pardoned, justified, and saved. He is the Divine Person whom God the Father has sealed to be the giver of everything that man requires for his soul. To Him are committed the keys of death and hell. In His favour is life. In Him alone there is hope of salvation for mankind. Without Him no child of Adam can be saved. "Other foundation can no man lay than that is laid, which is Jesus Christ." "He that hath the Son hath life, and he that hath not the Son hath not life." (1 Cor. iii. 11; 1 John v. 12.) And ought not man to think of Christ? Shall God the Father honour Him, and shall not man? I tell every reader of this tract that there is no person, living or dead, of such immense importance to all men as Christ. There is no person that men ought to think about so much as Christ.

All men ought to think of Christ, because of *what Christ has done for all men.* He thought upon man, when man was lost, bankrupt, and helpless by the fall, and undertook to come into the world to save sinners. In the fullness of time He was born of the Virgin Mary, and lived for man thirty-three years in this evil world. At the end of that time He suffered for sin on the cross, as man's substitute. He bore man's sins in His own body, and shed His own lifeblood to pay man's debt to God. He was made a curse for man, that man might be blessed. He died for man that man might live. He was counted a sinner for man that man might be counted righteous. And ought not man to think of Christ? I tell every reader of this tract that if Christ had not died for us, we might all of us, for anything we know, be lying at this moment in hell.

All men ought to think of Christ, because of *what Christ will yet do to all men.* He shall come again one day to this earth with power and glory, and raise the dead from their graves. All shall come forth at His bidding. Those who would not move when they heard the church-going bell, shall obey the voice of the Archangel and the trump of God. He shall set up His judgment-seat, and summon all mankind to stand before it. To Him every knee shall bow, and every tongue shall confess that He is Lord. Not one shall be able to escape that solemn assize. Not one but shall receive at the mouth of Christ an eternal sentence. Every one shall receive according to what he has done in the body, whether it be good or bad. And ought not men to think of Christ? I tell every reader of this tract, that whatever he may choose to think now, a day is soon coming when his eternal condition will hinge entirely on his relations to Christ.

But why should I say more on this subject? The time would fail me if I were to set down all the reasons why all men ought to think of Christ. Christ is the grand subject of the Bible. The Scriptures testify of Him.—Christ is the great object to whom all the Churches in Christendom profess to give honour. Even the worst and most corrupt branches of it will tell you that they are built on Christ.—Christ is the end and substance of all sacraments and ordinances.—Christ is the grand subject which every faithful minister exalts in the pulpit.—Christ is the object that every true pastor sets before dying people on their deathbeds.—Christ is the great source of light and peace and hope.

There is not a spark of spiritual comfort that has ever illumined a sinner's heart, that has not come from Christ. Surely it never can be a small matter whether we have any thoughts about Christ.

Reader, I leave this part of my subject here. There are many things which swallow up men's thoughts while they live, which they will think little of when they are dying. Hundreds are wholly absorbed in political schemes, and seem to care for nothing but the advancement of their own party.—Myriads are buried in business and money matters, and seem to neglect everything else but this world.

Thousands are always wrangling about the forms and ceremonies of religion, and are ready to cry down everybody who does not use their shibboleths, and worship in their way. But an hour is fast coming when only one subject will be minded, and that subject will be Christ! We shall all find—and many perhaps too late—that it mattered little what we thought about other things, so long as we did not think about Christ.

Reader, I tell you this Christmas, that all men ought to think about Christ. There is no one in whom all the world has such a deep interest. There is no one to whom all the world owes so much. High and low, rich and poor, old and young, gentle and simple,—all ought to think about Christ.

*II. Let us examine, secondly,
the common thoughts of many about Christ.*

To set down the whole list of thoughts about Christ, would indeed be thankless labour. It must content us to range them under a few general heads. This will save us both time and trouble. There were many strange thoughts about Christ when He was on earth. There are many strange and wrong thoughts about Christ now, when He is in heaven.

The thoughts of some people about Christ are simply *blasphemous.* They are not ashamed to deny His Divinity. They refuse to believe the miracles recorded of Him. They pretend to find fault with not a few of His sayings and doings. They even question the perfect honesty and sincerity of some things that He did. They tell us that He ought to be ranked with great Reformers and Philosophers, like Socrates, Seneca, and Confucius, but no higher.—Thoughts like these are purely ridiculous and absurd. They utterly fail to explain the enormous influence which Christ and Christianity have had for eighteen hundred years in this world. There is not the slightest comparison to be made between Christ and any other teacher of mankind that ever lived. The difference between Him and others is a gulf that cannot be spanned, and a height that cannot be measured. It is the difference between gold and clay,—between the sun and a candle. Nothing can account for Christ and Christianity, but the old belief that Christ is very God. Reader, are the thoughts I have just described your own? If they are, take care!

The thoughts of some people about Christ are *vague, dim, misty, and indistinct.* That there was such a Person they do not for a moment deny. That He was the Founder of Christianity, and the object of Christian worship, they are quite aware. That they hear of Him every time they go to public worship, and ought to have some opinion or belief about Him, they will fully admit. But they could not tell you what it is they believe. They could not accurately describe and define it. They have not thoroughly considered the subject They have not made up their minds!—Thoughts such as these are foolish, silly, and unreasonable. To be a dying sinner with an immortal soul, and to go on living without making up one's mind about the only Person who can save us, the Person who will at last judge us, is the conduct of a lunatic or an idiot, and not of a rational man. Reader, are the thoughts I have just described your own? If they are, take care!

The thoughts of some men about Christ are *mean and low.* They have, no doubt, a distinct opinion about His position in their system of Christianity. They consider that if they do their best, and live moral lives, and go to church pretty regularly, and use the ordinances of religion, Christ will deal mercifully with them at last, and make up any deficiencies.—Thoughts such as these utterly fail to explain why Christ died on the cross. They take the crown off Christ's head, and degrade Him into a kind of make-weight to man's soul. They overthrow the whole system of the Gospel, and pull up all its leading doctrines by the roots. They exalt man to an absurdly high position; as if he could pay some part of the price of his soul!—They rob man of all the comfort of the Gospel; as if he must needs do something and perform some work to justify his own soul!—They make Christ a sort of Judge far more than a Saviour, and place the cross and the atonement in a degraded and inferior position! Reader, are the thoughts I have just described your own? If they are, take care!

The thoughts of some men about Christ are *dishonouring and libellous.* They seem to think that we need a mediator between ourselves and our Saviour! They appear to suppose that Christ is so high, and awful, and exalted a Person, that poor, sinful man may not approach Him! They say that we must employ an Episcopacy ordained minister as a kind of go-between, to stand between us and Jesus, and manage for our souls! They send us to saints, or angels, or the Virgin Mary, as if they were more kind and accessible than Christ!—Thoughts such as these are a practical denial of Christ's priestly office. They overthrow the whole doctrine of His peculiar business, as man's Intercessor. They hide and bury out of sight His especial love to sinners and His boundless willingness to receive them. Instead of a gracious Saviour, they make Him out an austere and hard King. Reader, are the thoughts I have just described your own? If they are, take care!

The thoughts of some men about Christ are *wicked and unholy.* They seem to think that they may live as they please, because Christ died for sinners! They will indulge every kind of wickedness, and yet flatter themselves that they are not blameworthy for it, because Christ is a merciful Saviour! They will talk complacently of God's election, and the necessity of grace, and the impossibility of being justified by works and the fullness of Christ, and then make these glorious doctrines an excuse for lying, cheating, drunkenness, fornication, and every kind of immorality.—Thoughts such as these are as blasphemous and profane as downright infidelity. They actually make Christ the patron of sin. Reader, are the thoughts I have described your own? If they are, take care!

Reader, two general remarks apply to all these thoughts about Christ of which I have just been speaking. They all show a deplorable ignorance of Scripture. I defy any one to read the Bible honestly and find any warrant for them in that blessed Book. Men cannot know their Bibles when they hold such opinions.—They all help to prove the corruption and darkness of human nature. Man is ready to believe anything about Christ except the simple truth. He loves to set up an idol of his own, and bow down to it, rather than accept the Saviour whom God puts before him.

I leave this part of my subject here. It is a sorrowful and painful one, but not without its use. It is necessary to study morbid anatomy, if we would understand health. The ground must be cleared of rubbish before we build.

> *III. Let us now count up, lastly,*
> *the thoughts of true Christians about Christ.*

The thoughts I am going to describe are not the thoughts of many. I admit this most fully. It would be vain to deny it. The number of right thinkers about Christ in every age has been small. The true Christians among professing Christians have always been few. If it were not so, the Bible would have told an untruth. "Strait is the gate," says the Lord Jesus, "and narrow is the way that leadeth unto life, and few there be that find it.—Wide is the gate, and broad is the way, that leadeth unto destruction, and many there be that go in thereby." "Many walk," says Paul, "of whom I tell you, even weeping, that they are the enemies of the cross of Christ; whose end is destruction." (Matt vii. 13, 14. Phil. iii. 18, 19.)

True Christians have *high thoughts of Christ.* They see in Him a wondrous Person, far above all other beings in His nature,—a Person who is at one and the same time perfect God, mighty to save, and perfect Man, able to feel.—They see in Him an All-powerful Redeemer, who has paid their countless debts to God, and delivered their souls from guilt and hell.—They see in Him an Almighty Friend, who left heaven for them, lived for them, died for them, rose again for them,—that He might save them for evermore.—They see in Him an Almighty Physician, who washed away their sins in His own blood, put His own Spirit in their hearts, delivered them from the power of sin, and gave them power to become God's children.—Happy are they who have such thoughts! Reader, have you?

True Christians have *trustful thoughts of Christ*. They daily lean the weight of their souls upon Him by faith, for pardon and peace. They daily commit the care of their souls to Him, as a man commits a treasure to a safe keeper. They daily cling to Him by faith, as a child in a crowd clings to its mother's hand. They look to Him daily for mercy, grace, comfort, help, and strength, as Israel looked to the pillar of cloud and fire in the wilderness for guidance. Christ is the Rock under their feet, and the staff in their hands, their ark and their city of refuge, their sun and their shield, their bread and their medicine, their health and their light, their fountain and their shelter, their portion and their home, their door and their ladder, their root and their head, their advocate and their physician, their captain and their elder brother, their life, their hope, and their all. Happy are they who have such thoughts! Reader, have you?

True Christians have *experimental thoughts of Christ*. The things that they think of Him, they do not merely think with their heads. They have not learned them from schools, or picked them up from others. They think them because they have found them true by their own heart's experience. They have proved them, and tasted them, and tried them. They think what they have felt out for themselves. There is all the difference in the world between knowing that a man is a doctor or a lawyer, while we never have occasion to employ him, and knowing him as "our own," because we have gone to him for medicine or law. Just in the same way there is a wide difference between head knowledge and experimental thoughts of Christ. Happy are they who have such thoughts? Reader, have you?

True Christians have *loving and reverent thoughts of Christ*. They love to do the things that please Him. They like, in their poor weak way, to show their affection to Him by keeping His words. They love everything belonging to Him,—His day, His house, His ordinances, His people, His Book. They never find His yoke heavy, or His burden painful to bear, or His Commandments grievous. Love lightens all. They know something of the mind of Mr. Standfast, in "Pilgrim's Progress," when he said, as he stood in the river,—"I have loved to hear my Lord spoken of; and whenever I have seen the print of His shoe in the earth, then I have coveted to set my foot over it." Happy are they who have such thoughts? Reader, have you?

True Christians have *hopeful thoughts of Christ*. They expect yet to receive far more from Him than they have ever received yet. They hope that they shall be kept to the end, and never perish. But this is not all. They look forward to Christ's second coming and expect that then they shall see far more than they have seen, and enjoy far more than they have yet enjoyed. They have the earnest of an inheritance now in the Spirit dwelling in their heart. But they hope for a far fuller possession when this world has passed away. They have hopeful thoughts of Christ's second Advent, of their own resurrection from the grave of their reunion with all the saints who have gone before them, of eternal blessedness in Christ's kingdom. Happy are they who have such thoughts! They sweeten life, and lift men over many cares. Reader, have you such thoughts?

Reader, thoughts such as these are the property of all true Christians. Some of them know more of them and some of them know less. But all know something about them. They do not always feel them equally at all time! They do not always find such thoughts equally fresh and green in their minds. They have their winter as well as their summer, and their low tide as well as their high water. But all true Christians are, more or less, acquainted with these thoughts. In this matter churchmen and dissenters, rich and poor, all are agreed, if they are true Christians. In other things they may be unable to agree and see alike. But they all agree in their thoughts about Christ. One word they can all say, which is the same in every tongue. That word is "Hallelujah," praise to the Lord Christ! One answer they can all make, which in every tongue is equally the same. That word is, "Amen," so be it!

And now, reader, I shall wind up my Christmas tract, by simply bringing before your conscience the question which forms its title. I ask you this day,—"What think you of Christ?"

What others think about Him is not the question now. Their mistakes are no excuse for you.—Their correct views will not save your soul. The point you have before you is simply this,—"What do you think yourself?"

Reader, this Christmas may possibly be your last. Who can tell but you may never live to see another December come round? Who can tell but your place may be empty, when the family party next Christmas is gathered together? Do not, I entreat you, put off my question or turn away from it. It can do you no harm to look at it and consider it. What do you think of Christ?

Begin, I beseech you, this day to have right thoughts of Christ, if you never had them before. Let the time past suffice you to have lived without real and heartfelt religion.—Let this present Christmas be a starting point in your soul's history. Awake to see the value of your soul, and the immense importance of being saved. Break off sharp from sin and the world. Get down your Bible and begin to read it. Call upon the Lord Jesus Christ in prayer, and beseech Him to save your soul. Rest not, rest not till you have trustful, loving, experimental, hopeful thoughts of Christ.

Reader, mark my words! If you will only take the advice I have now given you, you will never repent it. Your life in future will be happier. Your heart will be lighter. Your Christmas gatherings will be more truly joyful. Nothing makes Christmas meetings so happy as to feel that we are all travelling on towards an eternal gathering in heaven.

Reader, I say for the last time, if you would have a happy Christmas, have right thoughts about Christ.

www.ingramcontent.com/pod-product-compliance
Lightning Source LLC
Chambersburg PA
CBHW022112040426
42450CB00006B/671